AWS Storage Gateway User Guide

A catalogue record for this book is available from the Hong Kong Public Libraries.

Published in Hong Kong by Samurai Media Limited.

Email: info@samuraimedia.org

ISBN 9789888407644

Contents

What Is AWS Storage Gateway?

AWS Storage Gateway connects an on-premises software appliance with cloud-based storage to provide seamless integration with data security features between your on-premises IT environment and the AWS storage infrastructure. You can use the service to store data in the AWS Cloud for scalable and cost-effective storage that helps maintain data security.

AWS Storage Gateway offers file-based, volume-based, and tape-based storage solutions:

File Gateway – A file gateway supports a file interface into Amazon Simple Storage Service (Amazon S3) and combines a service and a virtual software appliance. By using this combination, you can store and retrieve objects in Amazon S3 using industry-standard file protocols such as Network File System (NFS) and Server Message Block (SMB). The software appliance, or gateway, is deployed into your on-premises environment as a virtual machine (VM) running on VMware ESXi or Microsoft Hyper-V hypervisor. The gateway provides access to objects in S3 as files or file share mount points. With a file gateway, you can do the following:

- You can store and retrieve files directly using the NFS version 3 or 4.1 protocol.
- You can store and retrieve files directly using the SMB file system version, 2 and 3 protocol.
- You can access your data directly in Amazon S3 from any AWS Cloud application or service.
- You can manage your Amazon S3 data using lifecycle policies, cross-region replication, and versioning. You can think of a file gateway as a file system mount on S3.

A file gateway simplifies file storage in Amazon S3, integrates to existing applications through industry-standard file system protocols, and provides a cost-effective alternative to on-premises storage. It also provides low-latency access to data through transparent local caching. A file gateway manages data transfer to and from AWS, buffers applications from network congestion, optimizes and streams data in parallel, and manages bandwidth consumption. File gateways integrate with AWS services, for example with the following:

- Common access management using AWS Identity and Access Management (IAM)
- Encryption using AWS Key Management Service (AWS KMS)
- Monitoring using Amazon CloudWatch (CloudWatch)
- Audit using AWS CloudTrail (CloudTrail)
- Operations using the AWS Management Console and AWS Command Line Interface (AWS CLI)
- Billing and cost management

Volume Gateway – A volume gateway provides cloud-backed storage volumes that you can mount as Internet Small Computer System Interface (iSCSI) devices from your on-premises application servers. The gateway supports the following volume configurations:

- **Cached volumes** – You store your data in Amazon Simple Storage Service (Amazon S3) and retain a copy of frequently accessed data subsets locally. Cached volumes offer a substantial cost savings on primary storage and minimize the need to scale your storage on-premises. You also retain low-latency access to your frequently accessed data.
- **Stored volumes** – If you need low-latency access to your entire dataset, first configure your on-premises gateway to store all your data locally. Then asynchronously back up point-in-time snapshots of this data to Amazon S3. This configuration provides durable and inexpensive offsite backups that you can recover to your local data center or Amazon EC2. For example, if you need replacement capacity for disaster recovery, you can recover the backups to Amazon EC2.

Tape Gateway – With a tape gateway, you can cost-effectively and durably archive backup data in Amazon Glacier. A tape gateway provides a virtual tape infrastructure that scales seamlessly with your business needs and eliminates the operational burden of provisioning, scaling, and maintaining a physical tape infrastructure.

You can run AWS Storage Gateway either on-premises as a VM appliance, or in AWS as an Amazon Elastic Compute Cloud (Amazon EC2) instance. You deploy your gateway on an EC2 instance to provision iSCSI storage volumes in AWS. Gateways hosted on EC2 instances can be used for disaster recovery, data mirroring, and providing storage for applications hosted on Amazon EC2.

For an architectural overview, see How AWS Storage Gateway Works (Architecture). To see the wide range of use cases that AWS Storage Gateway helps make possible, see the AWS Storage Gateway detail page.

To get started with Storage Gateway, see the following.

Topics

- Are You a First-Time AWS Storage Gateway User?
- How AWS Storage Gateway Works (Architecture)
- AWS Storage Gateway Pricing
- Plan Your Storage Gateway Deployment

Are You a First-Time AWS Storage Gateway User?

In the following documentation, you can find a Getting Started section that covers setup information common to all gateways and also gateway-specific setup sections. The Getting Started section shows you how to deploy, activate, and configure storage for a gateway. The management section shows you how to manage your gateway and resources:

- Creating a File Gateway provides instructions on how to create and use a file gateway. It shows you how to create a file share, map your drive to an Amazon S3 bucket, and upload files and folders to Amazon S3.
- Creating a Volume Gateway describes how to create and use a volume gateway. It shows you how to create storage volumes and back up data to the volumes.
- Creating a Tape Gateway provides instructions on how to create and use a tape gateway. It shows you how to back up data to virtual tapes and archive the tapes.
- Managing Your Gateway describes how to perform management tasks for all gateway types and resources.

In this guide, you can primarily find how to work with gateway operations by using the AWS Management Console. If you want to perform these operations programmatically, see the *AWS Storage Gateway API Reference.*

AWS Storage Gateway Pricing

For current information about pricing, see Pricing on the AWS Storage Gateway details page.

Plan Your Storage Gateway Deployment

By using the AWS Storage Gateway software appliance, you can connect your existing on-premises application infrastructure with scalable, cost-effective AWS cloud storage that provides data security features.

To deploy Storage Gateway, you first need to decide on the following two things:

1. **Your storage solution** – Choose from one of the following storage solutions:

   - **File Gateway** – You can use a file gateway to ingest files to Amazon S3 for use by object-based workloads and for cost-effective storage for traditional backup applications. You can also use it to tier on-premises file storage to S3. You can cost-effectively and durably store and retrieve your on-premises objects in Amazon S3 using industry-standard file protocols.

   - **Volume Gateway** – Using volume gateways, you can create storage volumes in the AWS Cloud. Your on-premises applications can access these as Internet Small Computer System Interface (iSCSI) targets. There are two options—cached and stored volumes.

     With cached volumes, you store volume data in AWS, with a small portion of recently accessed data in the cache on-premises. This approach enables low-latency access to your frequently accessed dataset. It also provides seamless access to your entire dataset stored in AWS. By using cached volumes, you can scale your storage resource without having to provision additional hardware.

With stored volumes, you store the entire set of volume data on-premises and store periodic point-in-time backups (snapshots) in AWS. In this model, your on-premises storage is primary, delivering low-latency access to your entire dataset. AWS storage is the backup that you can restore in the event of a disaster in your data center.

For an architectural overview of volume gateways, see Cached Volumes Architecture and Stored Volumes Architecture.

- **Tape Gateway** – If you are looking for a cost-effective, durable, long-term, offsite alternative for data archiving, deploy a tape gateway. With its virtual tape library (VTL) interface, you can use your existing tape-based backup software infrastructure to store data on virtual tape cartridges that you create. For more information, see Supported Third-Party Backup Applications for a Tape Gateway. When you archive tapes, you don't worry about managing tapes on your premises and arranging shipments of tapes offsite. For an architectural overview, see Tape Gateways.

2. **Hosting option** – You can run Storage Gateway either on-premises as a VM appliance, or in AWS as an Amazon EC2 instance. For more information, see Requirements. If your data center goes offline and you don't have an available host, you can deploy a gateway on an EC2 instance. Storage Gateway provides an Amazon Machine Image (AMI) that contains the gateway VM image.

Additionally, as you configure a host to deploy a gateway software appliance, you need to allocate sufficient storage for the gateway VM.

Before you continue to the next step, make sure that you have done the following:

1. For a gateway deployed on-premises, you chose the type of host, VMware ESXi Hypervisor or Microsoft Hyper-V. and set it up. For more information, see Requirements. If you deploy the gateway behind a firewall, make sure that ports are accessible to the gateway VM. For more information, see Requirements.

2. For a tape gateway, you have installed client backup software. For more information, see Supported Third-Party Backup Applications for a Tape Gateway.

How AWS Storage Gateway Works (Architecture)

Following, you can find an architectural overview of the available AWS Storage Gateway solutions.

Topics

- File Gateways
- Volume Gateways
- Tape Gateways

File Gateways

To use the file gateway, you start by downloading a VM image for the file storage gateway. You then activate the file gateway from the AWS Management Console or through the Storage Gateway API. File gateway is also available as an Amazon EC2 images.

After the file gateway is activated, you create and configure your file share and associate that share with your Amazon S3 bucket so that it is accessible by clients using either the NFS or SMB protocol. Files written to a file share become objects in Amazon S3, with the path as the key. There is a one-to-one mapping between files and objects, and the gateway asynchronously updates the objects in Amazon S3 as you change the files. Existing objects in the bucket appear as files in the file system, and the key becomes the path. Objects are encrypted with with Amazon S3–server-side encryption keys (SSE-S3). All data transfer is done through HTTPS.

The service optimizes data transfer between the gateway and AWS using multipart parallel uploads or byte-range downloads, to better use the available bandwidth.Local cache is maintained to provide low latency access to the recently accessed data and reduce data egress charges. CloudWatch metrics provide insight into resource use on the VM and data transfer to and from AWS. CloudTrail tracks all API calls.

With file gateway storage, you can do such tasks as ingesting cloud workloads to S3, performing backup and archive, tiering and migrating storage data to the AWS Cloud. The following diagram provides an overview of file storage deployment for Storage Gateway.

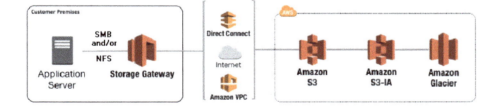

Volume Gateways

For volume gateways, you can use either cached volumes or stored volumes.

Topics

- Cached Volumes Architecture
- Stored Volumes Architecture

Cached Volumes Architecture

By using cached volumes, you can use Amazon S3 as your primary data storage, while retaining frequently accessed data locally in your storage gateway. Cached volumes minimize the need to scale your on-premises storage infrastructure, while still providing your applications with low-latency access to their frequently accessed data. You can create storage volumes up to 32 TiB in size and attach to them as iSCSI devices from your on-premises application servers. Your gateway stores data that you write to these volumes in Amazon S3 and retains recently read data in your on-premises storage gateway's cache and upload buffer storage.

Cached volumes can range from 1 GiB to 32 TiB in size and must be rounded to the nearest GiB. Each gateway configured for cached volumes can support up to 32 volumes for a total maximum storage volume of 1,024 TiB (1 PiB).

In the cached volumes solution, AWS Storage Gateway stores all your on-premises application data in a storage volume in Amazon S3. The following diagram provides an overview of the cached volumes deployment.

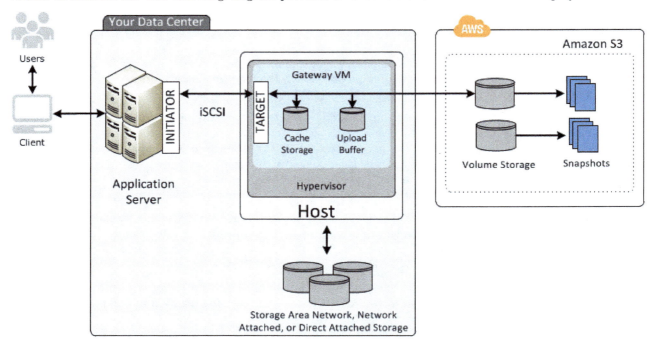

After you install the Storage Gateway software appliance—the VM—on a host in your data center and activate it, you use the AWS Management Console to provision storage volumes backed by Amazon S3. You can also provision storage volumes programmatically using the AWS Storage Gateway API or the AWS SDK libraries. You then mount these storage volumes to your on-premises application servers as iSCSI devices.

You also allocate disks on-premises for the VM. These on-premises disks serve the following purposes:

- **Disks for use by the gateway as cache storage** – As your applications write data to the storage volumes in AWS, the gateway first stores the data on the on-premises disks used for cache storage. Then the gateway uploads the data to Amazon S3. The cache storage acts as the on-premises durable store for data that is waiting to upload to Amazon S3 from the upload buffer.

  The cache storage also lets the gateway store your application's recently accessed data on-premises for low-latency access. If your application requests data, the gateway first checks the cache storage for the data before checking Amazon S3.

  You can use the following guidelines to determine the amount of disk space to allocate for cache storage. Generally, you should allocate at least 20 percent of your existing file store size as cache storage. Cache storage should also be larger than the upload buffer. This guideline helps make sure that cache storage is large enough to persistently hold all data in the upload buffer that has not yet been uploaded to Amazon S3.

- **Disks for use by the gateway as the upload buffer** – To prepare for upload to Amazon S3, your gateway also stores incoming data in a staging area, referred to as an *upload buffer*. Your gateway uploads this buffer data over an encrypted Secure Sockets Layer (SSL) connection to AWS, where it is stored encrypted in Amazon S3.

You can take incremental backups, called *snapshots*, of your storage volumes in Amazon S3. These point-in-time snapshots are also stored in Amazon S3 as Amazon EBS snapshots. When you take a new snapshot, only the data that has changed since your last snapshot is stored. You can initiate snapshots on a scheduled or one-time basis. When you delete a snapshot, only the data not needed for any other snapshots is removed. For information about Amazon EBS snapshots, see Amazon EBS Snapshots.

You can restore an Amazon EBS snapshot to a gateway storage volume if you need to recover a backup of your data. Alternatively, for snapshots up to 16 TiB in size, you can use the snapshot as a starting point for a new Amazon EBS volume. You can then attach this new Amazon EBS volume to an Amazon EC2 instance.

All gateway data and snapshot data for cached volumes is stored in Amazon S3 and encrypted at rest using server-side encryption (SSE). However, you can't access this data with the Amazon S3 API or other tools such as the Amazon S3 Management Console.

Stored Volumes Architecture

By using stored volumes, you can store your primary data locally, while asynchronously backing up that data to AWS. Stored volumes provide your on-premises applications with low-latency access to their entire datasets. At the same time, they provide durable, offsite backups. You can create storage volumes and mount them as iSCSI devices from your on-premises application servers. Data written to your stored volumes is stored on your on-premises storage hardware. This data is asynchronously backed up to Amazon S3 as Amazon Elastic Block Store (Amazon EBS) snapshots.

Stored volumes can range from 1 GiB to 16 TiB in size and must be rounded to the nearest GiB. Each gateway configured for stored volumes can support up to 32 volumes and a total volume storage of 512 TiB (0.5 PiB).

With stored volumes, you maintain your volume storage on-premises in your data center. That is, you store all your application data on your on-premises storage hardware. Then, using features that help maintain data security, the gateway uploads data to the AWS Cloud for cost-effective backup and rapid disaster recovery. This solution is ideal if you want to keep data locally on-premises, because you need to have low-latency access to all your data, and also to maintain backups in AWS.

The following diagram provides an overview of the stored volumes deployment.

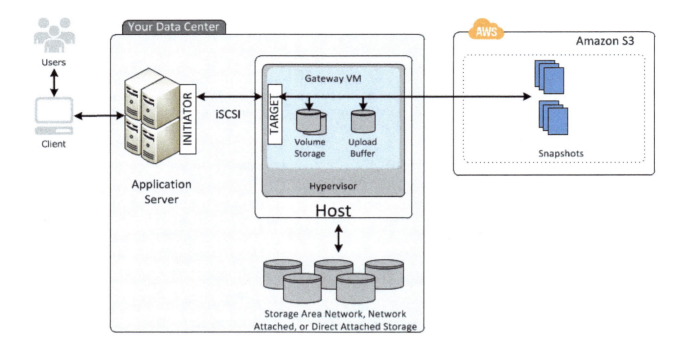

After you install the AWS Storage Gateway software appliance—the VM—on a host in your data center and activated it, you can create gateway *storage volumes*. You then map them to on-premises direct-attached storage (DAS) or storage area network (SAN) disks. You can start with either new disks or disks already holding data. You can then mount these storage volumes to your on-premises application servers as iSCSI devices. As your on-premises applications write data to and read data from a gateway's storage volume, this data is stored and retrieved from the volume's assigned disk.

To prepare data for upload to Amazon S3, your gateway also stores incoming data in a staging area, referred to as an *upload buffer*. You can use on-premises DAS or SAN disks for working storage. Your gateway uploads data from the upload buffer over an encrypted Secure Sockets Layer (SSL) connection to the AWS Storage Gateway service running in the AWS Cloud. The service then stores the data encrypted in Amazon S3.

You can take incremental backups, called *snapshots*, of your storage volumes. The gateway stores these snapshots in Amazon S3 as Amazon EBS snapshots. When you take a new snapshot, only the data that has changed since your last snapshot is stored. You can initiate snapshots on a scheduled or one-time basis. When you delete a snapshot, only the data not needed for any other snapshot is removed.

You can restore an Amazon EBS snapshot to an on-premises gateway storage volume if you need to recover a backup of your data. You can also use the snapshot as a starting point for a new Amazon EBS volume, which you can then attach to an Amazon EC2 instance.

Tape Gateways

Tape Gateway offers a durable, cost-effective solution to archive your data in the AWS Cloud. With its virtual tape library (VTL) interface, you use your existing tape-based backup infrastructure to store data on virtual tape cartridges that you create on your tape gateway. Each tape gateway is preconfigured with a media changer and tape drives. These are available to your existing client backup applications as iSCSI devices. You add tape cartridges as you need to archive your data.

The following diagram provides an overview of tape gateway deployment.

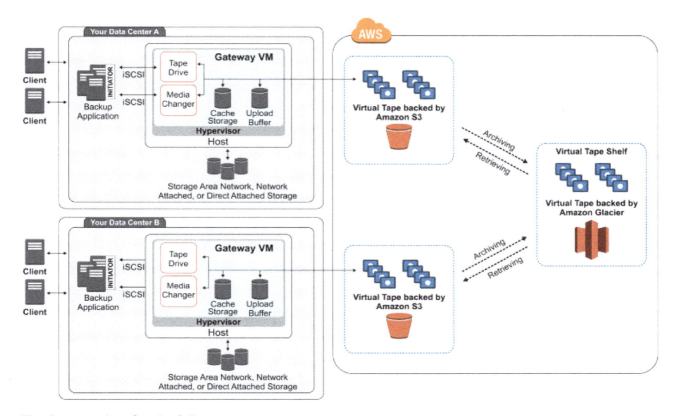

The diagram identifies the following tape gateway components:

- **Virtual tape** – A virtual tape is like a physical tape cartridge. However, virtual tape data is stored in the AWS Cloud. Like physical tapes, virtual tapes can be blank or can have data written on them. You can create virtual tapes either by using the Storage Gateway console or programmatically by using the Storage Gateway API. Each gateway can contain up to 1500 tapes or up to 1 PiB of total tape data at a time. The size of each virtual tape, which you can configure when you create the tape, is between 100 GiB and 2.5 TiB.

- **Virtual tape library (VTL)** – A VTL is like a physical tape library available on-premises with robotic arms and tape drives. Your VTL includes the collection of stored virtual tapes. Each tape gateway comes with one VTL.

  The virtual tapes that you create appear in your gateway's VTL. Tapes in the VTL are backed up by Amazon S3. As your backup software writes data to the gateway, the gateway stores data locally and then asynchronously uploads it to virtual tapes in your VTL—that is, Amazon S3.

  - **Tape drive** – A VTL tape drive is analogous to a physical tape drive that can perform I/O and seek operations on a tape. Each VTL comes with a set of 10 tape drives, which are available to your backup application as iSCSI devices.
  - **Media changer** – A VTL media changer is analogous to a robot that moves tapes around in a physical tape library's storage slots and tape drives. Each VTL comes with one media changer, which is available to your backup application as an iSCSI device.

- **Archive** – Archive is analogous to an offsite tape holding facility. You can archive tapes from your gateway's VTL to the archive. If needed, you can retrieve tapes from the archive back to your gateway's VTL.

  - **Archiving tapes** – When your backup software ejects a tape, your gateway moves the tape to the archive for long-term storage. The archive is located in the AWS Region in which you activated the gateway. Tapes in the archive are stored in the Virtual Tape Shelf, which is backed by Amazon

Glacier, a low-cost storage service for data archiving and backup. For more information, see Amazon Glacier.

- **Retrieving tapes** – You can't read archived tapes directly. To read an archived tape, you must first retrieve it to your tape gateway either by using the Storage Gateway console or by using the Storage Gateway API. A retrieved tape is available in your VTL in about three to five hours after you start retrieval.

After you deploy and activate a tape gateway, you mount the virtual tape drives and media changer on your on-premises application servers as iSCSI devices. You create virtual tapes as needed. Then you use your existing backup software application to write data to the virtual tapes. The media changer loads and unloads the virtual tapes into the virtual tape drives for read and write operations.

Allocating Local Disks for the Gateway VM

Your gateway VM needs local disks, which you allocate for the following purposes:

- **Cache storage** – The cache storage acts as the durable store for data that is waiting to upload to Amazon S3 from the upload buffer.

  If your application reads data from a virtual tape, the gateway saves the data to the cache storage. The gateway stores recently accessed data in the cache storage for low-latency access. If your application requests tape data, the gateway first checks the cache storage for the data before downloading the data from AWS.

- **Upload buffer** – The upload buffer provides a staging area for the gateway before it uploads the data to a virtual tape. The upload buffer is also critical for creating recovery points that you can use to recover tapes from unexpected failures. For more information, see You Need to Recover a Virtual Tape from a Malfunctioning Tape Gateway.

As your backup application writes data to your gateway, the gateway copies data to both the cache storage and the upload buffer. It then acknowledges completion of the write operation to your backup application.

For guidelines on the amount of disk space to allocate for the cache storage and upload buffer, see Deciding the Amount of Local Disk Storage.

Getting Started

In this section, you can find instructions about how to get started with AWS Storage Gateway. To get started, you first sign up for AWS. If you are a first-time user, we recommend that you read the regions and requirements section.

Topics

- Sign Up for AWS Storage Gateway
- Regions
- Requirements
- Accessing AWS Storage Gateway

Sign Up for AWS Storage Gateway

To use AWS Storage Gateway, you need an AWS account that gives you access to all AWS resources, forums, support, and usage reports. You aren't charged for any of the services unless you use them. If you already have an AWS account, you can skip this step.

To sign up for AWS account

1. Open https://aws.amazon.com/, and then choose **Create an AWS Account. Note**
   This might be unavailable in your browser if you previously signed into the AWS Management Console. In that case, choose **Sign in to a different account**, and then choose **Create a new AWS account**.

2. Follow the online instructions.

   Part of the sign-up procedure involves receiving a phone call and entering a PIN using the phone keypad.

For information about pricing, see AWS Storage Gateway Pricing on the AWS Storage Gateway detail page.

Regions

AWS Storage Gateway stores volume, snapshot, tape, and file data in the AWS Region in which your gateway is activated. File data is stored in the AWS Region where your Amazon S3 bucket is located. You select an AWS Region at the upper right of the AWS Storage Gateway Management Console before you start deploying your gateway. The following are the available AWS Regions for AWS Storage Gateway.

Region Name	Region String	File Gateway	Volume Gateway	Tape Gateway
US East (Ohio)	us-east-2	yes	yes	yes
US East (N. Virginia)	us-east-1	yes	yes	yes
US West (N. California)	us-west-1	yes	yes	yes
US West (Oregon)	us-west-2	yes	yes	yes
Canada (Central)	ca-central-1	yes	yes	yes
EU (Ireland)	eu-west-1	yes	yes	yes
EU (Frankfurt)	eu-central-1	yes	yes	yes
EU (London)	eu-west-2	yes	yes	yes
EU (Paris)	eu-west-3	yes	yes	yes
Asia Pacific (Tokyo)	ap-northeast-1	yes	yes	yes
Asia Pacific (Seoul)	ap-northeast-2	yes	yes	yes
Asia Pacific (Singapore)	ap-southeast-1	yes	yes	yes
Asia Pacific (Sydney)	ap-southeast-2	yes	yes	yes
Asia Pacific (Mumbai)	ap-south-1	yes	yes	yes
South America (São Paulo)	sa-east-1	yes	yes	no

Requirements

Unless otherwise noted, the following requirements are common to all gateway configurations.

Topics

- Hardware and Storage Requirements
- Network and Firewall Requirements
- Supported Hypervisors and Host Requirements
- Supported NFS Clients for a File Gateway
- Supported SMB Clients for a File Gateway
- Supported File System Operations for a File Gateway
- Supported iSCSI Initiators
- Supported Third-Party Backup Applications for a Tape Gateway

Hardware and Storage Requirements

In this section, you can find information about the minimum hardware and settings for your gateway and the minimum amount of disk space to allocate for the required storage.

Hardware Requirements

When deploying your gateway on-premises, you must make sure that the underlying hardware on which you deploy the gateway VM can dedicate the following minimum resources:

- Four virtual processors assigned to the VM.
- 16 GiB of reserved RAM assigned to the VM.
- 80 GiB of disk space for installation of VM image and system data.

For more information, see Optimizing Gateway Performance. For information about how your hardware affects the performance of the gateway VM, see AWS Storage Gateway Limits.

Amazon EC2 Instance Type Requirements

When deploying your gateway on Amazon EC2, the instance size must be at least **xlarge** for your gateway to function. However, for the compute-optimized instance family the size must be at least

2xlarge. Use one of the following instance types recommended for your gateway type.

Recommended for file gateway types

- General-purpose instance family— m4 or m5 instance type.
- Compute-optimized instance family— c4 or c5 instance types. Select the **2xlarge** instance size or higher to meet the required RAM requirements.
- Memory-optimized instance family—r3 instance types.

Recommended for cached volumes and tape gateway types

- General-purpose instance family—m4 instance types. We don't recommend using the **m4.16xlarge** instance type.
- Compute-optimized instance family—c4 instance types. Select the **2xlarge** instance size or higher to meet the required RAM requirements.
- Storage-optimized instance family—d2 or i2 instance types

Note

When deploying your gateway on an Amazon EC2 instance, you must make sure that you allocate the following minimum resources:

If you have more than 5 million objects in your Amazon S3 bucket and you are using a General Purposes SSD volume, a minimum root EBS volume of 350 GiB is needed for acceptable performance of your gateway during start up. For information about how to increase your volume size, see Modifying an EBS Volume from the Console.

Storage Requirements

In addition to 80 GiB disk space for the VM, you also need additional disks for your gateway.

The following table recommends sizes for local disk storage for your deployed gateway.

Gateway Type	Cache (Minimum)	Cache (Maximum)	Upload Buffer (Minimum)	Upload Buffer (Maximum)	Other Required Local Disks
File gateway	150 GiB	16 TiB	—	—	—
Cached volume gateway	150 GiB	16 TiB	150 GiB	2 TiB	—
Stored volume gateway	—	—	150 GiB	2 TiB	1 or more for stored volume or volumes
Tape gateway	150 GiB	16 TiB	150 GiB	2 TiB	—

Note

You can configure one or more local drives for your cache and upload buffer, up to the maximum capacity. When adding cache or upload buffer to an existing gateway, it's important to create new disks in your host (hypervisor or Amazon EC2 instance). Don't change the size of existing disks if the disks have been previously allocated as either a cache or upload buffer.

For information about gateway limits, see AWS Storage Gateway Limits.

Network and Firewall Requirements

Your gateway requires access to the internet, local networks, Domain Name Service (DNS) servers, firewalls, routers, and so on. Following, you can find information about required ports and how to allow access through firewalls and routers.

Topics

- Port Requirements
- Allowing AWS Storage Gateway Access Through Firewalls and Routers
- Configuring Security Groups for Your Amazon EC2 Gateway Instance

Port Requirements

AWS Storage Gateway requires certain ports to be allowed for its operation. The following illustrations show the required ports that you must allow for each type of gateway. Some ports are required by all gateway types, and others are required by specific gateway types. For more information about port requirements, see Port Requirements.

File gateways

The following illustration shows the ports to open for a file gateway.

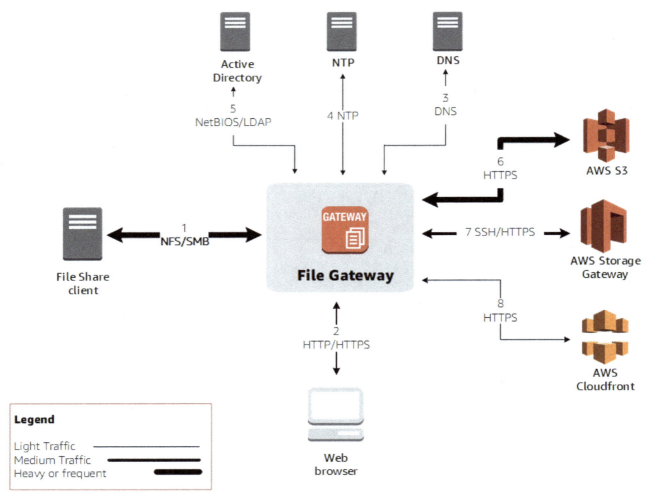

Active Directory is only required when you want to allow domain users to access an SMB file share. Your file gateway may be joined to any valid Windows domain (resolvable by DNS). You can also use the AWS Directory Service to create an AWS Managed Microsoft AD in the AWS Cloud. For most AWS Managed AD deployments you will need to configure the DHCP service for your VPC. Instructions on how to create a DHCP options set may be found here.

Volume gateways and tape Gateways

The following illustration shows the ports to open for volume and tape gateways.

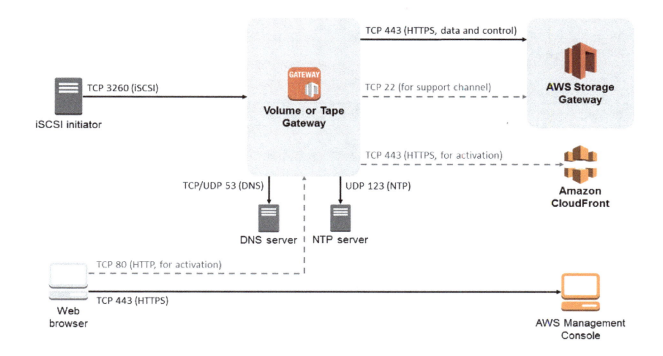

Allowing AWS Storage Gateway Access Through Firewalls and Routers

Your gateway requires access to the following endpoints to communicate with AWS. If you use a firewall or router to filter or limit network traffic, you must configure your firewall and router to allow these service endpoints for outbound communication to AWS.

The following service endpoints are required by all gateways for control path (anon-cp, client-cp, proxy-app) and data path (dp-1) operations.

```
1 anon-cp.storagegateway.region.amazonaws.com:443
2 client-cp.storagegateway.region.amazonaws.com:443
3 proxy-app.storagegateway.region.amazonaws.com:443
4 dp-1.storagegateway.region.amazonaws.com:443
```

The following service endpoint is required to make API calls.

```
1 storagegateway.region.amazonaws.com:443
```

The Amazon S3 service endpoint, shown following, is used by file gateways only. A file gateway requires this endpoint to access the S3 bucket that a file share maps to.

If your gateway can't determine the AWS Region where your S3 bucket is located, this endpoint defaults to us-east-1.s3.amazonaws.com. We recommend that you whitelist the us-east-1 region in addition to AWS Regions where your gateway is activated, and where your S3 bucket is located.

```
1 region.s3.amazonaws.com
```

The Amazon CloudFront endpoint following is required for Storage Gateway to get the list of available AWS Regions.

```
1 https://d4kdq0yaxexbo.cloudfront.net/
```

A Storage Gateway VM is configured to use the following NTP servers.

```
1  0.amazon.pool.ntp.org
2  1.amazon.pool.ntp.org
3  2.amazon.pool.ntp.org
4  3.amazon.pool.ntp.org
```

The following table provides a list of region strings for the available AWS Regions.

Region Name	Region String	File Gateway	Volume Gateway	Tape Gateway
US East (Ohio)	us-east-2	yes	yes	yes
US East (N. Virginia)	us-east-1	yes	yes	yes
US West (N. California)	us-west-1	yes	yes	yes
US West (Oregon)	us-west-2	yes	yes	yes
Canada (Central)	ca-central-1	yes	yes	yes
EU (Ireland)	eu-west-1	yes	yes	yes
EU (Frankfurt)	eu-central-1	yes	yes	yes
EU (London)	eu-west-2	yes	yes	yes
EU (Paris)	eu-west-3	yes	yes	yes
Asia Pacific (Tokyo)	ap-northeast-1	yes	yes	yes
Asia Pacific (Seoul)	ap-northeast-2	yes	yes	yes
Asia Pacific (Singapore)	ap-southeast-1	yes	yes	yes
Asia Pacific (Sydney)	ap-southeast-2	yes	yes	yes
Asia Pacific (Mumbai)	ap-south-1	yes	yes	yes
South America (São Paulo)	sa-east-1	yes	yes	no

Depending on your gateway's AWS Region, replace *region* in the endpoint with the corresponding region string. For example, if you create a gateway in the US West (Oregon) region, the endpoint looks like this: `storagegateway.us-west-2.amazonaws.com:443`.

Configuring Security Groups for Your Amazon EC2 Gateway Instance

A security group controls traffic to your Amazon EC2 gateway instance. When you create an instance from the Amazon Machine Image (AMI) for AWS Storage Gateway from AWS Marketplace, you have two choices for launching the instance. To launch the instance by using the **1-Click Launch** feature of AWS Marketplace, follow the steps in Deploying a Volume or Tape Gateway on an Amazon EC2 Host . We recommend that you use this **1-Click Launch** feature.

You can also launch an instance by using the **Manual Launch** feature in AWS Marketplace. In this case, an autogenerated security group that is named `AWS Storage Gateway-1-0-AutogenByAWSMP-` is created. This security group has the correct rule for port 80 to activate your gateway. For more information about security groups, see Security Group Concepts in the *Amazon EC2 User Guide for Linux Instances*.

Regardless of the security group that you use, we recommend the following:

- The security group should not allow incoming connections from the outside internet. It should allow only instances within the gateway security group to communicate with the gateway. If you need to allow instances to connect to the gateway from outside its security group, we recommend that you allow connections only on ports 3260 (for iSCSI connections) and 80 (for activation).

- If you want to activate your gateway from an EC2 host outside the gateway security group, allow incoming connections on port 80 from the IP address of that host. If you cannot determine the activating host's IP address, you can open port 80, activate your gateway, and then close access on port 80 after completing activation.
- Allow port 22 access only if you are using AWS Support for troubleshooting purposes. For more information, see You Want AWS Support to Help Troubleshoot Your EC2 Gateway.

In some cases, you might use an Amazon EC2 instance as an initiator (that is, to connect to iSCSI targets on a gateway that you deployed on Amazon EC2). In such a case, we recommend a two-step approach:

1. You should launch the initiator instance in the same security group as your gateway.

2. You should configure access so the initiator can communicate with your gateway.

For information about the ports to open for your gateway, see Port Requirements.

Supported Hypervisors and Host Requirements

You can run AWS Storage Gateway either on-premises as a virtual machine (VM) appliance, or in AWS as an Amazon Elastic Compute Cloud (Amazon EC2) instance.

AWS Storage Gateway supports the following hypervisor versions and hosts:

- VMware ESXi Hypervisor (version 4.1, 5.0, 5.1, 5.5, 6.0 or 6.5)—A free version of VMware is available on the VMware website. For this setup, you also need a VMware vSphere client to connect to the host.
- Microsoft Hyper-V Hypervisor (version 2008 R2, 2012, or 2012 R2)—A free, standalone version of Hyper-V is available at the Microsoft Download Center. For this setup, you need a Microsoft Hyper-V Manager on a Microsoft Windows client computer to connect to the host.
- EC2 instance—AWS Storage Gateway provides an Amazon Machine Image (AMI) that contains the gateway VM image. Only file, cached volume, and tape gateway types can be deployed on Amazon EC2. For information about how to deploy a gateway on Amazon EC2, see Deploying a Volume or Tape Gateway on an Amazon EC2 Host.

Note
AWS Storage Gateway doesn't support recovering a gateway from a VM that was created from a snapshot or clone of another gateway VM or from your Amazon EC2 AMI. If your gateway VM malfunctions, activate a new gateway and recover your data to that gateway. For more information, see Recovering from an Unexpected Virtual Machine Shutdown.

Supported NFS Clients for a File Gateway

File gateways support the following Network File System (NFS) clients:

- Amazon Linux

- Mac OS X

- RHEL 7

- SUSE Linux Enterprise Server 11 and SUSE Linux Enterprise Server 12

- Ubuntu 14.04

- Microsoft Windows 10 Enterprise, Windows Server 2012, and Windows Server 2016. Native clients only support NFS version 3.

- Windows 7 Enterprise and Windows Server 2008.

  Native clients only support NFS v3. The maximum supported NFS I/O size is 32 KB, so you might experience degraded performance on these versions of Windows.

Supported SMB Clients for a File Gateway

File gatewayssupport the following Service Message Block (SMB) clients:

- Microsoft Windows Server 2003 and later
- Windows desktop versions: 10, 8, 7, Vista, and XP
- Windows Terminal Server running on Windows Server 2003 and later

Supported File System Operations for a File Gateway

Your NFS or SMB client can write, read, delete, and truncate files. Clients send writes to Amazon S3 through optimized multipart uploads by using a write-back cache. Reads are first served through the local cache. If data is not available, it's fetched through Amazon S3 as a read-through cache.

Writes and reads are optimized in that only the parts that are changed or requested are transferred through your gateway. Deletes remove objects from S3. Directories are managed as folder objects in S3, using the same syntax as in the Amazon S3 Management Console.

HTTP operations such as `GET`, `PUT`, `UPDATE`, and `DELETE` can modify files in a file share. These operations conform to the atomic create, read, update, and delete (CRUD) functions.

Supported iSCSI Initiators

When you deploy a cached volume or stored volume gateway, you can create iSCSI storage volumes on your gateway. When you deploy a tape gateway, the gateway is preconfigured with one media changer and 10 tape drives. These tape drives and the media changer are available to your existing client backup applications as iSCSI devices.

To connect to these iSCSI devices, AWS Storage Gateway supports the following iSCSI initiators:

- Windows Server 2012 and Windows Server 2012 R2
- Windows Server 2008 and Windows Server 2008 R2
- Windows 7
- Red Hat Enterprise Linux 5
- Red Hat Enterprise Linux 6
- Red Hat Enterprise Linux 7
- VMware ESX Initiator, which provides an alternative to using initiators in the guest operating systems of your VMs

Important
Storage Gateway doesn't support Microsoft Multipath I/O (MPIO) from Windows clients.
Storage Gateway supports connecting multiple hosts to the same volume if the hosts coordinate access by using Windows Server Failover Clustering (WSFC). However, you can't connect multiple hosts to that same volume (for example, sharing a nonclustered NTFS/ext4 file system) without using WSFC.

Supported Third-Party Backup Applications for a Tape Gateway

You use a backup application to read, write, and manage tapes with a tape gateway. The following third-party backup applications are supported to work with tape gateways.

The type of medium changer you choose depends on the backup application you plan to use. The following table lists third-party backup applications that have been tested and found to be compatible with tape gateways. This table includes the medium changer type recommended for each backup application.

Backup Application	Medium Changer Type
Arcserve Backup	AWS-Gateway-VTL
Backup Exec 2012	STK-L700
Backup Exec 2014	AWS-Gateway-VTL
Backup Exec 15	AWS-Gateway-VTL
Backup Exec 16	AWS-Gateway-VTL
Commvault V11	STK-L700
Dell EMC NetWorker V8.x or V9.x	AWS-Gateway-VTL
Micro Focus (HPE) Data Protector 9.x	AWS-Gateway-VTL
Microsoft System Center 2012 R2 Data Protection Manager Data Protection Manager doesn't display barcodes for virtual tapes created in AWS Storage Gateway.	STK-L700
NovaStor DataCenter/Network 6.4 or 7.1	STK-L700
Quest NetVault Backup 10.0	STK-L700
Symantec NetBackup Version 7.x	AWS-Gateway-VTL
Veeam Backup & Replication V7	STK-L700
Veeam Backup & Replication V8	STK-L700
Veeam Backup & Replication V9 Update 2 or later	AWS-Gateway-VTL

Important

We highly recommend that you choose the medium changer that's listed for your backup application. Other medium changers might not function properly. You can choose a different medium changer after the gateway is activated. For more information, see Selecting a Medium Changer After Gateway Activation.

Accessing AWS Storage Gateway

You can use the AWS Storage Gateway Management Console to perform various gateway configuration and management tasks. The Getting Started section and various other sections of this guide use the console to illustrate gateway functionality.

Additionally, you can use the AWS Storage Gateway API to programmatically configure and manage your gateways. For more information about the API, see API Reference for AWS Storage Gateway.

You can also use the AWS SDKs to develop applications that interact with AWS Storage Gateway. The AWS SDKs for Java, .NET, and PHP wrap the underlying AWS Storage Gateway API to simplify your programming tasks. For information about downloading the SDK libraries, see Sample Code Libraries.

Creating Your Gateway

To create your gateway, open the AWS Storage Gateway Management Console and choose the AWS Region that you want to create your gateway in. If you haven't created a gateway in this AWS Region, the Storage Gateway service homepage is displayed.

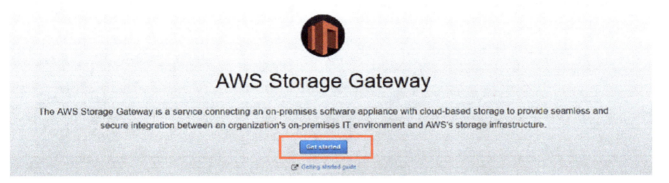

Choose **Get started** to open the **Create gateway** page. On this page, you choose a gateway type. If you have a gateway in the current AWS Region, the console shows your gateway in the console.

Topics

- Creating a File Gateway
- Creating a Volume Gateway
- Creating a Tape Gateway

Creating a File Gateway

In this section, you can find instructions about how to create and use a file gateway.

Topics

- Creating a Gateway
- Creating a File Share
- Using Your File Share

Creating a Gateway

In this section, you can find instructions about how to download, deploy, and activate a tape gateway.

Topics

- Choosing a Gateway Type
- Choosing a Host Platform and Downloading the VM
- Connecting to Your Gateway
- Activating Your Gateway
- Configuring Local Disks

Choosing a Gateway Type

For a tape gateway, you store and archive your data on virtual tapes in AWS. A tape gateway eliminates some of the challenges associated with owning and operating an on-premises physical tape infrastructure.

To create a tape gateway

1. Open the AWS Management Console at http://console.aws.amazon.com/storagegateway/home, and choose the AWS Region that you want to create your gateway in.

   If you have previously created a gateway in this AWS Region, the console shows your gateway. Otherwise, the console home page appears.

2. If you haven't created a gateway in the AWS Region you selected, choose **Get started**. If you already have a gateway in the AWS Region you selected, choose **Gateways** from the navigation pane, and then choose **Create gateway**.

3. On the **Select gateway type page**, choose **Tape gateway**, and then choose **Next**.

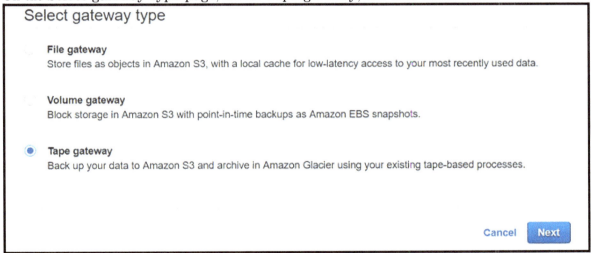

Choosing a Host Platform and Downloading the VM

If you create your gateway on-premises, you download and deploy the gateway VM and then activate the gateway. If you create your gateway on an Amazon EC2 instance, you launch an Amazon Machine Image (AMI) that contains the gateway VM image and then activate the gateway. For information about supported host platforms, see Supported Hypervisors and Host Requirements.

Note
You can run only file, cached volume, and tape gateways on an Amazon EC2 instance.

To select a host platform and download the VM

1. On the **Select host platform** page, choose the virtualization platform that you want to run your gateway on.

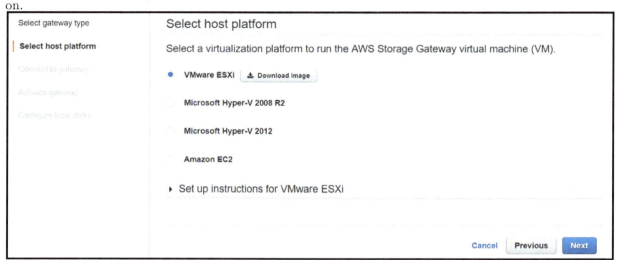

2. Choose **Download image** next to your virtualization platform to download a .zip file that contains the .ova file for your virtualization platform. **Note**
The .zip file is over 500 MB in size and might take some time to download, depending on your network connection.

   For EC2, you create an instance from the provided AMI.

3. Deploy the downloaded image to your hypervisor. You need to add at least one local disk for your cache and one local disk for your upload buffer during the deployment. A file gateway requires only one local disk for a cache. For information about local disk requirements, see Hardware and Storage Requirements.

   If you choose VMware, do the following:

   - Store your disk in **Thick provisioned format**. When you use thick provisioning, the disk storage is allocated immediately, resulting in better performance. In contrast, thin provisioning allocates storage on demand. On-demand allocation can affect the normal functioning of AWS Storage Gateway. For Storage Gateway to function properly, the VM disks must be stored in thick-provisioned format.
   - Configure your gateway VM to use paravirtualized disk controllers. For more information, see Configuring the AWS Storage Gateway VM to Use Paravirtualized Disk Controllers.

   If you choose Microsoft Hyper-V, do the following:

   - Configure the disk type as **Fixed size**. When you use fixed-size provisioning, the disk storage is allocated immediately, resulting in better performance. If you don't use fixed-size provisioning, the storage is allocated on demand. On-demand allocation can affect the functioning of AWS Storage Gateway. For Storage Gateway to function properly, the VM disks must be stored in fixed-size provisioned format.
   - When allocating disks, choose **virtual hard disk (.vhd) file**. Storage Gateway supports the .vhdx file type. By using this file type, you can create larger virtual disks than with other file types. If you create a .vhdx type virtual disk, make sure that the size of the virtual disks that you create doesn't exceed the recommended disk size for your gateway.

   For both VMware and Microsoft Hyper-V, synchronizing the VM time with the host time is required for successful gateway activation. Make sure that your host clock is set to the correct time and synchronize it with a Network Time Protocol (NTP) server.

For information about deploying your gateway to an Amazon EC2 host, see Deploy your gateway to an Amazon EC2 host.

36

Connecting to Your Gateway

To connect to your gateway, the first step is to get the IP address of your gateway VM. You use this IP address to activate your gateway. For gateways deployed and activated on an on-premises host, you can get the IP address from your gateway VM local console or your hypervisor client. For gateways deployed and activated on an Amazon EC2 instance, you can get the IP address from the Amazon EC2 console.

The activation process associates your gateway with your AWS account. Your gateway VM must be running for activation to succeed.

Make sure that you connect to the correct gateway type. The .ova files and AMIs for the gateway types are different and are not interchangeable.

To get the IP address for your gateway VM from the local console

1. Log on to your gateway VM local console. For detailed instructions, see the following:
    - VMware ESXi—Accessing the Gateway Local Console with VMware ESXi.
    - Microsoft Hyper-V—Access the Gateway Local Console with Microsoft Hyper-V.

2. Get the IP address from the top of the menu page, and make note of it for later use.

To get the IP address from an EC2 instance

1. Open the Amazon EC2 console at https://console.aws.amazon.com/ec2/.

2. In the navigation pane, choose **Instances**, and then choose the EC2 instance.

3. Choose the **Description** tab at the bottom, and then note the IP address. You use this IP address to activate the gateway.

For activation, you can use the public or private IP address assigned to a gateway. You must be able to reach the IP address that you use from the browser from which you perform the activation. In this walkthrough, we use the public IP address to activate the gateway.

To associate your gateway with your AWS account

1. If the **Connect to gateway** page isn't already open, open the console and navigate to that page.

2. Type the IP address of your gateway for **IP address**, and then choose **Connect gateway**.

Connect to gateway

Type the IP address of your gateway VM. Your web browser must be able to connect to this IP address. The IP address doesn't need to be accessible from outside your network.

🗗 Learn more

IP address   01.123.45.67

                                                    Cancel   Previous   **Connect to gateway**

For detailed information about how to get a gateway IP address, see Connecting to Your Gateway.

Activating Your Gateway

When your gateway VM is deployed and running, you can configure your gateway settings and activate your gateway. If activation fails, check that the IP address you entered is correct. If the IP address is correct, confirm that your network is configured to let your browser access the gateway VM. For more information on troubleshooting, see Troubleshooting On-Premises Gateway Issues or Troubleshooting Amazon EC2 Gateway Issues.

To configure your gateway settings

1. Type the information listed on the activation page to configure your gateway settings and complete the activation process.

   The following screenshot shows the activation page for tape gateways.

   Activate gateway

   Selected gateway configuration: VTL gateway

   Activation securely associates your gateway with your AWS account. Learn more

   Storage and data transfer pricing applies when you start using your gateway. Learn more

   AWS Region   US East (Ohio)

   Gateway time zone   GMT Western Europe Time, London, Lisbon,... ▼

   Gateway name   Gateway_VTL_Test

   Backup application   EMC Networker ▼ 🛈

   Tape drive type   IBM-ULT3580-TD5

                                                    Cancel   **Activate gateway**

   - **AWS Region** specifies the AWS Region where your gateway will be created and your data stored.

   - **Gateway time zone** specifies the time zone to use for your gateway.

   - **Gateway name** identifies your gateway. You use this name to manage your gateway in the console; you can change it after the gateway is activated. This name must be unique to your account.

   - **Backup application** specifies the backup application you want to use. Storage Gateway automatically chooses a compatible medium changer for your backup application. If your backup application is not listed, choose **Other** and choose a medium changer type.

Activate gateway

Selected gateway configuration: VTL gateway

Activation securely associates your gateway with your AWS account Learn more

Storage and data transfer pricing applies when you start using your gateway Learn more

AWS Region	US East (Ohio)
Gateway time zone	GMT Western Europe Time, London, Lisbon... ▼
Gateway name	Gateway_VTL_Test
Backup application	Other ▼ ❶
Medium changer type	● AWS-Gateway-VTL STK-L700
Tape drive type	IBM-ULT3580-TD5

Cancel   Activate gateway

Medium changer type specifies the type of medium changer to use for your backup application.

The type of medium changer you choose depends on the backup application you plan to use. The following table lists third-party backup applications that have been tested and found to be compatible with tape gateways. This table includes the medium changer type recommended for each backup application.
[See the AWS documentation website for more details] **Important**
We highly recommend that you choose the medium changer that's listed for your backup application. Other medium changers might not function properly. You can choose a different medium changer after the gateway is activated. For more information, see Selecting a Medium Changer After Gateway Activation.

- **Tape drive type** specifies the type of tape drive used by this gateway.

2. Choose **Activate gateway**.

   When the gateway is successfully activated, the AWS Storage Gateway console displays the **Configure local storage** page.

   If activation is not successful, see Troubleshooting Your Gateway for possible solutions.

Configuring Local Disks

When you deployed the VM, you allocated local disks for your gateway. Now you configure your gateway to use these disks.

Note
If you allocate local disks on a VMware host, make sure to configure the disks to use paravirtualized disk controllers.
When adding a cache or upload buffer to an existing gateway, make sure to create new disks in your host (hypervisor or Amazon EC2 instance). Don't change the size of existing disks if the disks have been previously allocated as either a cache or upload buffer.

To configure local disks

1. On the **Configure local disks** page, identify the disks you allocated and decide which ones you want to use for an upload buffer and cached storage. For information about disk size limits, see Configuration and

Performance Limits.

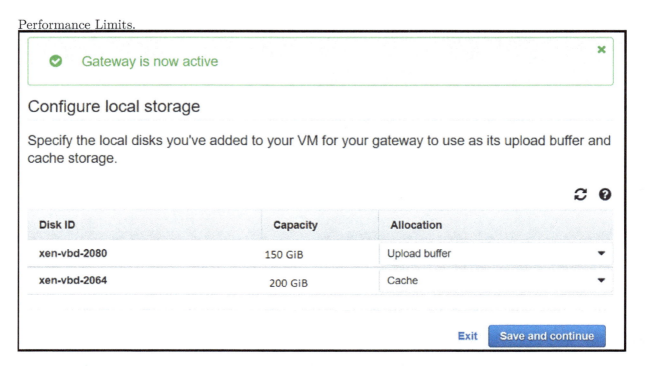

2. In the **Allocation** column next to your upload buffer disk, choose **Upload Buffer**.

3. Choose **Cache** for the disk you want to configure as cache storage.

   If you don't see your disks, choose **Refresh**.

4. Choose **Save and continue** to save your configuration settings.

Next Step

Creating Tapes

Creating a File Share

Topics

- Creating an NFS File Share
- Creating an SMB File Share

In this section, you can find instructions about how to create a file share. You can create a file share that can be accessed using either the NFS or SMB protocol.

For **NFS**:

- There is one type of NFS file share. When you create an NFS share, by default, anyone who has access to the NFS server can access the NFS file share. You can limit access to clients by IP address.

For **SMB**, you can have one of three different modes of authentication:

- A file share with Active Directory access. Any authenticated AD user will get access to this file share type.
- An SMB file share with limited access. Only certain domain users and groups that you speciffy are allowed access.
- An SMB file share with guest access. Any users who can provide the guest password will get access to this file share.

A file gateway can host one or more file shares of different types. You can have multiple NFS and/or SMB file shares on a file gateway, but only one form of SMB authentication is allowed per file gateway.

Important

To create a file share, a file gateway requires you to activate AWS Security Token Service (AWS STS). Make sure that AWS STS is activated in the AWS Region that you are creating your file gateway in. If AWS STS is not activated in that AWS Region, activate it. For information about how to activate AWS STS, see Activating and Deactivating AWS STS in an AWS Region in the *IAM User Guide*.

Note

You can use AWS Key Management Service (AWS KMS) to encrypt objects that the file gateway stores in Amazon S3. Currently, you can do this by using the AWS Storage Gateway API Reference. For more information, see the API Reference for instructions.

Creating an NFS File Share

To create an NSF file share

1. Open the AWS Storage Gateway console at https://console.aws.amazon.com/storagegateway/home.

2. Choose **Create file share**.

3. For **Amazon S3 bucket name**, provide the name for the Amazon S3 bucket for your gateway to store your files in and retrieve your files to. This name must be compliant with Domain Name Service (DNS). This bucket must also exist already in S3; it isn't created for you by File Gateway. For information on DNS-compliant names for buckets, see Rules for Bucket Naming in the *Amazon Simple Storage Service Developer Guide*.

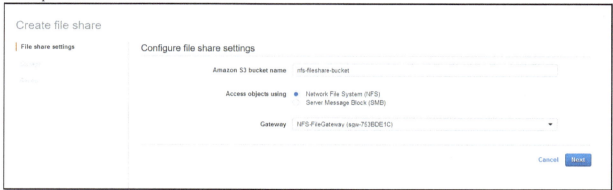

4. For **Access objects using**, choose **Network File System(NFS)**..

5. For **Gateway**, choose your file gateway from the list and choose **Next**.

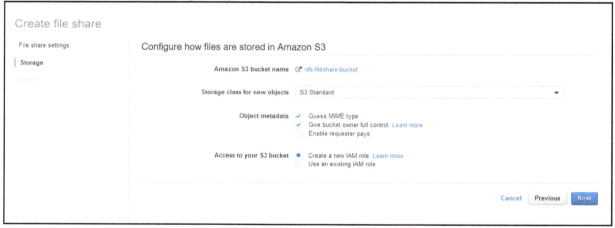

6. For **Storage class for new objects**, choose a storage class to use for new objects created in your Amazon S3 bucket:

   - Choose **S3 Standard** to store your frequently accessed object data redundantly in multiple Availability Zones that are geographically separated.
   - Choose **S3 Standard-IA** to store your infrequently accessed object data redundantly in multiple Availability Zones that are geographically separated.
   - Choose **S3 One Zone-IA** to store your infrequently accessed object data in a single Availability Zone.

   For more information, see Storage Classes in the *Amazon Simple Storage Service Developer Guide*.

7. For **Object metadata**, choose the metadata you want to use:

- Choose **Guess MIME type** to enable guessing of the MIME type for uploaded objects based on file extensions.
- Choose **Give bucket owner full control** to give full control to the owner of the S3 bucket that maps to the file NFS file share. For more information on using your file share to access objects in a bucket owned by another account, see Using a File Share for Cross-Account Access.
- Choose **Enable requester pays** if you are using this file share on a bucket that requires the requester or reader instead of bucket owner to pay for access charges. For more information, see Requester Pays Buckets.

8. For **Access to your bucket**, choose the AWS Identity and Access Management (IAM) role that you want your gateway to use to access your Amazon S3 bucket. This role allows the gateway to access your S3 bucket. A file gateway can create a new IAM role and access policy on your behalf. Or, if you have an IAM role you want to use, you can specify it in the **IAM role** box and set up the access policy manually. For more information, see Granting Access to an Amazon S3 Bucket. For information about IAM roles, see IAM Roles in the *IAM User Guide*.

9. Choose **Next** to review configuration settings for your file share. You can change the allowed NFS clients for **Allowed clients** as needed.

   To change **Squash level** and **Export as** under **Mount options** and to change **File metadata defaults** options, choose **Edit** by the option to change. **Note**
   For file shares mounted on a Microsoft Windows client, if you choose **Read-only** for **Export as**, you might see a message about an unexpected error keeping you from creating the folder. You can ignore this message.

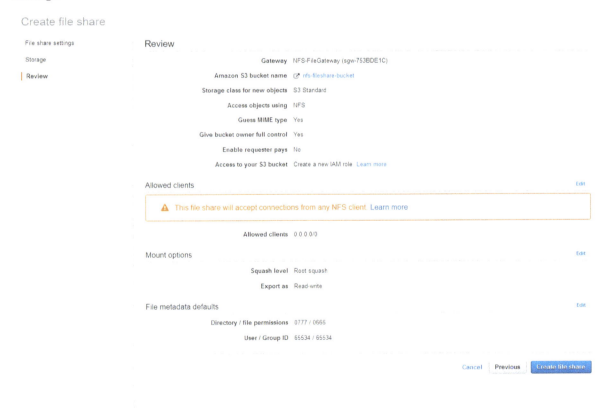

The next step is to review configuration settings for your file share. File gateway applies default settings to your file share. .

To change the configuration settings for your NFS file share do the following:

1. Choose **Edit** for the settings you want to change.

2. Configure **Allowed clients** to allow or restrict each client's access to your file share. For more information, see Editing Access Settings for Your NFS File Share.

3. (Optional) Modify the mount options for your file share as needed.

4. (Optional) Modify the file metadata defaults as needed. For more information, see Editing Metadata Defaults for Your NFS File Share.

5. Review your file share configuration settings, and then choose **Create file share**.

    After your file share is created, you can see your file share settings in the file share's **Details** tab.

Next Step

Mounting Your NFS File Share on Your Client

Creating an SMB File Share

Creating an SMB accessible file share is a *two-step process*. Before you create an SMB file share you need to configure your file gateway **SMB Settings** for either Active Directory or Guest access. A file share can provide one type of SMB access only. After setting the authentication methods you create your file share.

Note
An SMB file share will not operate correctly without the requisite ports open in you security group. For more information, see Port Requirements.

To configure your SMB file share for Active Directory access

1. Sign in to your console and on the **Gateway** page enable the check box next to the file gateway you wish to join to a domain.

2. Select **Actions**, choose then **Edit SMB Settings**.

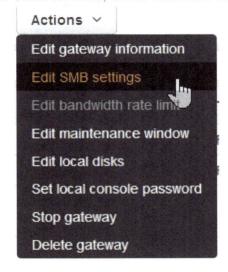

The **Edit SMB dialog box** appears as shown in the figure below.

3. For *Active Directory authentication* enable the **Join Domain** check box,

4. Enter your fully qualified domain name into the **Domain name** text field. **Note**
The AWS Directory Service allows you to create a hosted Active Directory domain service in the AWS cloud if you require that option.

Edit SMB settings ✖

Active Directory settings

Join domain ☐

Domain name *Fully qualified domain or realm*

Domain user

Domain password

Guest access settings

Set guest password ☐

Guest password

Cancel   **Save**

5. Enter your account name into the **Domain name** text box. This account must have the privilege of joining a server to a domain.

6. Type in your acccount password into the **Domain password** text box.

7. Then select **Save** to complete SMB file share Active Directory authentication.

   A message at the top of the Gateways section of your console indicates that your gateway successfully joined your AD domain.

To configure your SMB file share for Guest access

1. Sign in to your console and on the **Gateway** page enable the check box next to the file gateway you wish to join to a domain.

2. Select **Actions**, choose then **Edit SMB Settings**.

The **Edit SMB dialog box** appears as shown in the figure below.

Edit SMB settings   ✖

Active Directory settings
_____

Join domain   ☐

Domain name | _Fully qualified domain or realm_ |

Domain user | |

Domain password | |

Guest access settings
_____

Set guest password ☐

Guest password | |

                                        Cancel   [Save]

3. Enable *Guest access* for your SMB file share enable **Set guest password. Note**
   It is not necessary for a file gateway to be part of an AD domain if only guest access is provided. A file gateway that is a member of your AD domain can also be used to create file shares with guest access.

4. In Guest password enter a password that meets your organization's security requirements.

5. Choose **Save** to complete SMB file share Guest access authentication.

   A message at the top of the Gateways section of your console indicates that your gateway now allows guest access.

In the next procedure you will create an SMB file share with either Active Directory or Guest access using the **Create File Share** wizard. You should have completed the SMB file share settings (above) for your file gateway before peforming the steps below.

To create an SMB file share

1. Open the AWS Storage Gateway console at https://console.aws.amazon.com/storagegateway/home.

2. On the navigation pane, choose **Shares**, select the file gateway you wish to use, and then choose **Create**

file share. You can also choose **Create file share** from the Gateway tab.

The **Create file share** wizard appears with the **Configure file share settings** page open as shown below.

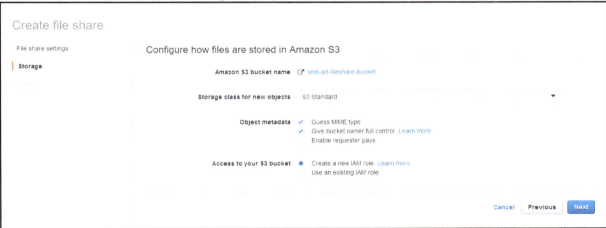

3. For **Amazon S3 bucket name**, provide a name for an existing Amazon S3 bucket for your gateway to store your files in and retrieve your files to.

   The Create file share wizard cannot create an S3 bucket automatically. You will need to create the bucket beforehand in the AWS S3 service.

4. Select **Server Message Block (SMB)** in the **Access Objects using** section.

5. If you have already selected the file gateway prior to starting the wizard its name will be populated into the Gateway list box. If not, then select the file gateway you wish to use from the list box, then select **Next**.

   The **Create file share** wizard **Storage** step appears as shown below.

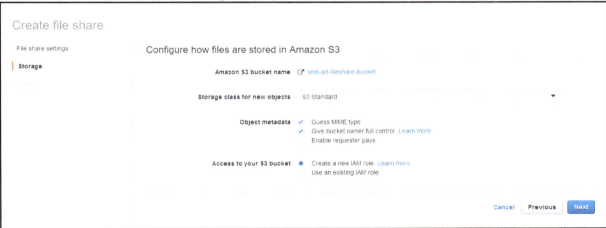

6. For **Storage class for new objects**, choose a storage class to use for new objects created in your Amazon S3 bucket:

   - Choose **S3 Standard** to store your frequently accessed object data redundantly in multiple Availability Zones that are geographically separated.
   - Choose **S3 Standard-IA** to store your infrequently accessed object data redundantly in multiple Availability Zones that are geographically separated.
   - Choose **S3 One Zone-IA** to store your infrequently accessed object data in a single Availability Zone.

   For more information, see Storage Classes in the *Amazon Simple Storage Service Developer Guide*.

7. For **Object metadata**, choose the metadata you want to use:

- Choose **Guess MIME type** to enable guessing of the MIME type for uploaded objects based on file extensions.
- Choose **Give bucket owner full control** to give full control to the owner of the S3 bucket that maps to the file NFS file share. For more information on using your file share to access objects in a bucket owned by another account, see Using a File Share for Cross-Account Access.
- Choose **Enable requester pays** if you are using this file share on a bucket that requires the requester or reader instead of bucket owner to pay for access charges. For more information, see Requester Pays Buckets.

8. For **Access to your bucket**, choose the AWS Identity and Access Management (IAM) role that you want your gateway to use to access your Amazon S3 bucket. This role allows the gateway to access your S3 bucket. A file gateway can create a new IAM role and access policy on your behalf. Or, if you have an IAM role you want to use, you can specify it in the **IAM role** box and set up the access policy manually. For more information, see Granting Access to an Amazon S3 Bucket. For information about IAM roles, see IAM Roles in the *IAM User Guide*.

9. Choose **Next** to view the **Review** configuration settings for your SMB file share.as shown in the figure below.

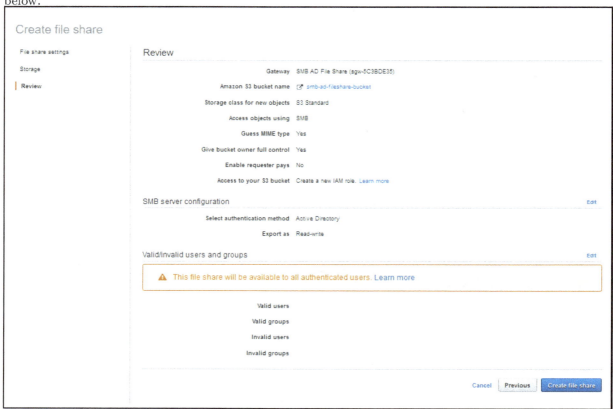

10. *Active Directory access* is the default authentication method. For AD authentication check that Active Directory is shown in the **Select authentication method** text box. **Note**
For Active Directory access your file gateway must be joined to a domain.
For Guest access you must have set a guest access password.

11. If you want to change to *Guest access* choose **Edit** in the **SMB server configuration** section, and then select **Guest acess** from the drop down menu.

12. Choose the **Read-write** (the default) or **Read-only** option. Choose **Close** to enforce your authentication settings.

13. Review your file share configuration settings, and then choose **Create file share**.

After your SMB file share is created, you can see your file share settings in the file share's Details tab. A green banner is posted that shows your new file share was successfully created as shown in the figure below.

The procedure above creates an Active Directory file share where anyone with domain credentials can access the file share. To limit access to certain users and groups see Editing Access Settings for Your SMB File Share

Next Step

Mounting Your SMB File Share on Your Client

Using Your File Share

Following, you can find instructions about how to mount your file share on your client, use your share, test your file gateway, and clean up resources as needed. For more information about supported Network File System (NFS) clients, see Supported NFS Clients for a File Gateway. For more information about supported Service Message Block (SMB) clients, see Supported SMB Clients for a File Gateway.

Example commands to mount your file share can be found in the Management Console. In following sections, you will see details on how to mount your file share on your client, use your share, test your file gateway, and clean up resources as needed.

Topics

- Mounting Your NFS File Share on Your Client
- Mounting Your SMB File Share on Your Client
- Working with File Shares on a Bucket with Pre-exisiting Objects
- Testing Your File Gateway
- Where Do I Go from Here?

Mounting Your NFS File Share on Your Client

Now you mount your NFS file share on a drive on your client and map it to your Amazon S3 bucket.

To mount a file share and map it to an Amazon S3 bucket

1. If you are using a Microsoft Windows client, turn on Services for NFS in Windows.

2. Mount your NFS file share:

   - For Windows clients, type the following command at the command prompt.

     mount –o nolock -o mtype=hard *[Your gateway VM IP address]:/[S3 bucket name] [Drive letter on your windows client]*

   - For Linux clients, type the following command at the command prompt.

     sudo mount -t nfs -o nolock *[Your gateway VM IP address]:/[S3 bucket name] [mount path on your client]*

   - For MacOS clients, type the following command at the command prompt.

     sudo mount_nfs -o vers=3,nolock,rwsize=65536 -v *[Your gateway VM IP address]:/[S3 bucket name] [mount path on your client]*

For example, suppose that on a Windows client your VM's IP address is 123.456.1.2 and your Amazon S3 bucket name is `test-bucket`. Suppose also that you want to map to drive T. In this case, your command looks like the following.

mount –o nolock 123.456.1.2:/test-bucket T: Note
When mounting file shares, be aware of the following:
You might have a case where a folder and an object exist in an Amazon S3 bucket and have the same name. In this case, if the object name doesn't contain a trailing slash, only the folder is visible in a file gateway. For example, if a bucket contains an object named `test` or `test/` and a folder named `test/test1`, only `test/` and `test/test1` are visible in a file gateway. You might need to remount your file share after a reboot of your client. By default Windows uses a soft mount for mounting your NFS share. Soft mounts time out more easily when there are connection issues. We recommend using a hard mount because a hard mount is safer and better preserves your data. The soft mount command omits the **-o mtype=hard** switch.

Next Step

Testing Your File Gateway

Mounting Your SMB File Share on Your Client

Now you mount your SMB file share and map to a drive accessible to your client. The file gateway console show the supported mount commands that you can use for SMB clients. This section offers some additional options for you to try.

You can use several different methods for mounting SMB file shares, including the following:

- The `net use` command – Doesn't persist across system reboots. The specific command that you use depends on whether you plan to use your file share for Microsoft Active Directory (AD) access or guest access.
- The `CmdKey` command line utility – Creates a persistent connection to a mounted SMB file share that remains after a reboot.
- A network drive mapped in File Explorer – Configures the mounted file share to reconnect at sign-in and to require that you enter your network credentials.
- PowerShell script – Can be persistent, and can be either visible or invisible to the operating system while mounted.

Note

If you are a Microsoft AD user, check with your administrator to ensure that you have access to the SMB file share before mounting the file share to your local system.

If you are a guest user, make sure that you have the guest user account password before attempting to mount the file share.

To mount your SMB file share for Microsoft AD users using the net use command

1. Make sure that you have access to the SMB file share before mounting the file share to your local system.

2. Mount your SMB file share:

   - For Windows clients, type the following command at the command prompt.

     net use *[WindowsDriveLetter]***:** *[Gateway IP Address]**[File share name]*

   - For Linux clients, type the following command at the command prompt.

     sudo mount -t smbfs *//[Gateway IP address]/[File Share name] [MountPath]*

   - For MacOS clients, type the following command at the command prompt.

     sudo mount_smbfs *//[Gateway IP address]:/[File Share name] [MountPath]*

To mount your SMB file share for guest users using the net use command

1. Make sure that you have the guest user account password before mounting the file share.

2. Mount your SMB file share:

   - For Windows clients, type the following command at the command prompt.

     net use *[WindowsDriveLetter]***:** \\\\$*[Gateway IP Address]*\\$*[path]* **/user:**$*[Gateway ID]***smbguest**

   - For Linux clients, type the following command at the command prompt.

     sudo mount -t smbfs *//[Gateway IP address]/[File Share name] [MountPath]*

   - For MacOS clients, type the following command at the command prompt.

     sudo mount_smbfs *//*$*[Gateway ID]]***;smbguest@***[File Gateway IP]*$*[path] [MountPath]*

To mount an SMB file share on Windows using CmdKey:

1. Press the Windows key and type **cmd** to view the command prompt menu item.

2. Open the context (right-click) menu for **Command Prompt** and choose **Run as administrator**.

3. Type the following command:

C:\\>cmdkey /add:*[Gateway VM IP address]* /user:*[DomainName][UserName]*
/pass:*[Password]***

Note

When mounting file shares, be aware of the following:

You might have a case where a folder and an object exist in an Amazon S3 bucket and have the same name. In this case, if the object name doesn't contain a trailing slash, only the folder is visible in a file gateway. For example, if a bucket contains an object named `test` or `test/` and a folder named `test/test1`, only `test/` and `test/test1` are visible in a file gateway. You might need to remount your file share after a reboot of your client.

To mount an SMB file share using Windows File Explorer

1. Press the Windows key and type **File Explorer** in the **Search Windows** box, or press **Win+E**.

2. In the navigation pane, choose **This PC**, then choose **Map Network Drive** for **Map Network Drive** in the **Computer** tab, as shown in the following screenshot.

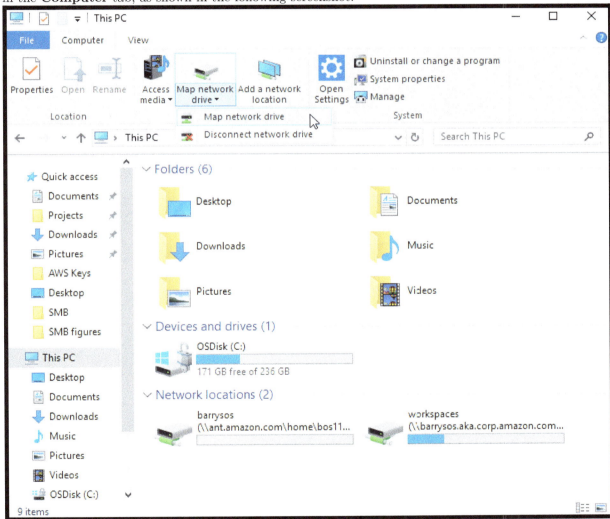

3. In the **Map Network Drive** dialog box, choose a drive letter for **Drive**.

4. For **Folder**, type *[File Gateway IP]**[SMB File Share Name]*, or choose **Browse** to select your SMB file share from the dialog box.

5. (Optional) Select **Reconnect at sign-up** if you want your mount point to persist after reboots.

6. (Optional) Select **Connect using different credentials** if you want a user to enter the Active Directory logon or guest account user password.

7. Choose **Finish** to complete your mount point.

You can edit file share settings, edit allowed and denied users and groups, and change the guest access password from the Storage Gateway Management Console. You can also refresh the data in the file share's cache and delete a file share from the console.

Note

It is important to understand that gateway level settings that you enter in the **Edit SMB Settings** for AD and guest access are different than the share level settings that you apply to a specific SMB file share from the file shares page. Do not mix up the general settings for those that apply to specific SMB file shares or you may provide access to file shares to people you don't intend to have that access.

To modify your SMB file share's properties

1. Open the AWS Storage Gateway console at https://console.aws.amazon.com/storagegateway/home.

2. On the navigation pane, choose **File Shares**.

3. On the **File Share** page, select the check box by the SMB file share that you want to modify.

4. For Actions, choose the action that you want:
   - Choose **Edit file share settings** to modify share access.
   - Choose **Edit allowed/denied users** to add or delete users and groups, and then type the allowed and denied users and groups into the **Allowed Users**, **Denied Users**, **Allowed Groups**, and **Denied Groups** boxes. Use the **Add Entry** buttons to create new access rights, and the **(X)** button to remove access.

5. When you're finished, choose **Save**.

   When you enter allowed users and groups you are creating a whitelist. Without a whitelist all authenticated AD users can acces the SMB file share. Any users and groups that are marked as denied are added to a blacklist and can't acess the SMB file share. In instances where a user or group is on the blacklist and whitelist, the blacklist always takes precedence.

Next Step

Testing Your File Gateway

Working with File Shares on a Bucket with Pre-exisiting Objects

You can export a file share on an Amazon S3 bucket with objects created outside of the file gateway using either NFS or SMB. Standard POSIX access and permissions are used in the file share. When files are written back to the Amazon S3 bucket they assume the properties and access rights that the person saving the files give them. Objects can be uploaded to an S3 bucket at any time. For the file share to display these newly added objects as files, you need to refresh the cache first.

Note
Be sure to read the *Can I have multiple writers to my Amazon S3 bucket?* in the FAQ section. This practice is not recommended.

To assign metadata defaults to objects accessed using **NFS**, refer to the section *Editing Metadata Defaults* iin the Managing Your File Gateway topic.

For **SMB** you can export a share using AD or guest access on an Amazon S3 bucket with preexisting objects. Objects in the bucket created outside of the gateway display as files in the SMB file system when they are accessed by your SMB clients. SMB file share files inherits ownership and permissions from the root ACL. The ower=smbguest, file permissions are 666 and directory permissions are 777 when there are no parent directories. In the case when there are directories into which objects were previously populated the object inherits the POSIX metadata of those parent directories.

Testing Your File Gateway

You can copy files and folders to your mapped drive. The files automatically upload to your Amazon S3 bucket.

To upload files from your windows client to Amazon S3

1. On your Windows client, navigate to the drive that you mounted your file share on. The name of your drive is preceded by the name of your S3 bucket.

2. Copy files or a folder to the drive.

3. On the Amazon S3 Management Console, navigate to your mapped bucket. You should see the files and folders that you copied in the Amazon S3 bucket that you specified.

    You can see the file share that you created in the **File shares** tab in the AWS Storage Gateway Management Console.

Your NFS or SMB client can write, read, delete, rename, and truncate files.

Note
File gateways don't support creating hard or symbolic links on a file share.

Keep in mind these points about how file gateways work with S3:

- Reads are served from a read-through cache. In other words, if data isn't available, it's fetched from S3 and added to the cache.
- Writes are sent to S3 through optimized multipart uploads by using a write-back cache.
- Read and writes are optimized so that only the parts that are requested or changed are transferred over the network.
- Deletes remove objects from S3.
- Directories are managed as folder objects in S3, using the same syntax as in the Amazon S3 console. You can rename empty directories.
- Recursive file system operation performance (for example `ls l`) depends on the number of objects in your bucket.

Next Step

Where Do I Go from Here?

Where Do I Go from Here?

After your tape gateway is in production, you can perform several maintenance tasks, such as adding and removing tapes, monitoring and optimizing gateway performance, and troubleshooting. For general information about these management tasks, see Managing Your Gateway.

You can perform some of the tape gateway maintenance tasks on the AWS Management Console, such as configuring your gateway's bandwidth rate limits and managing gateway software updates. If your tape gateway is deployed on-premises, you can perform some maintenance tasks on the gateway's local console. These include routing your tape gateway through a proxy and configuring your gateway to use a static IP address. If you are running your gateway as an Amazon EC2 instance, you can perform specific maintenance tasks on the Amazon EC2 console, such as adding and removing Amazon EBS volumes. For more information on maintaining your tape gateway, see Managing Your Tape Gateway.

If you plan to deploy your gateway in production, you should take your real workload into consideration in determining the disk sizes. For information on how to determine real-world disk sizes, see Managing Local Disks for Your AWS Storage Gateway. Also, consider cleaning up if you don't plan to continue using your tape gateway. Cleaning up lets you avoid incurring charges. For information on cleanup, see Cleaning Up Resources You Don't Need.

Cleaning Up Resources You Don't Need

If you created the gateway as an example exercise or a test, consider cleaning up to avoid incurring unexpected or unnecessary charges.

If you plan to continue using your tape gateway, see additional information in Where Do I Go from Here?

To clean up resources you don't need

1. Delete tapes from both your gateway's virtual tape library (VTL) and archive. For more information, see Deleting Your Gateway by Using the AWS Storage Gateway Console and Removing Associated Resources.

    1. Archive any tapes that have the **RETRIEVED** status in your gateway's VTL. For instructions, see Archiving Tapes.

    2. Delete any remaining tapes from your gateway's VTL. For instructions, see Deleting Tapes.

    3. Delete any tapes you have in the archive. For instructions, see Deleting Tapes.

2. Unless you plan to continue using the tape gateway, delete it: For instructions, see Deleting Your Gateway by Using the AWS Storage Gateway Console and Removing Associated Resources.

3. Delete the AWS Storage Gateway VM from your on-premises host. If you created your gateway on an Amazon EC2 instance, terminate the instance.

Creating a Volume Gateway

In this section, you can find instructions about how to create and use a volume gateway.

Topics

- Creating a Gateway
- Creating a Volume
- Using Your Volume

Creating a Volume

Previously, you allocated local disks that you added to the VM cache storage and upload buffer. Now you create a storage volume to which your applications read and write data. The gateway maintains the volume's recently accessed data locally in cache storage, and asynchronously transferred data to Amazon S3. For stored volumes, you allocated local disks that you added to the VM upload buffer and your application's data.

Note
You can use AWS Key Management Service (AWS KMS) to encrypt data written to a cached volume that is stored in Amazon S3. Currently, you can do this by using the AWS Storage Gateway API Reference. For more information, see CreateCachediSCSIVolume or create-cached-iscsi-volume.

To create a volume

1. Open the AWS Storage Gateway console at https://console.aws.amazon.com/storagegateway/home.

2. On the AWS Storage Gateway console, choose **Create volume**.

3. In the **Create volume** dialog box, choose a gateway for **Gateway**.

4. For the cached volumes, type the capacity in **Capacity**.

   For stored volumes, choose a **Disk ID** value from the list.

5. For **Volume content**, your choices depend on the type of gateway you are creating the volume for.

   For cached volumes, you have the following options:

   - **Create a new empty volume.**
   - **Create a volume based on an Amazon EBS snapshot**. If you choose this option, provide a value for **EBS snapshot ID**.
   - **Clone from last volume recovery point**. If you choose this option, choose a volume ID for **Source volume**. If there are no volumes in the region, this option doesn't appear.

   For stored volumes, you have the following options:

   - **Create a new empty volume.**
   - **Create a volume based on a snapshot**. If you choose this option, provide a value for **EBS snapshot ID**.
   - **Preserve existing data on the disk**

6. Type a name for **iSCSI target name**.

   The target name can contain lowercase letters, numbers, periods (.), and hyphens (-). This target name appears as the **iSCSI target node** name in the **Targets** tab of the **iSCSI Microsoft initiator** UI after discovery. For example, the name `target1` appears as `iqn.1007-05.com.amazon:target1`. Make sure that the target name is globally unique within your storage area network (SAN).

7. Verify that the **Network interface** setting has IP address selected, or choose an IP address for **Network interface**. For **Network interface**, one IP address appears for each adapter that is configured for the gateway VM. If the gateway VM is configured for only one network adapter, no **Network interface** list appears because there is only one IP address.

   Your iSCSI target will be available on the network adapter you choose.

   If you have defined your gateway to use multiple network adapters, choose the IP address that your storage applications should use to access your volume. For information about configuring multiple network adapters, see Configuring Your Gateway for Multiple NICs. **Note**
   After you choose a network adapter, you can't change this setting.

8. Choose **Create volume**.

If you have previously created volumes in this region, you can see them listed on the Storage Gateway console.

The **Configure CHAP Authentication** dialog box appears. You can configure Challenge-Handshake Authentication Protocol (CHAP) for your volume at this point, or you can choose **Cancel** and configure CHAP later. For more information on CHAP setup, see Configure CHAP Authentication for Your Volumes, following.

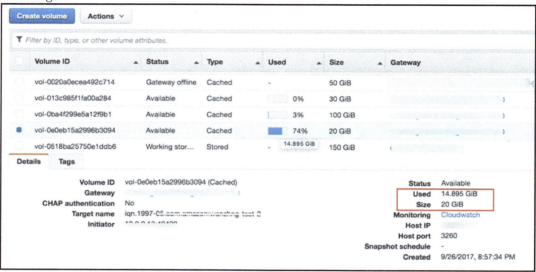

If you don't want to set up CHAP, get started using your volume. For more information, see Using Your Volume.

Configure CHAP Authentication for Your Volumes

CHAP provides protection against playback attacks by requiring authentication to access your storage volume targets. In the **Configure CHAP Authentication** dialog box, you provide information to configure CHAP for your volumes.

To configure CHAP

1. Choose the volume for which you want to configure CHAP.

2. For **Actions**, choose **Configure CHAP authentication**.

3. For **Initiator Name**, type the name of your initiator.

4. For **Initiator secret**, type the secret phrase you used to authenticate your iSCSI initiator.

5. For **Target secret**, type the secret phrase used to authenticate your target for mutual CHAP.

6. Choose **Save** to save your entries.

   For more information about setting up CHAP authentication, see Configuring CHAP Authentication for Your iSCSI Targets.

Next Step

Using Your Volume

Using Your Volume

Following, you can find instructions about how to use your volume. To use your volume, you first connect it to your client as an iSCSI target, then initialize and format it.

Topics

- Connecting Your Volumes to Your Client
- Initializing and Formatting Your Volume
- Testing Your Gateway
- Where Do I Go from Here?

Connecting Your Volumes to Your Client

You use the iSCSI initiator in your client to connect to your volumes. At the end of the following procedure, the volumes become available as local devices on your client.

Important
With AWS Storage Gateway, you can connect multiple hosts to the same volume if the hosts coordinate access by using Windows Server Failover Clustering (WSFC). You can't connect multiple hosts to the same volume without using WSFC, for example by sharing a nonclustered NTFS/ext4 file system.

Topics

- Connecting to a Microsoft Windows Client
- Connecting to a Red Hat Enterprise Linux Client

Connecting to a Microsoft Windows Client

The following procedure shows a summary of the steps that you follow to connect to a Windows client. For more information, see Connecting iSCSI Initiators.

To connect to a Windows client

1. Start iscsicpl.exe.

2. In the **iSCSI Initiator Properties** dialog box, choose the **Discovery** tab, and then choose **Discovery Portal**.

3. In the **Discover Target Portal** dialog box, type the IP address of your iSCSI target for IP address or DNS name.

4. Connect the new target portal to the storage volume target on the gateway.

5. Choose the target, and then choose **Connect**.

6. In the **Targets** tab, make sure that the target status has the value **Connected**, indicating the target is connected, and then choose **OK**.

Connecting to a Red Hat Enterprise Linux Client

The following procedure shows a summary of the steps that you follow to connect to a Red Hat Enterprise Linux (RHEL) client. For more information, see Connecting iSCSI Initiators.

To connect a Linux client to iSCSI targets

1. Install the iscsi-initiator-utils RPM package.

   You can use the following command to install the package.

```
1 sudo yum install iscsi-initiator-utils
```

2. Make sure that the iSCSI daemon is running.

   For RHEL 5 or 6, use the following command.

```
1 sudo /etc/init.d/iscsi status
```

   For RHEL 7, use the following command.

```
1 sudo service iscsid status
```

3. Discover the volume or VTL device targets defined for a gateway. Use the following discovery command.

```
1 sudo /sbin/iscsiadm --mode discovery --type sendtargets --portal [GATEWAY_IP]:3260
```

   The output of the discovery command should look like the following example output.

   For volume gateways: `[GATEWAY_IP]:3260, 1 iqn.1997-05.com.amazon:myvolume`

   For tape gateways: `iqn.1997-05.com.amazon:[GATEWAY_IP]-tapedrive-01`

4. Connect to a target.

   Make sure to specify the correct *[GATEWAY_IP]* and IQN in the connect command.

   Use the following command.

```
1 sudo /sbin/iscsiadm --mode node --targetname iqn.1997-05.com.amazon:[ISCSI_TARGET_NAME] --
      portal [GATEWAY_IP]:3260,1 --login
```

5. Verify that the volume is attached to the client machine (the initiator). To do so, use the following command.

```
1 ls -l /dev/disk/by-path
```

   The output of the command should look like the following example output.

   ```
   lrwxrwxrwx. 1 root root 9 Apr 16 19:31 ip-[GATEWAY_IP]:3260-iscsi-iqn.1997-05.com.
   amazon:myvolume-lun-0 -> ../../sda
   ```

   We highly recommend that after you set up your initiator you customize your iSCSI settings as discussed in Customizing Your Linux iSCSI Settings.

Initializing and Formatting Your Volume

After you use the iSCSI initiator in your client to connect to your volumes, you initialize and format your volume.

Topics

- Initializing and Formatting Your Volume on Microsoft Windows
- Initializing and Formatting Your Volume on Red Hat Enterprise Linux

Initializing and Formatting Your Volume on Microsoft Windows

Use the following procedure to initialize and format your volume on Windows.

To initialize and format your storage volume

1. Start **diskmgmt.msc** to open the **Disk Management** console.

2. In the **Initialize Disk** dialog box, initialize the volume as a **MBR (Master Boot Record)** partition. When selecting the partition style, you should take into account the type of volume you are connecting to—cached or stored—as shown in the following table.
[See the AWS documentation website for more details]

3. Create a simple volume:

    1. Bring the volume online to initialize it. All the available volumes are displayed in the disk management console.

    2. Open the context (right-click) menu for the disk, and then choose **New Simple Volume. Important** Be careful not to format the wrong disk. Check to make sure that the disk you are formatting matches the size of the local disk you allocated to the gateway VM and that it has a status of **Unallocated**.

    3. Specify the maximum disk size.

    4. Assign a drive letter or path to your volume, and format the volume by choosing **Perform a quick format. Important** We strongly recommend using **Perform a quick format** for cached volumes. Doing so results in less initialization I/O, smaller initial snapshot size, and the fastest time to a usable volume. It also avoids using cached volume space for the full format process. **Note** The time that it takes to format the volume depends on the size of the volume. The process might take several minutes to complete.

Initializing and Formatting Your Volume on Red Hat Enterprise Linux

Use the following procedure to initialize and format your volume on Red Hat Enterprise Linux (RHEL).

To initialize and format your storage volume

1. Change directory to the `/dev` folder.

2. Run the `sudo cfdisk` command.

3. Identify your new volume by using the following command. To find new volumes, you can list the partition layout of your volumes.

    `$ lsblk`

    An "unrecognized volumes label" error for the new unpartitioned volume appears.

4. Initialize your new volume. When selecting the partition style, you should take into account the size and type of volume you are connecting to—cached or stored—as shown in the following table.
[See the AWS documentation website for more details]

    For an MBR partition, use the following command: `sudo parted /dev/your volume mklabel msdos`

    For a GPT partition, use the following command: `sudo parted /dev/your volume mklabel gpt`

5. Create a partition by using the following command.

    `sudo parted -a opt /dev/your volume mkpart primary file system 0% 100%`

6. Assign a drive letter to the partition and create a file system by using the following command.

    `sudo mkfs drive letter datapartition /dev/your volume`

7. Mount the file system by using the following command.

    `sudo mount -o defaults /dev/your volume /mnt/your directory`

Testing Your Gateway

You test your volume gateway setup by performing the following tasks:

1. Write data to the volume.

2. Take a snapshot.

3. Restore the snapshot to another volume.

You verify the setup for a gateway by taking a snapshot backup of your volume and storing the snapshot in AWS. You then restore the snapshot to a new volume. Your gateway copies the data from the specified snapshot in AWS to the new volume.

Note

Restoring data from Amazon Elastic Block Store (Amazon EBS) volumes that are encrypted is not supported.

To create a snapshot of a storage volume on Microsoft Windows

1. On your Windows computer, copy some data to your mapped storage volume.

   The amount of data copied doesn't matter for this demonstration. A small file is enough to demonstrate the restore process.

2. In the navigation pane of the AWS Storage Gateway console, choose **Volumes**.

3. Choose the storage volume that you created for the gateway.

   This gateway should have only one storage volume. Choose the volume displays its properties.

4. For **Actions**, choose **Create Snapshot** to create a snapshot of the volume.

   Depending on the amount of data on the disk and the upload bandwidth, it might take a few seconds to complete the snapshot. Note the volume ID for the volume from which you create a snapshot. You use the ID to find the snapshot.

5. In the **Create Snapshot** dialog box, provide a description for your snapshot, and then choose **Create Snapshot**.

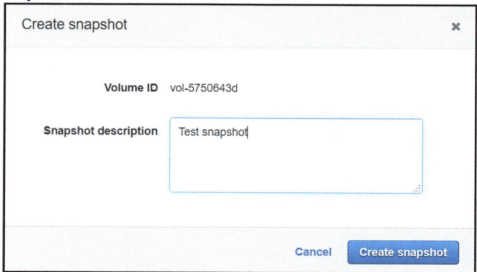

Your snapshot is stored as an Amazon EBS snapshot. Take note of your snapshot ID.

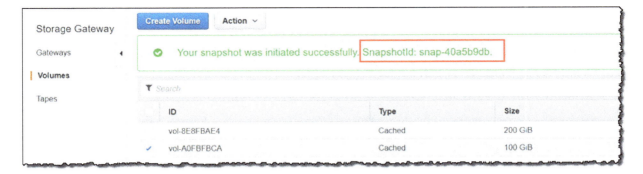

The number of snapshots created for your volume is displayed in the snapshot column.

6. For **Snapshot**, choose the link for the volume you created the snapshot for to see your EBS snapshot on the Amazon EC2 console.

Where Do I Go from Here?

In the preceding sections, you created and provisioned a gateway and then connected your host to the gateway's storage volume. You added data to the gateway's iSCSI volume, took a snapshot of the volume, and restored it to a new volume, connected to the new volume, and verified that the data shows up on it.

After you finish the exercise, consider the following:

- If you plan on continuing to use your gateway, read about sizing the upload buffer more appropriately for real-world workloads. For more information, see Sizing Your Volume Gateway's Storage for Real-World Workloads.
- If you don't plan on continuing to use your gateway, consider deleting the gateway to avoid incurring any charges. For more information, see Cleaning Up Resources You Don't Need.

Other sections of this guide include information about how to do the following:

- To learn more about storage volumes and how to manage them, see Managing Your Gateway.
- To troubleshoot gateway problems, see Troubleshooting Your Gateway.
- To optimize your gateway, see Optimizing Gateway Performance.
- To learn about Storage Gateway metrics and how you can monitor how your gateway performs, see Monitoring Your Gateway and Resources).
- To learn more about configuring your gateway's iSCSI targets to store data, see Connecting to Your Volumes to a Windows Client.

To learn about sizing your volume gateway's storage for real-world workloads and cleaning up resources you don't need, see the following sections.

Sizing Your Volume Gateway's Storage for Real-World Workloads

By this point, you have a simple, working gateway. However, the assumptions used to create this gateway are not appropriate for real-world workloads. If you want to use this gateway for real-world workloads, you need to do two things:

1. Size your upload buffer appropriately.

2. Set up monitoring for your upload buffer, if you haven't done so already.

Following, you can find how to do both of these tasks. If you activated a gateway for cached volumes, you also need to size your cache storage for real-world workloads.

To size your upload buffer and cache storage for a gateway-cached setup

- Use the formula shown in Adding and Removing Upload Buffer for sizing the upload buffer. We strongly recommend that you allocate at least 150 GiB for the upload buffer. If the upload buffer formula yields a value less than 150 GiB, use 150 GiB as your allocated upload buffer.

  The upload buffer formula takes into account the difference between throughput from your application to your gateway and throughput from your gateway to AWS, multiplied by how long you expect to write data. For example, assume that your applications write text data to your gateway at a rate of 40 MB per second for 12 hours a day and your network throughput is 12 MB per second. Assuming a compression factor of 2:1 for the text data, the formula specifies that you need to allocate approximately 675 GiB of upload buffer space.

To size your upload buffer for a stored setup

- Use the formula discussed in Adding and Removing Upload Buffer. We strongly recommend that you allocate at least 150 GiB for your upload buffer. If the upload buffer formula yields a value less than 150 GiB, use 150 GiB as your allocated upload buffer.

  The upload buffer formula takes into account the difference between throughput from your application to your gateway and throughput from your gateway to AWS, multiplied by how long you expect to write data. For example, assume that your applications write text data to your gateway at a rate of 40 MB per second for 12 hours a day and your network throughput is 12 MB per second. Assuming a compression factor of 2:1 for the text data, the formula specifies that you need to allocate approximately 675 GiB of upload buffer space.

To monitor your upload buffer

1. Open the AWS Storage Gateway console at https://console.aws.amazon.com/storagegateway/home.

2. Choose the **Gateway** tab, choose the **Details** tab, and then find the **Upload Buffer Used** field to view your gateway's current upload buffer.

3. Set one or more alarms to notify you about upload buffer use.

   We highly recommend that you create one or more upload buffer alarms in the Amazon CloudWatch console. For example, you can set an alarm for a level of use you want to be warned about and an alarm for a level of use that, if exceeded, is cause for action. The action might be adding more upload buffer space. For more information, see To set an upper threshold alarm for a gateway's upload buffer.

Cleaning Up Resources You Don't Need

If you created your gateway as an example exercise or a test, consider cleaning up to avoid incurring unexpected or unnecessary charges.

To clean up resources you don't need

1. Delete any snapshots. For instructions, see Deleting a Snapshot.

2. Unless you plan to continue using the gateway, delete it. For more information, see Deleting Your Gateway by Using the AWS Storage Gateway Console and Removing Associated Resources.

3. Delete the AWS Storage Gateway VM from your on-premises host. If you created your gateway on an Amazon EC2 instance, terminate the instance.

Creating a Tape Gateway

In this section, you can find instructions about how to create and use a tape gateway.

Topics

- Creating a Gateway
- Creating Tapes
- Using Your Tape Gateway

Creating Tapes

Note

You are charged only for the amount of data you write to the tape, not the tape capacity.

You can use AWS Key Management Service (AWS KMS) to encrypt data written to a virtual tape that is stored Amazon S3. Currently, you can do this by using the AWS Storage Gateway API Reference. For more information, see CreateTapes or create-tapes.

To create virtual tapes

1. In the navigation pane, choose the **Gateways** tab.

2. Choose **Create tapes** to open the **Create tape** dialog box.

3. For **Gateway**, choose a gateway. The tape is created for this gateway.

4. For **Number of tapes**, choose the number of tapes you want to create. For more information about tape limits, see AWS Storage Gateway Limits.

5. For **Capacity**, type the size of the virtual tape you want to create. Tapes must be larger than 100 GiB. For information about capacity limits, see AWS Storage Gateway Limits.

6. For **Barcode prefix**, type the prefix you want to prepend to the barcode of your virtual tapes. **Note** Virtual tapes are uniquely identified by a barcode. You can add a prefix to the barcode. The prefix is optional, but you can use it to help identify your virtual tapes. The prefix must be uppercase letters (A–Z) and must be one to four characters long.

7. Choose **Create tapes**.

8. In the navigation pane, choose the **Tapes** tab to see your tapes.

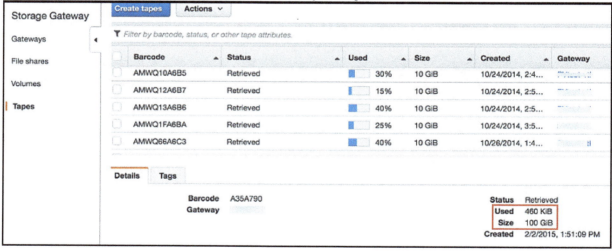

The status of the virtual tapes is initially set to **CREATING** when the virtual tapes are being created. After the tapes are created, their status changes to **AVAILABLE**. For more information, see Managing Your Tape Gateway.

Next Step

Using Your Tape Gateway

Using Your Tape Gateway

Following, you can find instructions about how to use your tape gateway.

Topics

- Connecting Your VTL Devices
- Testing Your Gateway Setup
- Where Do I Go from Here?

Connecting Your VTL Devices

Following, you can find instructions about how to connect your virtual tape library (VTL) devices to your Microsoft Windows or Red Hat Enterprise Linux (RHEL) client.

Topics

- Connecting to a Microsoft Windows Client
- Connecting to a Linux Client

Connecting to a Microsoft Windows Client

The following procedure shows a summary of the steps that you follow to connect to a Windows client.

To connect your VTL devices to a Windows client

1. Start iscsicpl.exe. **Note**
   You must have administrator rights on the client computer to run the iSCSI initiator.

2. Start the Microsoft iSCSI initiator service.

3. In the **iSCSI Initiator Properties** dialog box, choose the **Discovery** tab, and then choose the **Discover Portal** button.

4. Provide the IP address of your tape gateway for **IP address or DNS name**.

5. Choose the **Targets** tab, and then choose **Refresh**. All 10 tape drives and the medium changer appear in the **Discovered targets** box. The status for the targets is **Inactive**.

6. Choose the first device and connect it. You connect the devices one at a time.

7. Connect all of the targets.

On a Windows client, the driver provider for the tape drive must be Microsoft. Use the following procedure to verify the driver provider, and update the driver and provider if necessary:

To verify and update the driver and provider

1. On your Windows client, start Device Manager.

2. Expand **Tape drives**, open the context (right-click) menu for a tape drive, and choose **Properties**.

3. In the **Driver** tab of the **Device Properties** dialog box, verify **Driver Provider** is Microsoft.

4. If **Driver Provider** is not Microsoft, set the value as follows:

   1. Choose **Update Driver**.

   2. In the **Update Driver Software** dialog box, choose **Browse my computer for driver software**.

   3. In the **Update Driver Software** dialog box, choose **Let me pick from a list of device drivers on my computer**.

4. Choose **LTO Tape drive** and choose **Next**.

5. Choose **Close** to close the **Update Driver Software** window, and verify that the **Driver Provider** value is now set to Microsoft.

6. Repeat the steps to update driver and provider for all the tape drives.

Connecting to a Linux Client

The following procedure shows a summary of the steps that you follow to connect to an RHEL client.

To connect a Linux client to VTL devices

1. Install the iscsi-initiator-utils RPM package.

   You can use the following command to install the package.

   ```
   sudo yum install iscsi-initiator-utils
   ```

2. Make sure that the iSCSI daemon is running.

   For RHEL 5 or 6, use the following command.

   ```
   sudo /etc/init.d/iscsi status
   ```

   For RHEL 7, use the following command.

   ```
   sudo service iscsid status
   ```

3. Discover the volume or VTL device targets defined for a gateway. Use the following discovery command.

   ```
   sudo /sbin/iscsiadm --mode discovery --type sendtargets --portal [GATEWAY_IP]:3260
   ```

   The output of the discovery command looks like the following example output.

   For volume gateways: `[GATEWAY_IP]:3260, 1 iqn.1997-05.com.amazon:myvolume`

   For tape gateways: `iqn.1997-05.com.amazon:[GATEWAY_IP]-tapedrive-01`

4. Connect to a target.

   Make sure to specify the correct *[GATEWAY_IP]* and IQN in the connect command.

   Use the following command.

   ```
   sudo /sbin/iscsiadm --mode node --targetname iqn.1997-05.com.amazon:[ISCSI_TARGET_NAME] --
         portal [GATEWAY_IP]:3260,1 --login
   ```

5. Verify that the volume is attached to the client machine (the initiator). To do so, use the following command.

   ```
   ls -l /dev/disk/by-path
   ```

   The output of the command should look like the following example output.

   ```
   lrwxrwxrwx. 1 root root 9 Apr 16 19:31 ip-[GATEWAY_IP]:3260-iscsi-iqn.1997-05.com.
   amazon:myvolume-lun-0 -> ../../sda
   ```

   We highly recommend that after you set up your initiator you customize your iSCSI settings as discussed in Customizing Your Linux iSCSI Settings.

Next Step

Testing Your Gateway Setup

Testing Your Gateway Setup

You test your tape gateway setup by performing the following tasks using your backup application:

1. Configure the backup application to detect your storage devices. **Note**
   To improve I/O performance, we recommend setting the block size of the tape drives in your backup application to 128 KB, 256 KB, or 512 KB. For more information, see Use a Larger Block Size for Tape Drives.

2. Back up data to a tape.

3. Archive the tape.

4. Retrieve the tape from the archive.

5. Restore data from the tape.

To test your setup, use a compatible backup application, as described following.

Topics

- Testing Your Setup by Using Backup Exec
- Testing Your Setup by Using Arcserve Backup r17.0
- Testing Your Setup by Using Commvault
- Testing Your Setup by Using Dell EMC NetWorker
- Testing Your Setup by Using Micro Focus (HPE) Data Protector
- Testing Your Setup by Using Microsoft System Center 2012 R2 Data Protection Manager
- Testing Your Setup by Using Symantec NetBackup Version 7.x
- Testing Your Setup by Using NovaStor DataCenter/Network
- Testing Your Setup by Using Quest NetVault Backup
- Testing Your Setup by Using Veeam Backup & Replication

For more information about compatible backup applications, see Supported Third-Party Backup Applications for a Tape Gateway.

Testing Your Setup by Using Backup Exec

You can back up your data to virtual tapes, archive the tapes, and manage your virtual tape library (VTL) devices by using Symantec Backup Exec. In this topic, you can find basic documentation needed to perform backup and restore operations using the following versions of Backup Exec:

- Backup Exec 2014
- Backup Exec 15
- Backup Exec 16

The procedure for using these versions of Backup Exec with a tape gateway is the same. For detailed information about how to use Backup Exec, see the How to Create Secure Backups with Backup Exec video on the Backup Exec website. For Backup Exec support information on hardware compatibility, see the Software Compatibility Lists (SCL), Hardware Compatibility Lists (HCL), and Administrator Guides for Backup Exec (all versions) on the Backup Exec website. For information about best practices, see Best Practices for using Symantec Backup products (NetBackup, Backup Exec) with the Amazon Web Services (Tape Gateway) on the Symantec website.

For more information about supported backup applications, see Supported Third-Party Backup Applications for a Tape Gateway.

Topics

- Configuring Storage in Backup Exec
- Importing a Tape in Backup Exec
- Writing Data to a Tape in Backup Exec
- Archiving a Tape Using Backup Exec
- Restoring Data from a Tape Archived in Backup Exec
- Disabling a Tape Drive in Backup Exec

Configuring Storage in Backup Exec

After you have connected the virtual tape library (VTL) devices to the Windows client, you configure Backup Exec storage to recognize your devices. For information about how to connect VTL devices to the Windows client, see Connecting Your VTL Devices.

To configure storage

1. Start the Backup Exec software, and then choose the yellow icon in top-left corner on the toolbar.

2. Choose **Configuration and Settings**, and then choose **Backup Exec Services** to open the Backup Exec Service Manager.

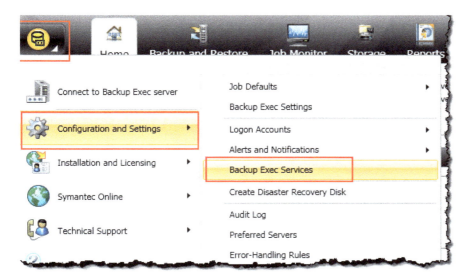

3. Choose **Restart All Services**. Backup Exec then recognizes the VTL devices (that is, the medium changer and tape drives). The restart process might take a few minutes. **Note**
Tape Gateway provides 10 tape drives. However, your Backup Exec license agreement might require your backup application to work with fewer than 10 tape drives. In that case, you must disable tape drives in the Backup Exec robotic library to leave only the number of tape drives allowed by your license agreement enabled. For instructions, see Disabling a Tape Drive in Backup Exec .

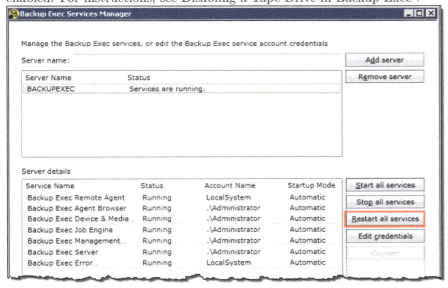

4. After the restart is completed, close the Backup Exec Service Manager.

Importing a Tape in Backup Exec

You are now ready to import a tape from your gateway into a slot.

1. Choose the **Storage** tab, and then expand the **Robotic library** tree to display the VTL devices. **Important**
Symantec Backup Exec software requires the Tape Gateway medium changer type. If the medium changer type listed under **Robotic library** is not Tape Gateway, you must change it before you configure storage in the backup application. For information about how to select a different medium changer type, see

Selecting a Medium Changer After Gateway Activation.

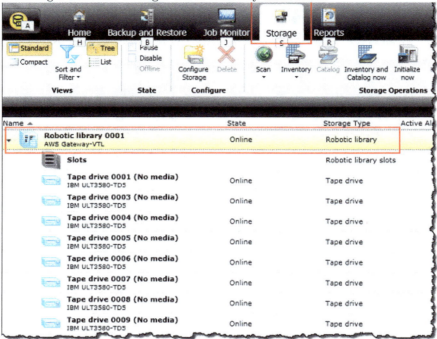

2. Choose the **Slots** icon to display all slots. **Note**
   When you import tapes into the robotic library, the tapes are stored in slots instead of tape drives. Therefore, the tape drives might have a message that indicates there is no media in the drives (No media). When you initiate a backup or restore job, the tapes are moved into the tape drives.
   You must have tapes available in your gateway tape library to import a tape into a storage slot. For instructions on how to create tapes, see Adding Virtual Tapes.

3. Open the context (right-click) menu for an empty slot, choose **Import**, and then choose **Import media now**. In the following screenshot, slot number **3** is empty. You can select more than one slot and import multiple tapes in a single import operation.

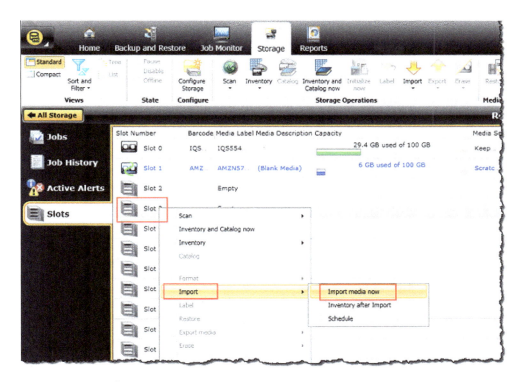

4. In the **Media Request** window that appears, choose **View details**.

5. In the **Action Alert: Media Intervention** window, choose **Respond OK** to insert the media into the slot.

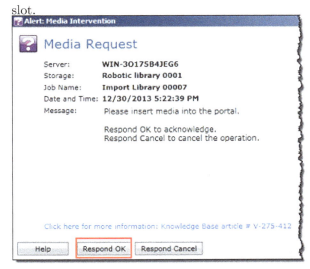

The tape appears in the slot you selected. **Note**
Tapes that are imported include empty tapes and tapes that have been retrieved from the archive to the gateway.

Writing Data to a Tape in Backup Exec

You write data to a tape gateway virtual tape by using the same procedure and backup policies you do with physical tapes. For detailed information, see the *Backup Exec Administrative Guide *in the documentation section in the Backup Exec software.

Archiving a Tape Using Backup Exec

When you archive a tape, tape gateway moves the tape from your gateway's virtual tape library (VTL) to the offline storage. You begin tape archival by exporting the tape using your Backup Exec software.

To archive your tape

1. Choose the **Storage** menu, choose **Slots**, open the context (right-click) menu for the slot you want to export the tape from, choose **Export media**, and then choose **Export media now**. You can select more than one slot and export multiple tapes in a single export operation.

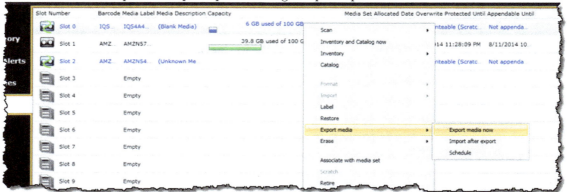

2. In the **Media Request** pop-up window, choose **View details**, and then choose **Respond OK** in the **Alert: Media Intervention** window.

   In the AWS Storage Gateway console, you can verify the status of the tape you are archiving. It might take some time to finish uploading data to AWS. During this time, the exported tape is listed in the tape gateway's VTL with the status **IN TRANSIT TO VTS**. When the upload is completed and the archiving process begins, the status changes to **ARCHIVING**. When data archiving has completed, the exported tape is no longer listed in the VTL.

3. Choose your gateway, and then choose **VTL Tape Cartridges** and verify that the virtual tape is no longer listed in your gateway.

4. On the Navigation pane of the AWS Storage Gateway console, choose **Tapes**. Verify that your tapes status is ARCHIVED.

Restoring Data from a Tape Archived in Backup Exec

Restoring your archived data is a two-step process.

To restore data from an archived tape

1. Retrieve the archived tape to a tape gateway. For instructions, see Retrieving Archived Tapes.

2. Use Backup Exec to restore the data. This process is the same as restoring data from physical tapes. For instructions, see the *Backup Exec Administrative Guide *in the documentation section in the Backup Exec software.

Disabling a Tape Drive in Backup Exec

A tape gateway provides 10 tape drives, but you might decide to use fewer tape drives. In that case, you disable the tape drives you don't use.

1. Open Backup Exec, and choose the **Storage** tab.

2. In the **Robotic library** tree, open the context (right-click) menu for the tape drive you want to disable, and then choose **Disable**.

Next Step

Cleaning Up Resources You Don't Need

Testing Your Setup by Using Arcserve Backup r17.0

You can back up your data to virtual tapes, archive the tapes, and manage your virtual tape library (VTL) devices by using Arcserve Backup r17.0. In this topic, you can find basic documentation to configure Arcserve Backup with a tape gateway and perform a backup and restore operation. For detailed information about to use Arcserve Backup r17.0, see Arcserve Backup r17 documentation in the *Arcserve Administration Guide. *

The following screenshot shows the Arcserve menus.

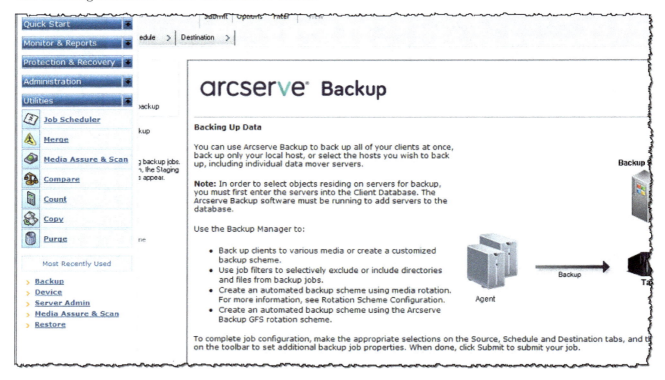

Topics

- Configuring Arcserve to Work with VTL Devices
- Loading Tapes into a Media Pool
- Backing Up Data to a Tape
- Archiving a Tape
- Restoring Data from a Tape

Configuring Arcserve to Work with VTL Devices

After you have connected your virtual tape library (VTL) devices to your client, you scan for your devices.

To scan for VTL devices

1. In the Arcserve Backup Manager, choose the **Utilities** menu.

2. Choose **Media Assure and Scan**.

Loading Tapes into a Media Pool

When the Arcserve software connects to your gateway and your tapes become available, Arcserve automatically loads your tapes. If your gateway is not found in the Arcserve software, try restarting the tape engine in Arcserve.

To restart the tape engine

1. Choose **Quick Start**, choose **Administration**, and then choose **Device**.

2. On the navigation menu, open the context (right-click) menu for your gateway and choose an import/export slot.

3. Choose **Quick Import** and assign your tape to an empty slot.

4. Open the context (right-click) menu for your gateway and choose **Inventory/Offline Slots**.

5. Choose **Quick Inventory** to retrieve media information from the database.

If you add a new tape, you need to scan your gateway for the new tape to have it appear in Arcserve. If the new tapes don't appear, you must import the tapes.

To import tapes

1. Choose the **Quick Start** menu, choose **Back up**, and then choose **Destination tap**.

2. Choose your gateway, open the context (right-click) menu for one tape, and then choose **Import/Export Slot**.

3. Open the context (right-click) menu for each new tape and choose **Inventory**.

4. Open the context (right-click) menu for each new tape and choose **Format**.

Each tape's barcode now appears in your Storage Gateway console, and each tape is ready to use.

Backing Up Data to a Tape

When your tapes have been loaded into Arcserve, you can back up data. The backup process is the same as backing up physical tapes.

To back up data to a tape

1. From the **Quick Start** menu, open the restore a backup session.

2. Choose the **Source** tab, and then choose the file system or database system that you want to back up.

3. Choose the **Schedule** tab and choose the repeat method you want to use.

4. Choose the **Destination** tab and then choose the tape you want to use. If the data you are backing up is larger than the tape can hold, Arcserve prompts you to mount a new tape.

5. Choose **Submit** to back up your data.

Archiving a Tape

When you archive a tape, your tape gateway moves the tape from the tape library to the offline storage. Before you eject and archive a tape, you might want to check the content on it.

To archive a tape

1. From the **Quick Start** menu, open the restore a backup session.

2. Choose the **Source** tab, and then choose the file system or database system you want to back up.

3. Choose the **Schedule** tab and choose the repeat method you want to use.

4. Choose your gateway, open the context (right-click) menu for one tape, and then choose **Import/Export Slot**.

5. Assign a mail slot to load the tape. The status in the Storage Gateway console changes to **Archive**. The archive process might take some time.

The archiving process can take some time to complete. The initial status of the tape appears as **IN TRANSIT TO VTS**. When archiving starts, the status changes to **ARCHIVING**. When archiving is completed, the tape is no longer listed in the VTL.

Restoring Data from a Tape

Restoring your archived data is a two-step process.

To restore data from an archived tape

1. Retrieve the archived tape to a tape gateway. For instructions, see Retrieving Archived Tapes.

2. Use Arcserve to restore the data. This process is the same as restoring data from physical tapes. For instructions, see the Arcserve Backup r17 documentation.

To restore data from a tape, use the following procedure.

To restore data from a tape

1. From the **Quick Start** menu, open the restore a restore session.

2. Choose the **Source** tab, and then choose the file system or database system you want to restore.

3. Choose the **Destination** tab and accept the default settings.

4. Choose the **Schedule** tab, choose the repeat method that you want to use, and then choose **Submit**.

Next Step

Cleaning Up Resources You Don't Need

Testing Your Setup by Using Commvault

You can back up your data to virtual tapes, archive the tapes, and manage your virtual tape library (VTL) devices by using Commvault version 11. In this topic, you can find basic documentation on how to configure the Commvault backup application for a tape gateway, perform a backup archive, and retrieve your data from archived tapes. For detailed information about how to use Commvault, see the Commvault documentation on the Commvault website.

Topics

- Configuring Commvault to Work with VTL Devices
- Creating a Storage Policy and a Subclient
- Backing Up Data to a Tape in Commvault
- Archiving a Tape in Commvault
- Restoring Data from a Tape

Configuring Commvault to Work with VTL Devices

After you connect the VTL devices to the Windows client, you configure Commvault to recognize them. For information about how to connect VTL devices to the Windows client, see Connecting Your VTL Devices to a Windows client.

The Commvault backup application doesn't automatically recognize VTL devices. You must manually add devices to expose them to the Commvault backup application and then discover the devices.

To configure Commvault

1. In the CommCell console main menu, choose **Storage**, and then choose** Expert Storage Configuration** to open the **Select MediaAgents** dialog box.

2. Choose the available media agent you want to use, choose **Add**, and then choose **OK**.

3. In the **Expert Storage Configuration** dialog box, choose **Start**, and then choose **Detect/Configure Devices**.

4. Leave the **Device Type** options selected, choose **Exhaustive Detection**, and then choose **OK**.

5. In the **Confirm Exhaustive Detection** confirmation box, choose **Yes**.

6. In the **Device Selection** dialog box, choose your library and all its drives, and then choose **OK**. Wait for your devices to be detected, and then choose **Close** to close the log report.

7. Right-click your library, choose **Configure**, and then choose **Yes**. Close the configuration dialog box.

8. In the **Does this library have a barcode reader?** dialog box, choose **Yes**, and then for device type, choose **IBM ULTRIUM V5**.

9. In the CommCell browser, choose **Storage Resources**, and then choose **Libraries** to see your tape library.

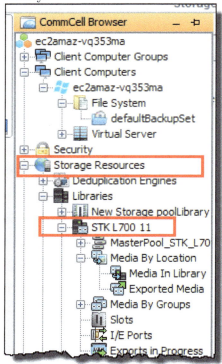

10. To see your tapes in your library, open the context (right-click) menu for your library, and then choose **Discover Media**, **Media location**, **Media Library**.

11. To mount your tapes, open the context (right-click) menu for your media, and then choose **Load**.

Creating a Storage Policy and a Subclient

Every backup and restore job is associated with a storage policy and a subclient policy.

A storage policy maps the original location of the data to your media.

To create a storage policy

1. In the CommCell browser, choose **Policies**.

2. Open the context (right-click) menu for **Storage Policies**, and then choose **New Storage Policy**.

3. In the Create Storage Policy wizard, choose **Data Protection and Archiving**, and then choose **Next**.

4. Type a name for **Storage Policy Name**, and then choose **Incremental Storage Policy**. To associate this storage policy with incremental loads, choose one of the options. Otherwise, leave the options unchecked, and then choose **Next**.

5. In the **Do you want to Use Global Deduplication Policy?** dialog box, choose your **Deduplication** preference, and then choose **Next**.

6. From **Library for Primary Copy**, choose your VTL library, and then choose **Next**.

7. Verify that your media agent settings are correct, and then choose **Next**.

8. Verify that your scratch pool settings are correct, and then choose **Next**.

9. Configure your retention policies in **iData Agent Backup data**, and then choose **Next**.

10. Review the encryption settings, and then choose **Next**.

11. To see your storage policy, choose **Storage Policies**.

You create a subclient policy and associate it with your storage policy. A subclient policy enables you to configure similar file system clients from a central template, so that you don't have to set up many similar file systems manually.

To create a subclient policy

1. In the CommCell browser, choose **Client Computers**, and then choose your client computer. Choose **File System**, and then choose **defaultBackupSet**.

2. Right-click **defaultBackupSet**, choose **All Tasks**, and then choose **New Subclient**.

3. In the **Subclient** properties box, type a name in **SubClient Name**, and then choose **OK**.

4. Choose **Browse**, navigate to the files that you want to back up, choose **Add**, and then close the dialog box.

5. In the **Subclient** property box, choose the **Storage Device** tab, choose a storage policy from **Storage policy**, and then choose **OK**.

6. In the **Backup Schedule** window that appears, associate the new subclient with a backup schedule.

7. Choose **Do Not Schedule** for one time or on-demand backups, and then choose **OK**.

   You should now see your subclient in the **defaultBackupSet** tab.

Backing Up Data to a Tape in Commvault

You create a backup job and write data to a virtual tape by using the same procedures you use with physical tapes. For detailed information about how to back up data, see the Commvault documentation.

Archiving a Tape in Commvault

You start the archiving process by ejecting the tape. When you archive a tape, tape gateway moves the tape from the tape library to offline storage. Before you eject and archive a tape, you might want to first check the content on the tape.

To archive a tape

1. In the CommCell browser, choose **Storage Resources**, **Libraries**, and then choose **Your library**. Choose **Media By Location**, and then choose **Media In Library**.

2. Open the context (right-click) menu for the tape you want to archive, choose **All Tasks**, choose **Export**, and then choose **OK**.

The archiving process can take some time to complete. The initial status of the tape appears as **IN TRANSIT TO VTS**. When archiving starts, the status changes to **ARCHIVING**. When archiving is completed, the tape is no longer listed in the VTL.

In the Commvault software, verify that the tape is no longer in the storage slot.

In the navigation pane of the Storage Gateway console, choose **Tapes**. Verify that your archived tape's status is **ARCHIVED**.

Restoring Data from a Tape

You can restore data from a tape that has never been archived and retrieved, or from a tape that has been archived and retrieved. For tapes that have never been archived and retrieved (nonretrieved tapes), you have two options to restore the data:

- Restore by subclient
- Restore by job ID

To restore data from a nonretrieved tape by subclient

1. In the CommCell browser, choose **Client Computers**, and then choose your client computer. Choose **File System**, and then choose **defaultBackupSet.**

2. Open the context (right-click) menu for your subclient, choose **Browse and Restore**, and then choose **View Content.**

3. Choose the files you want to restore, and then choose **Recover All Selected.**

4. Choose **Home**, and then choose **Job Controller** to monitor the status of your restore job.

To restore data from a nonretrieved tape by job ID

1. In the CommCell browser, choose **Client Computers**, and then choose your client computer. Right-click **File System**, choose **View**, and then choose **Backup History.**

2. In the **Backup Type** category, choose the type of backup jobs you want, and then choose **OK.** A tab with the history of backup jobs appears.

3. Find the **Job ID** you want to restore, right-click it, and then choose **Browse and Restore.**

4. In the **Browse and Restore Options** dialog box, choose **View Content.**

5. Choose the files that you want to restore, and then choose **Recover All Selected.**

6. Choose **Home**, and then choose **Job Controller** to monitor the status of your restore job.

To restore data from an archived and retrieved tape

1. In the CommCell browser, choose **Storage Resources**, choose **Libraries**, and then choose **Your library.** Choose **Media By Location**, and then choose **Media In Library.**

2. Right-click the retrieved tape, choose **All Tasks**, and then choose** Catalog.**

3. In the **Catalog Media** dialog box, choose **Catalog only**, and then choose **OK.**

4. Choose **CommCell Home**, and then choose **Job Controller** to monitor the status of your restore job.

5. After the job succeeds, open the context (right-click) menu for your tape, choose **View**, and then choose **View Catalog Contents.** Take note of the **Job ID** value for use later.

6. Choose **Recatalog/Merge.** Make sure that **Merge only** is chosen in the **Catalog Media** dialog box.

7. Choose **Home**, and then choose **Job Controller** to monitor the status of your restore job.

8. After the job succeeds, choose **CommCell Home**, choose **Control Panel**, and then choose **Browse/Search/Recovery.**

9. Choose **Show aged data during browse and recovery**, choose **OK**, and then close the **Control Panel.**

10. In the CommCell browser, right-click **Client Computers**, and then choose your client computer. Choose **View**, and then choose **Job History.**

11. In the **Job History Filter** dialog box, choose **Advanced.**

12. Choose **Include Aged Data**, and then choose **OK.**

13. In the **Job History** dialog box, choose **OK** to open the **history of jobs** tab.

14. Find the job that you want to restore, open the context (right-click) menu for it, and then choose **Browse and Restore**.

15. In the **Browse and Restore** dialog box, choose **View Content**.

16. Choose the files that you want to restore, and then choose **Recover All Selected.**

17. Choose **Home**, and then choose **Job Controller** to monitor the status of your restore job.

Testing Your Setup by Using Dell EMC NetWorker

You can back up your data to virtual tapes, archive the tapes and manage your virtual tape library (VTL) devices by using Dell EMC NetWorker version 8.x or 9.x. In this topic, you can find basic documentation on how to configure the Dell EMC NetWorker software to work with a tape gateway and perform a backup, including how to configure storage devices, write data to a tape, archive a tape and restore data from a tape. This documentation uses the Dell NetWorker V9.x as an example.

For detailed information about how to install and use the Dell EMC NetWorker software, see the *EMC NetWorker Administration Guide*.

For more information about compatible backup applications, see Supported Third-Party Backup Applications for a Tape Gateway.

Topics

- Configuring Dell EMC NetWorker to Work with VTL Devices
- Enabling Import of WORM Tapes into Dell EMC NetWorker
- Backing Up Data to a Tape in Dell EMC NetWorker
- Archiving a Tape in Dell EMC NetWorker
- Restoring Data from an Archived Tape in Dell EMC NetWorker

Configuring Dell EMC NetWorker to Work with VTL Devices

After you have connected your virtual tape library (VTL) devices to your Microsoft Windows client, you configure Dell EMC NetWorker to recognize your devices. For information about how to connect VTL devices to the Windows client, see Connecting Your VTL Devices.

Dell EMC NetWorker doesn't automatically recognize tape gateway devices. To expose your VTL devices to the NetWorker software and get the software to discover them, you manually configure the software. Following, we assume that you have correctly installed the Dell EMC NetWorker software and that you are familiar with the Dell EMC NetWorker Management Console. For more information about the Dell EMC NetWorker Management Console, see the NetWorker Management Console interface section of the *EMC NetWorker Administration Guide*.

The following screenshot shows the Dell EMC NetWorker V9.x Management Console.

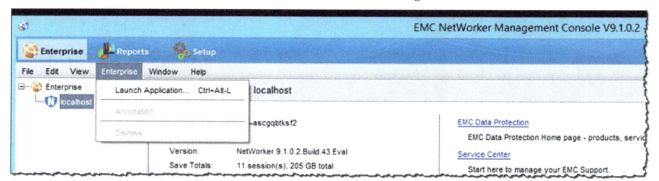

To configure the Dell EMC NetWorker software for VTL devices

1. Start the Dell EMC NetWorker Management Console application, choose **Enterprise** from the menu, and then choose **localhost** from the left pane.

2. Open the context (right-click) menu for **localhost**, and then choose **Launch Application**.

3. Choose the **Devices** tab, open the context (right-click) menu for **Libraries**, and then choose **Scan for Devices**.

4. In the Scan for Devices wizard, choose **Start Scan**, and then choose **OK** from the dialog box that appears.

5. Expand the **Libraries** folder tree to see all your libraries. This process might take a few seconds to load the devices into the library.

6. Open the context (right-click) menu for your library, and then choose **Configure All Libraries**.

7. In the **Provide General Configuration Information** box, choose the configuration settings you want, and then choose **Next**.

8. In the **Select Target Storage Nodes** box, verify that a storage node is selected, and then choose **Start Configuration**. The selected storage node will have **Configure** selected.

9. In the Start Configuration wizard, choose **Finish**.

10. Choose your library to see your tapes in the left pane and the corresponding empty volume slots list in the right pane. In this screenshot, the **AWS@3.0.0** library is selected.

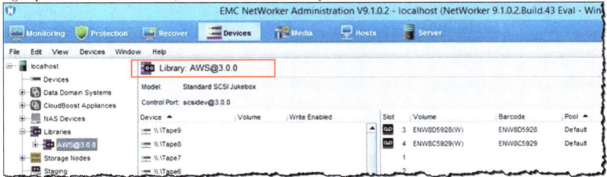

11. In the volume list, select the volumes you want to enable (selected volumes are highlighted), open the context (right-click) menu for the selected volumes, and then choose **Deposit**. This action moves the tape from the I/E slot into the volume slot.

12. In the dialog box that appears, choose **Yes**, and then in the **Load the Cartridges into** dialog box, choose **Yes**.

13. If you don't have any more tapes to deposit, choose **No** or **Ignore**. Otherwise, choose **Yes** to deposit additional tapes.

Enabling Import of WORM Tapes into Dell EMC NetWorker

You are now ready to import tapes from your tape gateway into the Dell EMC NetWorker library.

The virtual tapes are write once read many (WORM) tapes, but Dell EMC NetWorker expects non-WORM tapes. For Dell EMC NetWorker to work with your virtual tapes, you must enable import of tapes into non-WORM media pools.

To enable import of WORM tapes into non-WORM media pools

1. On NetWorker Console, choose **Media**, open the context (right-click) menu for **localhost**, and then choose **Properties**.

2. In the **NetWorker Sever Properties** window, choose the **Configuration** tab.

3. In the **Worm tape handling** section, clear the **WORM tapes only in WORM pools** box, and then choose **OK**.

Backing Up Data to a Tape in Dell EMC NetWorker

Backing up data to a tape is a two-step process.

1. Label the tapes you want to back up your data to, create the target media pool, and add the tapes to the pool.

   You create a media pool and write data to a virtual tape by using the same procedures you do with physical tapes. For detailed information, see the Backing Up Data section of the Dell EMC NetWorker Administration Guide.

2. Write data to the tape. You back up data by using the Dell EMC NetWorker User application instead of the Dell EMC NetWorker Management Console. The Dell EMC NetWorker User application installs as part of the NetWorker installation.

Note
You use the Dell EMC NetWorker User application to perform backups, but you view the status of your backup and restore jobs in the EMC Management Console. To view status, choose the **Devices** menu and view the status in the **Log** window.

Archiving a Tape in Dell EMC NetWorker

When you archive a tape, tape gateway moves the tape from the Dell EMC NetWorker tape library to the offline storage. You begin tape archival by ejecting a tape from the tape drive to the storage slot. You then withdraw the tape from the slot to the archive by using your backup application—that is, the Dell EMC NetWorker software.

To archive a tape by using Dell EMC NetWorker

1. On the **Devices** tab in the NetWorker Administration window, choose **localhost** or your EMC server, and then choose **Libraries**.

2. Choose the library you imported from your virtual tape library.

3. From the list of tapes that you have written data to, open the context (right-click) menu for the tape you want to archive, and then choose **Eject/Withdraw**.

4. In the confirmation box that appears, choose **OK**.

The archiving process can take some time to complete. The initial status of the tape appears as **IN TRANSIT TO VTS**. When archiving starts, the status changes to **ARCHIVING**. When archiving is completed, the tape is no longer listed in the VTL.

In the Dell EMC NetWorker software, verify that the tape is no longer in the storage slot.

In the navigation pane of the Storage Gateway console, choose **Tapes**. Verify that your archived tape's status is **ARCHIVED**.

Restoring Data from an Archived Tape in Dell EMC NetWorker

Restoring your archived data is a two-step process:

1. Retrieve the archived tape a tape gateway. For instructions, see Retrieving Archived Tapes.

2. Use the Dell EMC NetWorker software to restore the data. You do this by creating a restoring a folder file, as you do when restoring data from physical tapes. For instructions, see the Using the NetWorker User program section of the *EMC NetWorker Administration Guide.*

Next Step

Cleaning Up Resources You Don't Need

Testing Your Setup by Using Micro Focus (HPE) Data Protector

You can back up your data to virtual tapes, archive the tapes, and manage your virtual tape library (VTL) devices by using Micro Focus (HPE) Data Protector v9.x. In this topic, you can find basic documentation on how to configure the Micro Focus (HPE) Data Protector software for a tape gateway and perform a backup and restore operation. For detailed information about how to use the Micro Focus (HPE) Data Protector software, see the Hewlett Packard documentation. For more information about compatible backup applications, see Supported Third-Party Backup Applications for a Tape Gateway.

Topics

- Configuring Micro Focus (HPE) Data Protector to Work with VTL Devices
- Preparing Virtual Tapes for Use with HPE Data Protector
- Loading Tapes into a Media Pool
- Backing Up Data to a Tape
- Archiving a Tape
- Restoring Data from a Tape

Configuring Micro Focus (HPE) Data Protector to Work with VTL Devices

After you have connected the virtual tape library (VTL) devices to the client, you configure Micro Focus (HPE) Data Protector to recognize your devices. For information about how to connect VTL devices to the client, see Connecting Your VTL Devices.

The Micro Focus (HPE) Data Protector software doesn't automatically recognize tape gateway devices. To have the software recognize these devices, manually add the devices and then discover the VTL devices, as described following.

To add the VTL devices

1. In the Micro Focus (HPE) Data Protector main window, choose the **Devices & Media** shelf in the list at top left.

   Open the context (right-click) menu for **Devices**, and choose **Add Device**.

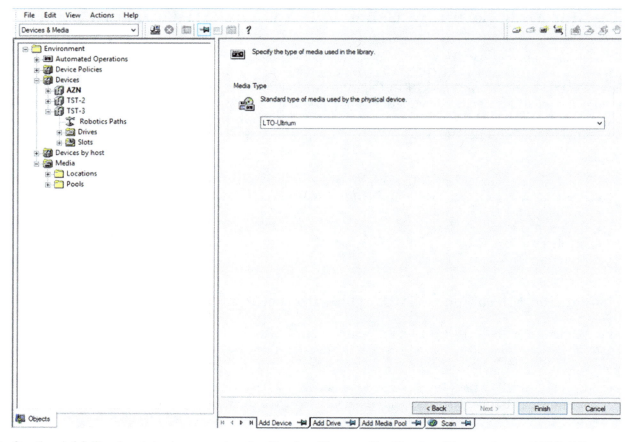

2. On the **Add Device** tab, type a value for **Device Name**. For **Device Type**, choose **SCSI Library**, and then choose **Next**.

3. On the next screen, do the following:

   1. For **SCSI address of the library robotic**, select your specific address.

   2. For **Select what action Data Protector should take if the drive is busy**, choose "Abort" or your preferred action.

   3. Choose to enable these options:

      - **Barcode reader support**
      - **Automatically discover changed SCSI address**
      - **SCSI Reserve/Release (robotic control)**

   4. Leave **Use barcode as medium label on initialization** clear (unchecked), unless your system requires it.

   5. Choose **Next** to continue.

4. On the next screen, specify the slots that you want to use with HP Data Protector. Use a hyphen ("-") between numbers to indicate a range of slots, for example 1–6. When you've specified slots to use, choose **Next**.

5. For the standard type of media used by the physical device, choose **LTO_Ultrium**, and then choose **Finish** to complete the setup.

Your tape library is now ready to use. To load tapes into it, see the next section.

Preparing Virtual Tapes for Use with HPE Data Protector

Before you can back up data to a virtual tape, you need to prepare the tape for use. Doing this involves the following actions:

- Load a virtual tape into a tape library
- Load the virtual tape into a slot
- Create a media pool
- Load the virtual tape into media pool

In the following sections, you can find steps to guide you through this process.

Loading Virtual Tapes into a Tape Library

Your tape library should now be listed under **Devices**. If you don't see it, press F5 to refresh the screen. When your library is listed, you can load virtual tapes into the library.

To load virtual tapes into your tape library

1. Choose the plus sign next to your tape library to display the nodes for robotics paths, drives, and slots.

2. Open the context (right-click) menu for **Drives**, choose **Add Drive**, type a name for your tape, and then choose **Next** to continue.

3. Choose the tape drive you want to add for **SCSI address of data drive**, choose **Automatically discover changed SCSI address**, and then choose **Next**.

4. On the following screen, choose **Advanced**. The **Advanced Options** pop-up screen appears.

    1. On the **Settings** tab, you should consider the following options:

        - **CRC Check** (to detect accidental data changes)
        - **Detect dirty drive** (to ensure the drive is clean before backup)
        - **SCSI Reserve/Release(drive)** (to avoid tape contention)

        For testing purposes, you can leave these options disabled (unchecked).

    2. On the **Sizes** tab, set the **Block size (kB)** to **Default (256)**.

    3. Choose **OK** to close the advanced options screen, and then choose **Next** to continue.

5. On the next screen, choose these options under **Device Policies**:

    - **Device may be used for restore**
    - **Device may be used as source device for object copy**

6. Choose **Finish** to finish adding your tape drive to your tape library.

Loading Virtual Tapes into Slots

Now that you have a tape drive in your tape library, you can load virtual tapes into slots.

To load a tape into a slot

1. In the tape library tree node, open the node labeled **Slots**. Each slot has a status represented by an icon:

    - A green tape means that a tape is already loaded into the slot.
    - A gray slot means that the slot is empty.
    - A cyan question mark means that the tape in that slot is not formatted.

2. For an empty slot, open the context (right-click) menu, and then choose **Enter**. If you have existing tapes, choose one to load into that slot.

Creating a Media Pool

A *media pool* is a logical group used to organize your tapes. To set up tape backup, you create a media pool.

To create a media pool

1. In the **Devices & Media** shelf, open the tree node for **Media**, open the context (right-click) menu for the **Pools** node, and then choose **Add Media Pool**.

2. For **Pool name**, type a name.

3. For **Media Type**, choose **LTO_Ultrium**, and then choose **Next**.

4. On the following screen, accept the default values, and then choose **Next**.

5. Choose **Finish** to finish creating a media pool.

Loading Tapes into a Media Pool

Before you can back up data onto your tapes, you must load the tapes into the media pool that you created.

To load a virtual tape into a media pool

1. On your tape library tree node, choose the **Slots** node.

2. Choose a loaded tape, one that has a green icon showing a loaded tape. Open the context (right-click) menu and choose **Format**, and then choose **Next**.

3. Choose the media pool you created, and then choose **Next**.

4. For **Medium Description**, choose **Use barcode**, and then choose **Next**.

5. For **Options**, choose **Force Operation**, and then choose **Finish**.

You should now see your chosen slot change from a status of unassigned (gray) to a status of tape inserted (green). A series of messages appear to confirm that your media is initialized.

At this point, you should have everything configured to begin using your virtual tape library with HPE Data Protector. To double-check that this is the case, use the following procedure.

To verify that your tape library is configured for use

- Choose **Drives**, then open the context (right-click) menu for your drive, and choose **Scan**.

If your configuration is correct, a message confirms that your media was successfully scanned.

Backing Up Data to a Tape

When your tapes have been loaded into a media pool, you can back up data to them.

To back up data to a tape

1. Choose the **Backup** shelf at top left of the screen.

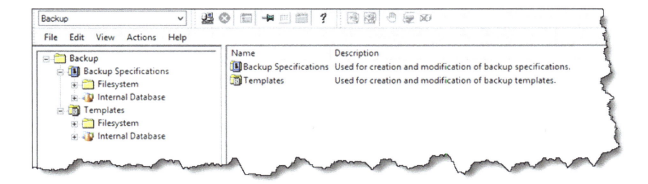

2. Open the context (right-click) menu for **Filesystem**, and choose **Add Backup**.

3. On the **Create New Backup** screen, under **Filesystem**, choose **Blank File System Backup**, and then choose **OK**.

4. On the tree node that shows your host system, select the file system or file systems that you want to back up, and choose **Next** to continue.

5. Open the tree node for the tape library you want to use, open the context (right-click) menu for the tape drive you want to use, and then choose **Properties**.

6. Choose your media pool, choose **OK**, and then choose **Next**.

7. For the next three screens, accept the default settings and choose **Next**.

8. On the **Perform finishing steps in your backup/template design** screen, choose **Save as** to save this session. In the pop-up window, give the backup a name and assign it to the group where you want to save your new backup specification.

9. Choose **Start Interactive Backup**.

If the host system contains a database system, you can choose it as your target backup system. The screens and selections are similar to the file-system backup just described.

Archiving a Tape

When you archive a tape, tape gateway moves the tape from the tape library to the offline storage. Before you eject and archive a tape, you might want to check the content on it.

To check a tape's content before archiving it

1. Choose **Slots** and then choose the tape you want to check.

2. Choose **Objects** and check what content is on the tape.

When you have chosen a tape to archive, use the following procedure.

To eject and archive a tape

1. Open the context (right-click) menu for that tape, and choose **Eject**.

2. On the AWS Storage Gateway console, choose your gateway, and then choose **VTL Tape Cartridges** and verify the status of the virtual tape you are archiving.

After the tape is ejected, it will be automatically archived in Amazon Glacier. The archiving process can take some time to complete. The initial status of the tape is shown as **IN TRANSIT TO VTS**. When archiving starts, the status changes to **ARCHIVING**. When archiving is completed, the tape is no longer listed in the VTL.

Restoring Data from a Tape

Restoring your archived data is a two-step process.

To restore data from an archived tape

1. Retrieve the archived tape to a tape gateway. For instructions, see Retrieving Archived Tapes.

2. Use HPE Data Protector to restore the data. This process is the same as restoring data from physical tapes.

To restore data from a tape, use the following procedure.

To restore data from a tape

1. Choose the **Restore** shelf at the top left of the screen.

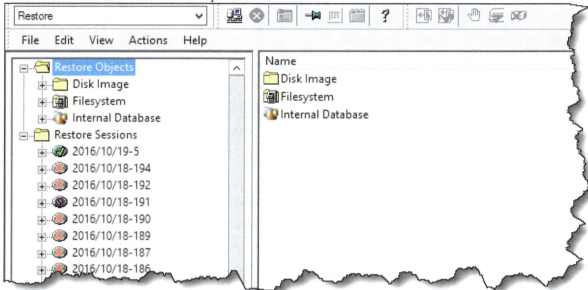

2. Choose the file system or database system you want to restore. For the backup that you want to restore, make sure that the box is selected. Choose **Restore**.

3. In the **Start Restore Session** window, choose **Needed Media**. Choose **All media**, and you should see the tape originally used for the backup. Choose that tape, and then choose **Close**.

4. In the **Start Restore Session** window, accept the default settings, choose **Next**, and then choose **Finish**.

Next Step

Cleaning Up Resources You Don't Need

Testing Your Setup by Using Microsoft System Center 2012 R2 Data Protection Manager

You can back up your data to virtual tapes, archive the tapes, and manage your virtual tape library (VTL) devices by using Microsoft System Center 2012 R2 Data Protection Manager (DPM). In this topic, you can find basic documentation on how to configure the DPM backup application for a tape gateway and perform a backup and restore operation.

For detailed information about how to use DPM, see the DPM documentation on the Microsoft System Center website. For more information about compatible backup applications, see Supported Third-Party Backup Applications for a Tape Gateway.

Topics

- Configuring DPM to Recognize VTL Devices
- Importing a Tape into DPM
- Writing Data to a Tape in DPM
- Archiving a Tape by Using DPM
- Restoring Data from a Tape Archived in DPM

Configuring DPM to Recognize VTL Devices

After you have connected the virtual tape library (VTL) devices to the Windows client, you configure DPM to recognize your devices. For information about how to connect VTL devices to the Windows client, see Connecting Your VTL Devices.

By default, the DPM server does not recognize tape gateway devices. To configure the server to work with the tape gateway devices, you perform the following tasks:

1. Update the device drivers for the VTL devices to expose them to the DPM server.

2. Manually map the VTL devices to the DPM tape library.

To update the VTL device drivers

- In Device Manager, update the driver for the medium changer. For instructions, see Updating the Device Driver for Your Medium Changer.

You use the DPMDriveMappingTool to map your tape drives to the DPM tape library.

To map tape drives to the DPM server tape library

1. Create at least one tape for your gateway. For information on how to do this on the console, see Creating Tapes.

2. Import the tape into the DPM library. For information on how to do this, see Importing a Tape into DPM.

3. If the DPMLA service is running, stop it by opening a command terminal and typing the following on the command line.

   net stop DPMLA

4. Locate the following file on the DPM server: `%ProgramFiles%\System Center 2012 R2\DPM\DPM\Config\DPMLA.xml`. **Note**
   If this file exists, the DPMDriveMappingTool overwrites it. If you want to preserve your original file, create a backup copy.

5. Open a command terminal, change the directory to `%ProgramFiles%\System Center 2012 R2\DPM\DPM\Bin`, and run the following command.

```
1
2 C:\Microsoft System Center 2012 R2\DPM\DPM\bin>DPMDriveMappingTool.exe
```

The output for the command looks like the following.

```
1
2 Performing Device Inventory ...
3 Mapping Drives to Library ...
4 Adding Standalone Drives ...
5 Writing the Map File ...
6 Drive Mapping Completed Successfully.
```

Importing a Tape into DPM

You are now ready to import tapes from your tape gateway into the DPM backup application library.

To import tapes into the DPM backup application library

1. On the DPM server, open the Management Console, choose **Rescan**, and then choose **Refresh**. Doing this displays your medium changer and tape drives.

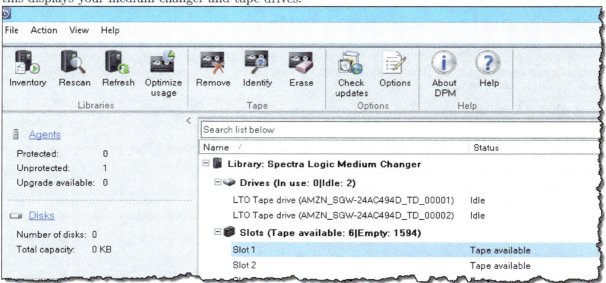

2. Open the context (right-click) menu for the media changer in the **Library** section, and then choose **Add tape (I/E port)** to add a tape to the **Slots** list. **Note**
The process of adding tapes can take several minutes to complete.

   The tape label appears as **Unknown**, and the tape is not usable. For the tape to be usable, you must identify it.

3. Open the context (right-click) menu for the tape you want to identify, and then choose **Identify unknown tape. Note**
The process of identifying tapes can take a few seconds or a few minutes.
Microsoft System Center 2012 R2 Data Protection Manager doesn't display barcodes for virtual tapes created in AWS Storage Gateway.

   When identification is complete, the tape label changes to **Free**. That is, the tape is free for data to be written to it.

In the following screenshot, the tape in slot 2 has been identified and is free to use but the tape in slot 3 is not.

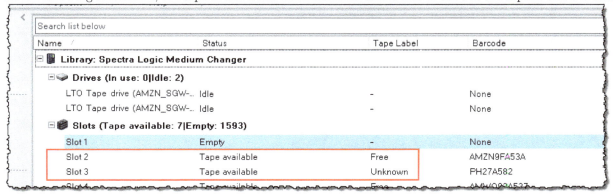

Writing Data to a Tape in DPM

You write data to a tape gateway virtual tape by using the same protection procedures and policies you do with physical tapes. You create a protection group and add the data you want to back up, and then back up the data by creating a recovery point. For detailed information about how to use DPM, see the DPM documentation on the Microsoft System Center website.

Archiving a Tape by Using DPM

When you archive a tape, tape gateway moves the tape from the DPM tape library to offline storage. You begin tape archival by removing the tape from the slot using your backup application—that is, DPM.

To archive a tape in DPM

1. Open the context (right-click) menu for the tape you want to archive, and then choose **Remove tape (I/E port)**.

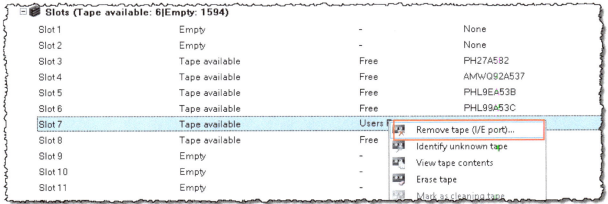

2. In the dialog box that appears, choose **Yes**. Doing this ejects the tape from the medium changer's storage slot and moves the tape into one of the gateway's I/E slots. When a tape is moved into the gateway's I/E slot, it is immediately sent for archiving.

3. On the AWS Storage Gateway console, choose your gateway, and then choose **VTL Tape Cartridges** and verify the status of the virtual tape you are archiving.

   The archiving process can take some time to complete. The initial status of the tape is shown as **IN TRANSIT TO VTS**. When archiving starts, the status changes to **ARCHIVING**. When archiving is completed, the tape is no longer listed in the VTL.

Restoring Data from a Tape Archived in DPM

Restoring your archived data is a two-step process.

To restore data from an archived tape

1. Retrieve the archived tape from archive to a tape gateway. For instructions, see Retrieving Archived Tapes.

2. Use the DPM backup application to restore the data. You do this by creating a recovery point, as you do when restoring data from physical tapes. For instructions, see Recovering Client Computer Data on the DPM website.

Next Step

Cleaning Up Resources You Don't Need

Testing Your Setup by Using Symantec NetBackup Version 7.x

You can back up your data to virtual tapes, archive the tapes, and manage your virtual tape library (VTL) devices by using Symantec NetBackup version 7.x. In this topic, you can find basic documentation on how to configure the NetBackup application for a tape gateway and perform a backup and restore operation. For detailed information about how to use NetBackup, see the Veritas Services and Operations Readiness Tools (SORT) on the Veritas website. For Symantec support information on hardware compatibility, see the NetBackup 7.0 - 7.6.x Hardware Compatibility List on the Veritas website.

For more information about compatible backup applications, see Supported Third-Party Backup Applications for a Tape Gateway.

Topics

- Configuring NetBackup Storage Devices
- Backing Up Data to a Tape
- Archiving the Tape
- Restoring Data from the Tape

Configuring NetBackup Storage Devices

After you have connected the virtual tape library (VTL) devices to the Windows client, you configure Symantec NetBackup version 7.x storage to recognize your devices. For information about how to connect VTL devices to the Windows client, see Connecting Your VTL Devices.

To configure NetBackup to use storage devices on your tape gateway

1. Open the NetBackup Administration Console and run it as an administrator.

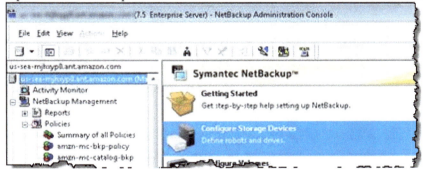

2. Choose **Configure Storage Devices** to open the Device Configuration wizard.

3. Choose **Next**. The NetBackup application detects your computer as a device host.

4. In the **Device Hosts** column, select your computer, and then choose **Next**. The NetBackup application scans your computer for devices and discovers all devices.

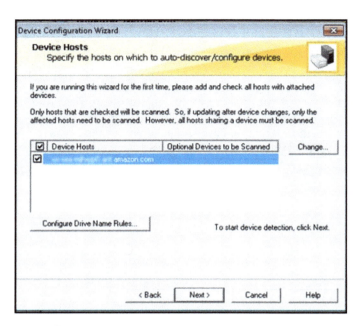

5. In the **Scanning Hosts** page, choose **Next**, and then choose **Next**. The NetBackup application finds all 10 tape drives and the medium changer on your computer.

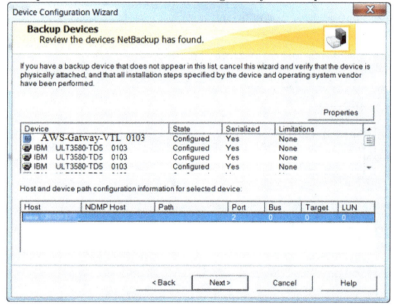

6. In the **Backup Devices** window, choose **Next**.

7. In the **Drag and Drop Configuration** window, verify that your medium changer is selected, and then choose **Next.**

8. In the dialog box that appears, choose **Yes** to save the configuration on your computer. The NetBackup application updates the device configuration.

9. When the update is completed, choose **Next** to make the devices available to the NetBackup application.

10. In the **Finished!** window, choose **Finish**.

To verify your devices in the NetBackup application

1. In the NetBackup Administration Console, expand the **Media and Device Management** node, and then expand the **Devices** node. Choose **Drives** to display all the tape drives.

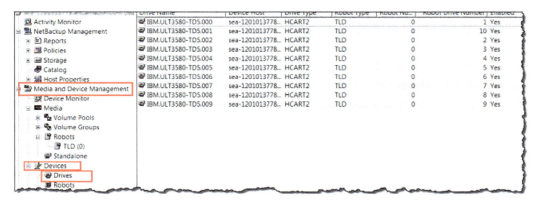

2. In the **Devices** node, choose **Robots** to display all your medium changers. In the NetBackup application, the medium changer is called a *robot*.

3. In the **All Robots** pane, open the context (right-click) menu for **TLD(0)** (that is, your robot), and then choose **Inventory Robot**.

4. In the **Robot Inventory** window, verify that your host is selected from the **Device-Host** list located in the **Select robot** category.

5. Verify that your robot is selected from the **Robot** list.

6. In the **Robot Inventory** window, select **Update volume configuration**, select **Preview changes**, select **Empty media access port prior to update**, and then choose **Start**.

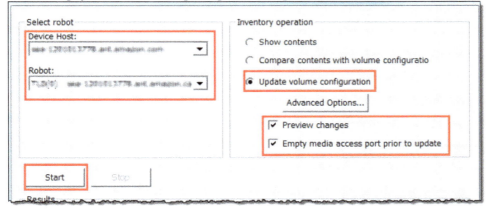

The process then inventories your medium changer and virtual tapes in the NetBackup Enterprise Media Management (EMM) database. NetBackup stores media information, device configuration, and tape status in the EMM.

7. In the **Robot Inventory** window, choose **Yes** once the inventory is complete. Choosing **Yes** here updates the configuration and moves virtual tapes found in import/export slots to the virtual tape library.

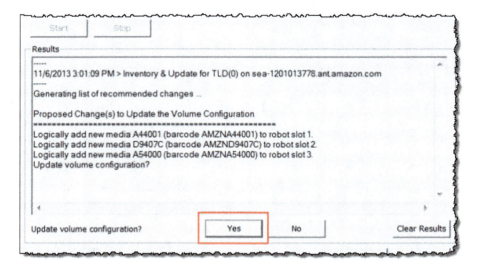

For example, the following screenshot shows three virtual tapes found in the import/export slots.

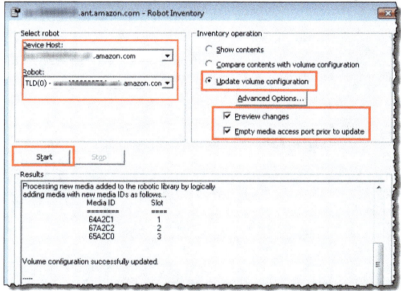

8. Close the **Robot Inventory** window.

9. In the **Media** node, expand the **Robots** node and choose **TLD(0)** to show all virtual tapes that are available to your robot (medium changer). **Note**
If you have previously connected other devices to the NetBackup application, you might have multiple robots. Make sure that you select the right robot.

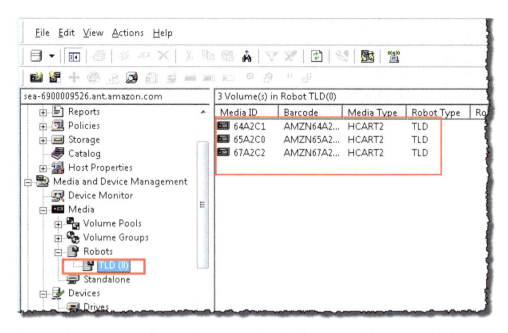

Now that you have connected your devices and made them available to your backup application, you are ready to test your gateway. To test your gateway, you back up data onto the virtual tapes you created and archive the tapes.

Backing Up Data to a Tape

You test the tape gateway setup by backing up data onto your virtual tapes.

Note
You should back up only a small amount of data for this Getting Started exercise, because there are costs associated with storing, archiving, and retrieving data. For pricing information, see Pricing on the AWS Storage Gateway detail page.

To create a volume pool

A *volume pool* is a collection of virtual tapes to use for a backup.

1. Start the NetBackup Administration Console.

2. Expand the **Media** node, open the context (right-click) menu for **Volume Pool**, and then choose **New**. The **New Volume Pool** dialog box appears.

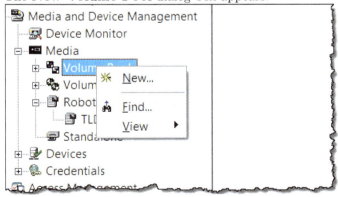

3. For **Name**, type a name for your volume pool.

4. For **Description**, type a description for the volume pool, and then choose **OK**. The volume pool you just created is added to the volume pool list.

The following screenshot shows a list of volume pools.

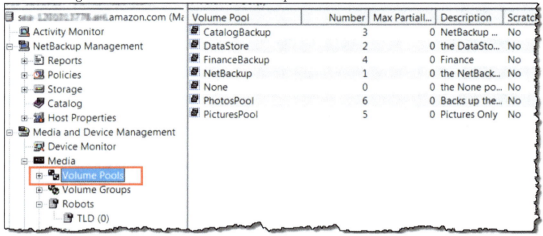

To add virtual tapes to a volume pool

1. Expand the **Robots** node, and select the **TLD(0)** robot to display the virtual tapes this robot is aware of.

   If you have previously connected a robot, your tape gateway robot might have a different name.

2. From the list of virtual tapes, open the context (right-click) menu for the tape you want to add to the volume pool, and choose **Change** to open the **Change Volumes** dialog box. The following screenshot shows the **Change Volumes** dialog box.

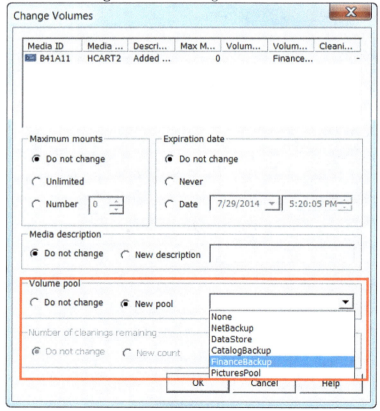

3. For **Volume Pool**, choose **New pool**.

4. For **New pool**, select the pool you just created, and then choose **OK**.

   You can verify that your volume pool contains the virtual tape that you just added by expanding the **Media** node and choosing your volume pool.

To create a backup policy

The backup policy specifies what data to back up, when to back it up, and which volume pool to use.

1. Choose your **Master Server** to return to the Symantec NetBackup console.

   The following screenshot shows the NetBackup console with **Create a Policy** selected.

2. Choose **Create a Policy** to open the **Policy Configuration Wizard** window.

3. Select **File systems, databases, applications**, and choose **Next**.

4. For **Policy Name**, type a name for your policy and verify that **MS-Windows** is selected from the **Select the policy type** list, and then choose **Next**.

5. In the **Client List** window, choose **Add**, type the host name of your computer in the **Name** column, and then choose **Next**. This step applies the policy you are defining to localhost (your client computer).

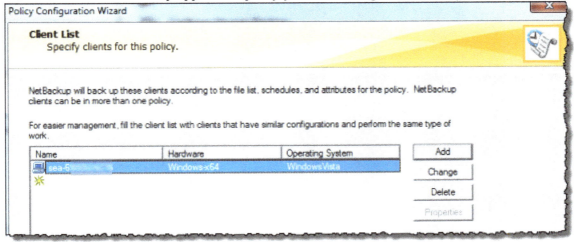

6. In the **Files** window, choose **Add**, and then choose the folder icon.

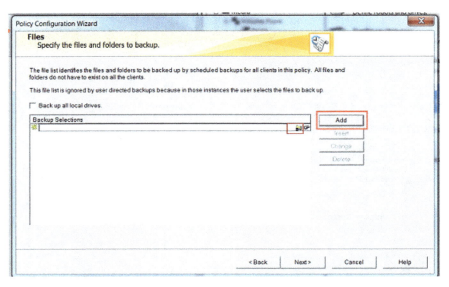

7. In the **Browse** window, browse to the folder or files you want to back up, choose **OK**, and then choose **Next**.

8. In the **Backup Types** window, accept the defaults, and then choose **Next**. **Note**
   If you want to initiate the backup yourself, select **User Backup**.

9. In the **Frequency and Retention** window, select the frequency and retention policy you want to apply to the backup. For this exercise, you can accept all the defaults and choose** Next**.

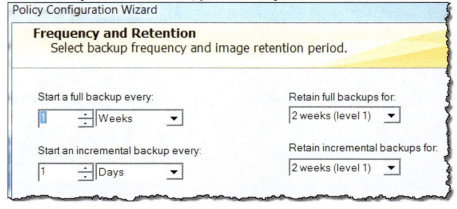

10. In the **Start** window, select **Off hours**, and then choose **Next**. This selection specifies that your folder should be backed up during off hours only.

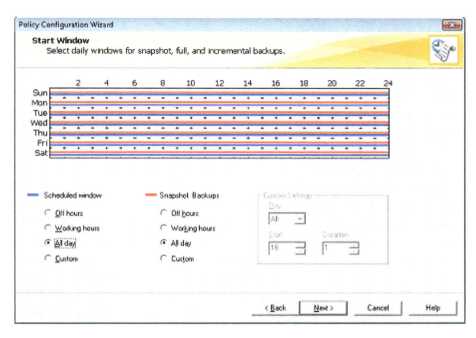

11. In the **Policy Configuration** wizard, choose **Finish**.

The policy runs the backups according to the schedule. You can also perform a manual backup at any time, which we do in the next step.

To perform a manual backup

1. On the navigation pane of the NetBackup console, expand the **NetBackup Management** node.

2. Expand the **Policies** node.

3. Open the context (right-click) menu for your policy, and choose **Manual Backup**.

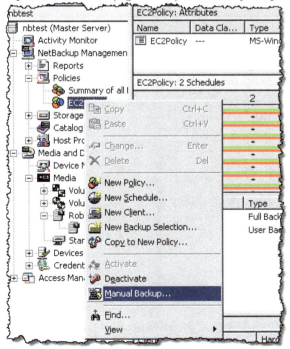

4. In the **Manual Backup** window, select a schedule, select a client, and then choose **OK**.

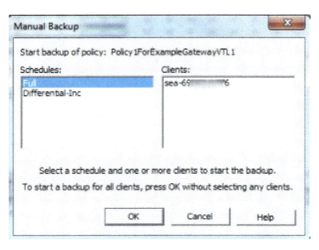

5. In the **Manual Backup Started** dialog box that appears, choose **OK**.

6. On the navigation pane, choose **Activity Monitor** to view the status of your backup in the **Job ID** column.

	Job ID	Type	Job State	State Details	Status	Job Policy	Job Schedule	Client
	18	Backup	Done		0	EC2Policy	Full	localhost
	17	Backup	Done		0	EC2Policy	Full	localhost
	14	Backup	Done		0	EC2Policy	Full	localhost
	10	Image Cleanup	Done		1			
	11	Image Cleanup	Done		1			

nbtest: 11 Jobs (0 Queued   0 Active   0 Waiting for Retry   0 Suspended   0 Incomplete   11 Done)

To find the barcode of the virtual tape where NetBackup wrote the file data during the backup, look in the **Job Details** window as described in the following procedure. You need this barcode in the procedure in the next section, where you archive the tape.

To find the barcode of a tape

1. In **Activity Monitor**, open the context (right-click) menu for the identifier of your backup job in the **Job ID** column, and then choose **Details**.

2. In the **Job Details** window, choose the **Detailed Status** tab.

3. In the **Status** box, locate the media ID. For example, in the following screenshot, the media ID is **87A222**. This ID helps you determine which tape you have written data to.

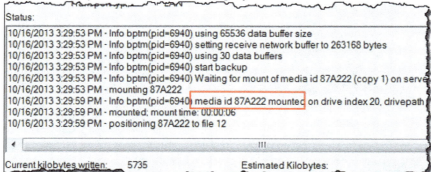

You have now successfully deployed a tape gateway, created virtual tapes, and backed up your data. Next, you can archive the virtual tapes and retrieve them from the archive.

Archiving the Tape

When you archive a tape, tape gateway moves the tape from your gateway's virtual tape library (VTL) to the archive, which provides offline storage. You initiate tape archival by ejecting the tape using your backup application.

To archive a virtual tape

1. In the NetBackup Administration console, expand the **Media and Device Management** node, and expand the **Media** node.

2. Expand **Robots** and choose **TLD**(0).

3. Open the context (right-click) menu for the virtual tape you want to archive, and choose **Eject Volume From Robot**.

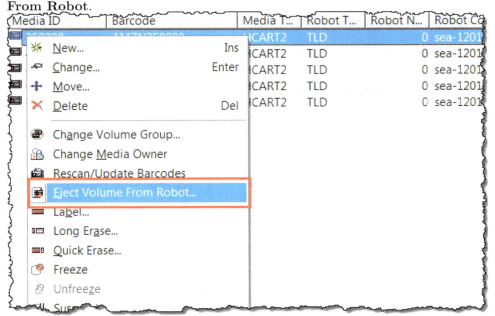

4. In the **Eject Volumes** window, make sure the **Media ID** matches the virtual tape you want to eject, and then choose **Eject**.

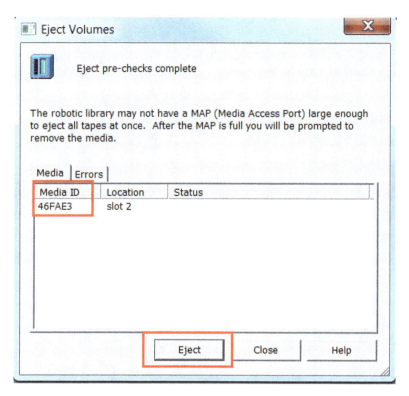

5. In the dialog box, choose **Yes**. The dialog box is shown following.

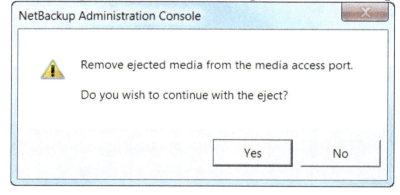

When the eject process is completed, the status of the tape in the **Eject Volumes** dialog box indicates that the eject succeeded.

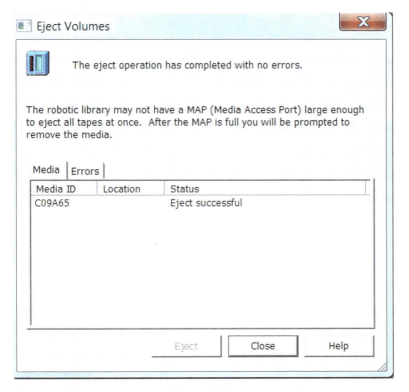

6. Choose **Close** to close the **Eject Volumes** window.

7. In the AWS Storage Gateway console, verify the status of the tape you are archiving in the gateway's VTL. It can take some time to finish uploading data to AWS. During this time, the ejected tape is listed in the gateway's VTL with the status **IN TRANSIT TO VTS**. When archiving starts, the status is **ARCHIVING**. Once data upload has completed, the ejected tape is no longer listed in the VTL.

8. To verify that the virtual tape is no longer listed in your gateway, choose your gateway, and then choose **VTL Tape Cartridges**.

9. In the navigation pane of the AWS Storage Gateway console, choose **Tapes**. Verify that your archived tape's status is **ARCHIVED**.

Restoring Data from the Tape

Restoring your archived data is a two-step process.

To restore data from an archived tape

1. Retrieve the archived tape to a tape gateway. For instructions, see Retrieving Archived Tapes.

2. Use the Backup, Archive, and Restore software installed with the Symantec NetBackup application. This process is the same as restoring data from physical tapes. For instructions, see Veritas Services and Operations Readiness Tools (SORT) on the Veritas website.

Next Step

Cleaning Up Resources You Don't Need

Testing Your Setup by Using NovaStor DataCenter/Network

You can back up your data to virtual tapes, archive the tapes, and manage your virtual tape library (VTL) devices by using NovaStor DataCenter/Network version 6.4 or 7.1. In this topic, you can find basic documentation on how to configure the NovaStor DataCenter/Network version 7.1 backup application for a tape gateway and perform backup and restore operations. For detailed information about how to use NovaStor DataCenter/Network version 7.1, see Documentation NovaStor DataCenter/Network.

Setting Up NovaStor DataCenter/Network

After you have connected your virtual tape library (VTL) devices to your Microsoft Windows client, you configure the NovaStor software to recognize your devices. For information about how to connect VTL devices to your Windows client, see Connecting Your VTL Devices.

NovaStor DataCenter/Network requires drivers from the driver manufacturers. You can use the Windows drivers, but you must first deactivate other backup applications.

Configuring NovaStor DataCenter/Network to Work with VTL Devices

When configuring your VTL devices to work with NovaStor DataCenter/Network version 6.4 or 7.1, you might see an error message that reads `External Program did not exit correctly`. This issue requires a workaround, which you need to perform before you continue.

You can prevent the issue by creating the workaround before you start configuring your VTL devices. For information about how to create the workaround, see Resolving an "External Program Did Not Exit Correctly" Error.

To configure NovaStor DataCenter/Network to work with VTL devices

1. In the NovaStor DataCenter/Network Admin console, choose **Media Management**, and then choose **Storage Management**.

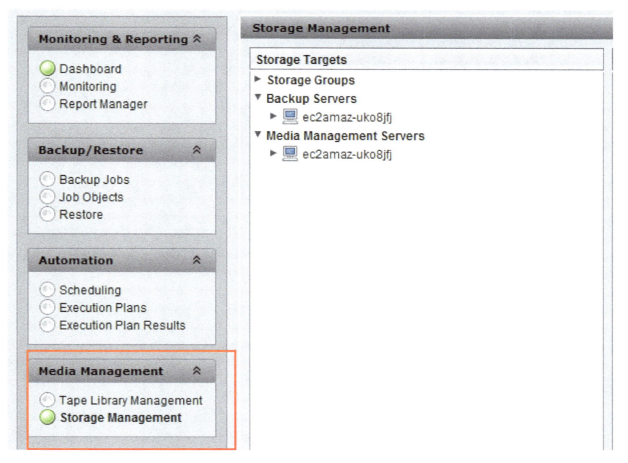

2. In the **Storage Targets** menu, open the context menu (right-click) for **Media Management Servers**, choose **New**, and choose **OK** to create and prepopulate a **storage** node.

   If you see an error message that says `External Program did not exit correctly`, resolve the issue before you continue. This issue requires a workaround. For information about how to resolve this issue, see Resolving an "External Program Did Not Exit Correctly" Error in the NovaStor documentation.
   Important
   This error occurs because the element assignment range from AWS Storage Gateway for storage drives and tape drives exceeds the number that NovaStor DataCenter/Network allows.

3. Open the context (right-click) menu for the **storage** node that was created, and choose **New Library**.

4. Choose the library server from the list. The library list is automatically populated.

5. Name the library and choose **OK**.

6. Choose the library to display all the properties of the Storage Gateway virtual tape library.

7. In the **Storage Targets** menu, expand **Backup Servers**, open the context (right-click) menu for the server, and choose **Attach Library**.

8. In the **Attach Library** dialog box that appears, choose the **LTO5** media type, and then choose **OK**.

115

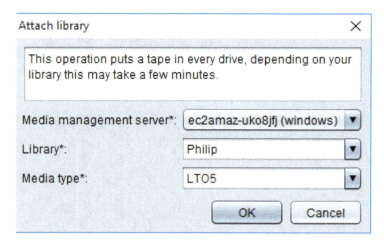

9. Expand **Backup Servers** to see the Storage Gateway virtual tape library and the library partition that shows all the mounted tape drives.

Creating a Tape Pool

A tape pool is dynamically created in the NovaStor DataCenter/Network software and so doesn't contain a fixed number of media. A tape pool that needs a tape gets it from its scratch pool. A *scratch pool* is a reservoir of tapes that are freely available for one or more tape pools to use. A tape pool returns to the scratch pool any media that have exceeded their retention times and that are no longer needed.

Creating a tape pool is a three-step task:

1. You create a scratch pool.

2. You assign tapes to the scratch pool.

3. You create a tape pool.

To create a scratch pool

1. In the left navigation menu, choose the **Scratch Pools** tab.

2. Open the context (right-click) menu for **Scratch Pools**, and choose **Create Scratch Pool**.

3. In the **Scratch Pools** dialog box, name your scratch pool, and then choose your media type.

4. Choose **Label Volume**, and create a low water mark for the scratch pool. When the scratch pool is emptied down to the low water mark, a warning appears.

5. In the warning dialog box that appears, choose **OK** to create the scratch pool.

To assign tapes to a scratch pool

1. In the left navigation menu, choose **Tape Library Management**.

2. Choose the **Library** tab to see your library's inventory.

3. Choose the tapes that you want to assign to the scratch pool. Make sure that the tapes are set to the correct media type.

4. Open the context (right-click) menu for the library and choose **Add to Scratch Pool**.

You now have a filled scratch pool that you can use for tape pools.

To create a tape pool

1. From the left navigation menu, choose **Tape Library Management**.

2. Open the context (right-click) menu for the **Media Pools** tab and choose **Create Media Pool**.

3. Name the media pool and choose **Backup Server**.

4. Choose a library partition for the media pool.

5. Choose the scratch pool that you want the pool to get the tapes from.

6. For **Schedule**, choose **Not Scheduled**.

Configuring Media Import and Export to Archive Tapes

NovaStor DataCenter/Network can use import/export slots if they are part of the media changer.

For an export, NovaStor DataCenter/Network must know which tapes are going to be physically taken out of the library.

For an import, NovaStor DataCenter/Network recognizes tape media that are exported in the tape library and offers to import them all, either from a data slot or an export slot. Your tape gateway archives tapes in the virtual tape shelf (VTS), which is backed by Amazon Glacier. The VTS is referred to as offsite location in NovaStor DataCenter/Network.

To configure media import and export

1. Navigate to **Tape Library Management**, choose a server for **Media Management Server**, and then choose **Library**.

2. Choose the **Off-site Locations** tab.

3. Open the context (right-click) menu for the white area, and choose **Add** to open a new panel.

4. In the panel, type **Glacier** and add an optional description in the text box.

Backing Up Data to Tape

You create a backup job and write data to a virtual tape by using the same procedures that you do with physical tapes. For detailed information about how to back up data using the NovaStor software, see Start Backup Job in the NovaStor documentation.

Archiving a Tape

When you archive a tape, a tape gateway ejects the tape from the tape drive to the storage slot. It then exports the tape from the slot to the archive by using your backup application—that is, NovaStor DataCenter/Network.

To archive a tape

1. In the left navigation menu, choose **Tape Library Management**.

2. Choose the **Library** tab to see the library's inventory.

3. Highlight the tapes you want to archive, open the context (right-click) menu for the tapes, and choose **Mail Slot Export to Glacier**.

The archiving process can take some time to complete. The initial status of the tape appears as **IN TRANSIT TO VTS**. When archiving starts, the status changes to **ARCHIVING**. When archiving is completed, the tape is no longer listed in the VTL.

In NovaStor DataCenter/Network, verify that the tape is no longer in the storage slot.

In the navigation pane of the Storage Gateway console, choose **Tapes**. Verify that your archived tape's status is **ARCHIVED**.

Restoring Data from an Archived and Retrieved Tape

Restoring your archived data is a two-step process.

To restore data from an archived tape

1. Retrieve the archived tape from archive to a tape gateway. For instructions, see Retrieving Archived Tapes.

2. Use the NovaStor DataCenter/Network software to restore the data. You do this by refreshing the mail slot and moving each tape you want to retrieve into an empty slot, as you do when restoring data from physical tapes. For instructions, see Restore the Example in the NovaStor documentation.

Writing Several Backup Jobs to a Tape Drive at the Same Time

In the NovaStor software, you can write several jobs to a tape drive at the same time using the multiplexing feature. This feature is available when a multiplexer is available for a media pool. For information about how to use multiplexing, see Define Backup Destination and Schedule in the NovaStor documentation.

Resolving an "External Program Did Not Exit Correctly" Error

When configuring your VTL devices to work with NovaStor DataCenter/Network version 6.4 or 7.1, you might see an error message that reads `External Program did not exit correctly`. This error occurs because the element assignment range from AWS Storage Gateway for storage drives and tape drives exceeds the number that NovaStor DataCenter/Network allows.

Storage Gateway returns 3200 storage and import/export slots, which is more than the 2400 limit that NovaStor DataCenter/Network allows. To resolve this issue, you add a configuration file that enables the NovaStor software to limit the number of storage and import/export slots and preconfigures the element assignment range.

To apply the workaround for an "external program did not exit correctly" error

1. Navigate to the Tape folder on your computer where you installed the NovaStor software.

2. In the Tape folder, create a text file and name it `hijacc.ini`.

3. Copy the following content, paste it into `hijacc.ini` file, and save the file.

```
1 port:12001
2 san:no
3 define: A3B0S0L0
4 *DRIVES: 10
5 *FIRST_DRIVE: 10000
6 *SLOTS: 200
7 *FIRST_SLOT: 20000
8 *HANDLERS: 1
9 *FIRST_HANDLER: 0
10 *IMP-EXPS: 30
11 *FIRST_IMP-EXP: 30000
```

4. Add and attach the library to the media management server.

5. Move a tape from the import/export slot into the library by using the following command as shown the screenshots below. In the command, replace VTL with the name of your library.

118

```
C:\Program Files\NovaStor\DataCenter\Hiback\tape>ophijacc.exe -c VTL-ec2amaz-uko8jfj-ec2amaz-uko8jfj.lcfg

1  Configuration
2  Status   Handler
3  Status   Import/Export
4  Status   Drive
5  Status   Slot
6  Mount    Medium
7  Unmount  Medium
8  Find     Address by Tag

9  Reset    Stacker
11 Move     Element
88 Inventory
99 Exit

   What (#[,#[,#]])? 1
Handlers      :   1   Address: 0
Import/Export:  30   Address: 30000
Drives        :  10   Address: 10000
Slots         : 200   Address: 20000
```

```
1  Configuration
2  Status   Handler
3  Status   Import/Export
4  Status   Drive
5  Status   Slot
6  Mount    Medium
7  Unmount  Medium
8  Find     Address by Tag

9  Reset    Stacker
11 Move     Element
88 Inventory
99 Exit

   What (#[,#[,#]])? 11
   Source        Address?  30000
   Destination Address?  20000

1  Configuration
2  Status   Handler
3  Status   Import/Export
4  Status   Drive
5  Status   Slot
6  Mount    Medium
7  Unmount  Medium
8  Find     Address by Tag

9  Reset    Stacker
```

6. Attach the library to the backup server.

7. In the NovaStor software, import all the tapes from import/export slots into the library.

Testing Your Setup by Using Quest NetVault Backup

You can back up your data to virtual tapes, archive the tapes, and manage your virtual tape library (VTL) devices by using Quest (formerly Dell) NetVault Backup version 10.0. In this topic, you can find basic documentation on how to configure the Quest NetVault Backup application for a tape gateway and perform a backup and restore operation.

For additional setup information, see Backing up to Amazon AWS with Quest NetVault Backup on the Quest (formerly Dell) website. For detailed information about how to use the Quest NetVault Backup application, see the Quest NetVault Backup 10.0.1 – Administration Guide. For more information about compatible backup applications, see Supported Third-Party Backup Applications for a Tape Gateway.

Topics

- Configuring Quest NetVault Backup to Work with VTL Devices
- Backing Up Data to a Tape in the Quest NetVault Backup
- Archiving a Tape by Using the Quest NetVault Backup
- Restoring Data from a Tape Archived in Quest NetVault Backup

Configuring Quest NetVault Backup to Work with VTL Devices

After you have connected the virtual tape library (VTL) devices to the Windows client, you configure Quest NetVault Backup to recognize your devices. For information about how to connect VTL devices to the Windows client, see Connecting Your VTL Devices.

The Quest NetVault Backup application doesn't automatically recognize tape gateway devices. You must manually add the devices to expose them to the Quest NetVault Backup application and then discover the VTL devices.

Adding VTL Devices

To add the VTL devices

1. In Quest NetVault Backup, choose **Manage Devices** in the **Configuration** tab.

2. On the Manage Devices page, choose **Add Devices**.

3. In the Add Storage Wizard, choose **Tape library / media changer**, and then choose **Next**.

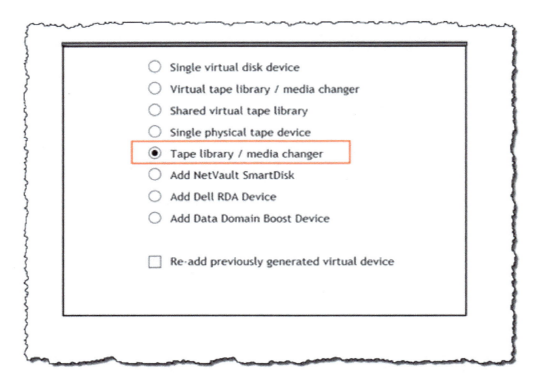

4. On the next page, choose the client machine that is physically attached to the library and choose **Next** to scan for devices.

5. If devices are found, they are displayed. In this case, your medium changer is displayed in the device box.

6. Choose your medium changer and choose **Next**. Detailed information about the device is displayed in the wizard.

7. On the Add Tapes to Bays page, choose **Scan For Devices**, choose your client machine, and then choose **Next**.

   All your drives are displayed on the page. Quest NetVault Backup displays the 10 bays to which you can add your drives. The bays are displayed one at a time.

Device	Serial Number
3-0.5.0 (IBM ULT3580-TD5)	AMZN_SGW- 54A94C3D_TD_00005
3-0.29.0 (IBM ULT3580-TD5)	AMZN_SGW- 54A94C3D_TD_00007
3-0.30.0 (IBM ULT3580-TD5)	AMZN_SGW- 54A94C3D_TD_00008
3-0.31.0 (IBM ULT3580-TD5)	AMZN_SGW- 54A94C3D_TD_00009
3-0.32.0 (IBM ULT3580-TD5)	AMZN_SGW- 54A94C3D_TD_00010
⁛ ◄ ► ►⁛	1 - 5 of 5 items

8. Choose the drive you want to add to the bay that is displayed, and then choose **Next**. **Important**

When you add a drive to a bay, the drive and bay numbers must match. For example, if bay 1 is displayed, you must add drive 1. If a drive is not connected, leave its matching bay empty.

9. When your client machine appears, choose it, and then choose **Next**. The client machine can appear multiple times.

10. When the drives are displayed, repeat steps 7 through 9 to add all the drives to the bays.

11. In the **Configuration** tab, choose **Manage devices** and on the **Manage Devices** page, expand your medium changer to see the devices that you added.

Backing Up Data to a Tape in the Quest NetVault Backup

You create a backup job and write data to a virtual tape by using the same procedures you do with physical tapes. For detailed information about how to back up data, see the Quest NetVault Backup documentation.

Archiving a Tape by Using the Quest NetVault Backup

When you archive a tape, a tape gateway ejects the tape from the tape drive to the storage slot. It then exports the tape from the slot to the archive by using your backup application—that is, the Quest NetVault Backup.

To archive a tape in Quest NetVault Backup

1. In the Quest NetVault Backup Configuration tab, choose and expand your medium changer to see your tapes.

2. On the **Slots** row, choose the settings icon to open the **Slots Browser** for the medium changer.

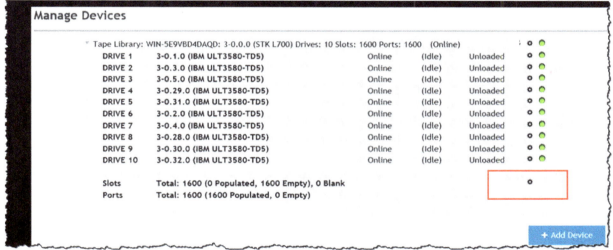

3. In the slots, locate the tape you want to archive, choose it, and then choose **Export**.

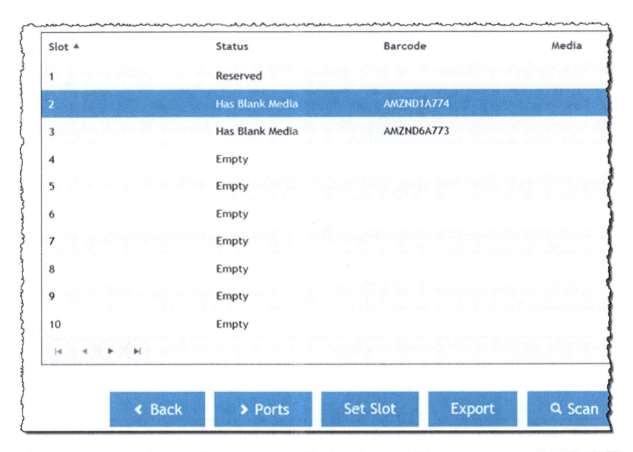

Slot ▲	Status	Barcode	Media
1	Reserved		
2	Has Blank Media	AMZND1A774	
3	Has Blank Media	AMZND6A773	
4	Empty		
5	Empty		
6	Empty		
7	Empty		
8	Empty		
9	Empty		
10	Empty		

‹ Back › Ports Set Slot Export 🔍 Scan

The archiving process can take some time to complete. The initial status of the tape appears as **IN TRANSIT TO VTS**. When archiving starts, the status changes to **ARCHIVING**. When archiving is completed, the tape is no longer listed in the VTL.

In the Quest NetVault Backup software, verify that the tape is no longer in the storage slot.

In the navigation pane of the Storage Gateway console, choose **Tapes**. Verify that your archived tape's status is **ARCHIVED**.

Restoring Data from a Tape Archived in Quest NetVault Backup

Restoring your archived data is a two-step process.

To restore data from an archived tape

1. Retrieve the archived tape from archive to a tape gateway. For instructions, see Retrieving Archived Tapes.

2. Use the Quest NetVault Backup application to restore the data. You do this by creating a restoring a folder file, as you do when restoring data from physical tapes. For instructions, see Quest NetVault Backup 10.0.1 – Administration Guide (Creating a restore job) in the Quest NetVault Backup documentation.

Next Step

Cleaning Up Resources You Don't Need

Testing Your Setup by Using Veeam Backup & Replication

You can back up your data to virtual tapes, archive the tapes, and manage your virtual tape library (VTL) devices by using Veeam Backup & Replication V7, V8, or V9 Update 2 or later. In this topic, you can find basic documentation on how to configure the Veeam Backup & Replication software for a tape gateway and perform a backup and restore operation. For detailed information about how to use the Veeam software, see the Veeam Backup & Replication documentation in the Veeam Help Center. For more information about compatible backup applications, see Supported Third-Party Backup Applications for a Tape Gateway.

Topics

- Configuring Veeam to Work with VTL Devices
- Importing a Tape into Veeam
- Backing Up Data to a Tape in Veeam
- Archiving a Tape by Using Veeam
- Restoring Data from a Tape Archived in Veeam

Configuring Veeam to Work with VTL Devices

After you have connected your virtual tape library (VTL) devices to the Windows client, you configure Veeam Backup & Replication to recognize your devices. For information about how to connect VTL devices to the Windows client, see Connecting Your VTL Devices.

Updating VTL Device Drivers

By default, the Veeam V7 and V8 backup application does not recognize tape gateway devices. To configure the software to work with tape gateway devices, you update the device drivers for the VTL devices to expose them to the Veeam software and then discover the VTL devices. In Device Manager, update the driver for the medium changer. For instructions, see Updating the Device Driver for Your Medium Changer.

Discovering VTL Devices

For the Veeam 9 backup application, you must use native SCSI commands instead of a Windows driver to discover your tape library if your media changer is unknown. For detailed instructions, see Working with Tape Libraries.

To discover VTL devices

1. In the Veeam software, choose **Backup Infrastructure**. When the tape gateway is connected, virtual tapes are listed in the **Backup Infrastructure** tab. **Note**
Depending on the version of the Veeam Backup & Replication you are using, the user interface might differ somewhat from that shown in the screenshots in this documentation.

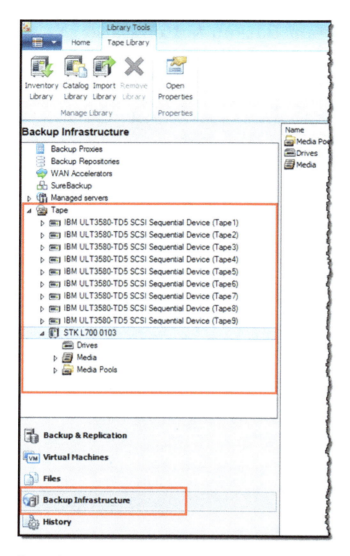

2. Expand the **Tape** tree to see your tape drives and medium changer.

3. Expand the medium changer tree. If your tape drives are mapped to the medium changer, the drives appear under **Drives**. Otherwise, your tape library and tape drives appear as separate devices.

   If the drives are not mapped automatically, follow the instructions on the Veeam website to map the drives.

Importing a Tape into Veeam

You are now ready to import tapes from your tape gateway into the Veeam backup application library.

To import a tape into the Veeam library

1. Open the context (right–click) menu for the medium changer, and choose **Import** to import the tapes to the I/E slots.

2. Open the context (right–click) menu for the medium charger, and choose **Inventory Library** to identify unrecognized tapes. When you load a new virtual tape into a tape drive for the first time, the tape is not recognized by the Veeam backup application. To identify the unrecognized tape, you inventory the tapes in the tape library.

Backing Up Data to a Tape in Veeam

Backing data to a tape is a two-step process:

1. You create a media pool and add the tape to the media pool.

2. You write data to the tape.

You create a media pool and write data to a virtual tape by using the same procedures you do with physical tapes. For detailed information about how to back up data, see the Veeam documentation in the Veeam Help Center.

Archiving a Tape by Using Veeam

When you archive a tape, tape gateway moves the tape from the Veeam tape library to the offline storage. You begin tape archival by ejecting from the tape drive to the storage slot and then exporting the tape from the slot to the archive by using your backup application—that is, the Veeam software.

To archive a tape in the Veeam library

1. Choose **Backup Infrastructure**, and choose the media pool that contains the tape you want to archive.

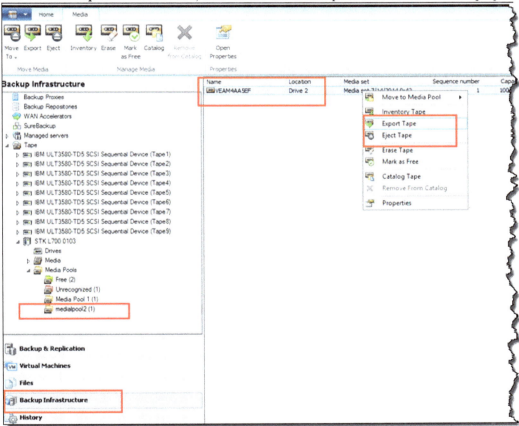

2. Open the context (right–click) menu for the tape that you want to archive, and then choose **Eject Tape**.

3. For **Ejecting tape**, choose **Close**. The location of the tape changes from a tape drive to a slot.

4. Open the context (right–click) menu for the tape again, and then choose **Export**. The status of the tape changes from **Tape drive **to **Offline**.

5. For **Exporting tape**, choose **Close**. The location of the tape changes from **Slot** to **Offline**.

6. On the AWS Storage Gateway console, choose your gateway, and then choose **VTL Tape Cartridges** and verify the status of the virtual tape you are archiving.

The archiving process can take some time to complete. The initial status of the tape appears as **IN TRANSIT TO VTS**. When archiving starts, the status changes to **ARCHIVING**. When archiving is completed, the tape is no longer listed in the VTL.

Restoring Data from a Tape Archived in Veeam

Restoring your archived data is a two-step process.

To restore data from an archived tape

1. Retrieve the archived tape from archive to a tape gateway. For instructions, see Retrieving Archived Tapes.

2. Use the Veeam software to restore the data. You do this by creating a restoring a folder file, as you do when restoring data from physical tapes. For instructions, see Restoring Data from Tape in the Veeam Help Center.

Next Step

Cleaning Up Resources You Don't Need

Managing Your Gateway

Managing your gateway includes tasks such as configuring cache storage and upload buffer space, working with volumes or virtual tapes, and doing general maintenance. If you haven't created a gateway, see Getting Started.

Topics

- Managing Your File Gateway
- Managing Your Volume Gateway
- Managing Your Tape Gateway

Managing Your File Gateway

Following, you can find information about how to manage your file gateway resources.

Topics

- Adding a File Share
- Deleting a File Share
- Editing Storage Settings for Your File Share
- Editing Metadata Defaults for Your NFS File Share
- Editing Access Settings for Your NFS File Share
- Editing Access Settings for Your SMB File Share
- Refreshing Objects in Your Amazon S3 Bucket
- Understanding File Share Status
- File Share Best Practices

Adding a File Share

After your file gateway is activated and running, you can add additional file shares and grant access to Amazon S3 buckets. Buckets that you can grant access to include buckets in a different AWS account than your file share. For information about how to add a file share, see Creating a File Share.

Topics

- Granting Access to an Amazon S3 Bucket
- Using a File Share for Cross-Account Access

Granting Access to an Amazon S3 Bucket

When you create a file share, your file gateway requires access to upload files into your Amazon S3 bucket. To grant this access, your file gateway assumes an AWS Identity and Access Management (IAM) role that is associated with an IAM policy that grants this access.

The role requires this IAM policy and a security token service trust (STS) relationship for it. The policy determines which actions the role can perform. In addition, your S3 bucket must have an access policy that allows the IAM role to access the S3 bucket.

You can create the role and access policy yourself, or your file gateway can create them for you. If your file gateway creates the policy for you, the policy contains a list of S3 actions. For information about roles and permissions, see Creating a Role to Delegate Permissions to an AWS Service in the *IAM User Guide*.

The following example is a trust policy that allows your file gateway to assume an IAM role.

```
1  {
2    "Version": "2012-10-17",
3    "Statement": [
4      {
5        "Sid": "",
6        "Effect": "Allow",
7        "Principal": {
8          "Service": "storagegateway.amazonaws.com"
9        },
10       "Action": "sts:AssumeRole"
11     }
12   ]
13 }
```

If you don't want your file gateway to create a policy on your behalf, you create your own policy and attach it to your file share. For more information about how to do this, see Creating a File Share.

The following example policy allows your file gateway to perform all the Amazon S3 actions listed in the policy. The first part of the statement allows all the actions listed to be performed on the S3 bucket named `TestBucket`. The second part allows the listed actions on all objects in `TestBucket`.

```
{
    "Version": "2012-10-17",
    "Statement": [
        {
            "Action": [
                "s3:GetAccelerateConfiguration",
                "s3:GetBucketLocation",
                "s3:GetBucketVersioning",
                "s3:ListBucket",
                "s3:ListBucketVersions",
                "s3:ListBucketMultipartUploads"
            ],
            "Resource": "arn:aws:s3:::TestBucket",
            "Effect": "Allow"
        },
        {
            "Action": [
                "s3:AbortMultipartUpload",
                "s3:DeleteObject",
                "s3:DeleteObjectVersion",
                "s3:GetObject",
                "s3:GetObjectAcl",
                "s3:GetObjectVersion",
                "s3:ListMultipartUploadParts",
                "s3:PutObject",
                "s3:PutObjectAcl"
            ],
            "Resource": "arn:aws:s3:::TestBucket/*",
            "Effect": "Allow"
        }
    ]
}
```

Using a File Share for Cross-Account Access

Cross-account access is when an AWS account and users for that account are granted access to resources that belong to another AWS account. With file gateways, you can use a file share in one AWS account to access objects in an Amazon S3 bucket that belongs to a different AWS account.

To use a file share owned by one AWS account to access an S3 bucket in a different AWS account

1. Make sure that the S3 bucket owner has granted your AWS account access to the S3 bucket that you need to access and the objects in that bucket. For information about how to grant this access, see Example 2: Bucket Owner Granting Cross-Account Bucket Permissions in the *Amazon Simple Storage Service Developer Guide*. For a list of the required permissions, see Granting Access to an Amazon S3 Bucket.

2. Make sure that the IAM role that your file share uses to access the S3 bucket includes permissions for operations such as `s3:GetObjectAcl` and `s3:PutObjectAcl`. In addition, make sure that the IAM role

includes a trust policy that allows your account to assume that IAM role. For an example of such a trust policy, see Granting Access to an Amazon S3 Bucket.

3. Open the AWS Storage Gateway console at https://console.aws.amazon.com/storagegateway/home.

4. Choose **Give bucket owner full control** in the **Object metadata** settings in the **Configure file share setting** dialog box.

When you have created or updated your file share for cross-account access and mounted the file share on-premises, we highly recommend that you test your setup. You can do this by listing directory contents or writing test files and making sure the files show up as objects in the S3 bucket.

Important
Make sure to set up the policies correctly to grant cross-account access to the account used by your file share. If you don't, updates to files through your on-premises applications don't propagate to the Amazon S3 bucket that you're working with.

Resources

For additional information about access policies and access control lists, see the following:

Guidelines for Using the Available Access Policy Options in the *Amazon Simple Storage Service Developer Guide*

Access Control List (ACL) Overview in the *Amazon Simple Storage Service Developer Guide*

Deleting a File Share

If you no longer need a file share, you can delete it from the AWS Storage Gateway Management Console. When you delete a file share, the gateway is detached from the Amazon S3 bucket that the file share maps to. However, the S3 bucket and its contents aren't deleted.

If your gateway is uploading data to a S3 bucket when you delete a file share, the delete process doesn't complete until all the data is uploaded. The file share has the DELETING status until the data is completely uploaded.

If you want your data to be completely uploaded, use the **To delete a file share** procedure directly following. If you don't want to wait for your data to be completely uploaded, see the **To forcibly delete a file share** procedure later in this topic.

To delete a file share

1. Open the AWS Storage Gateway console at https://console.aws.amazon.com/storagegateway/home.

2. Choose **File shares**, and choose the file share that you want to delete.

3. For **Actions**, choose **Delete file share**. The following confirmation dialog box appears.

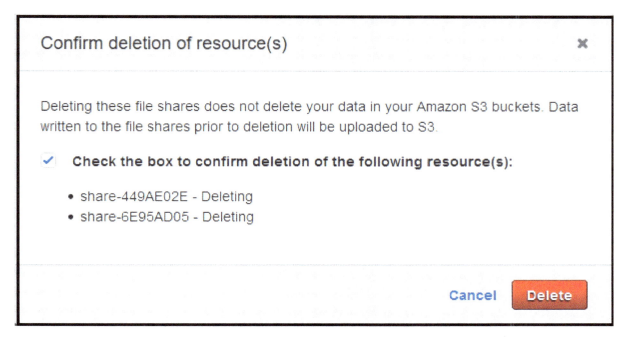

4. In the confirmation dialog box, select the check box for the file share or shares that you want to delete, and then choose **Delete**.

In certain cases, you might not want to wait until all the data written to files on the Network File System (NFS) file share is uploaded before deleting the file share. For example, you might want to intentionally discard data that was written but has not yet been uploaded. In another example, the Amazon S3 bucket or objects that back the file share might have already been deleted, meaning that uploading the specified data is no longer possible.

In these cases, you can forcibly delete the file share by using the AWS Management Console or the `DeleteFileShare` API operation. This operation aborts the data upload process. When it does, the file share enters the FORCE_DELETING status. To forcibly delete a file share from the console, see the procedure following.

To forcibly delete a file share

1. Open the AWS Storage Gateway console at https://console.aws.amazon.com/storagegateway/home.

2. Choose **File shares**, and choose the file share that you want to forcibly delete and wait for a few seconds. A delete message is displayed in the **Details** tab.

Note
You cannot undo the force delete operation.

3. In the message that appears in the **Details** tab, verify the ID of the file share that you want to forcibly delete, select the confirmation box, and choose **Force delete now**.

You can also use the DeleteFileShare API operation to forcibly delete the file share.

Editing Storage Settings for Your File Share

You can edit the default storage class for your Amazon S3 bucket, the squash level setting, and the **Export as** option for your file share. Possible **Export as** options include, for example, **Read-write**.

To edit the file share settings

1. Open the AWS Storage Gateway console at https://console.aws.amazon.com/storagegateway/home.

2. Choose **File shares**, and then choose the file share that you want to update.

3. For **Actions**, choose **Edit storage settings**.

4. Do one or more of the following:

   - For **Storage class for new objects**, choose a default storage class for your S3 bucket, and choose **Save**.

     Possible values for the storage class for new objects are the following:

     - **S3 Standard **– Store your frequently accessed object data redundantly in multiple Availability Zones that are geographically separated.

     - **S3 Standard_IA **– Store your infrequently accessed object data redundantly in multiple Availability Zones that are geographically separated.

     - **S3 One Zone_IA** – Store your infrequently accessed object data a single Availability Zone.

     For more information, see Storage Classes in the *Amazon Simple Storage Service Developer Guide*.

   - For **Object metadata**, choose the metadata that you want to use:

     - Choose **Guess MIME type** to enable guessing of the MIME type for uploaded objects based on file extensions.
     - Choose **Give bucket owner full control** to give full control to the owner of the S3 bucket that maps to the file NFS/SMB file share. For more information on using your file share to access objects in a bucket owned by another account, see Using a File Share for Cross-Account Access.
     - Choose **Enable requester pays** if you are using this file share on a bucket that requires the requester or reader instead of bucket owner to pay for access charges. For more information, see Requester Pays Buckets.

   - For **Squash level**, choose the squash level setting that you want for your NFS file share, and then choose **Save**. **Note**
     You can choose a squash level setting for NFS file shares only. SMB file shares don't use squash settings.

     Possible values are the following:

     - **Root squash (default)** – Access for the remote superuser (root) is mapped to UID (65534) and GID (65534).
     - **No root squash** – The remote superuser (root) receives access as root.
     - **All squash – **All user access is mapped to UID (65534) and GID (65534).

     The default value for squash level is **Root squash**.

   - For **Export as**, choose an option for your file share, and then choose **Save**. The default value is **Read-write**. **Note**
     For file shares mounted on a Microsoft Windows client, if you select **Read-only** for **Export as**, you might see an error message about an unexpected error keeping you from creating the folder. This error message is a known issue with NFS version 3. You can ignore the message.

Editing Metadata Defaults for Your NFS File Share

If you don't set metadata values for your files or directories in your bucket, your file gateway sets default metadata values. These values include Unix permissions for files and folders. You can edit the metadata defaults on the AWS Storage Gateway Management Console.

When your file gateway stores files and folders in Amazon S3, the Unix file permissions are stored in object metadata. When your file gateway discovers objects that weren't stored by the file gateway, these objects are assigned default Unix file permissions. You can find the default Unix permissions in the following table.

Metadata	Description
Directory permissions	The Unix directory mode in the form "nnnn". For example, "0666" represents the access mode for all directories inside the file share. The default value is 0777.
File permissions	The Unix file mode in the form "nnnn". For example, "0666" represents the file mode inside the file share. The default value is 0666.
User ID	The default owner ID for files in the file share. The default value is 65534.
Group ID	The default group ID for the file share. The default value is 65534.

To edit metadata defaults

1. Open the AWS Storage Gateway console at https://console.aws.amazon.com/storagegateway/home.

2. Choose **File shares**, and then choose the file share that you want to update.

3. For **Actions**, choose **Edit file metadata defaults**.

4. In the **Edit file metadata defaults** dialog box, provide the metadata information and choose **Save**.

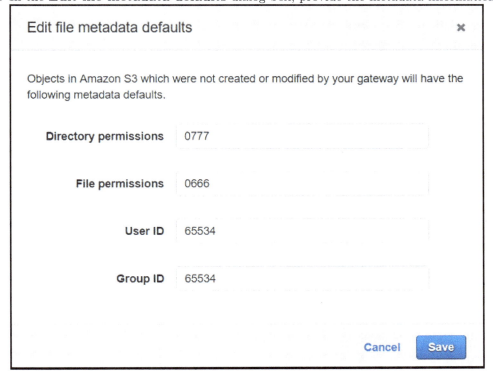

Editing Access Settings for Your NFS File Share

We recommend changing the allowed NFS client settings for your NFS file share. If you don't, any client on your network can mount to your file share.

To edit NFS access settings

1. Open the AWS Storage Gateway console at https://console.aws.amazon.com/storagegateway/home.

2. Choose **File shares**, and then choose the NFS file share that you want to edit.

3. For **Actions**, choose **Edit share access settings**.

4. In the **Edit allowed clients** dialog box, choose **Add entry**, provide the IP address or CIDR notation for the client that you want to allow, and then choose **Save**.

Editing Access Settings for Your SMB File Share

A file gateway provides Microsoft Active Directory (AD) access or guest access (also known as anonymous access) authentication modes for accessing an SMB file share. You can provide unlimited access to the SMB file share for all Microsoft AD users or limit access to specific users and groups.

To use your corporate Active Directory for user authenticated access to your SMB file share, edit the SMB settings for your gateway with your Microsoft AD domain credentials. Doing this allows your gateway to join your Active Directory domain and allows members of the domain to access the SMB file share.

Note
Using AWS Directory Service, you can create a hosted Active Directory domain service in the AWS Cloud.

Anyone who can provide the correct password gets guest access to the SMB file share.

To enable Active Directory authentication

1. Open the AWS Storage Gateway console at https://console.aws.amazon.com/storagegateway/home.

2. Choose the gateway that you want to use to join the domain.

3. For **Actions**, choose **Edit SMB settings** to open the **Edit SMB settings** dialog box.

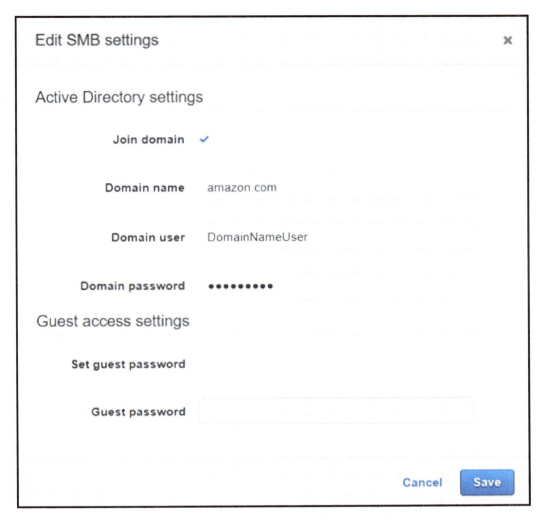

4. In the **Active Directory settings** section, choose **Join domain**.

5. For **Domain name**, provide the domain that you want the gateway to join.

6. Provide the domain user and the domain password, and then choose **Save**.

   A message at the top of the **Gateways** section of your console indicates that your gateway successfully joined your AD domain.

To limit file share access to specific AD users and groups

1. Choose the file share that you want to limit access to.

2. For **Actions**, choose **Edit SMB settings** to open the **Edit Valid/invalid users and groups** dialog box.

3. For **Valid users**, choose **Add entry** and provide the list of AD users that you want to allow file share access.

4. For **Valid groups**, choose **Add entry** and provide the list of AD groups that you want to allow file share access.

5. For **Invalid users**, choose **Add entry** and provide the list of AD users that you want to deny file share access.

6. For **Invalid groups**, choose **Add entry** and provide the list of AD users that you want to deny file share access.

7. When you finish adding your entries, choose **Save**.

If you don't specify valid or invalid users or groups, any authenticated Active Directory user can export the file share.

If you want to provide only guest access, your file gateway doesn't have to be part of a Microsoft AD domain. You can also use a file gateway that is a member of your AD domain to create file shares with guest access. Before you create a file share using guest access, you are required to change the default password.

To change the guest access password

1. Open the AWS Storage Gateway console at https://console.aws.amazon.com/storagegateway/home.

2. Choose the gateway that you want to use to join the domain.

3. For **Actions**, choose **Edit SMB settings**.

4. In the **Guest access settings** section, choose **Set guest password**, provide the password, and then choose **Save**.

Refreshing Objects in Your Amazon S3 Bucket

As your NFS/SMB client performs file system operations, your gateway maintains an inventory of the objects in the Amazon S3 bucket associated with your file share. Your gateway uses this cached inventory to reduce the latency and frequency of S3 requests.

To refresh the S3 bucket for your file share, you can use the AWS Storage Gateway console or the RefreshCache operation in the AWS Storage Gateway API.

To refresh objects in a S3 bucket from the console

1. Open the AWS Storage Gateway console at https://console.aws.amazon.com/storagegateway/home.

2. Choose **File shares**, and then choose the file share associated with the S3 bucket that you want to refresh.

3. For **Actions**, choose **Refresh cache**. The time that it takes to refresh depends on the number of objects that the S3 bucket contains.

Understanding File Share Status

Each file share has an associated status that tells you at a glance what the health of the file share is. Most of the time, the status indicates that the file share is functioning normally and that no action is needed on your part. In some cases, the status indicates a problem that might or might not require action on your part.

You can see file share status on the AWS Storage Gateway console. File share status appears in the **Status** column for each file share in your gateway. A file share that is functioning normally has the status of AVAILABLE.

In the following table, you can find a description of each file share status, and if and when you should act based on the status. A file share should have AVAILABLE status all or most of the time it's in use.

Status	Meaning
AVAILABLE	The file share is configured properly and is available to use. The AVAILABLE status is the normal running status for a file share.
CREATING	The file share is being created and is not ready for use. The CREATING status is transitional. No action is required. If file share is stuck in this status, it's probably because the gateway VM lost connection to AWS.

Status	Meaning
UPDATING	The file share configuration is being updated. If a file share is stuck in this status, it's probably because the gateway VM lost connection to AWS.
DELETING	The file share is being deleted. The file share is not deleted until all data is uploaded to AWS. The DELETING status is transitional, and no action is required.
FORCE_DELETING	The file share is being deleted forcibly. The file share is deleted immediately and uploading to AWS is aborted. The FORCE_DELETING status is transitional, and no action is required.
UNAVAILABLE	The file share is in an unhealthy state. Certain issues can cause the file share to go into an unhealthy state. For example, role policy errors can cause this, or if the file share maps to an Amazon S3 bucket that doesn't exist. When the issue that caused the unhealthy state is resolved, the file returns to AVAILABLE state.

File Share Best Practices

In this section, you can find information about best practices for creating file shares.

Topics

- Preventing Multiple File Shares Writing to Your Amazon S3 Bucket
- Allowing Specific NFS Clients to Mount Your File Share

Preventing Multiple File Shares Writing to Your Amazon S3 Bucket

When you create a file share, we recommend that you configure your Amazon S3 bucket so that only one file share can write to it. If you configure your S3 bucket to be written to by multiple file shares, unpredictable results can occur. To prevent this, create an S3 bucket policy that denies all roles except the role used for the file share to put or delete objects in the bucket. Then attach this policy to the S3 bucket.

The following example policy denies all roles except the role that created the bucket to write to the S3 bucket. The `s3:DeleteObject` and `s3:PutObject` actions are denied for all roles except `"TestUser"`. The policy applies to all objects in the `"arn:aws:s3:::test-bucket/*"` bucket.

```
1  {
2    "Version":"2012-10-17",
3    "Statement":[
4      {
5        "Sid":"DenyMultiWrite",
6        "Effect":"Deny",
7        "Principal":"*",
8        "Action":[
9          "s3:DeleteObject",
10         "s3:PutObject"
11       ],
```

```
12        "Resource":"arn:aws:s3:::TestBucket/*",
13        "Condition":{
14          "StringNotLike":{
15            "aws:userid":"TestUser:*"
16          }
17        }
18     }
19   ]
20 }
```

Allowing Specific NFS Clients to Mount Your File Share

We recommend that you change the allowed NFS client settings for your file share. If you don't, any client on your network can mount your file share. For information about how to edit your NFS client settings, see Editing Access Settings for Your NFS File Share.

Managing Your Volume Gateway

Following, you can find information about how to manage your volume gateway resources.

Cached volumes are volumes in Amazon Simple Storage Service (Amazon S3) that are exposed as iSCSI targets on which you can store your application data. You can find information following about how to add and delete volumes for your cached setup. You can also learn how to add and remove Amazon Elastic Block Store (Amazon EBS) volumes in Amazon EC2 gateways.

Topics

- Adding a Volume
- Expanding the Size of a Volume
- Cloning a Volume
- Viewing Volume Usage
- Deleting a Volume
- Reducing the Amount of Billed Storage on a Volume
- Creating a One-Time Snapshot
- Editing a Snapshot Schedule
- Deleting a Snapshot
- Understanding Volume Status

Important

If a cached volume keeps your primary data in Amazon S3, you should avoid processes that read or write all data on the entire volume. For example, we don't recommend using virus-scanning software that scans the entire cached volume. Such a scan, whether done on demand or scheduled, causes all data stored in Amazon S3 to be downloaded locally for scanning, which results in high bandwidth usage. Instead of doing a full disk scan, you can use real-time virus scanning—that is, scanning data as it is read from or written to the cached volume.

Resizing a volume is not supported. To change the size of a volume, create a snapshot of the volume, and then create a new cached volume from the snapshot. The new volume can be bigger than the volume from which the snapshot was created. For steps describing how to remove a volume, see To remove a volume. For steps describing how to add a volume and preserve existing data, see Deleting a Volume.

All cached volume data and snapshot data is stored in Amazon S3 and is encrypted at rest using server-side encryption (SSE). However, you cannot access this data by using the Amazon S3 API or other tools such as the Amazon S3 console.

Adding a Volume

As your application needs grow, you might need to add more volumes to your gateway. As you add more volumes, you must consider the size of the cache storage and upload buffer you allocated to the gateway. The gateway must have sufficient buffer and cache space for new volumes. For more information, see Adding and Removing Upload Buffer.

You can add volumes using the AWS Storage Gateway console or AWS Storage Gateway API. For information on using the AWS Storage Gateway API to add volumes, see CreateCachediSCSIVolume. For instructions on how to add a volume using the AWS Storage Gateway console, see Creating a Volume.

Expanding the Size of a Volume

As your application needs grow, you might want to expand your volume instead of adding more volumes to your gateway. In this case, you can do one of the following:

- Create a snapshot of the volume you want to expand and then use the snapshot to create a new volume of a larger size. For information about how to create a snapshot, see Creating a One-Time Snapshot. For information about how to use a snapshot to create a new volume, see Creating a Volume.
- Use the cached volume you want to expand to clone a new volume of a larger size. For information about how to clone a volume, see Cloning a Volume. For information about how to create a volume, see Creating a Volume.

Cloning a Volume

You can create a new volume from any existing cached volume in the same AWS Region. The new volume is created from the most recent recovery point of the selected volume. A *volume recovery point* is a point in time at which all data of the volume is consistent. To clone a volume, you choose the **Clone from last recovery point** option in the **Create volume** dialog box, then select the volume to use as the source. The following screenshot shows the **Create volume** dialog box.

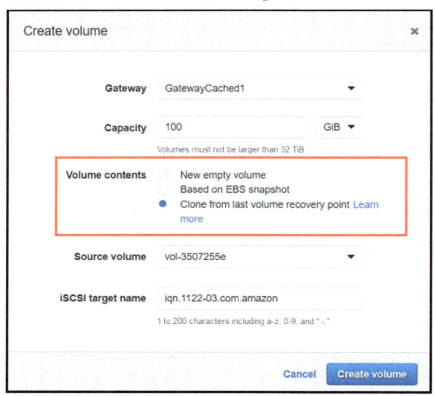

Cloning from an existing volume is faster and more cost-effective than creating an Amazon EBS snapshot. Cloning does a byte-to-byte copy of your data from the source volume to the new volume, using the most recent recovery point from the source volume. Storage Gateway automatically creates recovery points for your cached volumes. To see when the last recovery point was created, check the `TimeSinceLastRecoveryPoint` metric in Amazon CloudWatch.

The cloned volume is independent of the source volume. That is, changes made to either volume after cloning have no effect on the other. For example, if you delete the source volume, it has no effect on the cloned volume. You can clone a source volume while initiators are connected and it is in active use. Doing so doesn't affect the performance of the source volume. For information about how to clone a volume, see Creating a Volume.

You can also use the cloning process in recovery scenarios. For more information, see Your Cached Gateway is Unreachable And You Want to Recover Your Data.

Cloning From a Volume Recovery Point

The following procedure shows you how to clone a volume from a volume recovery point and use that volume.

To clone and use a volume from an unreachable gateway

1. Open the AWS Storage Gateway console at https://console.aws.amazon.com/storagegateway/home.

2. On the AWS Storage Gateway console, choose **Create volume**.

3. In the **Create volume** dialog box, choose a gateway for **Gateway**.

4. For **Capacity**, type the capacity for your volume. The capacity must be at least the same size as the source volume.

5. Choose **Clone from last recovery point** and select a volume ID for **Source volume**. The source volume can be any cached volume in the selected AWS Region.

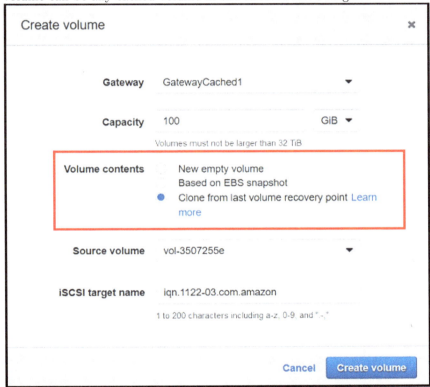

6. Type a name for **iSCSI target name**.

   The target name can contain lowercase letters, numbers, periods (.), and hyphens (-). This target name appears as the **iSCSI target node** name in the **Targets** tab of the **iSCSI Microsoft initiator** UI after discovery. For example, the name `target1` appears as `iqn.1007-05.com.amazon:target1`. Ensure that the target name is globally unique within your storage area network (SAN).

7. Verify that the **Network interface** setting is the IP address of your gateway, or choose an IP address for **Network interface**.

   If you have defined your gateway to use multiple network adapters, choose the IP address that your storage applications use to access the volume. Each network adapter defined for a gateway represents one IP address that you can choose.

   If the gateway VM is configured for more than one network adapter, the **Create volume** dialog box displays a list for **Network interface**. In this list, one IP address appears for each adapter configured for the gateway VM. If the gateway VM is configured for only one network adapter, no list appears because there's only one IP address.

8. Choose **Create volume**. The **Configure CHAP Authentication** dialog box appears. You can configure CHAP later. For information, see Configuring CHAP Authentication for Your iSCSI Targets.

The next step is to connect your volume to your client. For more information, see Connecting Your Volumes to Your Client.

Creating a Recovery Snapshot

The following procedure shows you how to create a snapshot from a volume recovery point and using that snapshot. You can take snapshots on a one-time, ad hoc basis or set up a snapshot schedule for the volume.

To create and use a recovery snapshot of a volume from an unreachable gateway

1. Open the AWS Storage Gateway console at https://console.aws.amazon.com/storagegateway/home.

2. In the navigation pane, choose **Gateways**.

3. Choose the unreachable gateway, and then choose the **Details** tab.

   A recovery snapshot message is displayed in the tab.

4. Choose **Create recovery snapshot** to open the **Create recovery snapshot** dialog box.

5. From the list of volumes displayed, choose the volume you want to recover, and then choose **Create snapshots**.

   AWS Storage Gateway initiates the snapshot process.

6. Find and restore the snapshot.

Viewing Volume Usage

When you write data to a volume, you can view the amount of data stored on the volume in the AWS Storage Gateway Management Console. The **Details** tab for each volume shows the volume usage information.

To view amount of data written to a volume

1. Open the AWS Storage Gateway console at https://console.aws.amazon.com/storagegateway/home.

2. In the navigation pane, choose **Volumes** and then choose the volume you are interested in.

3. Choose the **Details** tab.

   The following fields provide information about the volume:

   - **Size:** The total capacity of the selected volume.

- **Used:** The size of data stored on the volume. **Note**
  These values are not available for volumes created before May 13, 2015, until you store data on the volume.

Deleting a Volume

You might need to delete a volume as your application needs change—for example, if you migrate your application to use a larger storage volume. Before you delete a volume, make sure that there are no applications currently writing to the volume. Also, make sure that there are no snapshots in progress for the volume. If a snapshot schedule is defined for the volume, you can check it on the **Snapshot Schedules** tab of the AWS Storage Gateway console. For more information, see Editing a Snapshot Schedule.

You can delete volumes using the AWS Storage Gateway console or the AWS Storage Gateway API. For information on using the AWS Storage Gateway API to remove volumes, see Delete Volume. The following procedure demonstrates using the console.

Before you delete a volume, back up your data or take a snapshot of your critical data. For stored volumes, your local disks aren't erased. After you delete a volume, you can't get it back.

To remove a volume

1. Open the AWS Storage Gateway console at https://console.aws.amazon.com/storagegateway/home.

2. On the **Volumes** tab, choose the volume and choose the confirmation box. Make sure that the volume listed is the volume you intend to delete.

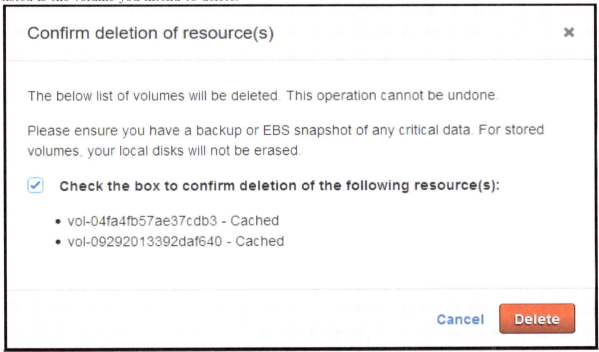

3. Choose **Delete** to delete the volume.

Reducing the Amount of Billed Storage on a Volume

Deleting files from your file system doesn't necessarily delete data from the underlying block device or reduce the amount of data stored on your volume. If you want to reduce the amount of billed storage on your volume, we recommend overwriting your files with zeros to compress the storage to a negligible amount of actual storage. AWS Storage Gateway charges for volume usage based on compressed storage.

Note
If you use a delete tool that overwrites the data on your volume with random data, your usage will not be reduced. This is because the random data is not compressible.

Creating a One-Time Snapshot

In addition to scheduled snapshots, for volume gateways you can take one-time, ad hoc snapshots. By doing this, you can back up your storage volume immediately without waiting for the next scheduled snapshot.

To take a one-time snapshot of your storage volume

1. Open the AWS Storage Gateway console at https://console.aws.amazon.com/storagegateway/home.

2. In the navigation pane, choose **Volumes**, and then choose the volume you want to create the snapshot from.

3. On the **Actions** menu, choose **Create snapshot**.

4. In the **Create snapshot** dialog box, type the snapshot description, and then choose **Create snapshot**.

   You can verify that the snapshot was created using the console.

Your snapshot is listed in the **Snapshots** in the same row as the volume.

Editing a Snapshot Schedule

For stored volumes, AWS Storage Gateway creates a default snapshot schedule of once a day. This schedule helps ensure that your gateway can keep up with the rate of incoming write operations on your local storage volumes.

Note
You can't remove the default snapshot schedule. Stored volumes require at least one snapshot schedule. However, you can change a snapshot schedule by specifying either the time the snapshot occurs each day or the frequency (every 1, 2, 4, 8, 12, or 24 hours), or both.

For cached volumes, AWS Storage Gateway doesn't create a default snapshot schedule. No default schedule is created because your data is stored in Amazon S3, so you don't need snapshots or a snapshot schedule for disaster recovery purposes. However, you can set up a snapshot schedule at any time if you need to. Creating snapshot for your cached volume provides an additional way to recover your data if necessary.

By using the following steps, you can edit the snapshot schedule for a volume.

To edit the snapshot schedule for a volume

1. Open the AWS Storage Gateway console at https://console.aws.amazon.com/storagegateway/home.

2. In the navigation pane, choose **Volumes**, and then choose the volume the snapshot was created from.

3. On the **Actions** menu, choose **Edit snapshot schedule**.

4. In the **Edit snapshot schedule** dialog box, modify the schedule, and then choose **Save**.

Deleting a Snapshot

You can delete a snapshot of your storage volume. For example, you might want to do this if you have taken many snapshots of a storage volume over time and you don't need the older snapshots. Because snapshots are incremental backups, if you delete a snapshot, only the data that is not needed in other snapshots is deleted.

Topics

- Deleting Snapshots by Using the AWS SDK for Java
- Deleting Snapshots by Using the AWS SDK for .NET
- Deleting Snapshots by Using the AWS Tools for Windows PowerShell

On the Amazon EBS console, you can delete snapshots one at a time. For information about how to delete snapshots using the Amazon EBS console, see Deleting an Amazon EBS Snapshot in the *Amazon EC2 User Guide*.

To delete multiple snapshots at a time, you can use one of the AWS SDKs that supports AWS Storage Gateway operations. For examples, see Deleting Snapshots by Using the AWS SDK for Java, Deleting Snapshots by Using the AWS SDK for .NET, and Deleting Snapshots by Using the AWS Tools for Windows PowerShell.

Deleting Snapshots by Using the AWS SDK for Java

To delete many snapshots associated with a volume, you can use a programmatic approach. The example following demonstrates how to delete snapshots using the AWS SDK for Java. To use the example code, you should be familiar with running a Java console application. For more information, see Getting Started in the *AWS SDK for Java Developer Guide*. If you need to just delete a few snapshots, use the console as described in Deleting a Snapshot.

Example : Deleting Snapshots by Using the AWS SDK for Java

The following Java code example lists the snapshots for each volume of a gateway and whether the snapshot start time is before or after a specified date. It uses the AWS SDK for Java API for AWS Storage Gateway and Amazon EC2. The Amazon EC2 API includes operations for working with snapshots.

Update the code to provide the service endpoint, your gateway Amazon Resource Name (ARN), and the number of days back you want to save snapshots. Snapshots taken before this cutoff are deleted. You also need to specify the Boolean value `viewOnly`, which indicates whether you want to view the snapshots to be deleted or to actually perform the snapshot deletions. Run the code first with just the view option (that is, with `viewOnly` set to `true`) to see what the code deletes. For a list of AWS service endpoints you can use with AWS Storage Gateway, see Regions and Endpoints in the *AWS General Reference*.

```
1  import java.io.IOException;
2  import java.util.ArrayList;
3  import java.util.Calendar;
4  import java.util.Collection;
5  import java.util.Date;
6  import java.util.GregorianCalendar;
7  import java.util.List;
8
9  import com.amazonaws.auth.PropertiesCredentials;
10 import com.amazonaws.services.ec2.AmazonEC2Client;
11 import com.amazonaws.services.ec2.model.DeleteSnapshotRequest;
12 import com.amazonaws.services.ec2.model.DescribeSnapshotsRequest;
13 import com.amazonaws.services.ec2.model.DescribeSnapshotsResult;
14 import com.amazonaws.services.ec2.model.Filter;
15 import com.amazonaws.services.ec2.model.Snapshot;
16 import com.amazonaws.services.storagegateway.AWSStorageGatewayClient;
17 import com.amazonaws.services.storagegateway.model.ListVolumesRequest;
18 import com.amazonaws.services.storagegateway.model.ListVolumesResult;
19 import com.amazonaws.services.storagegateway.model.VolumeInfo;
20
21 public class ListDeleteVolumeSnapshotsExample {
22
23     public static AWSStorageGatewayClient sgClient;
24     public static AmazonEC2Client ec2Client;
25     static String serviceURLSG = "https://storagegateway.us-east-1.amazonaws.com";
```

```
26      static String serviceURLEC2 = "https://ec2.us-east-1.amazonaws.com";
27
28      // The gatewayARN
29      public static String gatewayARN = "*** provide gateway ARN ***";
30
31      // The number of days back you want to save snapshots. Snapshots before this cutoff are
            deleted
32      // if viewOnly = false.
33      public static int daysBack = 10;
34
35      // true = show what will be deleted; false = actually delete snapshots that meet the
            daysBack criteria
36      public static boolean viewOnly = true;
37
38      public static void main(String[] args) throws IOException {
39
40          // Create a storage gateway and amazon ec2 client
41          sgClient = new AWSStorageGatewayClient(new PropertiesCredentials(
42              ListDeleteVolumeSnapshotsExample.class.getResourceAsStream("AwsCredentials.
                    properties")));
43          sgClient.setEndpoint(serviceURLSG);
44
45          ec2Client = new AmazonEC2Client(new PropertiesCredentials(
46              ListDeleteVolumeSnapshotsExample.class.getResourceAsStream("AwsCredentials.
                    properties")));
47          ec2Client.setEndpoint(serviceURLEC2);
48
49          List<VolumeInfo> volumes = ListVolumesForGateway();
50          DeleteSnapshotsForVolumes(volumes, daysBack);
51
52      }
53      public static List<VolumeInfo> ListVolumesForGateway()
54      {
55          List<VolumeInfo> volumes = new ArrayList<VolumeInfo>();
56
57          String marker = null;
58          do {
59              ListVolumesRequest request = new ListVolumesRequest().withGatewayARN(gatewayARN);
60              ListVolumesResult result = sgClient.listVolumes(request);
61              marker = result.getMarker();
62
63              for (VolumeInfo vi : result.getVolumeInfos())
64              {
65                  volumes.add(vi);
66                  System.out.println(OutputVolumeInfo(vi));
67              }
68          } while (marker != null);
69
70          return volumes;
71      }
72      private static void DeleteSnapshotsForVolumes(List<VolumeInfo> volumes,
73              int daysBack2) {
74
75          // Find snapshots and delete for each volume
```

```
76      for (VolumeInfo vi : volumes) {
77
78          String volumeARN = vi.getVolumeARN();
79          String volumeId = volumeARN.substring(volumeARN.lastIndexOf("/")+1).toLowerCase();
80          Collection<Filter> filters = new ArrayList<Filter>();
81          Filter filter = new Filter().withName("volume-id").withValues(volumeId);
82          filters.add(filter);
83
84          DescribeSnapshotsRequest describeSnapshotsRequest =
85              new DescribeSnapshotsRequest().withFilters(filters);
86          DescribeSnapshotsResult describeSnapshotsResult =
87              ec2Client.describeSnapshots(describeSnapshotsRequest);
88
89          List<Snapshot> snapshots = describeSnapshotsResult.getSnapshots();
90          System.out.println("volume-id = " + volumeId);
91          for (Snapshot s : snapshots){
92              StringBuilder sb = new StringBuilder();
93              boolean meetsCriteria = !CompareDates(daysBack, s.getStartTime());
94              sb.append(s.getSnapshotId() + ", " + s.getStartTime().toString());
95              sb.append(", meets criteria for delete? " + meetsCriteria);
96              sb.append(", deleted? ");
97              if (!viewOnly & meetsCriteria) {
98                  sb.append("yes");
99                  DeleteSnapshotRequest deleteSnapshotRequest =
100                     new DeleteSnapshotRequest().withSnapshotId(s.getSnapshotId());
101                 ec2Client.deleteSnapshot(deleteSnapshotRequest);
102             }
103             else {
104                 sb.append("no");
105             }
106             System.out.println(sb.toString());
107         }
108     }
109 }
110
111 private static String OutputVolumeInfo(VolumeInfo vi) {
112
113     String volumeInfo = String.format(
114             "Volume Info:\n" +
115             "   ARN: %s\n" +
116             "   Type: %s\n",
117             vi.getVolumeARN(),
118             vi.getVolumeType());
119     return volumeInfo;
120 }
121
122 // Returns the date in two formats as a list
123 public static boolean CompareDates(int daysBack, Date snapshotDate) {
124     Date today = new Date();
125     Calendar cal = new GregorianCalendar();
126     cal.setTime(today);
127     cal.add(Calendar.DAY_OF_MONTH, -daysBack);
128     Date cutoffDate = cal.getTime();
129     return (snapshotDate.compareTo(cutoffDate) > 0) ? true : false;
```

```
130        }
131
132 }
```

Deleting Snapshots by Using the AWS SDK for .NET

To delete many snapshots associated with a volume, you can use a programmatic approach. The following example demonstrates how to delete snapshots using the AWS SDK for .NET version 2 and 3. To use the example code, you should be familiar with running a .NET console application. For more information, see Getting Started in the *AWS SDK for .NET Developer Guide*. If you need to just delete a few snapshots, use the console as described in Deleting a Snapshot.

Example : Deleting Snapshots by Using the AWS SDK for .NET

In the following C# code example, an AWS Identity and Access Management (IAM) user can list the snapshots for each volume of a gateway. The user can then determine whether the snapshot start time is before or after a specified date (retention period) and delete snapshots that have passed the retention period. The example uses the AWS SDK for .NET API for AWS Storage Gateway and Amazon EC2. The Amazon EC2 API includes operations for working with snapshots.

The following code example uses the AWS SDK for .NET version 2 and 3. You can migrate older versions of .NET to the newer version. For more information, see Migrating Your Code to the Latest Version of the AWS SDK for .NET.

Update the code to provide the service endpoint, your gateway Amazon Resource Name (ARN), and the number of days back you want to save snapshots. Snapshots taken before this cutoff are deleted. You also need to specify the Boolean value `viewOnly`, which indicates whether you want to view the snapshots to be deleted or to actually perform the snapshot deletions. Run the code first with just the view option (that is, with `viewOnly` set to `true`) to see what the code deletes. For a list of AWS service endpoints you can use with AWS Storage Gateway, see Regions and Endpoints in the *AWS General Reference*.

First, you create an IAM user and attach the minimum IAM policy to the IAM user. Then you schedule automated snapshots for your gateway.

The following code creates the minimum policy that allows an IAM user to delete snapshots. In this example, the policy is named **sgw-delete-snapshot**.

```
 1 {
 2      "Version": "2012-10-17",
 3      "Statement": [
 4          {
 5              "Sid": "StmtEC2Snapshots",
 6              "Effect": "Allow",
 7              "Action": [
 8                  "ec2:DeleteSnapshot",
 9                  "ec2:DescribeSnapshots"
10              ],
11              "Resource": [
12                  "*"
13              ]
14          },
15          {
16              "Sid": "StmtSgwListVolumes",
17              "Effect": "Allow",
18              "Action": [
19                  "storagegateway:ListVolumes"
20              ],
21              "Resource": [
22                  "*"
23              ]
```

150

```
24            }
25        ]
26    }
```

The following C# code finds all snapshots in the specified gateway that match the volumes and the specified cut-off period and then deletes them.

```csharp
1  using System;
2  using System.Collections.Generic;
3  using System.Text;
4  using Amazon.EC2;
5  using Amazon.EC2.Model;
6  using Amazon.StorageGateway.Model;
7  using Amazon.StorageGateway;
8
9  namespace DeleteStorageGatewaySnapshotNS
10 {
11     class Program
12     {
13         /*
14          * Replace the variables below to match your environment.
15          */
16
17         /* IAM AccessKey */
18         static String AwsAccessKey = "AKIA...............";
19
20         /* IAM SecretKey */
21         static String AwsSecretKey = "***********************";
22
23         /* AWS Account number, 12 digits, no hyphen */
24         static String OwnerID = "123456789012";
25
26         /* Your Gateway ARN. Use a Storage Gateway ID, sgw-XXXXXXXX* */
27         static String GatewayARN = "arn:aws:storagegateway:ap-southeast-2:123456789012:gateway/
              sgw-XXXXXXXX";
28
29         /* Snapshot status: "completed", "pending", "error" */
30         static String SnapshotStatus = "completed";
31
32         /* AWS Region where your gateway is activated */
33         static String AwsRegion = "ap-southeast-2";
34
35         /* Minimum age of snapshots before they are deleted (retention policy) */
36         static int daysBack = 30;
37
38         /*
39          * Do not modify the four lines below.
40          */
41         static AmazonEC2Config ec2Config;
42         static AmazonEC2Client ec2Client;
43         static AmazonStorageGatewayClient sgClient;
44         static AmazonStorageGatewayConfig sgConfig;
45
46         static void Main(string[] args)
47         {
```

```
48          // Create an EC2 client.
49          ec2Config = new AmazonEC2Config();
50          ec2Config.ServiceURL = "https://ec2." + AwsRegion + ".amazonaws.com";
51          ec2Client = new AmazonEC2Client(AwsAccessKey, AwsSecretKey, ec2Config);
52
53          // Create a Storage Gateway client.
54          sgConfig = new AmazonStorageGatewayConfig();
55          sgConfig.ServiceURL = "https://storagegateway." + AwsRegion + ".amazonaws.com";
56          sgClient = new AmazonStorageGatewayClient(AwsAccessKey, AwsSecretKey, sgConfig);
57
58          List<VolumeInfo> StorageGatewayVolumes = ListVolumesForGateway();
59          List<Snapshot> StorageGatewaySnapshots = ListSnapshotsForVolumes(
                StorageGatewayVolumes,
60                                                    daysBack);
61          DeleteSnapshots(StorageGatewaySnapshots);
62      }
63
64      /*
65       * List all volumes for your gateway
66       * returns: A list of VolumeInfos, or null.
67       */
68      private static List<VolumeInfo> ListVolumesForGateway()
69      {
70          ListVolumesResponse response = new ListVolumesResponse();
71          try
72          {
73              ListVolumesRequest request = new ListVolumesRequest();
74              request.GatewayARN = GatewayARN;
75              response = sgClient.ListVolumes(request);
76
77              foreach (VolumeInfo vi in response.VolumeInfos)
78              {
79                  Console.WriteLine(OutputVolumeInfo(vi));
80              }
81          }
82          catch (AmazonStorageGatewayException ex)
83          {
84              Console.WriteLine(ex.Message);
85          }
86          return response.VolumeInfos;
87      }
88
89      /*
90       * Gets the list of snapshots that match the requested volumes
91       * and cutoff period.
92       */
93      private static List<Snapshot> ListSnapshotsForVolumes(List<VolumeInfo> volumes, int
            snapshotAge)
94      {
95          List<Snapshot> SelectedSnapshots = new List<Snapshot>();
96          try
97          {
98              foreach (VolumeInfo vi in volumes)
99              {
```

```
100             String volumeARN = vi.VolumeARN;
101             String volumeID = volumeARN.Substring(volumeARN.LastIndexOf("/") + 1).
                    ToLower();
102
103             DescribeSnapshotsRequest describeSnapshotsRequest = new
                    DescribeSnapshotsRequest();
104
105             Filter ownerFilter = new Filter();
106             List<String> ownerValues = new List<String>();
107             ownerValues.Add(OwnerID);
108             ownerFilter.Name = "owner-id";
109             ownerFilter.Values = ownerValues;
110             describeSnapshotsRequest.Filters.Add(ownerFilter);
111
112             Filter statusFilter = new Filter();
113             List<String> statusValues = new List<String>();
114             statusValues.Add(SnapshotStatus);
115             statusFilter.Name = "status";
116             statusFilter.Values = statusValues;
117             describeSnapshotsRequest.Filters.Add(statusFilter);
118
119             Filter volumeFilter = new Filter();
120             List<String> volumeValues = new List<String>();
121             volumeValues.Add(volumeID);
122             volumeFilter.Name = "volume-id";
123             volumeFilter.Values = volumeValues;
124             describeSnapshotsRequest.Filters.Add(volumeFilter);
125
126             DescribeSnapshotsResponse describeSnapshotsResponse =
127               ec2Client.DescribeSnapshots(describeSnapshotsRequest);
128
129             List<Snapshot> snapshots = describeSnapshotsResponse.Snapshots;
130             Console.WriteLine("volume-id = " + volumeID);
131             foreach (Snapshot s in snapshots)
132             {
133                 if (IsSnapshotPastRetentionPeriod(snapshotAge, s.StartTime))
134                 {
135                     Console.WriteLine(s.SnapshotId + ", " + s.VolumeId + ",
136                       " + s.StartTime + ", " + s.Description);
137                     SelectedSnapshots.Add(s);
138                 }
139             }
140         }
141     }
142     catch (AmazonEC2Exception ex)
143     {
144         Console.WriteLine(ex.Message);
145     }
146     return SelectedSnapshots;
147 }
148
149 /*
150  * Deletes a list of snapshots.
151  */
```

```
152    private static void DeleteSnapshots(List<Snapshot> snapshots)
153    {
154        try
155        {
156            foreach (Snapshot s in snapshots)
157            {
158
159                DeleteSnapshotRequest deleteSnapshotRequest = new DeleteSnapshotRequest(s.
                        SnapshotId);
160                DeleteSnapshotResponse response = ec2Client.DeleteSnapshot(
                        deleteSnapshotRequest);
161                Console.WriteLine("Volume: " +
162                        s.VolumeId +
163                        " => Snapshot: " +
164                        s.SnapshotId +
165                        " Response: "
166                        + response.HttpStatusCode.ToString());
167            }
168        }
169        catch (AmazonEC2Exception ex)
170        {
171            Console.WriteLine(ex.Message);
172        }
173    }
174
175    /*
176     * Checks if the snapshot creation date is past the retention period.
177     */
178    private static Boolean IsSnapshotPastRetentionPeriod(int daysBack, DateTime snapshotDate
            )
179    {
180        DateTime cutoffDate = DateTime.Now.Add(new TimeSpan(-daysBack, 0, 0, 0));
181        return (DateTime.Compare(snapshotDate, cutoffDate) < 0) ? true : false;
182    }
183
184    /*
185     * Displays information related to a volume.
186     */
187    private static String OutputVolumeInfo(VolumeInfo vi)
188    {
189        String volumeInfo = String.Format(
190            "Volume Info:\n" +
191            "  ARN: {0}\n" +
192            "  Type: {1}\n",
193            vi.VolumeARN,
194            vi.VolumeType);
195        return volumeInfo;
196    }
197 }
198 }
```

Deleting Snapshots by Using the AWS Tools for Windows PowerShell

To delete many snapshots associated with a volume, you can use a programmatic approach. The example following demonstrates how to delete snapshots using the AWS Tools for Windows PowerShell. To use the example script, you should be familiar with running a PowerShell script. For more information, see Getting Started in the *AWS Tools for Windows PowerShell*. If you need to delete just a few snapshots, use the console as described in Deleting a Snapshot.

Example : Deleting Snapshots by Using the AWS Tools for Windows PowerShell

The following PowerShell script example lists the snapshots for each volume of a gateway and whether the snapshot start time is before or after a specified date. It uses the AWS Tools for Windows PowerShell cmdlets for AWS Storage Gateway and Amazon EC2. The Amazon EC2 API includes operations for working with snapshots. You need to update the script and provide your gateway Amazon Resource Name (ARN) and the number of days back you want to save snapshots. Snapshots taken before this cutoff are deleted. You also need to specify the Boolean value `viewOnly`, which indicates whether you want to view the snapshots to be deleted or to actually perform the snapshot deletions. Run the code first with just the view option (that is, with `viewOnly` set to `true`) to see what the code deletes.

```
1  <#
2  .DESCRIPTION
3      Delete snapshots of a specified volume that match given criteria.
4
5  .NOTES
6      PREREQUISITES:
7      1) AWS Tools for PowerShell from http://console.aws.amazon.com/powershell/
8      2) Credentials and AWS Region stored in session using Initialize-AWSDefault.
9      For more info see, http://docs.aws.amazon.com/powershell/latest/userguide//specifying-your-
               aws-credentials.html
10
11 .EXAMPLE
12      powershell.exe .\SG_DeleteSnapshots.ps1
13 #>
14
15 # Criteria to use to filter the results returned.
16 $daysBack = 18
17 $gatewayARN = "*** provide gateway ARN ***"
18 $viewOnly = $true;
19
20 #ListVolumes
21 $volumesResult = Get-SGVolume -GatewayARN $gatewayARN
22 $volumes = $volumesResult.VolumeInfos
23 Write-Output("`nVolume List")
24 foreach ($volumes in $volumesResult)
25    { Write-Output("`nVolume Info:")
26      Write-Output("ARN:  " + $volumes.VolumeARN)
27      write-Output("Type: " + $volumes.VolumeType)
28    }
29
30 Write-Output("`nWhich snapshots meet the criteria?")
31 foreach ($volume in $volumesResult)
32    {
33      $volumeARN = $volume.VolumeARN
34
35      $volumeId = ($volumeARN-split"/")[3].ToLower()
36
37      $filter = New-Object Amazon.EC2.Model.Filter
```

```
38      $filter.Name = "volume-id"
39      $filter.Value.Add($volumeId)
40
41      $snapshots = get-EC2Snapshot -Filter $filter
42      Write-Output("`nFor volume-id = " + $volumeId)
43      foreach ($s in $snapshots)
44      {
45          $d = ([DateTime]::Now).AddDays(-$daysBack)
46          $meetsCriteria = $false
47          if ([DateTime]::Compare($d, $s.StartTime) -gt 0)
48          {
49              $meetsCriteria = $true
50          }
51
52          $sb = $s.SnapshotId + ", " + $s.StartTime + ", meets criteria for delete? " +
                  $meetsCriteria
53          if (!$viewOnly -AND $meetsCriteria)
54          {
55              $resp = Remove-EC2Snapshot -SnapshotId $s.SnapshotId
56              #Can get RequestId from response for troubleshooting.
57              $sb = $sb + ", deleted? yes"
58          }
59          else {
60              $sb = $sb + ", deleted? no"
61          }
62          Write-Output($sb)
63      }
64  }
```

Understanding Volume Status

Each volume has an associated status that tells you at a glance what the health of the volume is. Most of the time, the status indicates that the volume is functioning normally and that no action is needed on your part. In some cases, the status indicates a problem with the volume that might or might not require action on your part. You can find information following to help you decide when you need to act.

Topics

- Understanding Cached Volume Status Transitions
- Understanding Stored Volume Status Transitions

You can see volume status on the AWS Storage Gateway console or by using one of the Storage Gateway API operations, for example DescribeCachediSCSIVolumes or DescribeStorediSCSIVolumes. The following example shows volume status on the Storage Gateway console. Volume status appears in the **Status** column for each storage volume on your gateway. A volume that is functioning normally has a status of AVAILABLE.

In the following table, you can find a description of each storage volume status, and if and when you should act based on each status. The AVAILABLE status is the normal status of a volume. A volume should have this status all or most of the time it's in use.

Status	Meaning
AVAILABLE	The volume is available for use. This status is the normal running status for a volume. When a BOOTSTRAPPING phase is completed, the volume returns to AVAILABLE state. That is, the gateway has synchronized any changes made to the volume since it first entered PASS THROUGH status.
BOOTSTRAPPING	The gateway is synchronizing data locally with a copy of the data stored in AWS. You typically don't need to take action for this status, because the storage volume automatically sees the AVAILABLE status in most cases. The following are scenarios when a volume status is BOOTSTRAPPING: [See the AWS documentation website for more details]
CREATING	The volume is currently being created and is not ready for use. The CREATING status is transitional. No action is required.
DELETING	The volume is currently being deleted. The DELETING status is transitional. No action is required.
IRRECOVERABLE	An error occurred from which the volume cannot recover. For information on what to do in this situation, see Troubleshooting Volume Issues.
PASS THROUGH	Data maintained locally is out of sync with data stored in AWS. Data written to a volume while the volume is in PASS THROUGH status remains in the cache until the volume status is BOOTSTRAPPING, and starts to upload to AWS when BOOTSTRAPPING status begins. The PASS THROUGH status can occur for several reasons, listed following: [See the AWS documentation website for more details]
RESTORING	The volume is being restored from an existing snapshot. This status applies only for stored volumes. For more information, see How AWS Storage Gateway Works (Architecture). If you restore two storage volumes at the same time, both storage volumes show RESTORING as their status. Each storage volume changes to the AVAILABLE status automatically when it is finished being created. You can read and write to a storage volume and take a snapshot of it while it has the RESTORING status.

Status	Meaning
RESTORING PASS THROUGH	The volume is being restored from an existing snapshot and has encountered an upload buffer issue. This status applies only for stored volumes. For more information, see How AWS Storage Gateway Works (Architecture). One reason that can cause the RESTORING PASS THROUGH status is if your gateway has run out of upload buffer space. Your applications can continue to read from and write data to your storage volumes while they have the RESTORING PASS THROUGH status. However, you can't take snapshots of a storage volume during the RESTORING PASS THROUGH status period. For information about what action to take when your storage volume has the RESTORING PASS THROUGH status because upload buffer capacity has been exceeded, see Troubleshooting Volume Issues. Infrequently, the RESTORING PASS THROUGH status can indicate that a disk allocated for an upload buffer has failed. For information about what action to take in this scenario, see Troubleshooting Volume Issues.
UPLOAD BUFFER NOT CONFIGURED	You can't create or use the volume because the gateway doesn't have an upload buffer configured. For information on how to add upload buffer capacity for volumes in a cached volume setup, see Adding and Removing Upload Buffer. For information on how to add upload buffer capacity for volumes in a stored volume setup, see Adding and Removing Upload Buffer.

Understanding Cached Volume Status Transitions

Use the following state diagram to understand the most common transitions between statuses for volumes in cached gateways. You don't need to understand the diagram in detail to use your gateway effectively. Rather, the diagram provides detailed information if you are interested in knowing more about how volume gateways work.

The diagram doesn't show the UPLOAD BUFFER NOT CONFIGURED status or the DELETING status. Volume states in the diagram appear as green, yellow, and red boxes. You can interpret the colors as described following.

Color	Volume Status
Green	The gateway is operating normally. The volume status is AVAILABLE or eventually becomes AVAILABLE.

Color	Volume Status
Yellow	The volume has the PASS THROUGH status, which indicates there is a potential issue with the storage volume. If this status appears because the upload buffer space is filled, then in some cases buffer space becomes available again. At that point, the storage volume self-corrects to the AVAILABLE status. In other cases, you might have to add more upload buffer space to your gateway to allow the storage volume status to become AVAILABLE. For information on how to troubleshoot a case when upload buffer capacity has been exceeded, see Troubleshooting Volume Issues. For information on how to add upload buffer capacity, see Adding and Removing Upload Buffer.
Red	The storage volume has the IRRECOVERABLE status. In this case, you should delete the volume. For information on how to do this, see To remove a volume.

In the diagram, a transition between two states is depicted with a labeled line. For example, the transition from the CREATING status to the AVAILABLE status is labeled as *Create Basic Volume or Create Volume from Snapshot*. This transition represents creating a cached volume. For more information about creating storage volumes, see Adding a Volume.

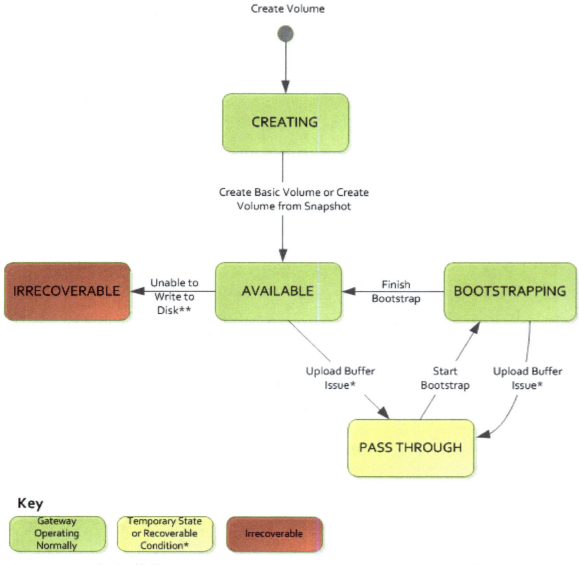

Key

| Gateway Operating Normally | Temporary State or Recoverable Condition* | Irrecoverable |

* e.g. run out of upload buffer
** e.g. lost connectivity

Note
The volume status of PASS THROUGH appears as yellow in this diagram. However, this doesn't match the color of this status icon in the **Status** box of the Storage Gateway console.

Understanding Stored Volume Status Transitions

Use the following state diagram to understand the most common transitions between statuses for volumes in stored gateways. You don't need to understand the diagram in detail to use your gateway effectively. Rather, the diagram provides detailed information if you are interested in understanding more about how volume gateways work.

The diagram doesn't show the UPLOAD BUFFER NOT CONFIGURED status or the DELETING status. Volume states in the diagram appear as green, yellow, and red boxes. You can interpret the colors as described following.

Color	Volume Status
Green	The gateway is operating normally. The volume status is AVAILABLE or eventually becomes AVAILABLE.
Yellow	When you are creating a storage volume and preserving data, then the path from the CREATING status to the PASS THROUGH status occurs if another volume is bootstrapping. In this case, the volume with the PASS THROUGH status goes to the BOOTSTRAPPING status and then to the AVAILABLE status when the first volume is finished bootstrapping. Other than the specific scenario mentioned, yellow (PASS THROUGH status) indicates that there is a potential issue with the storage volume, the most common one being an upload buffer issue. If upload buffer capacity has been exceeded, then in some cases buffer space becomes available again. At that point, the storage volume self-corrects to the AVAILABLE status. In other cases, you might have to add more upload buffer capacity to your gateway to return the storage volume to the AVAILABLE status. For information on how to troubleshoot a case when upload buffer capacity has been exceeded, see Troubleshooting Volume Issues. For information on how to add upload buffer capacity, see Adding and Removing Upload Buffer.
Red	The storage volume has the IRRECOVERABLE status. In this case, you should delete the volume. For information on how to do this, see Deleting a Volume.

In the following diagram, a transition between two states is depicted with a labeled line. For example, the transition from the CREATING status to the AVAILABLE status is labeled as *Create Basic Volume* and represents creating a storage volume without preserving data or creating the volume from a snapshot.

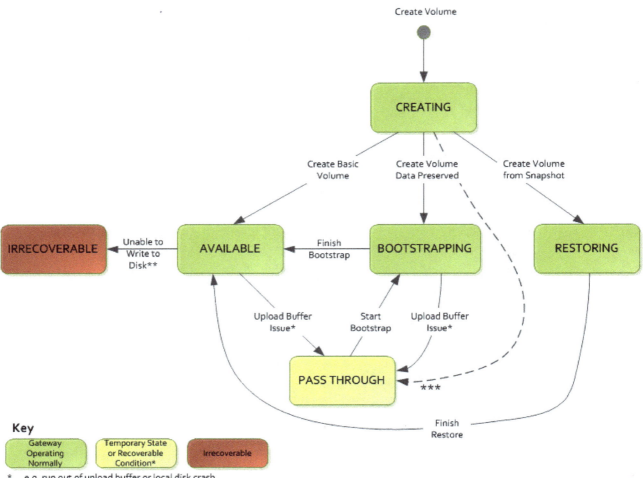

Key

Gateway Operating Normally	Temporary State or Recoverable Condition*	Irrecoverable

*   e.g. run out of upload buffer or local disk crash
** e.g. lost connectivity or disk crash
*** transition occurs only if another volume is bootstrapping

Note

The volume status of PASS THROUGH appears as yellow in this diagram. However, this doesn't match the color of this status icon in the **Status** box of the Storage Gateway console.

Managing Your Tape Gateway

Following, you can find information about how to manage your tape gateway resources.

Topics

- Adding Virtual Tapes
- Retrieving Archived Tapes
- Viewing Tape Usage
- Deleting Tapes
- Disabling Your Tape Gateway
- Understanding Tape Status

Adding Virtual Tapes

You can add tapes in your tape gateway when you need them. For information about how to create tapes, see Creating Tapes. After your tape is created, information about your tape is displayed in the columns and in the **Details** tab of your tape library. For information about tape gateway tape limits, see AWS Storage Gateway Limits.

Retrieving Archived Tapes

To access data stored on an archived virtual tape, you must first retrieve the tape that you want to your tape gateway. Your tape gateway provides one virtual tape library (VTL) for each gateway. You can restore a tape to a tape gateway.

If you have multiple tape gateways in an AWS Region, you can retrieve a tape to only one gateway.

The retrieved tape is write-protected; you can only read the data on the tape.

Important
It takes up to three to five hours for the tape to be available in your tape gateway.

Note
There is a charge for retrieving tapes from archive. For detailed pricing information, see AWS Storage Gateway Pricing.

To retrieve an archived tape to your gateway

1. Open the AWS Storage Gateway console at https://console.aws.amazon.com/storagegateway/home.

2. In the navigation pane, choose **Tapes**. To display all virtual tapes that have been archived by all your gateways, use search.

3. Choose the virtual tape you want to retrieve, and choose **Retrieve Tape** for **Actions**. **Note**
   The status of the virtual tape that you want to retrieve must be ARCHIVED.

4. In the **Retrieve tape** dialog box, for **Barcode**, verify that the barcode identifies the virtual tape you want to retrieve.

5. For **Gateway**, choose the gateway that you want to retrieve the archived tape to, and then choose **Retrieve tape**.

The status of the tape changes from ARCHIVED to RETRIEVING. At this point, your data is being moved from the virtual tape shelf (backed by Amazon Glacier) to the virtual tape library (backed by Amazon S3). After all the data is moved, the status of the virtual tape in the archive changes to RETRIEVED.

Note
Retrieved virtual tapes are read-only.

163

Viewing Tape Usage

When you write data to a tape, you can view the amount of data stored on the tape in the AWS Storage Gateway Management Console. The **Details** tab for each tape shows the tape usage information.

To view the amount of data stored on a tape

1. Open the AWS Storage Gateway console at https://console.aws.amazon.com/storagegateway/home.

2. In the navigation pane, choose **Tapes** and select the tape that you are interested in.

3. Choose the **Details** tab.

4. The following fields provide information about the tape:

   - **Size:** The total capacity of the selected tape.
   - **Used:** The size of data written to the tape by your backup application. **Note** This value is not available for tapes created before May 13, 2015.

Deleting Tapes

You can delete virtual tapes from your tape gateway by using the AWS Storage Gateway console.

Note
If the tape you want to delete from your tape gateway has a status of RETRIEVED, you must first eject the tape using your backup application before deleting the tape. For instructions on how to eject a tape using the Symantec NetBackup software, see Archiving the Tape. After the tape is ejected, the tape status changes back to ARCHIVED. You can then delete the tape.

Make copies of your data before you delete your tapes. After you delete a tape, you can't get it back.

To delete a virtual tape Warning
This procedure permanently deletes the selected virtual tape.

1. Open the AWS Storage Gateway console at https://console.aws.amazon.com/storagegateway/home.

2. In the navigation pane, choose **Tapes**.

3. Choose the virtual tape that you want to delete.

4. On the **Actions** menu, choose **Delete tape**. A confirmation box appears, as shown following.

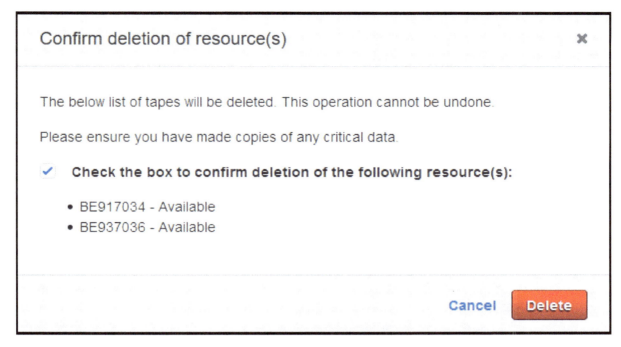

The below list of tapes will be deleted. This operation cannot be undone.

Please ensure you have made copies of any critical data.

☑ **Check the box to confirm deletion of the following resource(s):**

- BE917034 - Available
- BE937036 - Available

Cancel   **Delete**

5. Make sure that the tape listed is the tape you intend to delete, select the confirmation check box, and then choose **Delete**.

After the tape is deleted, it disappears from the tape gateway.

Disabling Your Tape Gateway

You disable a tape gateway if the tape gateway has failed and you want to recover the tapes from the failed gateway to another gateway.

To recover the tapes, you must first disable the failed gateway. Disabling a tape gateway locks down the virtual tapes in that gateway. That is, any data that you might write to these tapes after disabling the gateway isn't sent to AWS. You can only disable a gateway on the Storage Gateway console if the gateway is no longer connected to AWS. If the gateway is connected to AWS, you can't disable the tape gateway.

You disable a tape gateway as part of data recovery. For more information about recovering tapes, see You Need to Recover a Virtual Tape from a Malfunctioning Tape Gateway.

To disable your gateway

1. Open the AWS Storage Gateway console at https://console.aws.amazon.com/storagegateway/home.

2. In the navigation pane, choose **Gateways**, and then choose the failed gateway.

3. Choose the **Details** tab for the gateway to display the disable gateway message.

4. Choose **Create recovery tapes**.

5. Choose **Disable gateway**.

Understanding Tape Status

Each tape has an associated status that tells you at a glance what the health of the tape is. Most of the time, the status indicates that the tape is functioning normally and that no action is needed on your part. In some cases, the status indicates a problem with the tape that might require action on your part. You can find information following to help you decide when you need to act.

165

Topics

- Understanding Tape Status Information in a VTL
- Determining Tape Status in an Archive

Understanding Tape Status Information in a VTL

A tape's status must be AVAILABLE for you to read or write to the tape. The following table lists and describes possible status values.

Status	Description	Tape Data Is Stored In
CREATING	The virtual tape is being created. The tape can't be loaded into a tape drive, because the tape is being created.	—
AVAILABLE	The virtual tape is created and ready to be loaded into a tape drive.	Amazon S3
IN TRANSIT TO VTS	The virtual tape has been ejected and is being uploaded for archive. At this point, your tape gateway is uploading data to AWS. If the amount of data being uploaded is small, this status might not appear. When the upload is completed, the status changes to ARCHIVING.	Amazon S3
ARCHIVING	The virtual tape is being moved by your tape gateway to the archive, which is backed by Amazon Glacier. This process happens after the data upload to AWS is completed.	Data is being moved from Amazon S3 to Amazon Glacier
DELETING	The virtual tape is being deleted.	Data is being deleted from Amazon S3
DELETED	The virtual tape has been successfully deleted.	—
RETRIEVING	The virtual tape is being retrieved from the archive to your tape gateway. The virtual tape can be retrieved only to a tape gateway.	Data is being moved from Amazon Glacier to Amazon S3
RETRIEVED	The virtual tape is retrieved from the archive. The retrieved tape is write-protected.	Amazon S3

Status	Description	Tape Data Is Stored In
RECOVERED	The virtual tape is recovered and is read-only. When your tape gateway is not accessible for any reason, you can recover virtual tapes associated with that tape gateway to another tape gateway. To recover the virtual tapes, first disable the inaccessible tape gateway.	Amazon S3
IRRECOVERABLE	The virtual tape can't be read from or written to. This status indicates an error in your tape gateway.	Amazon S3

Determining Tape Status in an Archive

You can use the following procedure to determine the status of a virtual tape in an archive.

To determine the status of a virtual tape

1. Open the AWS Storage Gateway console at https://console.aws.amazon.com/storagegateway/home.

2. In the navigation pane, choose **Tapes**.

3. In the **Status** column of the tape library grid, check the status of the tape.

   The tape status also appears in the **Details** tab of each virtual tape.

Following, you can find a description of the possible status values.

Status	Description
ARCHIVED	The virtual tape has been ejected and is uploaded to the archive.
RETRIEVING	The virtual tape is being retrieved from the archive. The virtual tape can be retrieved only to a tape gateway.
RETRIEVED	The virtual tape has been retrieved from the archive. The retrieved tape is read-only.

For additional information about how to work with tapes and VTL devices, see Working With Tapes.

Monitoring Your Gateway and Resources

In this section, you can find information about how to monitor a gateway, including monitoring resources associated with the gateway and monitoring the upload buffer and cache storage. You use the AWS Management Console to view metrics for your gateway. For example, you can view the number of bytes used in read and write operations, the time spent in read and write operations, and the time taken to retrieve data from the AWS cloud. With metrics, you can track the health of your gateway and set up alarms to notify you when one or more metrics fall outside a defined threshold.

Topics

- Understanding Gateway Metrics
- Monitoring the Upload Buffer
- Monitoring Cache Storage
- Monitoring Your File Share
- Monitoring Your Volume Gateway
- Monitoring Your Tape Gateway
- Logging AWS Storage Gateway API Calls by Using AWS CloudTrail

AWS Storage Gateway provides Amazon CloudWatch metrics at no additional charge. Storage Gateway metrics are recorded for a period of two weeks. By using these metrics, you can access historical information and get a better perspective on how your gateway and volumes are performing. For detailed information about CloudWatch, see the *Amazon CloudWatch User Guide*.

Understanding Gateway Metrics

For the discussion in this topic, we define *gateway* metrics as metrics that are scoped to the gateway—that is, they measure something about the gateway. Because a gateway contains one or more volumes, a gateway-specific metric is representative of all volumes on the gateway. For example, the `CloudBytesUploaded` metric is the total number of bytes that the gateway sent to the cloud during the reporting period. This metric includes the activity of all the volumes on the gateway.

When working with gateway metric data, you specify the unique identification of the gateway that you are interested in viewing metrics for. To do this, you specify both the `GatewayId` and the `GatewayName` values. When you want to work with metric for a gateway, you specify the gateway *dimension* in the metrics namespace, which distinguishes a gateway-specific metric from a volume-specific metric. For more information, see Using Amazon CloudWatch Metrics.

Topics

The following table describes the Storage Gateway metrics that you can use to get information about your gateway. The entries in the table are grouped functionally by measure.

Note
The reporting period for these metrics is 5 minutes.

Metric	Description	Applies To..
CacheHitPercent	Percent of application reads served from the cache. The sample is taken at the end of the reporting period. Units: Percent	File, Cached volumes and Tape.
CachePercentUsed	Percent use of the gateway's cache storage. The sample is taken at the end of the reporting period. Units: Percent	File, Cached volumes and Tape.

Metric	Description	Applies To..
CachePercentDirty	Percent of the gateway's cache that has not been persisted to AWS. The sample is taken at the end of the reporting period. Units: Percent	File. Cached volumes and Tape.
CloudBytesDownloaded	The total number of compressed bytes that the gateway downloaded from AWS during the reporting period. Use this metric with the **Sum** statistic to measure throughput and with the **Samples** statistic to measure input/output operations per second (IOPS). Units: Bytes	File, Cached volumes, Stored volumes and Tape.
CloudDownloadLatency	The total number of milliseconds spent reading data from AWS during the reporting period. Use this metric with the **Average** statistic to measure latency. Units: Milliseconds	File, Cached volumes, Stored volumes and Tape.
CloudBytesUploaded	The total number of compressed bytes that the gateway uploaded to AWS during the reporting period. Use this metric with the **Sum** statistic to measure throughput and with the **Samples** statistic to measure IOPS. Units: Bytes	File, Cached volumes, Stored volumes and Tape.
UploadBufferFree	The total amount of unused space in the gateway's upload buffer. The sample is taken at the end of the reporting period. Units: Bytes	Cached volumes and Tape.
CacheFree	The total amount of unused space in the gateway's cache storage. The sample is taken at the end of the reporting period. Units: Bytes	File, Cached volumes, and Tape.
UploadBufferPercentUsed	Percent use of the gateway's upload buffer. The sample is taken at the end of the reporting period. Units: Percent	Cached volumes and Tape.
UploadBufferUsed	The total number of bytes being used in the gateway's upload buffer. The sample is taken at the end of the reporting period. Units: Bytes	Cached volumes and Tape.
CacheUsed	The total number of bytes being used in the gateway's cache storage. The sample is taken at the end of the reporting period. Units: Bytes	File, Cached volumes and Tape.

Metric	Description	Applies To..
QueuedWrites	The number of bytes waiting to be written to AWS, sampled at the end of the reporting period for all volumes in the gateway. These bytes are kept in your gateway's working storage. Units: Bytes	File, Cached volumes, Stored volumes and Tape.
ReadBytes	The total number of bytes read from your on-premises applications in the reporting period for all volumes in the gateway. Use this metric with the `Sum` statistic to measure throughput and with the `Samples` statistic to measure IOPS. Units: Bytes	File, Cached volumes, Stored volumes and Tape.
ReadTime	The total number of milliseconds spent to do read operations from your on-premises applications in the reporting period for all volumes in the gateway. Use this metric with the `Average` statistic to measure latency. Units: Milliseconds	File, Cached volumes, Stored volumes and Tape.
TotalCacheSize	The total size of the cache in bytes. The sample is taken at the end of the reporting period. Units: Bytes	File, Cached volumes, and Tape.
WriteBytes	The total number of bytes written to your on-premises applications in the reporting period for all volumes in the gateway. Use this metric with the `Sum` statistic to measure throughput and with the `Samples` statistic to measure IOPS. Units: Bytes	File, Cached volumes, Stored volumes and Tape.
WriteTime	The total number of milliseconds spent to do write operations from your on-premises applications in the reporting period for all volumes in the gateway. Use this metric with the `Average` statistic to measure latency. Units: Milliseconds	File, Cached volumes, Stored volumes and Tape.
TimeSinceLastRecoveryPoint	The time since the last available recovery point. For more information, see Your Cached Gateway is Unreachable And You Want to Recover Your Data. Units: Seconds	Cached volumes and Stored volumes.

Metric	Description	Applies To..
WorkingStorageFree	The total amount of unused space in the gateway's working storage. The sample is taken at the end of the reporting period. Units: Bytes	Stored volumes only.
WorkingStoragePercentUsed	Percent use of the gateway's upload buffer. The sample is taken at the end of the reporting period. Units: Percent	Stored volumes only.
WorkingStorageUsed	The total number of bytes being used in the gateway's upload buffer. The sample is taken at the end of the reporting period. Units: Bytes	Stored volumes only.

Monitoring the Upload Buffer

You can find information following about how to monitor a gateway's upload buffer and how to create an alarm so that you get a notification when the buffer exceeds a specified threshold. By using this approach, you can proactively add buffer storage to a gateway before it fills completely and your storage application stops backing up to AWS.

You monitor the upload buffer in the same way in both the cached volume and tape gateway architectures. For more information, see How AWS Storage Gateway Works (Architecture).

Note
The `WorkingStoragePercentUsed`, `WorkingStorageUsed`, and `WorkingStorageFree` metrics represent the upload buffer for the stored volumes setup only before the release of the cached-volume feature in Storage Gateway. Now you should use the equivalent upload buffer metrics `UploadBufferPercentUsed`, `UploadBufferUsed`, and `UploadBufferFree`. These metrics apply to both gateway architectures.

Item of Interest	How to Measure
Upload buffer usage	Use the `UploadBufferPercentUsed`, `UploadBufferUsed`, and `UploadBufferFree` metrics with the **Average** statistic. For example, use the `UploadBufferUsed` with the **Average** statistic to analyze the storage usage over a time period.

To measure upload buffer percent used

1. Open the CloudWatch console at https://console.aws.amazon.com/cloudwatch/.

2. Choose the **StorageGateway: Gateway Metrics** dimension, and find the gateway that you want to work with.

3. Choose the `UploadBufferPercentUsed` metric.

4. For **Time Range**, choose a value.

5. Choose the **Average** statistic.

6. For **Period**, choose a value of 5 minutes to match the default reporting time.

The resulting time-ordered set of data points contains the percent used of the upload buffer.

Using the following procedure, you can create an alarm using the CloudWatch console. To learn more about alarms and thresholds, see Creating CloudWatch Alarms.

To set an upper threshold alarm for a gateway's upload buffer

1. Open the CloudWatch console at https://console.aws.amazon.com/cloudwatch/.

2. Choose **Create Alarm** to start the Create Alarm Wizard.

3. Specify a metric for your alarm.

    1. On the **Select Metric** page of the Create Alarm Wizard, choose the **AWS/StorageGateway:GatewayId,GatewayName** dimension, and then find the gateway that you want to work with.

    2. Choose the `UploadBufferPercentUsed` metric. Use the `Average` statistic and a period of 5 minutes.

    3. Choose **Continue**.

4. Define the alarm name, description, and threshold.

    1. On the **Define Alarm** page of the Create Alarm Wizard, identify your alarm by giving it a name and description in the **Name** and **Description** boxes.

    2. Define the alarm threshold.

    3. Choose **Continue**.

5. Configure an email action for the alarm.

    1. In the **Configure Actions** page of the Create Alarm Wizard, choose **Alarm** for **Alarm State**.

    2. Choose **Choose or create email topic** for **Topic**.

        To create an email topic means that you set up an Amazon Simple Notification Service (Amazon SNS) topic. For more information about Amazon SNS, see Set Up Amazon SNS.

    3. For **Topic**, type a descriptive name for the topic.

    4. Choose **Add Action**.

    5. Choose **Continue**.

6. Review the alarm settings, and then create the alarm.

    1. In the **Review** page of the Create Alarm Wizard, review the alarm definition, metric, and associated actions from this step. Associated actions include, for example, sending an email notification.

    2. After reviewing the alarm summary, choose **Save Alarm**.

7. Confirm your subscription to the alarm topic.

    1. Open the Amazon Simple Notification Service (Amazon SNS) email topic that is sent to the email address that you specified when creating the topic.

        The following image shows a notification.

2. Confirm your subscription by clicking the link in the email.

   A subscription confirmation appears.

Monitoring Cache Storage

You can find information following about how to monitor a gateway's cache storage and how to create an alarm so that you get a notification when parameters of the cache pass specified thresholds. Using this alarm, you know when to proactively add cache storage to a gateway.

You only monitor cache storage in the cached volumes architecture. For more information, see How AWS Storage Gateway Works (Architecture).

Item of Interest	How to Measure
Total usage of cache	Use the `CachePercentUsed` and `TotalCacheSize` metrics with the `Average` statistic. For example, use the `CachePercentUsed` with the `Average` statistic to analyze the cache usage over a period of time. The `TotalCacheSize` metric changes only when you add cache to the gateway.
Percentage of read requests that are served from the cache	Use the `CacheHitPercent` metric with the `Average` statistic. Typically, you want `CacheHitPercent` to remain high.
Percentage of cache that is dirty—that is, it contains content that has not been uploaded to AWS	Use the `CachePercentDirty` metrics with the `Average` statistic. Typically, you want `CachePercentDirty` to remain low.

To measure the cache's percentage dirty for a gateway and all its volumes

1. Open the CloudWatch console at https://console.aws.amazon.com/cloudwatch/.

2. Choose the **StorageGateway: Gateway Metrics** dimension, and find the gateway that you want to work with.

3. Choose the `CachePercentDirty` metric.

4. For **Time Range**, choose a value.

5. Choose the `Average` statistic.

6. For **Period**, choose a value of 5 minutes to match the default reporting time.

The resulting time-ordered set of data points contains the percentage of the cache that is dirty over the 5 minutes.

To measure the cache's percentage dirty for a volume

1. Open the CloudWatch console at https://console.aws.amazon.com/cloudwatch/.

2. Choose the **StorageGateway: Volume Metrics** dimension, and find the volume that you want to work with.

3. Choose the `CachePercentDirty` metric.

4. For **Time Range**, choose a value.

5. Choose the `Average` statistic.

6. For **Period**, choose a value of 5 minutes to match the default reporting time.

The resulting time-ordered set of data points contains the percentage of the cache that is dirty over the 5 minutes.

Monitoring Your File Share

You can monitor your file share by using Amazon CloudWatch metrics and use Amazon CloudWatch Events to get notified when your file operations are done. For information about file gateway type metrics, see Monitoring Your Gateway and Resources.

Topics

- Getting Notification for File Operations
- Understanding File Share Metrics

Getting Notification for File Operations

AWS Storage Gateway can send a notification through CloudWatch Events when your file operations are done.

- You can get notified when the gateway finishes uploading your files to your file share. You can use the NotifyWhenUploaded API to request a file upload notification.
- You can get notified when the gateway finishes refreshing the cache for your S3 bucket. You can use the RefreshCache API to request a cache refresh notification.

When the file operation your requested is done, AWS Storage Gateway sends you notification through CloudWatch Events. You can configure CloudWatch Events to send the notification through event targets such as Amazon SNS, Amazon SQS or AWS Lambda function. For example, you can configure an Amazon SNS target, to send the notification Amazon SNS consumers such as email and text message. For information about CloudWatch Events, see What is Amazon CloudWatch Events?

To set up CloudWatch Events notification

1. Create a target such as an Amazon SNS topic or Lambda function to invoke when the event you requested in AWS Storage Gateway is triggered.

2. Create a rule in the Amazon CloudWatch Events Console to invoke targets based on an event in AWS Storage Gateway.

3. In the rule, create an event patten for the event type. The notification is triggered when the event matches this rule pattern.

4. Select the target and configure the settings.

The following example shows a rule that triggers the specified event type in the specified gateway and in the specified AWS Region. For example, you could specify the `Storage Gateway File Upload Event` as the event type.

```
1  {
2      "source":[
3          "aws.storagegateway"
4      ],
5      "resources":[
6          "arn:aws:storagegateway:AWS Region:account-id
7                      :gateway/gateway-id"
8      ],
9      "detail-type":[
10         "Event type"
11     ]
12 }
```

For information about how to create a CloudWatch Events see Getting Started with Amazon CloudWatch Events.

Getting File Upload Notification

For file notification use case, you could have two file gateways that mapped to the same Amazon S3 bucket and the NFS client for Gateway1 uploads new files to S3. The files will upload to S3 but they will not appear in Gateway2 because it uses a locally cached version of files in S3. To make the files visible in gateway2, you can use the NotifyWhenUploaded API to request file upload notification from Gateway1 to notify you when the upload is done. You can then use the CloudWatch Events to automatically issue RefreshCache request for the file share on Gateway2. When the RefreshCache request completes the new files will be visible in Gateway2.

Example Example—File Upload Notification

The following example shows a file upload notification that is sent to you through when the event matches the rule you created. This notification is in JSON format. You can configure this notification to be delivered to the target message.

```
1  {
2      "id" : "2649b160-d59d-c97f-3f64-8aaa9ea6aed3",
3      "version" : "0",
4      "account" : "209870788375",
5      "source" : "aws.storagegateway",
6      "resources" : [
7        "arn:aws:storagegateway:us-east-1:123456789011:share/share-F123D451",
8        "arn:aws:storagegateway:us-east-1:346332347513:gateway/sgw-712345DA",
9        "arn:aws:s3:::mybucket-sgw-aabbcc"
10     ],
11     "detail" : {
12       "event-type" : "upload-complete",
13       "notification-id" : "da8db69f-6351-4205-829b-4e82607a00fe",
14       "completed" : "2017-11-06T21:34:53Z",
15       "request-received" : "2017-11-06T21:34:42Z"
16     },
17     "detail-type" : "Storage Gateway File Upload Event",
18     "region" : "us-east-1",
19    "time" : "2017-11-06T21:34:42Z"
20  }
```

Getting Refresh Cache Notification

For refresh cache notification use case, you could have two file gateways that map to the same Amazon S3 bucket and the NFS client for Gateway1 uploads new files to the S3 bucket. The files will upload to S3 but they will not appear in Gateway2 until you refresh the cache. This is because Gateway2 uses a locally cached version of the files in S3. You might want to do something with the files in Gateway2 when the refresh cache is done. Large files could take a while to show up in gateway2 so you might want to be notified when the cache refresh is done. You can request refresh cache notification from Gateway2 to notify you when all the files are visible in Gateway2.

For information about how to create a CloudWatch Events see Getting Started with Amazon CloudWatch Events.

Example Example—Refresh Cache Notification

The following example shows a refresh cache notification that is sent to you through when the event matches the rule you created. This notification is in JSON format. You can configure this notification to be delivered to the target message.

```
1  {
2      "id" : "2649b160-d59d-c97f-3f64-8aaa9ea6aed3",
3      "version" : "0",
4      "account" : "209870788375",
```

```
5      "source" : "aws.storagegateway",
6      "resources" : [
7         "arn:aws:storagegateway:us-east-2:123456789011:share/share-F123D451",
8         "arn:aws:storagegateway:us-east-2:346332347513:gateway/sgw-712345DA"
9      ],
10     "detail" : {
11        "event-type" :"refresh-cache-complete",
12        "notification-id" : "da8db69f-6351-4205-829b-4e82607a00fe",
13        "completed" : "2018-02-06T21:34:53Z",
14        "request-received" : "2018-02-06T21:34:42Z"
15     },
16     "detail-type" : "Storage Gateway Refresh Cache Event",
17     "region" : "us-east-2",
18    "time" : "2017-11-06T21:34:42Z"
19 }
```

Understanding File Share Metrics

You can find information following about the Storage Gateway metrics that cover file shares. Each file share has a set of metrics associated with it. Some file share-specific metrics have the same name as certain gateway-specific metrics. These metrics represent the same kinds of measurements but are scoped to the file share instead. Always specify whether you want to work with either a gateway or a file share metric before working with a metric. Specifically, when working with file share metrics, you must specify the `File share` ID that identifies the file share for which you are interested in viewing metrics. For more information, see Using Amazon CloudWatch Metrics.

The following table describes the Storage Gateway metrics that you can use to get information about your file shares.

Metric	Description
CacheHitPercent	Percent of application read operations from the file shares that are served from cache. The sample is taken at the end of the reporting period. When there are no application read operations from the file share, this metric reports 100 percent. Units: Percent
CachePercentDirty	The file share's contribution to the overall percentage of the gateway's cache that has not been persisted to AWS. The sample is taken at the end of the reporting period. Use the `CachePercentDirty` metric of the gateway to view the overall percentage of the gateway's cache that has not been persisted to AWS. For more information, see Understanding Gateway Metrics. Units: Percent
CachePercentUsed	The file share's contribution to the overall percent use of the gateway's cache storage. The sample is taken at the end of the reporting period. Use the `CachePercentUsed` metric of the gateway to view overall percent use of the gateway's cache storage. For more information, see Understanding Gateway Metrics. Units: Percent

Metric	Description
CloudBytesUploaded	The total number of bytes that the gateway uploaded to AWS during the reporting period. Use this metric with the Sum statistic to measure throughput and with the Samples statistic to measure IOPS. Units: Bytes
CloudBytesDownloaded	The total number of bytes that the gateway downloaded from AWS during the reporting period. Use this metric with the Sum statistic to measure throughput and with the Samples statistic to measure input/output operations per second (IOPS). Units: Bytes
ReadBytes	The total number of bytes read from your on-premises applications in the reporting period for a file share. Use this metric with the Sum statistic to measure throughput and with the Samples statistic to measure IOPS. Units: Bytes
WriteBytes	The total number of bytes written to your on-premises applications in the reporting period. Use this metric with the Sum statistic to measure throughput and with the Samples statistic to measure IOPS. Units: Bytes

Monitoring Your Volume Gateway

In this section, you can find information about how to monitor a gateway in a cached volumes or stored volumes setup, including monitoring the volumes associated with the gateway and monitoring the upload buffer. You use the AWS Management Console to view metrics for your gateway. For example, you can view the number of bytes used in read and write operations, the time spent in read and write operations, and the time taken to retrieve data from the AWS cloud. With metrics, you can track the health of your gateway and set up alarms to notify you when one or more metrics fall outside a defined threshold.

Topics

- Using Amazon CloudWatch Metrics
- Measuring Performance Between Your Application and Gateway
- Measuring Performance Between Your Gateway and AWS
- Understanding Volume Metrics

Storage Gateway provides CloudWatch metrics at no additional charge. Storage Gateway metrics are recorded for a period of two weeks. By using these metrics, you can access historical information and get a better perspective on how your gateway and volumes are performing. For detailed information about CloudWatch, see the *Amazon CloudWatch User Guide.*

Using Amazon CloudWatch Metrics

You can get monitoring data for your gateway using either the AWS Management Console or the CloudWatch API. The console displays a series of graphs based on the raw data from the CloudWatch API. You can also use the CloudWatch API through one of the Amazon AWS Software Development Kits (SDKs) or the Amazon CloudWatch API tools. Depending on your needs, you might prefer to use either the graphs displayed in the console or retrieved from the API.

Regardless of which method you choose to use to work with metrics, you must specify the following information:

- The metric dimension to work with. A *dimension* is a name-value pair that helps you to uniquely identify a metric. The dimensions for Storage Gateway are `GatewayId`, `GatewayName`, and `VolumeId`. In the CloudWatch console, you can use the `Gateway Metrics` and `Volume Metrics` views to easily select gateway-specific and volume-specific dimensions. For more information about dimensions, see Dimensions in the *Amazon CloudWatch User Guide>*.
- The metric name, such as `ReadBytes`.

The following table summarizes the types of Storage Gateway metric data that you can use.

[See the AWS documentation website for more details]

Working with gateway and volume metrics is similar to working with other service metrics. You can find a discussion of some of the most common metrics tasks in the CloudWatch documentation listed following:

- Viewing Available Metrics
- Getting Statistics for a Metric
- Creating CloudWatch Alarms

Measuring Performance Between Your Application and Gateway

Data throughput, data latency, and operations per second are three measures that you can use to understand how your application storage that is using your gateway is performing. When you use the correct aggregation statistic, you can use Storage Gateway metrics to measure these values.

A *statistic* is an aggregation of a metric over a specified period of time. When you view the values of a metric in CloudWatch, use the `Average` statistic for data latency (milliseconds), use the `Sum` statistic for data throughput (bytes per second), and use the `Samples` statistic for input/output operations per second (IOPS). For more information, see Statistics in the *Amazon CloudWatch User Guide*.

The following table summarizes the metrics and corresponding statistic you can use to measure the throughput, latency, and IOPS between your applications and gateways.

Item of Interest	How to Measure
Throughput	Use the `ReadBytes` and `WriteBytes` metrics with the `Sum` CloudWatch statistic. For example, the `Sum` value of the `ReadBytes` metric over a sample period of 5 minutes divided by 300 seconds gives you the throughput as a rate in bytes per second.
Latency	Use the ReadTime and WriteTime metrics with the Average CloudWatch statistic. For example, the Average value of the ReadTime metric gives you the latency per operation over the sample period of time.
IOPS	Use the ReadBytes and WriteBytes metrics with the Samples CloudWatch statistic. For example, the Samples value of the ReadBytes metric over a sample period of 5 minutes divided by 300 seconds gives you IOPS.

For the average latency graphs and average size graphs, the average is calculated over the total number of operations (read or write, whichever is applicable to the graph) that completed during the period.

To measure the data throughput from an application to a volume

1. Open the CloudWatch console at https://console.aws.amazon.com/cloudwatch/.

2. Choose **Metrics**, then choose the **All metrics** tab and then choose **Storage Gateway**.

3. Choose the **Volume metrics** dimension, and find the volume that you want to work with.

4. Choose the `ReadBytes` and `WriteBytes` metrics.

5. For **Time Range**, choose a value.

6. Choose the `Sum` statistic.

7. For **Period**, choose a value of 5 minutes or greater.

8. In the resulting time-ordered sets of data points (one for `ReadBytes` and one for `WriteBytes`), divide each data point by the period (in seconds) to get the throughput at the sample point. The total throughput is the sum of the throughputs.

The following image shows the `ReadBytes` and `WriteBytes` metrics for a volume with the `Sum` statistic. In the image, the cursor over a data point displays information about the data point including its value and the number of bytes. Divide the bytes value by the **Period** value (5 minutes) to get the data throughput at that sample point. For the point highlighted, the read throughput is 2,384,199,680 bytes divided by 300 seconds, which is 7.6 megabytes per second.

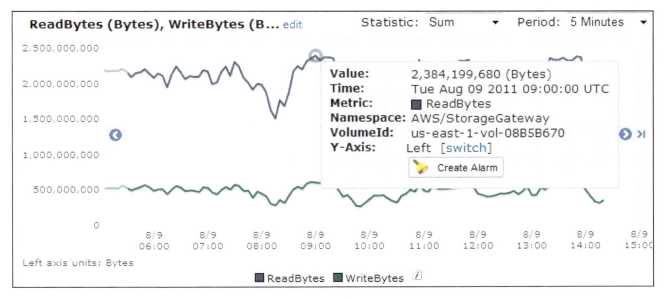

To measure the data input/output operations per second from an application to a volume

1. Open the CloudWatch console at https://console.aws.amazon.com/cloudwatch/.

2. Choose **Metrics**, then choose the **All metrics** tab and then choose **Storage Gateway**.

3. Choose the **Volume metrics** dimension, and find the volume that you want to work with.

4. Choose the `ReadBytes` and `WriteBytes` metrics.

5. For **Time Range**, choose a value.

6. Choose the `Samples` statistic.

7. For **Period**, choose a value of 5 minutes or greater.

8. In the resulting time-ordered sets of data points (one for `ReadBytes` and one for `WriteBytes`), divide each data point by the period (in seconds) to get IOPS.

The following image shows the `ReadBytes` and `WriteBytes` metrics for a storage volume with the `Samples` statistic. In the image, the cursor over a data point displays information about the data point, including its value and the number of samples. Divide the samples value by the **Period** value (5 minutes) to get the operations per second at that sample point. For the point highlighted, the number of write operations is 24,373 bytes divided by 300 seconds, which is 81 write operations per second.

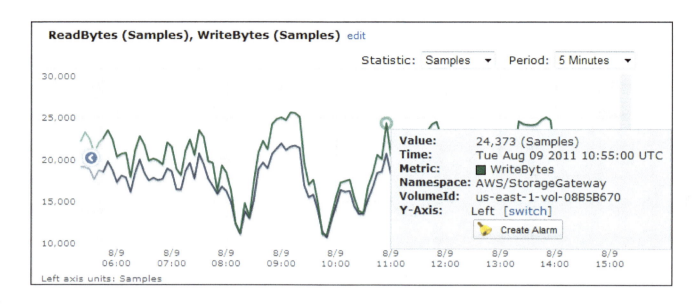

Measuring Performance Between Your Gateway and AWS

Data throughput, data latency, and operations per second are three measures that you can use to understand how your application storage using the Storage Gateway is performing. These three values can be measured using the Storage Gateway metrics provided for you when you use the correct aggregation statistic. The following table summarizes the metrics and corresponding statistic to use to measure the throughput, latency, and input/output operations per second (IOPS) between your gateway and AWS.

Item of Interest	How to Measure
Throughput	Use the `ReadBytes` and `WriteBytes` metrics with the `Sum` CloudWatch statistic. For example, the `Sum` value of the `ReadBytes` metric over a sample period of 5 minutes divided by 300 seconds gives you the throughput as a rate in bytes per second.
Latency	Use the ReadTime and WriteTime metrics with the Average CloudWatch statistic. For example, the Average value of the ReadTime metric gives you the latency per operation over the sample period of time.
IOPS	Use the ReadBytes and WriteBytes metrics with the Samples CloudWatch statistic. For example, the Samples value of the ReadBytes metric over a sample period of 5 minutes divided by 300 seconds gives you IOPS.
Throughput to AWS	Use the CloudBytesDownloaded and CloudBytesUploaded metrics with the Sum CloudWatch statistic. For example, the Sum value of the CloudBytesDownloaded metric over a sample period of 5 minutes divided by 300 seconds gives you the throughput from AWS to the gateway as bytes per second.

Item of Interest	How to Measure
Latency of data to AWS	Use the CloudDownloadLatency metric with the Average statistic. For example, the Average statistic of the CloudDownloadLatency metric gives you the latency per operation.

To measure the upload data throughput from a gateway to AWS

1. Open the CloudWatch console at https://console.aws.amazon.com/cloudwatch/.

2. Choose **Metrics**, then choose the **All metrics** tab and then choose **Storage Gateway**.

3. Choose the **Gateway metrics** dimension, and find the volume that you want to work with.

4. Choose the `CloudBytesUploaded` metric.

5. For **Time Range**, choose a value.

6. Choose the `Sum` statistic.

7. For **Period**, choose a value of 5 minutes or greater.

8. In the resulting time-ordered set of data points, divide each data point by the period (in seconds) to get the throughput at that sample period.

The following image shows the `CloudBytesUploaded` metric for a gateway volume with the `Sum` statistic. In the image, the cursor over a data point displays information about the data point, including its value and bytes uploaded. Divide this value by the **Period** value (5 minutes) to get the throughput at that sample point. For the point highlighted, the throughput from the gateway to AWS is 555,544,576 bytes divided by 300 seconds, which is 1.7 megabytes per second.

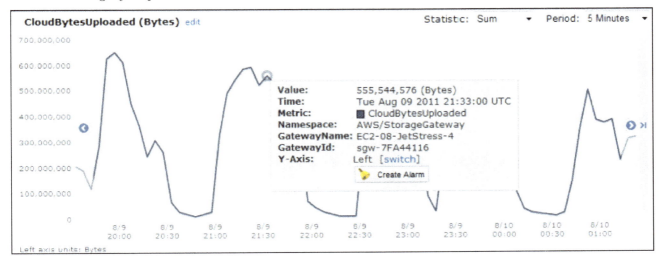

To measure the latency per operation of a gateway

1. Open the CloudWatch console at https://console.aws.amazon.com/cloudwatch/.

2. Choose **Metrics**, then choose the **All metrics** tab and then choose **Storage Gateway**.

3. Choose the **Gateway metrics** dimension, and find the volume that you want to work with.

4. Choose the `ReadTime` and `WriteTime` metrics.

5. For **Time Range**, choose a value.

6. Choose the `Average` statistic.

7. For **Period**, choose a value of 5 minutes to match the default reporting time.

8. In the resulting time-ordered set of points (one for `ReadTime` and one for `WriteTime`), add data points at the same time sample to get to the total latency in milliseconds.

To measure the data latency from a gateway to AWS

1. Open the CloudWatch console at https://console.aws.amazon.com/cloudwatch/.

2. Choose **Metrics**, then choose the **All metrics** tab and then choose **Storage Gateway**.

3. Choose the **Gateway metrics** dimension, and find the volume that you want to work with.

4. Choose the `CloudDownloadLatency` metric.

5. For **Time Range**, choose a value.

6. Choose the `Average` statistic.

7. For **Period**, choose a value of 5 minutes to match the default reporting time.

The resulting time-ordered set of data points contains the latency in milliseconds.

To set an upper threshold alarm for a gateway's throughput to AWS

1. Open the CloudWatch console at https://console.aws.amazon.com/cloudwatch/.

2. Choose **Alarms**.

3. Choose **Create Alarm** to start the Create Alarm Wizard.

4. Choose the **Storage Gateway** dimension, and find the gateway that you want to work with.

5. Choose the `CloudBytesUploaded` metric.

6. To define the alarm, define the alarm state when the `CloudBytesUploaded` metric is greater than or equal to a specified value for a specified time. For example, you can define an alarm state when the `CloudBytesUploaded` metric is greater than 10 MB for 60 minutes.

7. Configure the actions to take for the alarm state. For example, you can have an email notification sent to you.

8. Choose **Create Alarm**.

To set an upper threshold alarm for reading data from AWS

1. Open the CloudWatch console at https://console.aws.amazon.com/cloudwatch/.

2. Choose **Create Alarm** to start the Create Alarm Wizard.

3. Choose the **StorageGateway: Gateway Metrics** dimension, and find the gateway that you want to work with.

4. Choose the `CloudDownloadLatency` metric.

5. Define the alarm by defining the alarm state when the `CloudDownloadLatency` metric is greater than or equal to a specified value for a specified time. For example, you can define an alarm state when the `CloudDownloadLatency` is greater than 60,000 milliseconds for greater than 2 hours.

6. Configure the actions to take for the alarm state. For example, you can have an email notification sent to you.

7. Choose **Create Alarm**.

Understanding Volume Metrics

You can find information following about the Storage Gateway metrics that cover a volume of a gateway. Each volume of a gateway has a set of metrics associated with it. Note that some volume-specific metrics have the same name as certain gateway-specific metrics. These metrics represent the same kinds of measurements but are scoped to the volume instead of the gateway. You must always specify whether you want to work with either a gateway or a volume metric before working with a metric. Specifically, when working with volume metrics, you must specify the `VolumeId` that identifies the storage volume for which you are interested in viewing metrics. For more information, see Using Amazon CloudWatch Metrics.

The following table describes the Storage Gateway metrics that you can use to get information about your storage volumes.

Metric	Description	Cached volumes	Stored volumes
CacheHitPercent	Percent of application read operations from the volume that are served from cache. The sample is taken at the end of the reporting period. When there are no application read operations from the volume, this metric reports 100 percent. Units: Percent	yes	no
CachePercentDirty	The volume's contribution to the overall percentage of the gateway's cache that has not been persisted to AWS. The sample is taken at the end of the reporting period. Use the `CachePercentDirty` metric of the gateway to view the overall percentage of the gateway's cache that has not been persisted to AWS. For more information, see Understanding Gateway Metrics. Units: Percent	yes	no

Metric	Description	Cached volumes	Stored volumes
CachePercentUsed	The volume's contribution to the overall percent use of the gateway's cache storage. The sample is taken at the end of the reporting period. Use the `CachePercentUsed` metric of the gateway to view overall percent use of the gateway's cache storage. For more information, see Understanding Gateway Metrics. Units: Percent	yes	no
ReadBytes	The total number of bytes read from your on-premises applications in the reporting period. Use this metric with the `Sum` statistic to measure throughput and with the `Samples` statistic to measure IOPS. Units: Bytes	yes	yes
ReadTime	The total number of milliseconds spent to do read operations from your on-premises applications in the reporting period. Use this metric with the `Average` statistic to measure latency. Units: Milliseconds	yes	yes
WriteBytes	The total number of bytes written to your on-premises applications in the reporting period. Use this metric with the `Sum` statistic to measure throughput and with the `Samples` statistic to measure IOPS. Units: Bytes	yes	yes

Metric	Description	Cached volumes	Stored volumes
WriteTime	The total number of milliseconds spent to do write operations from your on-premises applications in the reporting period. Use this metric with the **Average** statistic to measure latency. Units: Milliseconds	yes	yes
QueuedWrites	The number of bytes waiting to be written to AWS, sampled at the end of the reporting period. Units: Bytes	yes	yes

Monitoring Your Tape Gateway

In this section, you can find information about how to monitor your tape gateway, virtual tapes associated with your tape gateway, cache storage, and the upload buffer. You use the AWS Management Console to view metrics for your tape gateway. With metrics, you can track the health of your tape gateway and set up alarms to notify you when one or more metrics are outside a defined threshold.

Storage Gateway provides CloudWatch metrics at no additional charge. Storage Gateway metrics are recorded for a period of two weeks. By using these metrics, you can access historical information and get a better perspective of how your tape gateway and virtual tapes are performing. For detailed information about CloudWatch, see the *Amazon CloudWatch User Guide*.

Topics

- Using Amazon CloudWatch Metrics
- Measuring Performance Between Your Tape Gateway and AWS

Using Amazon CloudWatch Metrics

You can get monitoring data for your tape gateway by using either the AWS Management Console or the CloudWatch API. The console displays a series of graphs based on the raw data from the CloudWatch API. The CloudWatch API can also be used through one of the Amazon AWS Software Development Kits (SDKs) or the Amazon CloudWatch API tools. Depending on your needs, you might prefer to use either the graphs displayed in the console or retrieved from the API.

Regardless of which method you choose to use to work with metrics, you must specify the following information:

- The metric dimension to work with. A *dimension* is a name-value pair that helps you to uniquely identify a metric. The dimensions for Storage Gateway are `GatewayId` and `GatewayName`. In the CloudWatch console, you can use the `Gateway Metrics` view to easily select gateway-specific and tape-specific dimensions. For more information about dimensions, see Dimensions in the *Amazon CloudWatch User Guide*.
- The metric name, such as `ReadBytes`.

The following table summarizes the types of Storage Gateway metric data that are available to you.

Amazon CloudWatch Namespace	Dimension	Description
AWS/StorageGateway	GatewayId, GatewayName	These dimensions filter for metric data that describes aspects of the tape gateway. You can identify a tape gateway to work with by specifying both the `GatewayId` and the `GatewayName` dimensions. Throughput and latency data of a tape gateway is based on all the virtual tapes in the tape gateway. Data is available automatically in 5-minute periods at no charge.

Working with gateway and tape metrics is similar to working with other service metrics. You can find a discussion of some of the most common metrics tasks in the CloudWatch documentation listed following:

- Viewing Available Metrics

- Getting Statistics for a Metric
- Creating CloudWatch Alarms

Measuring Performance Between Your Tape Gateway and AWS

Data throughput, data latency, and operations per second are measures that you can use to understand how your application storage that is using your tape gateway is performing. When you use the correct aggregation statistic, these values can be measured by using the Storage Gateway metrics that are provided for you.

A *statistic* is an aggregation of a metric over a specified period of time. When you view the values of a metric in CloudWatch, use the `Average` statistic for data latency (milliseconds), and use the `Samples` statistic for input/output operations per second (IOPS). For more information, see Statistics in the Amazon CloudWatch User Guide

The following table summarizes the metrics and the corresponding statistic you can use to measure the throughput, latency, and IOPS between your tape gateway and AWS.

Item of Interest	How to Measure
Latency	Use the ReadTime and WriteTime metrics with the Average CloudWatch statistic. For example, the Average value of the ReadTime metric gives you the latency per operation over the sample period of time.
Throughput to AWS	Use the CloudBytesDownloaded and CloudBytesUploaded metrics with the Sum CloudWatch statistic. For example, the Sum value of the CloudBytesDownloaded metric over a sample period of 5 minutes divided by 300 seconds gives you the throughput from AWS to the tape gateway as a rate in bytes per second.
Latency of data to AWS	Use the CloudDownloadLatency metric with the Average statistic. For example, the Average statistic of the CloudDownloadLatency metric gives you the latency per operation.

To measure the upload data throughput from a tape gateway to AWS

1. Open the CloudWatch console at https://console.aws.amazon.com/cloudwatch/.

2. Choose the **Metrics** tab.

3. Choose the **StorageGateway: Gateway Metrics** dimension, and find the tape gateway that you want to work with.

4. Choose the `CloudBytesUploaded` metric.

5. For **Time Range**, choose a value.

6. Choose the `Sum` statistic.

7. For **Period**, choose a value of 5 minutes or greater.

8. In the resulting time-ordered set of data points, divide each data point by the period (in seconds) to get the throughput at that sample period.

The following image shows the `CloudBytesUploaded` metric for a gateway tape with the `Sum` statistic. In the image, placing the cursor over a data point displays information about the data point, including its value and the number of bytes uploaded. Divide this value by the **Period** value (5 minutes) to get the throughput at that sample point. For the point highlighted, the throughput from the tape gateway to AWS is 555,544,576 bytes divided by 300 seconds, which is 1.7 megabytes per second.

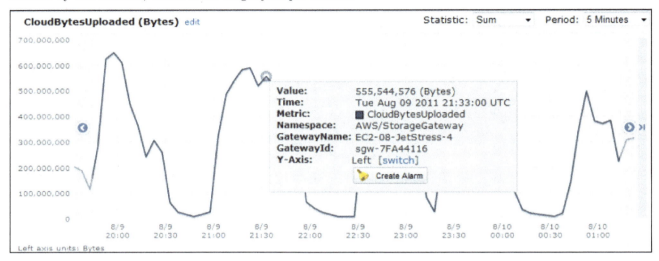

To measure the data latency from a tape gateway to AWS

1. Open the CloudWatch console at https://console.aws.amazon.com/cloudwatch/.

2. Choose the **Metrics** tab.

3. Choose the **StorageGateway: GatewayMetrics** dimension, and find the tape gateway that you want to work with.

4. Choose the `CloudDownloadLatency` metric.

5. For **Time Range**, choose a value.

6. Choose the `Average` statistic.

7. For **Period**, choose a value of 5 minutes to match the default reporting time.

The resulting time-ordered set of data points contains the latency in milliseconds.

To set an upper threshold alarm for a tape gateway's throughput to AWS

1. Open the CloudWatch console at https://console.aws.amazon.com/cloudwatch/.

2. Choose **Create Alarm** to start the Create Alarm Wizard.

3. Choose the **StorageGateway: Gateway Metrics** dimension, and find the tape gateway that you want to work with.

4. Choose the `CloudBytesUploaded` metric.

5. Define the alarm by defining the alarm state when the `CloudBytesUploaded` metric is greater than or equal to a specified value for a specified time. For example, you can define an alarm state when the `CloudBytesUploaded` metric is greater than 10 megabytes for 60 minutes.

6. Configure the actions to take for the alarm state. For example, you can have an email notification sent to you.

7. Choose **Create Alarm**.

To set an upper threshold alarm for reading data from AWS

1. Open the CloudWatch console at https://console.aws.amazon.com/cloudwatch/.

2. Choose **Create Alarm** to start the Create Alarm Wizard.

3. Choose the **StorageGateway: Gateway Metrics** dimension, and find the tape gateway that you want to work with.

4. Choose the `CloudDownloadLatency` metric.

5. Define the alarm by defining the alarm state when the `CloudDownloadLatency` metric is greater than or equal to a specified value for a specified time. For example, you can define an alarm state when the `CloudDownloadLatency` is greater than 60,000 milliseconds for greater than 2 hours.

6. Configure the actions to take for the alarm state. For example, you can have an email notification sent to you.

7. Choose **Create Alarm**.

Logging AWS Storage Gateway API Calls by Using AWS CloudTrail

Storage Gateway is integrated with AWS CloudTrail, a service that captures API calls made by or on behalf of Storage Gateway in your AWS account and delivers the log files to an Amazon S3 bucket that you specify. CloudTrail captures API calls from the Storage Gateway console or from the Storage Gateway API. Using the information collected by CloudTrail, you can determine what request was made to Storage Gateway, the source IP address from which the request was made, who made the request, when it was made, and so on. To learn more about CloudTrail, including how to configure and enable it, see the http://docs.aws.amazon.com/awscloudtrail/latest/userguide/.

Storage Gateway Information in CloudTrail

When CloudTrail logging is enabled in your AWS account, API calls made to Storage Gateway actions are tracked in log files. Storage Gateway records are written together with other AWS service records in a log file. CloudTrail determines when to create and write to a new file based on a time period and file size.

All of the Storage Gateway actions are logged and are documented in the Actions topic. For example, calls to the `ActivateGateway`, `ListGateways`, and `ShutdownGateway` actions generate entries in the CloudTrail log files.

Every log entry contains information about who generated the request. The user identity information in the log helps you determine whether the request was made with root or IAM user credentials, with temporary security credentials for a role or federated user, or by another AWS service. For more information, see the **userIdentity** field in the CloudTrail Event Reference in the *AWS CloudTrail User Guide*.

You can store your log files in your bucket for as long as you want, but you can also define Amazon S3 lifecycle rules to archive or delete log files automatically. By default, your log files are encrypted by using Amazon S3 server-side encryption (SSE).

You can choose to have CloudTrail publish Amazon Simple Notification Service (Amazon SNS) notifications when new log files are delivered if you want to take quick action upon log file delivery. For more information, see Configuring Amazon SNS Notifications.

You can also aggregate Storage Gateway log files from multiple AWS regions and multiple AWS accounts into a single Amazon S3 bucket. For more information, see Aggregating CloudTrail Log Files to a Single Amazon S3 Bucket.

Understanding Storage Gateway Log File Entries

CloudTrail log files can contain one or more log entries where each entry is made up of multiple JSON-formatted events. A log entry represents a single request from any source and includes information about the requested action, any parameters, the date and time of the action, and so on. The log entries are not guaranteed to be in any particular order. That is, they are not an ordered stack trace of the public API calls.

The following example shows a CloudTrail log entry that demonstrates the `ActivateGateway` action.

```
1  { "Records": [{
2              "eventVersion": "1.02",
3              "userIdentity": {
4              "type": "IAMUser",
5              "principalId": "AIDAII5AUEPBH2M7JTNVC",
6              "arn": "arn:aws:iam::111122223333:user/StorageGateway-team/JohnDoe",
7              "accountId": "111122223333",
8              "accessKeyId": "AKIAIOSFODNN7EXAMPLE",
9               "userName": "JohnDoe"
10             },
11              "eventTime": "2014-12-04T16:19:00Z",
```

```
12          "eventSource": "storagegateway.amazonaws.com",
13          "eventName": "ActivateGateway",
14          "awsRegion": "us-east-2",
15          "sourceIPAddress": "192.0.2.0",
16          "userAgent": "aws-cli/1.6.2 Python/2.7.6 Linux/2.6.18-164.el5",
17           "requestParameters": {
18                              "gatewayTimezone": "GMT-5:00",
19                              "gatewayName": "cloudtrailgatewayvtl",
20                              "gatewayRegion": "us-east-2",
21                              "activationKey": "EHFBX-1NDD0-P0IVU-PI259-DHK88",
22                              "gatewayType": "VTL"
23                                  },
24                              "responseElements": {
25                                              "gatewayARN": "arn:aws:
                                                  storagegateway:us-east
                                                  -2:111122223333:
                                                  gateway/
                                                  cloudtrailgatewayvtl"
26                                  },
27                              "requestID": "54
                                  BTFGNQI71987UJD2IHTCT8NF1Q8GLLE1QEU3KPGG6F0KSTAUU
                                  ",
28                              "eventID": "635f2ea2-7e42-45f0-bed1-8b17d7b74265
                                  ",
29                              "eventType": "AwsApiCall",
30                              "apiVersion": "20130630",
31                              "recipientAccountId": "444455556666"
32                      }
33              ]
34 }
```

The following example shows a CloudTrail log entry that demonstrates the ListGateways action.

```
1 {
2  "Records": [{
3              "eventVersion": "1.02",
4              "userIdentity": {
5                              "type": "IAMUser",
6                              "principalId": "AIDAII5AUEPBH2M7JTNVC",
7                              "arn": "arn:aws:iam::111122223333:user/StorageGateway-team/
                                  JohnDoe",
8                              "accountId:" 111122223333", " accessKeyId ":"
                                  AKIAIOSFODNN7EXAMPLE",
9                              " userName ":" JohnDoe "
10                             },
11
12                             " eventTime ":" 2014 - 12 - 03T19: 41: 53Z ",
13                             " eventSource ":" storagegateway.amazonaws.com ",
14                             " eventName ":" ListGateways ",
15                             " awsRegion ":" us-east-2 ",
16                             " sourceIPAddress ":" 192.0.2.0 ",
17                             " userAgent ":" aws - cli / 1.6.2 Python / 2.7.6 Linux / 2.6.18
                                  - 164.el5 ",
18                             " requestParameters ":null,
19                             " responseElements ":null,
```

```
20          "requestID ":" 6
               U2N42CU37KAO8BG6V1I23FRSJ1Q8GLLE1QEU3KPGG6FOKSTAUUO ",
21          " eventID ":" f76e5919 - 9362 - 48ff - a7c4 - d203a189ec8d ",
22          " eventType ":" AwsApiCall ",
23          " apiVersion ":" 20130630 ",
24          " recipientAccountId ":" 444455556666"
25      }]
26  }
```

Maintaining Your Gateway

Maintaining your gateway includes tasks such as configuring cache storage and upload buffer space, and doing general maintenance your gateway's performance. These tasks are common to all gateway types. If you haven't created a gateway, see Creating Your Gateway.

Topics

- Shutting Down Your Gateway VM
- Managing Local Disks for Your AWS Storage Gateway
- Optimizing Gateway Performance
- Managing Bandwidth for Your Gateway
- Managing Gateway Updates Using the AWS Storage Gateway Console
- Performing Maintenance Tasks on the Local Console
- Deleting Your Gateway by Using the AWS Storage Gateway Console and Removing Associated Resources

Shutting Down Your Gateway VM

You might need to shutdown or reboot your VM for maintenance, such as when applying a patch to your hypervisor. Before you shutdown the VM, you must first stop the gateway. For file gateway, you just shutdown your VM. Although this section focuses on starting and stopping your gateway using the AWS Storage Gateway Management Console, you can also and stop your gateway by using your VM local console or AWS Storage Gateway API. When you power on your VM, remember to restart your gateway.

- Gateway VM local console—see Logging in to the Local Console Using Default Credentials.
- AWS Storage Gateway API—-see ShutdownGateway

Note
If you stop your gateway while your backup software is writing or reading from a tape, the write or read task might not succeed. Before you stop your gateway, you should check your backup software and the backup schedule for any tasks in progress.

For file gateway, you simply shutdown your VM. You don't shutdown the gateway.

Starting and Stopping a Volume or Tape Gateway

The following instructions apply to volume and tape gateways only.

To stop a volume or tape gateway

1. Open the AWS Storage Gateway console at https://console.aws.amazon.com/storagegateway/home.

2. In the navigation pane, choose **Gateways**, and then choose the gateway to stop. The status of the gateway is **Running**.

3. On the **Actions** menu, choose **Stop gateway** and verify the id of the gateway from the dialog box, and then choose **Stop gateway**.

   While the gateway is stopping, you might see a message that indicates the status of the gateway. When the gateway shuts down, a message and a **Start gateway** button appears in the **Details** tab.

When you stop your gateway, the storage resources will not be accessible until you start your storage. If the gateway was uploading data when it was stopped, the upload will resume when you start the gateway.

To start a volume or tape gateway

1. Open the AWS Storage Gateway console at https://console.aws.amazon.com/storagegateway/home.

2. In the navigation pane, choose **Gateways** and then choose the gateway to start. The status of the gateway is **Shutdown**.

3. Choose **Details**. and then choose **Start gateway**.

Managing Local Disks for Your AWS Storage Gateway

The gateway virtual machine (VM) uses the local disks that you allocate on-premises for buffering and storage. For cached volumes and tape gateways, you allocate two disks, one disk for the upload buffer and the other for cache storage. For stored volumes, you allocate one disk for the upload buffer.

Important
When adding cache or upload buffer to an existing gateway, it is important to create new disks in your host (hypervisor or Amazon EC2 instance). Don't change the size of existing disks if the disks have been previously allocated as either a cache or upload buffer. Do not remove cache disks that have been allocated as cache storage.

Topics

- Deciding the Amount of Local Disk Storage
- Configuring Local Storage for Your Gateway
- Adding and Removing Upload Buffer
- Adding Cache Storage

Deciding the Amount of Local Disk Storage

In this step, you decide the number and size of disks to allocate for your gateway. Depending on the storage solution you deploy (see Plan Your Storage Gateway Deployment), the gateway requires the following additional storage:

- File gateways require at least one disk to use as a cache.
- Volume gateways:
  - Stored gateways require at least one disk to use as an upload buffer.
  - Cached gateways require at least two disks. One to use as a cache, and one to use as an upload buffer.
- Tape gateways require at least two disks. One to use as a cache, and one to use as an upload buffer.

For information about recommended disk sizes, see Recommended Local Disk Sizes For Your Gateway. If you plan to deploy your gateway in production, you should consider your real workload in determining disk sizes. For information about disk size guidelines, see Adding and Removing Upload Buffer and Adding Cache Storage.

For more information about how gateways use local storage, see How AWS Storage Gateway Works (Architecture). In the next step, you allocate the local disk storage to the gateway VM you deployed.

The following table recommends sizes for local disk storage for your deployed gateway. Before going to the next step, decide the number and size of disks to allocate. You can add more local storage after you set the gateway up, and as your workload demands.

Local Storage	Description	Gateway Type
Upload buffer	The upload buffer provides a staging area for the data before the gateway uploads the data to Amazon S3. Your gateway uploads this buffer data over an encrypted Secure Sockets Layer (SSL) connection to AWS.	[See the AWS documentation website for more details]

197

Local Storage	Description	Gateway Type
Cache storage	The cache storage acts as the on-premises durable store for data that is pending upload to Amazon S3 from the upload buffer. When your application performs I/O on a volume or tape, the gateway saves the data to the cache storage for low-latency access. When your application requests data from a volume or tape, the gateway first checks the cache storage for the data before downloading the data from AWS.	[See the AWS documentation website for more details]

Note
When you provision disks, we strongly recommend that you do not provision local disks for the upload buffer and cache storage that use the same underlying physical storage resource (that is, the same disk). Underlying physical storage resources are represented as a data store in VMware. When you deploy the gateway VM, you choose a data store on which to store the VM files. When you provision a local disk (for example, to use as cache storage or upload buffer), you have the option to store the virtual disk in the same data store as the VM or a different data store.

If you have more than one data store, we strongly recommend that you choose one data store for the cache storage and another for the upload buffer. A data store that is backed by only one underlying physical disk, or that is backed by a less-performant RAID configuration such as RAID 1, can lead to poor performance in some situations when used to back both the cache storage and upload buffer.

After the initial configuration and deployment of your gateway, you might find that you need to adjust the local storage by adding or removing disks for an upload buffer or adding disks for cache storage.

Configuring Local Storage for Your Gateway

When you created your gateway, you allocated disks for your gateway to use as upload buffer or cache storage. The upload buffer and cache storage are created from local disks you provisioned for your gateway VM when you first created your gateway. After your gateway is up and running, you might decide to configure additional upload buffer or cache storage for your gateway. You use the suggested sizing formula in deciding the disk sizes. For more information on sizing storage, see Adding and Removing Upload Buffer or Adding Cache Storage. If you are configuring local storage for the first time, see Configuring Local Disks for instructions.

Important
When adding cache or upload buffer to an existing gateway, it is important to create new disks in your host (hypervisor or Amazon EC2 instance). Don't change the size of existing disks if the disks have been previously allocated as either a cache or upload buffer. Do not remove cache disks that have been allocated as cache storage.

Configuring an Upload Buffer or Cache Storage

After your gateway is activated, you might need to add additional disks and configure them as local storage. The following procedure shows you how to configure an upload buffer or cache storage for your gateway.

To configure upload buffer or cache storage

1. Open the AWS Storage Gateway console at https://console.aws.amazon.com/storagegateway/home.

2. In the navigation pane, choose **Gateways**.

3. In the **Actions** menu, choose **Edit local disks**.

4. In the Edit local disks dialog box, identify the disks you provisioned and decide which one you want to use for upload buffer or cached storage. **Note**
For stored volumes, only the upload buffer is displayed because stored volumes have no cache disks.

5. In the drop-down list box, in the **Allocate to** column, choose **Upload Buffer** for the disk to use as upload buffer.

6. For gateways created with cached volumes and tape gateway, choose **Cache** for the disk you want to use as a cache storage.

   If you don't see your disks, choose the **Refresh** button.

7. Choose **Save** to save your configuration settings.

For stored volumes, you configure one of the two disks for use by your application's data and the other disk as an upload buffer.

Adding and Removing Upload Buffer

After you configure your initial gateway, you can allocate and configure additional upload buffer capacity or reduce the capacity as your application needs change. To learn more about how to size your upload buffer based on your application needs, see Sizing the Upload Buffer.

Topics

- Adding Upload Buffer Capacity
- Removing Upload Buffer Capacity
- Sizing the Upload Buffer

Adding Upload Buffer Capacity

As your application needs change and you add more volume capacity, you might need to increase the gateway's upload buffer capacity as well. You can add more buffer capacity to your gateway without interrupting existing gateway functions. Note that when you add more upload buffer capacity, you do so with the gateway VM turned on. However, when you reduce the amount of upload buffer capacity, you must first turn off the VM. You can add more upload buffer capacity by using the Storage Gateway console or the Storage Gateway API:

- For information on adding buffer capacity with the console, see To configure upload buffer or cache storage . This procedure assumes that your gateway has at least one local disk available on its VM that you can allocate as an upload buffer to the gateway.
- For information on adding buffer capacity with the API, see AddUploadBuffer.

Removing Upload Buffer Capacity

As your application needs change and you change the volume configuration for a gateway, you might need to decrease the gateway's upload buffer capacity. Or, a local disk allocated as upload buffer space might fail and you might need to remove that disk from your upload buffer and assign a new local disk. In both cases, you can remove buffer capacity using the Storage Gateway console.

The following procedure assumes that your activated gateway has at least one local disk allocated as an upload buffer for the gateway. In the procedure, you start on the Storage Gateway console, leave the console and use the VMware vSphere client or the Microsoft Hyper-V Manager to remove the disk, and then return to the console.

To find the ID of a disk allocated as an upload buffer

1. Open the AWS Storage Gateway console at https://console.aws.amazon.com/storagegateway/home.

2. In the navigation pane, choose **Gateways**.

3. On the **Actions** menu, choose **Edit local Disks**.

4. In the **Edit local disks** dialog box, note the value of the virtual device node for the local disk to be removed. You can find the node value in the **Disk ID** column.

   You use the disk's virtual device node in the vSphere client to help ensure that you remove the correct disk.

5. Stop the gateway by following the steps in the Shutting Down Your Gateway VM procedure. **Note** Before you stop the gateway, ensure that no application is writing data to it and that no snapshots are in progress. You can check the snapshot schedule of volumes on the **Snapshot Schedules** tab of the Storage Gateway console. For more information, see Editing a Snapshot Schedule.

6. To remove the underlying local disk, do one of the following procedures. [See the AWS documentation website for more details]

7. On the Storage Gateway console, turn on the gateway. **Important** After removing a disk used as an upload buffer, you must turn the gateway back on before adding new disks to the VM.

   After a gateway restart, a storage volume might go through the PASS THROUGH and BOOTSTRAPPING states as the gateway adjusts to the upload buffer disk that you removed. A volume that passes through these two states will eventually come to the ACTIVE state. You can use a volume during the PASS THROUGH and BOOTSTRAPPING states. However, you cannot take snapshots of the volume in these states. You can monitor your volume status in the **Volumes** tab on the Storage Gateway console.

Sizing the Upload Buffer

You can determine the size of your upload buffer by using an upload buffer formula. We strongly recommend that you allocate at least 150 GiB of upload buffer. If the formula returns a value less than 150 GiB, use 150 GiB as the amount you allocate to the upload buffer. You can configure up to 2 TiB of upload buffer capacity for each gateway.

Note
For volume gateways, when the upload buffer reaches its capacity, your volume goes to PASS THROUGH status. In this status, new data that your application writes is persisted locally but not uploaded to AWS immediately. Thus, you cannot take new snapshots. When the upload buffer capacity frees up, the volume goes through BOOTSTRAPPING status. In this status, any new data that was persisted locally is uploaded to AWS. Finally, the volume returns to ACTIVE status. Storage Gateway then resumes normal synchronization of the data stored locally with the copy stored in AWS, and you can start taking new snapshots. For more information about volume status, see Understanding Volume Status.
For tape gateways, when the upload buffer reaches its capacity, your applications can continue to read from and write data to your storage volumes. However, the tape gateway does not write any of your volume data to its upload buffer and does not upload any of this data to AWS until Storage Gateway synchronizes the data stored locally with the copy of the data stored in AWS. This synchronization occurs when the volumes are in BOOTSTRAPPING status.

To estimate the amount of upload buffer, you can determine the expected incoming and outgoing data rates and plug them into the following formula.

Rate of incoming data
This rate refers to the application throughput, the rate at which your on-premises applications write data to your gateway over some period of time.

Rate of outgoing data
This rate refers to the network throughput, the rate at which your gateway is able to upload data to AWS. This rate depends on your network speed, utilization, and whether you've enabled bandwidth throttling. This rate

should be adjusted for compression. When uploading data to AWS, the gateway applies data compression where possible. For example, if your application data is text-only, you might get an effective compression ratio of about 2:1. However, if you are writing videos, the gateway might not be able to achieve any data compression and might require more upload buffer for the gateway.

If your incoming rate is higher than the outgoing rate, or if the formula returns a value less than 150 GiB, we strongly recommend that you allocate at least 150 GiB of upload buffer space.

$$\left(\begin{array}{c} \text{Application} \\ \text{Throughput} \\ \text{(MB/s)} \end{array} - \begin{array}{c} \text{Network} \\ \text{Throughput} \\ \text{to AWS (MB/s)} \end{array} \times \begin{array}{c} \text{Compression} \\ \text{Factor} \end{array}\right) \times \begin{array}{c} \text{Duration} \\ \text{of writes} \\ \text{(s)} \end{array} = \begin{array}{c} \text{Upload} \\ \text{Buffer} \\ \text{(MB)} \end{array}$$

For example, assume that your business applications write text data to your gateway at a rate of 40 MB a second for 12 hours a day and your network throughput is 12 MB a second. Assuming a compression factor of 2:1 for the text data, you need to allocate approximately 690 GiB of space for the upload buffer.

Example

1. 1. ((40 MB/sec) - (12 MB/sec * 2)) * (12 hours * 3600 seconds/hour) = 691200 megabytes

Note that you can initially use this approximation to determine the disk size that you want to allocate to the gateway as upload buffer space. Add more upload buffer space as needed using the Storage Gateway console. Also, you can use the Amazon CloudWatch operational metrics to monitor upload buffer usage and determine additional storage requirements. For information on metrics and setting the alarms, see Monitoring the Upload Buffer.

If you decide that you need to change your upload buffer capacity, take one of the following actions.

To	Do This
Add more upload buffer capacity to your gateway.	Follow the steps in Adding Upload Buffer Capacity.
Remove a disk allocated as upload buffer space.	Follow the steps in Removing Upload Buffer Capacity.

Adding Cache Storage

The cache storage acts as the on-premises durable store for data that is pending upload to Amazon S3 from the upload buffer.

Important
Gateways created with stored volumes don't require cache storage.

Important
When adding cache or upload buffer to an existing gateway, it is important to create new disks in your host (hypervisor or Amazon EC2 instance). Don't change the size of existing disks if the disks have been previously allocated as either a cache or upload buffer. Do not remove cache disks that have been allocated as cache storage.

Topics

- Sizing Cache Storage
- Adding Cache Storage for Your Gateway

The following diagram highlights the cache storage in the larger picture of the cached volumes architecture. For more information, see How AWS Storage Gateway Works (Architecture).

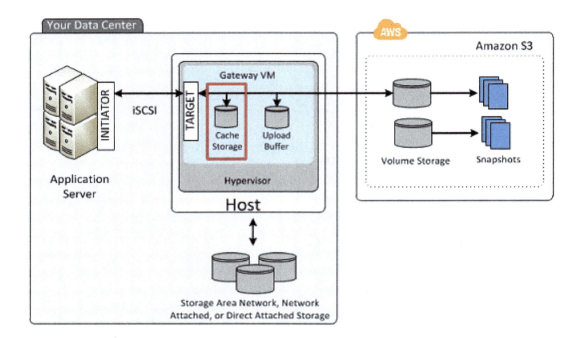

The following diagram highlights the cache storage in the larger picture of the tape gateway architecture. For more information, see How AWS Storage Gateway Works (Architecture).

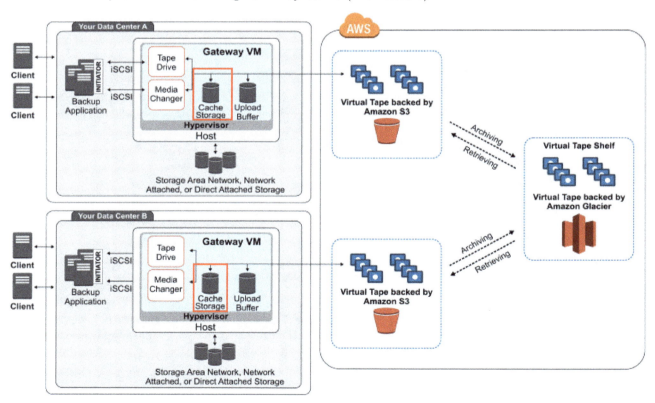

The amount of cache storage your gateway requires depends on how much of your application data you want to provide low-latency access to. The cache storage must be at least the size of the upload buffer. This guideline helps ensure that the cache storage is large enough to persistently hold all data that has not yet been uploaded to Amazon S3. When your cache storage has filled up with dirty data (that is, data that has not been uploaded to AWS), application write operations to your volumes or tapes are blocked until more cache storage becomes available. However, application read operations from the volume or tapes are still allowed.

Here are some guidelines you can follow to help ensure you have adequate cache storage allocated for your gateway.

- **Use the sizing formula.** – As your application needs change, you should periodically review the recommended formula for sizing cache storage. For more information, see Sizing Cache Storage.
- **Use Amazon CloudWatch metrics.** – You can proactively avoid filling up cache storage with dirty data by monitoring how cache storage is being used—particularly, by reviewing cache misses. CloudWatch provides usage metrics such as the `CachePercentDirty` and `CacheHitPercent` metrics for monitoring how much of the gateway's cache storage has not been uploaded to Amazon S3. You can set an alarm to trigger a notification to you when the percentage of the cache that is dirty exceeds a threshold or the cache hit percentage falls below a threshold. Both of these can indicate that the cache storage size is not adequate for the gateway. For a full list of Storage Gateway metrics, see Monitoring Your Gateway and Resources.

Sizing Cache Storage

Your gateway uses its cache storage to provide low-latency access to your recently accessed data. The cache storage acts as the on-premises durable store for data that is pending upload to Amazon S3 from the upload buffer. Generally speaking, you size the cache storage at 1.1 times the upload buffer size. For more information about how to estimate your cache storage size, see Sizing the Upload Buffer.

You can initially use this approximation to provision disks for the cache storage. You can then use Amazon CloudWatch operational metrics to monitor the cache storage usage and provision more storage as needed using the console. For information on using the metrics and setting up alarms, see Monitoring Cache Storage.

If you decide that you need to increase your gateway's cache storage capacity, follow the steps in Adding Cache Storage for Your Gateway.

Adding Cache Storage for Your Gateway

After you configure your initial gateway cache storage as described in Configuring an Upload Buffer or Cache Storage, you can add cache storage to your gateway as your application needs change. To learn more about how to size your cache storage based on your application needs, see Adding Cache Storage.

You can add more cache storage to your gateway without interrupting existing gateway functions and with the gateway VM turned on.

You can add more cache storage by using the Storage Gateway console or the Storage Gateway API:

- For information on adding cache storage using the console, To configure upload buffer or cache storage . This procedure assumes that your activated gateway has at least one local disk available on its VM that you can allocate as cache storage for the gateway. Don't remove cache disks that have been allocated as cache storage.
- For information on adding cache storage by using the API, see AddCache.

Optimizing Gateway Performance

You can find information following about how to optimize the performance of your gateway. The guidance is based on adding resources to your gateway and adding resources to your application server.

Add Resources to Your Gateway

Use higher-performance disks

To optimize gateway performance, you can add high performance disks such as solid-state drives (SSDs) and a NVMe controller. You can also attach virtual disks to your VM directly from a storage area network (SAN) instead of the Microsoft Hyper-V NTFS. Improved disk performance generally results in better throughput and more input/output operations per second (IOPS). To measure throughput, use the `ReadBytes` and `WriteBytes` metrics with the `Samples` Amazon CloudWatch statistic. For example, the `Samples` statistic of the `ReadBytes` metric over a sample period of 5 minutes divided by 300 seconds gives you the IOPS. As a general rule, when you review these metrics for a gateway, look for low throughput and low IOPS trends to indicate disk-related bottlenecks. For more information about gateway metrics, see Measuring Performance Between Your Tape Gateway and AWS.

CloudWatch metrics are not available for all gateways. For information about gateway metrics, see Monitoring Your Gateway and Resources

Add CPU resources to your gateway host

The minimum requirement for a gateway host server is four virtual processors. To optimize gateway performance, you should confirm that the four virtual processors that are assigned to the gateway VM are backed by four cores and that you are not oversubscribing the CPUs of the host server. When you add additional CPUs to your gateway host server, you increase the processing capability of the gateway to deal with, in parallel, both storing data from your application to your local storage and uploading this data to Amazon S3. Additional CPUs also help ensure that your gateway gets enough CPU resources when the host is shared with other VMs. Providing enough CPU resources has the general effect of improving throughput.

AWS Storage Gateway supports using 24 CPUs in your gateway host server. You can use 24 CPUs to significantly improve the performance of your gateway. We recommend the following gateway configuration for your gateway host server:

- 24 CPUs
- 16 GiB of reserved RAM
- Disk 1 attached to paravirtual controller 1, to be used as the gateway cache as follows:
  - SSD using an NVMe controller
- Disk 2 attached to paravirtual controller 1, to be used as the gateway upload buffer as follows:
  - SSD using an NVMe controller
- Disk 3 attached to paravirtual controller 2, to be used as the gateway upload buffer as follows:
  - SSD using an NVMe controller
- Network adapter 1 configured on VM network 1:
  - Use VM network 1 and add VMXnet3 (10 Gbps) to be used for ingestion
- Network adapter 2 configured on VM network 2:
  - Use VM network 2 and add a VMXnet3 (10 Gbps) to be used to connect to AWS

Back gateway virtual disks with separate physical disks

When you provision disks in a gateway setup, we strongly recommend that you do not provision local disks for the upload buffer and cache storage that use the same underlying physical storage disk. For example, for VMware ESXi, the underlying physical storage resources are represented as a data store. When you deploy the gateway VM, you choose a data store on which to store the VM files. When you provision a virtual disk (for example, to use as an upload buffer), you have the option to store the virtual disk in the same data store as the VM or a different data store. If you have more than one data store, then we strongly recommend that you choose one data store for each type of local storage you are creating. A data store that is backed by only one underlying physical disk, or that is backed by a less-performant RAID configuration such as RAID 1, can lead to poor performance—for example, when used to back both the cache storage and upload buffer in a gateway setup.

Change the volumes configuration

For volumes gateways, if you find that adding more volumes to a gateway reduces the throughput to the gateway, consider adding the volumes to a separate gateway. In particular, if a volume is used for a high-throughput application, consider creating a separate gateway for the high-throughput application. However, as a general rule, you should not use one gateway for all of your high-throughput applications and another gateway for all of your low-throughput applications. To measure your volume throughput, use the `ReadBytes` and `WriteBytes` metrics. For more information on these metrics, see Measuring Performance Between Your Application and Gateway.

Use a Larger Block Size for Tape Drives

For tape gateway, the default block size for a tape drive is 64 KB but you can increase the block size to improve I/O performance. We recommend setting the block size of the tape drives in the your backup software to either 128 KB or 256 KB or 512 KB. The size you choose depends on the block size limitations of your backup software. For more information, see the documentation for your backup software.

Add Resources to Your Application Environment

Increase the bandwidth between your application server and your gateway

To optimize gateway performance, ensure that the network bandwidth between your application and the gateway can sustain your application needs. You can use the `ReadBytes` and `WriteBytes` metrics of the gateway to measure the total data throughput (for more information on these metrics, see Measuring Performance Between Your Tape Gateway and AWS). For your application, compare the measured throughput with the desired throughput. If the measured throughput is less than the desired throughput, then increasing the bandwidth between your application and gateway can improve performance if the network is the bottleneck. Similarly, you can increase the bandwidth between your VM and your local disks, if they're not direct-attached.

Add CPU resources to your application environment

If your application can make use of additional CPU resources, then adding more CPUs can help your application to scale its I/O load.

Managing Bandwidth for Your Gateway

You can limit (or throttle) the upload throughput from the gateway to AWS or the download throughput from your AWS to your gateway. Using bandwidth throttling helps you to control the amount of network bandwidth used by your gateway. By default, an activated gateway has no rate limits on upload or download.

You can specify the rate limit by using the AWS Management Console, or programmatically by using either the AWS Storage Gateway API (see UpdateBandwidthRateLimit) or an AWS Software Development Kit (SDK). By throttling bandwidth programmatically, you can change limits automatically throughout the day**—**for example, by scheduling tasks to change the bandwidth. As described directly following, you can change these limits by using the AWS Storage Gateway console. Or, for information about changing bandwidth rate limits programmatically, see the following topics.

Topics

- Updating Gateway Bandwidth Rate Limits Using the AWS SDK for Java
- Updating Gateway Bandwidth Rate Limits Using the AWS SDK for .NET
- Updating Gateway Bandwidth Rate Limits Using the AWS Tools for Windows PowerShell

Note

Configuring bandwidth rate limit is currently not supported in the file gateway type.

To change a gateway's bandwidth throttling using the console

1. Open the AWS Storage Gateway console at https://console.aws.amazon.com/storagegateway/home.

2. In the navigation pane, choose **Gateways**, and then choose the gateway you want to manage.

3. On the **Actions** menu, choose **Edit Bandwidth Rate Limit**.

4. In the **Edit Rate Limits** dialog box, type new limit values, and then choose **Save**. Your changes appear in the **Details** tab for your gateway.

Updating Gateway Bandwidth Rate Limits Using the AWS SDK for Java

By updating bandwidth rate limits programmatically, you can adjust limits automatically over a period of time—for example, by using scheduled tasks. The following example demonstrates how to update a gateway's bandwidth rate limits using the AWS SDK for Java. To use the example code, you should be familiar with running a Java console application. For more information, see Getting Started in the *AWS SDK for Java Developer Guide*.

Example : Updating Gateway Bandwidth Limits Using the AWS SDK for Java

The following Java code example updates a gateway's bandwidth rate limits. You need to update the code and provide the service endpoint, your gateway Amazon Resource Name (ARN), and the upload and download limits. For a list of AWS service endpoints you can use with AWS Storage Gateway, see Regions and Endpoints in the *AWS General Reference*.

```
1  import java.io.IOException;
2
3  import com.amazonaws.AmazonClientException;
4  import com.amazonaws.auth.PropertiesCredentials;
5  import com.amazonaws.services.storagegateway.AWSStorageGatewayClient;
6  import com.amazonaws.services.storagegateway.model.UpdateBandwidthRateLimitRequest;
7  import com.amazonaws.services.storagegateway.model.UpdateBandwidthRateLimitResult;
8
9
10 public class UpdateBandwidthExample {
11
```

```
12      public static AWSStorageGatewayClient sgClient;
13
14      // The gatewayARN
15      public static String gatewayARN = "*** provide gateway ARN ***";
16
17      // The endpoint
18      static String serviceURL = "https://storagegateway.us-east-1.amazonaws.com";
19
20      // Rates
21      static long uploadRate = 51200;   // Bits per second, minimum 51200
22      static long downloadRate = 102400;    // Bits per second, minimum 102400
23
24      public static void main(String[] args) throws IOException {
25
26          // Create a storage gateway client
27          sgClient = new AWSStorageGatewayClient(new PropertiesCredentials(
28                  ListDeleteVolumeSnapshotsExample.class.getResourceAsStream("AwsCredentials.
                        properties")));
29          sgClient.setEndpoint(serviceURL);
30
31          UpdateBandwidth(gatewayARN, uploadRate, downloadRate);
32
33      }
34
35      private static void UpdateBandwidth(String gatewayARN2, long uploadRate2,
36              long downloadRate2) {
37          try
38          {
39              UpdateBandwidthRateLimitRequest updateBandwidthRateLimitRequest =
40                  new UpdateBandwidthRateLimitRequest()
41                  .withGatewayARN(gatewayARN)
42                  .withAverageDownloadRateLimitInBitsPerSec(downloadRate)
43                  .withAverageUploadRateLimitInBitsPerSec(uploadRate);
44
45              UpdateBandwidthRateLimitResult updateBandwidthRateLimitResult = sgClient.
                    updateBandwidthRateLimit(updateBandwidthRateLimitRequest);
46              String returnGatewayARN = updateBandwidthRateLimitResult.getGatewayARN();
47              System.out.println("Updated the bandwidth rate limits of " + returnGatewayARN);
48              System.out.println("Upload bandwidth limit = " + uploadRate + " bits per second");
49              System.out.println("Download bandwidth limit = " + downloadRate + " bits per second
                    ");
50          }
51          catch (AmazonClientException ex)
52          {
53              System.err.println("Error updating gateway bandwith.\n" + ex.toString());
54          }
55      }
56 }
```

Updating Gateway Bandwidth Rate Limits Using the AWS SDK for .NET

By updating bandwidth rate limits programmatically, you can adjust limits automatically over a period of time—for example, by using scheduled tasks. The following example demonstrates how to update a gateway's bandwidth rate limits by using the AWS Software Development Kit (SDK) for .NET. To use the example code, you should be familiar with running a .NET console application. For more information, see Getting Started in the *AWS SDK for .NET Developer Guide*.

Example : Updating Gateway Bandwidth Limits by Using the AWS SDK for .NET
The following C# code example updates a gateway's bandwidth rate limits. You need to update the code and provide the service endpoint, your gateway Amazon Resource Name (ARN), and the upload and download limits. For a list of AWS service endpoints you can use with AWS Storage Gateway, see Regions and Endpoints in the *AWS General Reference*.

```csharp
using System;
using System.Collections.Generic;
using System.Linq;
using System.Text;
using Amazon.StorageGateway;
using Amazon.StorageGateway.Model;

namespace AWSStorageGateway
{
    class UpdateBandwidthExample
    {
        static AmazonStorageGatewayClient sgClient;
        static AmazonStorageGatewayConfig sgConfig;

        // The gatewayARN
        public static String gatewayARN = "*** provide gateway ARN ***";

        // The endpoint
        static String serviceURL = "https://storagegateway.us-east-1.amazonaws.com";

        // Rates
        static long uploadRate = 51200;   // Bits per second, minimum 51200
        static long downloadRate = 102400;    // Bits per second, minimum 102400

        public static void Main(string[] args)
        {
            // Create a storage gateway client
            sgConfig = new AmazonStorageGatewayConfig();
            sgConfig.ServiceURL = serviceURL;
            sgClient = new AmazonStorageGatewayClient(sgConfig);

            UpdateBandwidth(gatewayARN, uploadRate, downloadRate);

            Console.WriteLine("\nTo continue, press Enter.");
            Console.Read();
        }

        public static void UpdateBandwidth(string gatewayARN, long uploadRate, long downloadRate
            )
        {
            try
            {
                UpdateBandwidthRateLimitRequest updateBandwidthRateLimitRequest =
                    new UpdateBandwidthRateLimitRequest()
                    .WithGatewayARN(gatewayARN)
                    .WithAverageDownloadRateLimitInBitsPerSec(downloadRate)
```

```
46              .WithAverageUploadRateLimitInBitsPerSec(uploadRate);
47
48          UpdateBandwidthRateLimitResponse updateBandwidthRateLimitResponse = sgClient.
                UpdateBandwidthRateLimit(updateBandwidthRateLimitRequest);
49          String returnGatewayARN = updateBandwidthRateLimitResponse.
                UpdateBandwidthRateLimitResult.GatewayARN;
50          Console.WriteLine("Updated the bandwidth rate limits of " + returnGatewayARN);
51          Console.WriteLine("Upload bandwidth limit = " + uploadRate + " bits per second")
                ;
52          Console.WriteLine("Download bandwidth limit = " + downloadRate + " bits per
                second");
53      }
54      catch (AmazonStorageGatewayException ex)
55      {
56          Console.WriteLine("Error updating gateway bandwith.\n" + ex.ToString());
57      }
58   }
59 }
60 }
```

Updating Gateway Bandwidth Rate Limits Using the AWS Tools for Windows PowerShell

By updating bandwidth rate limits programmatically, you can adjust limits automatically over a period of time—for example, by using scheduled tasks. The following example demonstrates how to update a gateway's bandwidth rate limits using the AWS Tools for Windows PowerShell. To use the example code, you should be familiar with running a PowerShell script. For more information, see Getting Started in the *AWS Tools for Windows PowerShell User Guide*.

Example : Updating Gateway Bandwidth Limits by Using the AWS Tools for Windows PowerShell

The following PowerShell script example updates a gateway's bandwidth rate limits. You need to update the script and provide your gateway Amazon Resource Name (ARN), and the upload and download limits.

```
1 <#
2 .DESCRIPTION
3     Update Gateway bandwidth limits.
4
5 .NOTES
6     PREREQUISITES:
7     1) AWS Tools for PowerShell from http://aws.amazon.com/powershell/
8     2) Credentials and region stored in session using Initialize-AWSDefault.
9     For more info see, http://docs.aws.amazon.com/powershell/latest/userguide/specifying-your-
            aws-credentials.html
10
11 .EXAMPLE
12     powershell.exe .\SG_UpdateBandwidth.ps1
13 #>
14
15 $UploadBandwidthRate = 51200
16 $DownloadBandwidthRate = 102400
17 $gatewayARN = "*** provide gateway ARN ***"
18
19 #Update Bandwidth Rate Limits
```

```
20 Update-SGBandwidthRateLimit -GatewayARN $gatewayARN `
21                             -AverageUploadRateLimitInBitsPerSec $UploadBandwidthRate `
22                             -AverageDownloadRateLimitInBitsPerSec $DownloadBandwidthRate
23
24 $limits =  Get-SGBandwidthRateLimit -GatewayARN $gatewayARN
25
26 Write-Output("`nGateway: " + $gatewayARN);
27 Write-Output("`nNew Upload Rate: " + $limits.AverageUploadRateLimitInBitsPerSec)
28 Write-Output("`nNew Download Rate: " + $limits.AverageDownloadRateLimitInBitsPerSec)
```

Managing Gateway Updates Using the AWS Storage Gateway Console

AWS Storage Gateway periodically releases important software updates for your gateway. You can either manually apply updates on the AWS Storage Gateway Management Console or the updates will be automatically applied during the configured weekly maintenance time. Although Storage Gateway checks for updates every week, it will only go through maintenance and restart if there are updates. Before any update is applied to your gateway, AWS notifies you with a message on the AWS Storage Gateway Console and your AWS Personal Health Dashboard. For more information, see AWS Personal Health Dashboard. The VM will not reboot, but the gateway will be unavailable for a short period while it is being updated and restarted.

When you deploy and activate your gateway, a default weekly maintenance schedule is set. You can modify the maintenance schedule at any time. When updates are available, the **Details** tab displays a maintenance message and an **Apply update now** button. You can see the date and time that the last successful update was applied to your gateway on the **Details** tab.

Important
You can minimize the chance of any disruption to your applications due to the gateway restart by increasing the timeouts of your iSCSI initiator. For more information about increasing iSCSI initiator timeouts for Windows and Linux, see Customizing Your Windows iSCSI Settings and Customizing Your Linux iSCSI Settings.

To modify the maintenance schedule

1. On the navigation menu, choose **Gateways**, and choose the gateway you want to modify the update schedule for.

2. On the **Actions** menu, choose **Edit maintenance window**.

3. Modify the values for **Day of the week** and **Time**. Your changes appear in the **Details** tab for the gateway.

Performing Maintenance Tasks on the Local Console

You can perform the following maintenance tasks using the host's local console. Local console tasks can be performed on the VM host or the Amazon EC2 instance. Many of the task are common to the hosts but there are also some differences.

Topics

- Performing Maintenance Tasks on the VMware Local Console
- Performing Maintenance Tasks on the Hyper V Local Console
- Performing Common Maintenance Tasks on the VM Local Console
- Performing Maintenance Tasks on the Amazon EC2 Gateway Local Console

Performing Maintenance Tasks on the VMware Local Console

For a gateway deployed on-premises, you can perform the following maintenance tasks using the VMware host local console.

Topics

- Accessing the Gateway Local Console with VMware ESXi
- Configuring Your Gateway for Multiple NICs in a VMware ESXi Host

Accessing the Gateway Local Console with VMware ESXi

To access your gateway's local console with VMware ESXi

1. In the VMware vSphere client, select your gateway VM.

2. Ensure that the gateway is turned on. **Note**
   If your gateway VM is turned on, a green arrow icon appears with the VM icon, as shown in the following screenshot. If your gateway VM is not turned on, you can turn it on by choosing the green **Power On** icon on the **Toolbar** menu.

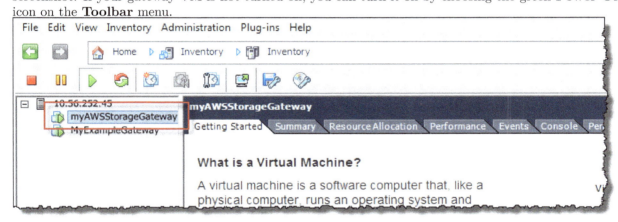

3. Choose the **Console** tab.

4. After a few moments, the VM is ready for you to log in. **Note**
   To release the cursor from the console window, press **Ctrl+Alt**.

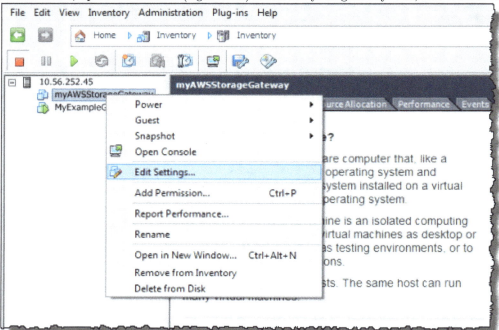

```
AWS Storage Gateway

Login to change your network configuration and other gateway settings.

For more information, please see:
https://docs.aws.amazon.com/console/storagegateway/LocalConsole

localhost login: _
```

5. To log in using the default credentials, continue to the procedure Logging in to the Local Console Using Default Credentials.

Configuring Your Gateway for Multiple NICs in a VMware ESXi Host

The following procedure assumes that your gateway VM already has one network adapter defined and that you are adding a second adapter. The following procedure shows how to add an adapter for VMware ESXi.

To configure your gateway to use an additional network adapter in VMware ESXi host

1. Shut down the gateway. For instructions, see To stop a volume or tape gateway.

2. In the VMware vSphere client, select your gateway VM.

   The VM can remain turned on for this procedure.

3. In the client, open the context (right-click) menu for your gateway VM, and choose **Edit Settings**.

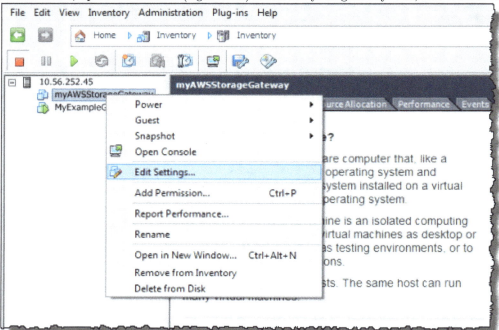

4. On the **Hardware** tab of the **Virtual Machine Properties** dialog box, choose **Add** to add a device.

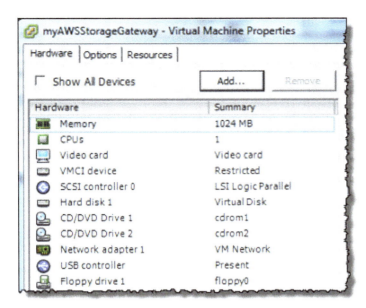

5. Follow the Add Hardware wizard to add a network adapter.

   1. In the **Device Type** pane, choose **Ethernet Adapter** to add an adapter, and then choose **Next**.

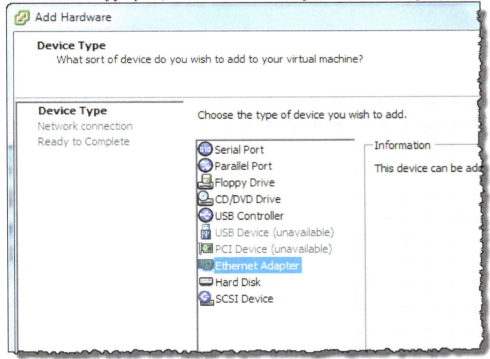

   2. In the **Network Type** pane, ensure that **Connect at power on** is selected for **Type**, and then choose **Next**.

      We recommend that you use the E1000 network adapter with Storage Gateway. For more information on the adapter types that might appear in the adapter list, see Network Adapter Types in the ESXi and vCenter Server Documentation.

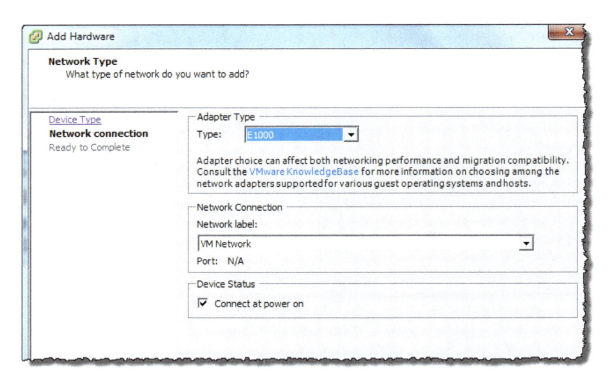

3. In the **Ready to Complete** pane, review the information, and then choose **Finish**.

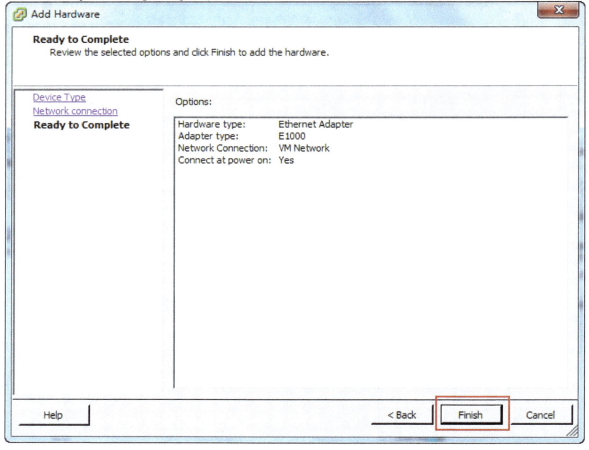

6. Choose the **Summary** tab of the VM, and choose **View All** next to the **IP Address** box. A **Virtual**

Machine IP Addresses window displays all the IP addresses you can use to access the gateway. Confirm that a second IP address is listed for the gateway. **Note**

It might take several moments for the adapter changes to take effect and the VM summary information to refresh.

The following image is for illustration only. In practice, one of the IP addresses will be the address by which the gateway communicates to AWS and the other will be an address in a different subnet.

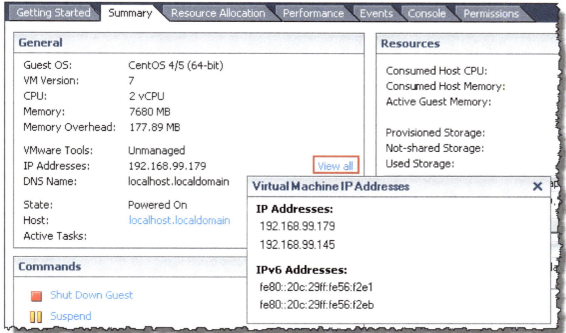

7. On the Storage Gateway console, turn on the gateway. For instructions, see To start a volume or tape gateway.

8. In the **Navigation** pane of the Storage Gateway console, choose **Gateways** and choose the gateway to which you added the adapter. Confirm that the second IP address is listed in the **Details** tab.

For information about local console tasks common to VMware and Hyper-V host, see Performing Common Maintenance Tasks on the VM Local Console

Performing Maintenance Tasks on the Hyper V Local Console

For a gateway deployed on-premises, you can perform the following maintenance tasks using the Hyper V host local console.

Topics

- Access the Gateway Local Console with Microsoft Hyper-V
- Synchronizing Your Gateway VM Time
- Configuring Your Gateway for Multiple NICs in Microsoft Hyper-V Host

Access the Gateway Local Console with Microsoft Hyper-V

To access your gateway's local console (Microsoft Hyper-V)

1. In the **Virtual Machines** list of the Microsoft Hyper-V Manager, select your gateway VM.

2. Ensure the gateway is turned on. **Note**
   If your gateway VM is turned on, `Running` is displayed as the **State** of the VM, as shown in the following screenshot. If your gateway VM is not turned on, you can turn it on by choosing **Start** in the **Actions** pane.

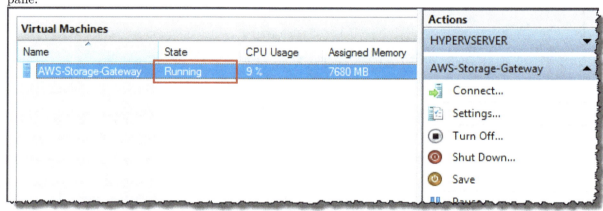

3. In the **Actions** pane, choose **Connect**.

   The **Virtual Machine Connection** window appears. If an authentication window appears, type the user name and password provided to you by the hypervisor administrator.

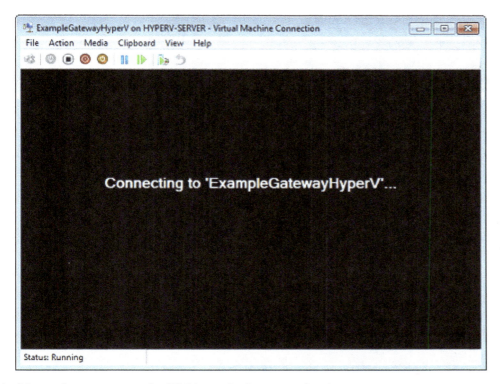

4. After a few moments, the VM is ready for you to log in.

5. To log in default credentials, continue to the procedure Logging in to the Local Console Using Default Credentials.

Synchronizing Your Gateway VM Time

For a gateway deployed on VMware ESXi, setting the hypervisor host time and synchronizing the VM time to the host is sufficient to avoid time drift. For more information, see Synchronizing VM Time with Host Time. For a gateway deployed on Microsoft Hyper-V, you should periodically check your VM's time using the procedure described following.

To view and synchronize the time of a Hyper-V gateway VM to an NTP server

1. Log in to your gateway's local console.

   - VMware ESXi—for more information, see Accessing the Gateway Local Console with VMware ESXi.
   - Microsoft Hyper-V—for more information, see Access the Gateway Local Console with Microsoft Hyper-V.

2. On the **AWS Storage Gateway Configuration** main menu, type **4** for **System Time Management**.

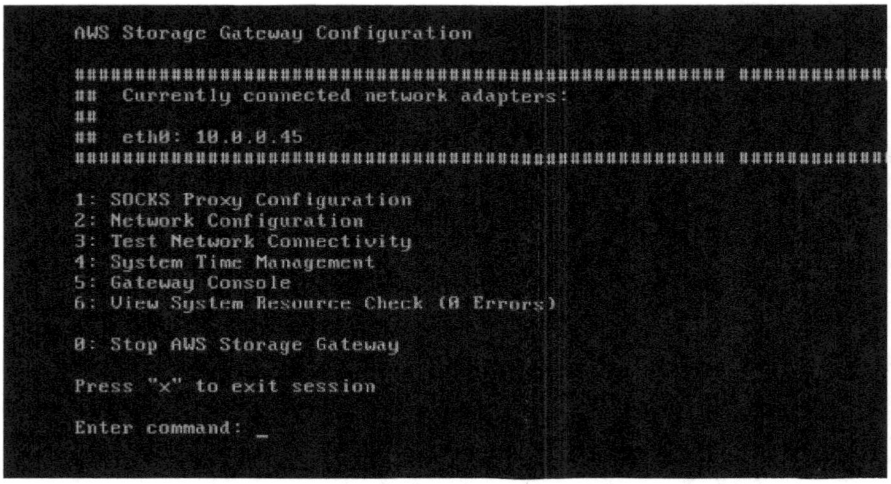

```
AWS Storage Gateway Configuration

############################################## #############
##   Currently connected network adapters:
##
##   eth0: 10.0.0.45
############################################## #############

1: SOCKS Proxy Configuration
2: Network Configuration
3: Test Network Connectivity
4: System Time Management
5: Gateway Console
6: View System Resource Check (0 Errors)

0: Stop AWS Storage Gateway

Press "x" to exit session

Enter command: _
```

3. On the **System Time Management** menu, type **1** for **View and Synchronize System Time**.

```
System Time Management

1: View and Synchronize System Time

Press "x" to exit

Enter command: _
```

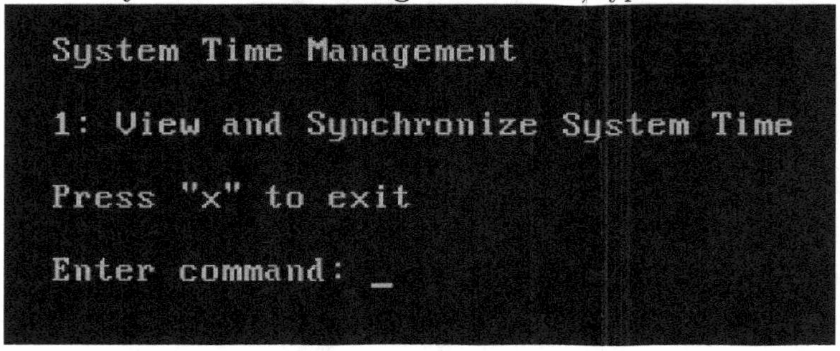

4. If the result indicates that you should synchronize your VM's time to the Network Time Protocol (NTP) time, type **y**. Otherwise, type **n**.

   If you type **y** to synchronize, the synchronization might take a few moments.

   The following screenshot shows a VM that does not require time synchronization.

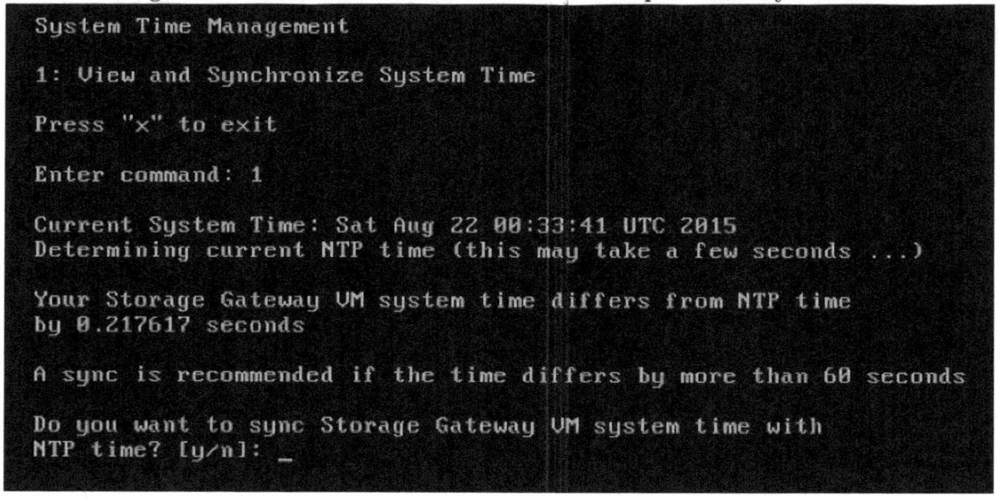

```
System Time Management

1: View and Synchronize System Time

Press "x" to exit

Enter command: 1

Current System Time: Sat Aug 22 00:33:41 UTC 2015
Determining current NTP time (this may take a few seconds ...)

Your Storage Gateway VM system time differs from NTP time
by 0.217617 seconds

A sync is recommended if the time differs by more than 60 seconds

Do you want to sync Storage Gateway VM system time with
NTP time? [y/n]: _
```

The following screenshot shows a VM that does require time synchronization.

```
System Time Management

1: View and Synchronize System Time

Press "x" to exit

Enter command: 1

Current System Time: Sat Aug 22 00:33:41 UTC 2015
Determining current NTP time (this may take a few seconds ...)

Your Storage Gateway VM system time differs from NTP time
by 61.217617 seconds

A sync is recommended if the time differs by more than 60 seconds

Do you want to sync Storage Gateway VM system time with
NTP time? [y/n]: _
```

Configuring Your Gateway for Multiple NICs in Microsoft Hyper-V Host

The following procedure assumes that your gateway VM already has one network adapter defined and that you are adding a second adapter. This procedure shows how to add an adapter for a Microsoft Hyper-V host.

To configure your gateway to use an additional network adapter in a Microsoft Hyper-V Host

1. On the Storage Gateway console, turn off the gateway. For instructions, see To stop a volume or tape gateway.

2. In the Microsoft Hyper-V Manager, select your gateway VM.

3. If the VM isn't turned off already, open the context (right-click) menu for your gateway and choose **Turn Off**.

4. In the client, open the context menu for your gateway VM and choose **Settings**.

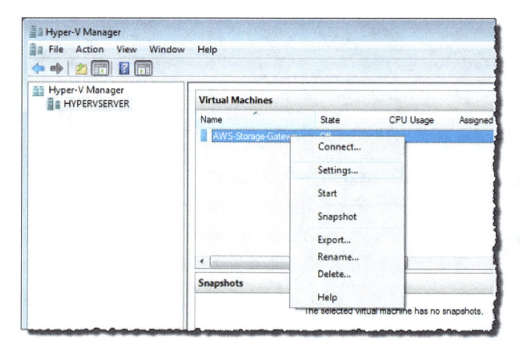

5. In the **Settings** dialog box for the VM, for **Hardware**, choose **Add Hardware**.

6. In the **Add Hardware** pane, choose **Network Adapter**, and then choose **Add** to add a device.

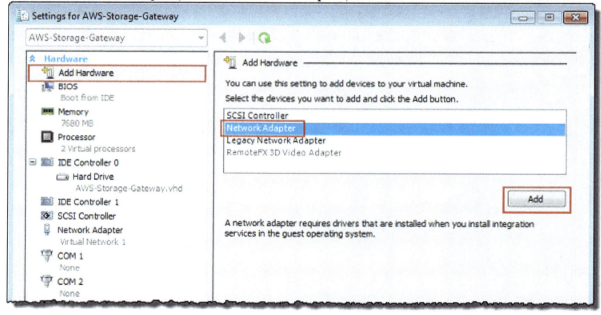

7. Configure the network adapter, and then choose **Apply** to apply settings.

   In the following example, **Virtual Network 2** is selected for the new adapter.

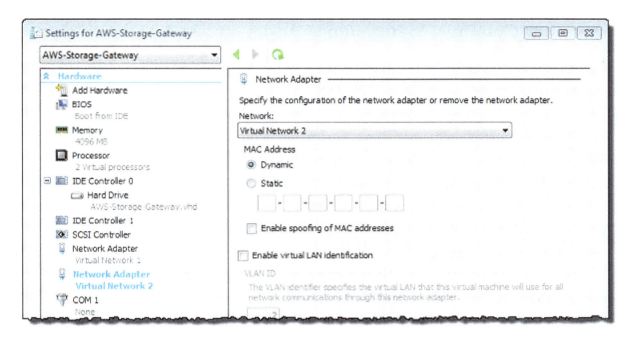

8. In the **Settings** dialog box, for **Hardware**, confirm that the second adapter was added, and then choose **OK**.

9. On the Storage Gateway console, turn on the gateway. For instructions, see To start a volume or tape gateway.

10. In the **Navigation** pane choose **Gateways**, then select the gateway to which you added the adapter. Confirm that the second IP address is listed in the **Details** tab.

For information about local console tasks common to VMware and Hyper-V host, see Performing Common Maintenance Tasks on the VM Local Console

Performing Common Maintenance Tasks on the VM Local Console

For a gateway deployed on-premises, you can perform the following maintenance tasks using the VM host's local console. These tasks are common to VMware and Hyper-V hosts.

Topics

- Logging in to the Local Console Using Default Credentials
- Setting the Local Console Password from the Storage Gateway Console
- Routing Your On-Premises Gateway Through a Proxy
- Configuring Your Gateway Network
- Testing Your Gateway Connection to the Internet
- Synchronizing Your Gateway VM Time
- Running Storage Gateway Commands on the Local Console
- Viewing Your Gateway System Resource Status
- Configuring Network Adapters for Your Gateway

Logging in to the Local Console Using Default Credentials

When the VM is ready for you to log in, the login screen is displayed. If this is your first time logging in to the local console, you use the default user name and password to log in. These default login credentials give you access to menus where you can configure gateway network settings and change the password from the local console. Storage Gateway enables you to set your own password from the AWS Storage Gateway console instead of changing the password from the local console. You don't need to know the default password to set a new password. For more information, see Setting the Local Console Password from the Storage Gateway Console.

```
AWS Storage Gateway


Login to change your network configuration and other gateway settings.

For more information, please see:
https://docs.aws.amazon.com/console/storagegateway/LocalConsole


localhost login: _
```

To log in to the gateway's local console

- If this is your first time logging in to the local console, log in to the VM with the user name *sguser* and password *sgpassword*. Otherwise, use your credentials to log in.

After you log in, you see the **Storage Gateway Configuration** main menu, as shown in the following screenshot.

```
AWS Storage Gateway Configuration

###############################################################  ############
##   Currently connected network adapters:
##
##   eth0: 10.0.0.45
###############################################################  ############

1: SOCKS Proxy Configuration
2: Network Configuration
3: Test Network Connectivity
4: System Time Management
5: Gateway Console
6: View System Resource Check (0 Errors)

0: Stop AWS Storage Gateway

Press "x" to exit session

Enter command: _
```

Note
We recommend changing the default password. You do this by running the `passwd` command from the Gateway Console menu (item 5 on the main menu). For information about how to run the command, see Running Storage Gateway Commands on the Local Console. You can also set your own password from the AWS Storage Gateway console. For more information, see Setting the Local Console Password from the Storage Gateway Console.

To	See
Configure a SOCKS proxy for your gateway	Routing Your On-Premises Gateway Through a Proxy.
Configure your network	Configuring Your Gateway Network.
Test network connectivity	Testing Your Gateway Connection to the Internet.
Manage VM time	Synchronizing Your Gateway VM Time.
Run Storage Gateway console commands	Running Storage Gateway Commands on the Local Console.
View system resource check	Viewing Your Gateway System Resource Status.

To shut down the gateway, type **0**.

To exit the configuration session, type **x** to exit the menu.

Setting the Local Console Password from the Storage Gateway Console

When you log in to the local console for the first time, you log in to the VM with the default credentials—the user name **admin** and the password **password**. We recommend that you set a new password. You can set this password from the AWS Storage Gateway console rather than the local console if you want. You don't need to know the default password to set a new password.

Note
If you created your gateway before June 20th, 2018 the default credentials are – user name **sguser** and password **sgpassword**

We recommend that you set a new password. You can set this password from the AWS Storage Gateway console rather than the local console, if you want. You don't need to know the default password to set a new password.

To set the local console password on the Storage Gateway console

1. Open the AWS Storage Gateway console at https://console.aws.amazon.com/storagegateway/home.

2. On the navigation pane, choose **Gateways** then choose the gateway for which you want to set a new password.

3. On the **Actions** menu, choose **Set Local Console Password**.

4. In the **Set Local Console Password** dialog box, type a new password, confirm the password and then choose **Save**. Your new password replaces the default password. AWS Storage Gateway does not save the password but rather safely transmits it to the VM. **Note**
   The password can consist of any character on the keyboard and can be 1 to 512 characters long.

Routing Your On-Premises Gateway Through a Proxy

Volume gateways and tape gateways support configuration of a Socket Secure version 5 (SOCKS5) proxy between your on-premises gateway and AWS. File gateways support configuration of an HyperText Transfer Protocol (HTTP) proxy.

Note
The only proxy configurations AWS Storage Gateway supports are SOCKS5 and HTTP.

If your gateway must use a proxy server to communicate to the Internet, then you need to configure the SOCKS or HTTP proxy settings for your gateway. You do this by specifying an IP address and port number for the host running your proxy. After you do so, AWS Storage Gateway routes all HTTP traffic through your proxy server. For information about network requirements for your gateway, see Network and Firewall Requirements.

The following procedure shows you how to configure SOCKS proxy for volume gateway and tape gateway. For instructions on how to configure HTTP proxy for file gateway, see To configure an HTTP proxy for a file gateway.

To configure a SOCKS5 proxy for volume and tape gateways

1. Log in to your gateway's local console.

   - VMware ESXi—for more information, see Accessing the Gateway Local Console with VMware ESXi.
   - Microsoft Hyper-V—for more information, see Access the Gateway Local Console with Microsoft Hyper-V.

2. On the **AWS Storage Gateway Configuration** main menu, type **1** to begin configuring the SOCKS proxy.

```
AWS Storage Gateway Configuration

###############################################  ############
##   Currently connected network adapters:
##
##   eth0: 10.0.0.45
###############################################  ############

1: SOCKS Proxy Configuration
2: Network Configuration
3: Test Network Connectivity
4: System Time Management
5: Gateway Console
6: View System Resource Check (0 Errors)

0: Stop AWS Storage Gateway

Press "x" to exit session

Enter command: _
```

3. Choose one of the following options on the **AWS Storage Gateway SOCKS Proxy Configuration** menu.

```
AWS Storage Gateway SOCKS Proxy Configuration

1: Configure SOCKS Proxy
2: View Current SOCKS Proxy Configuration
3: Remove SOCKS Proxy Configuration

Press "x" to exit

Enter command: _
```

[See the AWS documentation website for more details]

The following procedure shows you how to configure an HTTP proxy for a file gateway. For instructions on how to configure SOCKS proxy for a volume gateway or tape gateway, see To configure a SOCKS5 proxy for volume and tape gateways.

To configure an HTTP proxy for a file gateway

1. Log in to your gateway's local console.

   - VMware ESXi—for more information, see Accessing the Gateway Local Console with VMware ESXi.
   - Microsoft Hyper-V—for more information, see Access the Gateway Local Console with Microsoft Hyper-V.

2. On the **AWS Storage Gateway Configuration** main menu, type **1** to begin configuring the HTTP proxy.

```
AWS Storage Gateway Configuration

###############################################################
##   Currently connected network adapters:
##
##   eth0: 10.0.0.252
###############################################################

1: HTTP Proxy Configuration
2: Network Configuration
3: Test Network Connectivity
4: System Time Management
5: Gateway Console
6: View System Resource Check (0 Errors)

Press "x" to exit session

Enter command: ▮
```

3. Choose one of the following options on the **AWS Storage Gateway HTTP Proxy Configuration** menu:

```
AWS Storage Gateway HTTP Proxy Configuration

1: Configure HTTP Proxy
2: View Current HTTP Proxy Configuration
3: Remove HTTP Proxy Configuration

Press "x" to exit

Enter command: █
```

[See the AWS documentation website for more details]

4. Restart your VM to apply your HTTP configuration.

Configuring Your Gateway Network

The default network configuration for the gateway is Dynamic Host Configuration Protocol (DHCP). With DHCP, your gateway is automatically assigned an IP address. In some cases, you might need to manually assign your gateway's IP as a static IP address, as described following.

To configure your gateway to use static IP addresses

1. Log in to your gateway's local console.

   - VMware ESXi—for more information, see Accessing the Gateway Local Console with VMware ESXi.
   - Microsoft Hyper-V—for more information, see Access the Gateway Local Console with Microsoft Hyper-V.

2. On the **AWS Storage Gateway Configuration** main menu, type option **2** to begin configuring a static IP address.

```
AWS Storage Gateway Configuration

#################################################### ############
##   Currently connected network adapters:
##
##   eth0: 10.0.0.45
#################################################### ############

1: SOCKS Proxy Configuration
2: Network Configuration
3: Test Network Connectivity
4: System Time Management
5: Gateway Console
6: View System Resource Check (0 Errors)

0: Stop AWS Storage Gateway

Press "x" to exit session

Enter command: _
```

3. Choose one of the following options on the **AWS Storage Gateway Network Configuration** menu:

```
AWS Storage Gateway Network Configuration

1: Describe Adapter
2: Configure DHCP
3: Configure Static IP
4: Reset all to DHCP
5: Set Default Adapter
6: View DNS Configuration
7: View Routes

Press "x" to exit

Enter command: _
```

[See the AWS documentation website for more details]

Testing Your Gateway Connection to the Internet

You can use your gateway's local console to test your Internet connection. This test can be useful when you are troubleshooting network issues with your gateway.

To test your gateway's connection to the Internet

1. Log in to your gateway's local console.

   - VMware ESXi—for more information, see Accessing the Gateway Local Console with VMware ESXi.
   - Microsoft Hyper-V—for more information, see Access the Gateway Local Console with Microsoft Hyper-V.

2. On the **AWS Storage Gateway Configuration** main menu, type option **3** to begin testing network connectivity.

```
AWS Storage Gateway Configuration

########################################################### ###########
##   Currently connected network adapters:
##
##   eth0: 10.0.0.45
########################################################### ###########

1: SOCKS Proxy Configuration
2: Network Configuration
3: Test Network Connectivity
4: System Time Management
5: Gateway Console
6: View System Resource Check (0 Errors)

0: Stop AWS Storage Gateway

Press "x" to exit session

Enter command: _
```

The console displays the available regions.

3. Select the region you want to test. Following are the available regions for gateways deployed on-premises. [See the AWS documentation website for more details]

   Each endpoint in the selected region displays either a PASSED or FAILED message, as shown following. [See the AWS documentation website for more details]

For information about network and firewall requirements, see Network and Firewall Requirements.

229

Synchronizing Your Gateway VM Time

After your gateway is deployed and running, in some scenarios the gateway VM's time can drift. For example, if there is a prolonged network outage and your hypervisor host and gateway do not get time updates, then the gateway VM's time will be different from the true time. When there is a time drift, a discrepancy occurs between the stated times when operations such as snapshots occur and the actual times that the operations occur.

For a gateway deployed on VMware ESXi, setting the hypervisor host time and synchronizing the VM time to the host is sufficient to avoid time drift. For more information, see Synchronizing VM Time with Host Time.

For a gateway deployed on Microsoft Hyper-V, you should periodically check your VM's time. For more information, see Synchronizing Your Gateway VM Time.

Running Storage Gateway Commands on the Local Console

The AWS Storage Gateway console helps provide a secure environment for configuring and diagnosing issues with your gateway. Using the console commands, you can perform maintenance tasks such as saving routing tables or connecting to AWS Support.

To run a configuration or diagnostic command

1. Log in to your gateway's local console.

   - VMware ESXi—for more information, see Accessing the Gateway Local Console with VMware ESXi.
   - Microsoft Hyper-V—for more information, see Access the Gateway Local Console with Microsoft Hyper-V.

2. On the **AWS Storage Gateway Configuration** main menu, type option **5** for **Gateway Console**.

```
AWS Storage Gateway Configuration

##########################################################  ###########
##   Currently connected network adapters:
##
##   eth0: 10.0.0.45
##########################################################  ###########

1: SOCKS Proxy Configuration
2: Network Configuration
3: Test Network Connectivity
4: System Time Management
5: Gateway Console
6: View System Resource Check (0 Errors)

0: Stop AWS Storage Gateway

Press "x" to exit session

Enter command: _
```

3. On the AWS Storage Gateway console, type **h**, and then press the **Return** key.

The console displays the **Available Commands** menu with the available commands and after the menu a **Gateway Console** prompt, as shown in the following screenshot.

```
AVAILABLE COMMANDS
type 'man <command name>' to find out more information about commands

ip                      Show / manipulate routing, devices, and tunnels
save-routing-table      Save newly added routing table entry
ifconfig                View or configure network interfaces
iptables                Administration tool for IPv4 packet filtering and NAT
save-iptables           Persist IP tables
testconn                Test network connectivity
man                     Display command manual pages
passwd                  Update authentication tokens
open-support-channel    Connect to Storage Gateway Support
h                       Display available command list
exit                    Return to Storage Gateway Configuration menu

Gateway Console: _
```

4. To learn about a command, type **man** + *command name* at the **Gateway Console** prompt.

Viewing Your Gateway System Resource Status

When your gateway starts, it checks its virtual CPU cores, root volume size, and RAM and determines whether these system resources are sufficient for your gateway to function properly. You can view the results of this check on the gateway's local console.

To view the status of a system resource check

1. Log in to your gateway's local console.

   - VMware ESXi—for more information, see Accessing the Gateway Local Console with VMware ESXi.
   - Microsoft Hyper-V—for more information, see Access the Gateway Local Console with Microsoft Hyper-V.

2. In the **AWS Storage Gateway Configuration** main menu, type **6** to view the results of a system resource check.

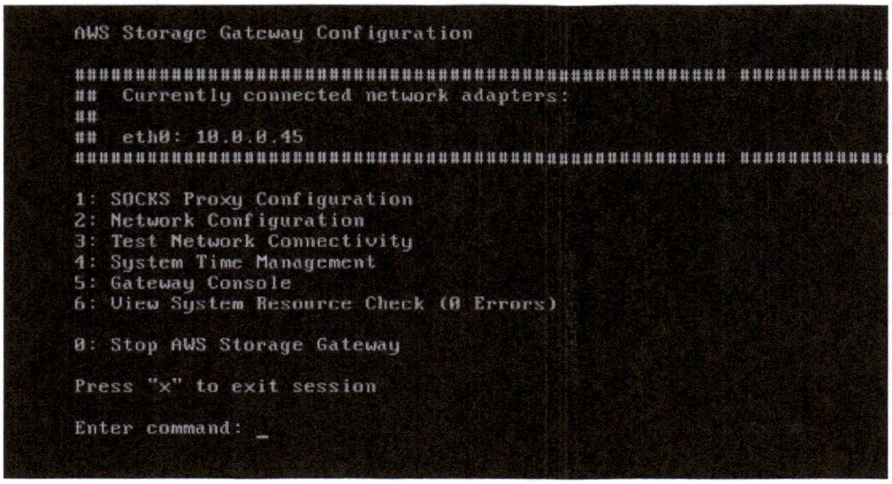

```
AWS Storage Gateway Configuration

####################################################### ##########
##   Currently connected network adapters:
##
##   eth0: 10.0.0.45
####################################################### ##########

1: SOCKS Proxy Configuration
2: Network Configuration
3: Test Network Connectivity
4: System Time Management
5: Gateway Console
6: View System Resource Check (0 Errors)

0: Stop AWS Storage Gateway

Press "x" to exit session

Enter command: _
```

The console displays an [**OK**], [**WARNING**], or [**FAIL**] message for each resource as described in the table following.
[See the AWS documentation website for more details]

The console also displays the number of errors and warnings next to the resource check menu option.

The following screenshot shows a [**FAIL**] message and the accompanying error message.

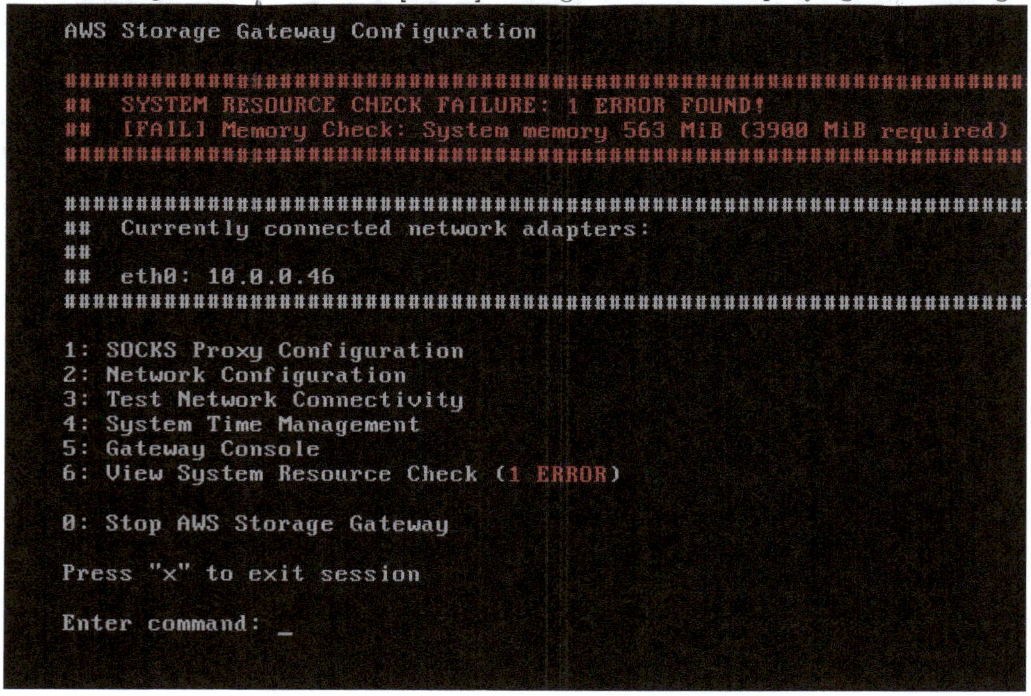

```
AWS Storage Gateway Configuration

#######################################################################
##   SYSTEM RESOURCE CHECK FAILURE: 1 ERROR FOUND!
##   [FAIL] Memory Check: System memory 563 MiB (3900 MiB required)
#######################################################################


#######################################################################
##   Currently connected network adapters:
##
##   eth0: 10.0.0.46
#######################################################################

1: SOCKS Proxy Configuration
2: Network Configuration
3: Test Network Connectivity
4: System Time Management
5: Gateway Console
6: View System Resource Check (1 ERROR)

0: Stop AWS Storage Gateway

Press "x" to exit session

Enter command: _
```

Configuring Network Adapters for Your Gateway

By default, AWS Storage Gateway is configured to use the E1000 network adapter type, but you can reconfigure your gateway to use the VMXNET3 (10 GbE) network adapter. You can also configure Storage Gateway so it can be accessed by more than one IP address. You do this by configuring your gateway to use more than one network adapter.

Topics

- Configuring Your Gateway to Use the VMXNET3 Network Adapter
- Configuring Your Gateway for Multiple NICs

Configuring Your Gateway to Use the VMXNET3 Network Adapter

AWS Storage Gateway supports the E1000 network adapter type in both VMware ESXi and Microsoft Hyper-V Hypervisor hosts. However, the VMXNET3 (10 GbE) network adapter type is supported in VMware ESXi hypervisor only. If your gateway is hosted on a VMware ESXi hypervisor, you can reconfigure your gateway to use the VMXNET3 (10 GbE) adapter type. For more information on this adapter, see the VMware website.

Important
To select VMXNET3, your guest operating system type must be **Other Linux64**.

Following are the steps you take to configure your gateway to use the VMXNET3 adapter:

1. Remove the default E1000 adapter.

2. Add the VMXNET3 adapter.

3. Restart your gateway.

4. Configure the adapter for the network.

Details on how to perform each step follow.

To remove the default E1000 adapter and configure your gateway to use the VMXNET3 adapter

1. In VMware, open the context (right-click) menu for your gateway and choose **Edit Settings**.

2. In the **Virtual Machine Properties** window, choose the **Hardware** tab.

3. For **Hardware**, choose **Network adapter**. Notice that the current adapter is E1000 in the **Adapter Type** section. You will replace this adapter with the VMXNET3 adapter.

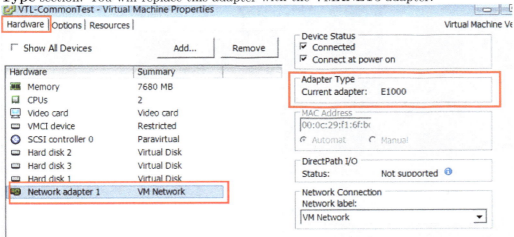

4. Choose the E1000 network adapter, and then choose **Remove**. In this example, the E1000 network adapter is **Network adapter 1**. **Note**
   Although you can run the E1000 and VMXNET3 network adapters in your gateway at the same time, we don't recommend doing so because it can cause network problems.

5. Choose **Add** to open the Add Hardware wizard.

6. Choose **Ethernet Adapter**, and then choose **Next**.

7. In the Network Type wizard, select **VMXNET3** for **Adapter Type**, and then choose **Next**.

8. In the Virtual Machine properties wizard, verify in the **Adapter Type** section that **Current Adapter** is set to **VMXNET3**, and then choose **OK**.

9. In the VMware VSphere client, shut down your gateway.

10. In the VMware VSphere client, restart your gateway.

After your gateway restarts, reconfigure the adapter you just added to make sure that network connectivity to the Internet is established.

To configure the adapter for the network

1. In the VSphere client, choose the **Console** tab to start the local console. You will use the default login credentials to log in to the gateway's local console for this configuration task. For information about how to log in using the default credentials, see Logging in to the Local Console Using Default Credentials.

```
AWS Storage Gateway


Login to change your network configuration and other gateway settings.

For more information, please see:
https://docs.aws.amazon.com/console/storagegateway/LocalConsole


localhost login: _
```

```
   AWS Storage Gateway Configuration

   ##################################################### ###########
   ## Currently connected network adapters:
   ##
   ##  eth0: 10.0.0.45
   ##################################################### ###########

   1: SOCKS Proxy Configuration
   2: Network Configuration
   3: Test Network Connectivity
   4: System Time Management
   5: Gateway Console
   6: View System Resource Check (0 Errors)

   0: Stop AWS Storage Gateway

   Press "x" to exit session

   Enter command: _
```

2. At the prompt, type **2** to select **Network Configuration**, and then press **Enter** to open the network configuration menu.

3. At the prompt, type **4** to select **Reset to DHCP**, and then type **y** (for yes) at the prompt to reset the adapter you just added to use Dynamic Host Configuration Protocol (DHCP). You can type **5** to set all adapters to DHCP.

4. At the **Enter the adapter** prompt, type **eth0**, and then press **Enter** to continue. The only adapter available is **eth0**.

```
AWS Storage Gateway Network Configuration

1: Describe Adapter
2: Configure DHCP
3: Configure Static IP
4: Reset all to DHCP
5: Set Default Adapter
6: View DNS Configuration
7: View Routes

Press "x" to exit

Enter command: 2

Available adapters: eth0
Enter Network Adapter: eth0

Reset to DHCP [y/n]: y

Adapter eth0 set to use DHCP

You must exit Network Configuration to complete this configuration.

Press Return to Continue_
```

If your gateway is already activated, you must shut it down and restart it from the AWS Storage Gateway Management Console. After the gateway restarts, you must test network connectivity to the Internet. For information about how to test network connectivity, see Testing Your Gateway Connection to the Internet.

Configuring Your Gateway for Multiple NICs

If you configure your gateway to use multiple network adapters (NICs), it can be accessed by more than one IP address. You might want to do this in the following situations:

- **Maximizing throughput** – You might want to maximize throughput to a gateway when network adapters are a bottleneck.
- **Application separation** – You might need to separate how your applications write to a gateway's volumes. For example, you might choose to have a critical storage application exclusively use one particular adapter defined for your gateway.
- **Network constraints** – Your application environment might require that you keep your iSCSI targets and the initiators that connect to them in an isolated network that is different from the network by which the gateway communicates with AWS.

In a typical multiple-adapter use case, one adapter is configured as the route by which the gateway communicates with AWS (that is, as the default gateway). Except for this one adapter, initiators must be in the same subnet as the adapter that contains the iSCSI targets to which they connect. Otherwise, communication with the intended targets might not be possible. If a target is configured on the same adapter that is used for communication with AWS, then iSCSI traffic for that target and AWS traffic will flow through the same adapter.

When you configure one adapter to connect to the AWS Storage gateway console and then add a second adapter, storage gateway automatically configures the route table to use the second adapter as the preferred route. For instructions on how to configure multiple-adapters, see the following sections.

- Configuring Your Gateway for Multiple NICs in a VMware ESXi Host
- Configuring Your Gateway for Multiple NICs in Microsoft Hyper-V Host

Performing Maintenance Tasks on the Amazon EC2 Gateway Local Console

Some maintenance tasks require that you log in to the local console when running a gateway deployed on an Amazon EC2 instance. In this section, you can find information about how to log in to the local console and perform maintenance tasks.

Topics

- Logging In to Your Amazon EC2 Gateway Local Console
- Routing Your Gateway Deployed on Amazon EC2 Through a Proxy
- Testing Your Gateway Connectivity to the Internet
- Running Storage Gateway Commands on the Local Console
- Viewing Your Gateway System Resource Status

Logging In to Your Amazon EC2 Gateway Local Console

You can connect to your Amazon EC2 instance by using a Secure Shell (SSH) client. For detailed information, see Connect to Your Instance in the *Amazon EC2 User Guide*. To connect this way, you will need the SSH key pair you specified when you launched the instance. For information about Amazon EC2 key pairs, see Amazon EC2 Key Pairs in the *Amazon EC2 User Guide*.

To log in to the gateway local console

1. Log in to your local console. If you are connecting to your EC2 instance from a Windows computer, log in as *sguser*.

2. After you log in, you see the **AWS Storage Gateway Configuration** main menu, as shown in the following screenshot.

```
AWS Storage Gateway Configuration

########################################################
##   Currently connected network adapters:
##
##   eth0: 10.222.0.40
########################################################

1: SOCKS Proxy Configuration
2: Test Network Connectivity
3: Gateway Console
4: View System Resource Check (0 Errors)

0: Stop AWS Storage Gateway

Press "x" to exit session

Enter command: _
```

[See the AWS documentation website for more details]

To shut down the gateway, type **0**.

To exit the configuration session, type **x** to exit the menu.

Routing Your Gateway Deployed on Amazon EC2 Through a Proxy

AWS Storage Gateway supports the configuration of a Socket Secure version 5 (SOCKS5) proxy between your gateway deployed on Amazon EC2 and AWS.

Note
The only proxy configuration AWS Storage Gateway supports is SOCKS5.

If your gateway must use a proxy server to communicate to the Internet, then you need to configure the SOCKS proxy settings for your gateway. You do this by specifying an IP address and port number for the host running your proxy. After you do so, AWS Storage Gateway will route all HyperText Transfer Protocol Secure (HTTPS) traffic through your proxy server.

To route your gateway Internet traffic through a local proxy server

1. Log in to your gateway's local console. For instructions, see Logging In to Your Amazon EC2 Gateway Local Console.

2. On the **AWS Storage Gateway Configuration** main menu, type **1** to begin configuring the SOCKS proxy.

```
AWS Storage Gateway Configuration

###############################################################
##   Currently connected network adapters:
##
##   eth0: 10.222.0.40
###############################################################

1: SOCKS Proxy Configuration
2: Test Network Connectivity
3: Gateway Console
4: View System Resource Check (0 Errors)

0: Stop AWS Storage Gateway

Press "x" to exit session

Enter command: _
```

3. Choose one of the following options in the **AWS Storage Gateway SOCKS Proxy Configuration** menu:

```
AWS Storage Gateway SOCKS Proxy Configuration

1: Configure SOCKS Proxy
2: View Current SOCKS Proxy Configuration
3: Remove SOCKS Proxy Configuration

Press "x" to exit

Enter command: _
```

[See the AWS documentation website for more details]

Testing Your Gateway Connectivity to the Internet

You can use your gateway's local console to test your Internet connection. This test can be useful when you are troubleshooting network issues with your gateway.

To test your gateway's connection to the Internet

1. Log in to your gateway's local console. For instructions, see Logging In to Your Amazon EC2 Gateway Local Console.

2. In the **AWS Storage Gateway Configuration** main menu, type **2** to begin testing network connectivity.

```
AWS Storage Gateway Configuration

#########################################################M:###
##   Currently connected network adapters:
##
##   eth0: 10.222.0.40
###############################################################

1: SOCKS Proxy Configuration
2: Test Network Connectivity
3: Gateway Console
4: View System Resource Check <0 Errors>

0: Stop AWS Storage Gateway

Press "x" to exit session

Enter command: _
```

The console displays the available regions.

3. Select the region you want to test. Following are the available regions for gateways deployed an EC2 instance.
[See the AWS documentation website for more details]

Each endpoint in the region you select displays either a [**PASSED**] or [**FAILED**] message, as shown following.
[See the AWS documentation website for more details]

Running Storage Gateway Commands on the Local Console

The AWS Storage Gateway console helps provide a secure environment for configuring and diagnosing issues with your gateway. Using the console commands, you can perform maintenance tasks such as saving routing tables or connecting to AWS Support.

To run a configuration or diagnostic command

1. Log in to your gateway's local console. For instructions, see Logging In to Your Amazon EC2 Gateway Local Console.

2. In the **AWS Storage Gateway Configuration** main menu, type **3** for **Gateway Console**.

```
AWS Storage Gateway Configuration

#########################################################M:###
##   Currently connected network adapters:
##
##   eth0: 10.222.0.40
###############################################################

1: SOCKS Proxy Configuration
2: Test Network Connectivity
3: Gateway Console
4: View System Resource Check <0 Errors>

0: Stop AWS Storage Gateway

Press "x" to exit session

Enter command: _
```

3. In the Storage Gateway console, type **h**, and then press the **Return** key.

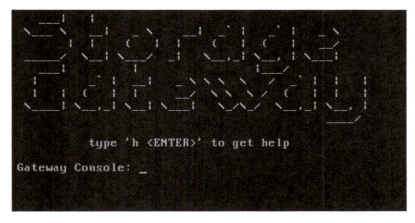

The console displays the **Available Commands** menu with the available commands. After the menu, a **Gateway Console** prompt appears, as shown in the following screenshot.

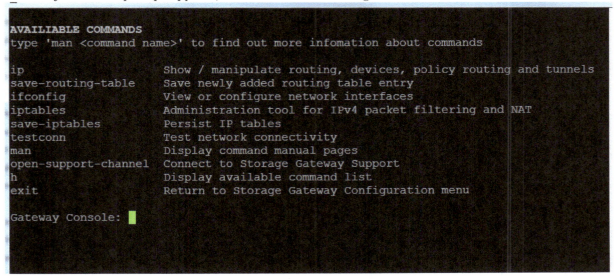

4. To learn about a command, type **man + command name** at the **Gateway Console** prompt.

Viewing Your Gateway System Resource Status

When your gateway starts, it checks its virtual CPU cores, root volume size, and RAM and determines whether these system resources are sufficient for your gateway to function properly. You can view the results of this check on the gateway's local console.

To view the status of a system resource check

1. Log in to your gateway's local console. For instructions, see Logging In to Your Amazon EC2 Gateway Local Console.

2. In the **AWS Storage Gateway Configuration** main menu, type **4** to view the results of a system resource check.

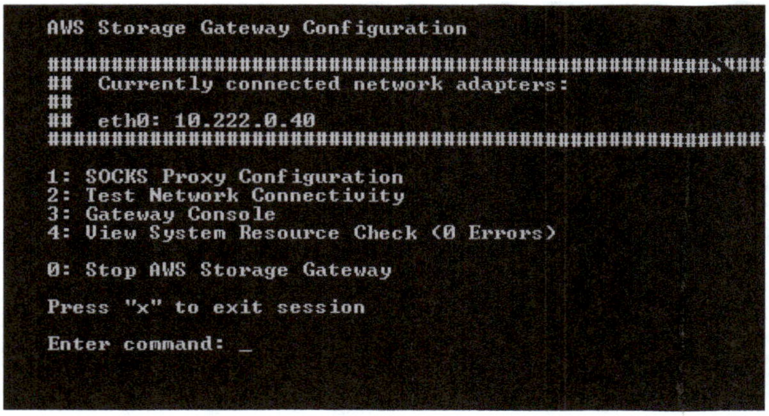

```
AWS Storage Gateway Configuration

###############################################################
## Currently connected network adapters:
##
## eth0: 10.222.0.40
###############################################################

1: SOCKS Proxy Configuration
2: Test Network Connectivity
3: Gateway Console
4: View System Resource Check (0 Errors)

0: Stop AWS Storage Gateway

Press "x" to exit session

Enter command: _
```

The console displays an [OK], [WARNING], or [FAIL] message for each resource as described in the table following.

[See the AWS documentation website for more details]

The console also displays the number of errors and warnings next to the resource check menu option.

The following screenshot shows a [FAIL] message and the accompanying error message.

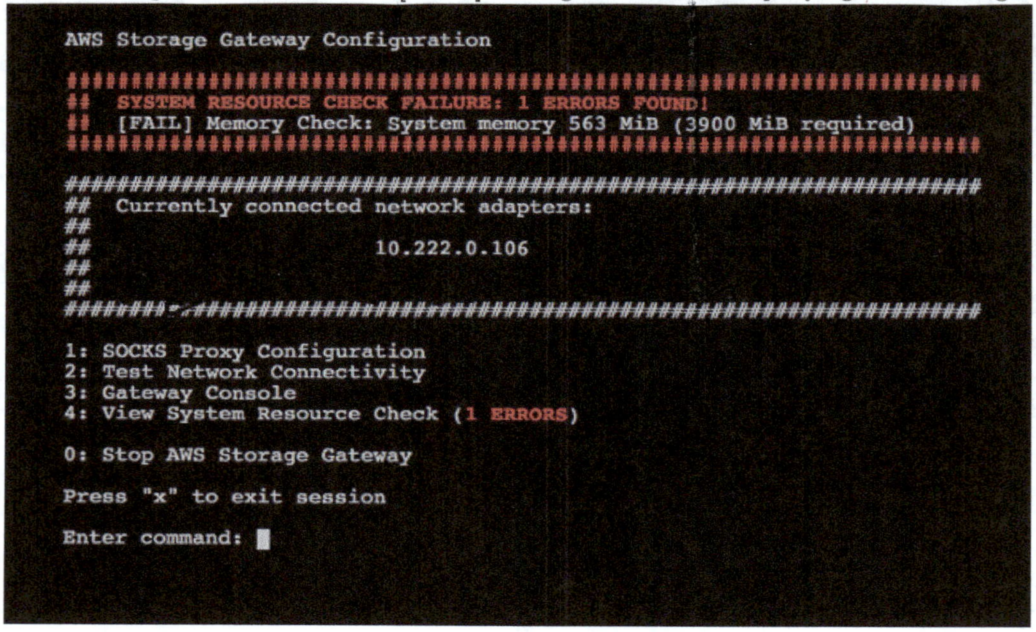

```
AWS Storage Gateway Configuration

###############################################################
##  SYSTEM RESOURCE CHECK FAILURE: 1 ERRORS FOUND!
##  [FAIL] Memory Check: System memory 563 MiB (3900 MiB required)
###############################################################

###############################################################
## Currently connected network adapters:
##
##                  10.222.0.106
##
##
###############################################################

1: SOCKS Proxy Configuration
2: Test Network Connectivity
3: Gateway Console
4: View System Resource Check (1 ERRORS)

0: Stop AWS Storage Gateway

Press "x" to exit session

Enter command: 
```

Deleting Your Gateway by Using the AWS Storage Gateway Console and Removing Associated Resources

If you don't plan to continue using your gateway, consider deleting the gateway and its associated resources. Removing resources avoids incurring charges for resources you don't plan to continue using and helps reduce your monthly bill.

When you delete a gateway, it no longer appears on the AWS Storage Gateway Management Console and its iSCSI connection to the initiator is closed. The procedure for deleting a gateway is the same for all gateway types; however, depending on the type of gateway you want to delete and the host it is deployed on, you follow specific instructions to remove associated resources.

You can delete a gateway using the Storage Gateway console or programmatically. You can find information following about how to delete a gateway using the Storage Gateway console. If you want to programmatically delete your gateway, see *AWS Storage Gateway API Reference.*

Topics

- Deleting Your Gateway by Using the AWS Storage Gateway Console
- Removing Resources from a Gateway Deployed On-Premises
- Removing Resources from a Gateway Deployed on an Amazon EC2 Instance

Deleting Your Gateway by Using the AWS Storage Gateway Console

The procedure for deleting a gateway is the same for all gateway types. However, depending on the type of gateway you want to delete and the host the gateway is deployed on, you might have to perform additional tasks to remove resources associated with the gateway. Removing these resources helps you avoid paying for resources you don't plan to use.

Note
For gateways deployed on a Amazon Elastic Compute Cloud (Amazon EC2) instance, the instance continues to exist until you delete it.
For gateways deployed on a virtual machine (VM), after you delete your gateway the gateway VM still exists in your virtualization environment. To remove the VM, use the VMware vSphere client or Microsoft Hyper-V Manager to connect to the host and remove the VM. Note that you can't reuse the deleted gateway's VM to activate a new gateway.

To delete a gateway

1. Open the AWS Storage Gateway console at https://console.aws.amazon.com/storagegateway/home.

2. In the navigation pane, choose **Gateways**, and then choose the gateway you want to delete.

3. On the **Actions** menu, choose **Delete gateway**.

4.

Important
Before you do this step, be sure that there are no applications currently writing to the gateway's volumes. If you delete the gateway while it is in use, data loss can occur. **Warning**
When a gateway is deleted, there is no way to get it back.

In the confirmation dialog box that appears, select the check box to confirm your deletion. Make sure the gateway ID listed specifies the gateway you want to delete. and then choose **Delete**.

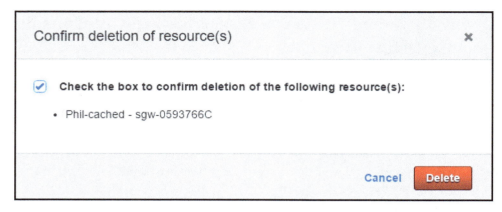

Important

You no longer pay software charges after you delete a gateway, but resources such as virtual tapes, Amazon Elastic Block Store (Amazon EBS) snapshots, and Amazon EC2 instances persist. You will continue to be billed for these resources. You can choose to remove Amazon EC2 instances and Amazon EBS snapshots by canceling your Amazon EC2 subscription. If you want to keep your Amazon EC2 subscription, you can delete your Amazon EBS snapshots using the Amazon EC2 console.

Removing Resources from a Gateway Deployed On-Premises

You can use the instructions following to remove resources from a gateway that is deployed on-premises.

Removing Resources from a Volume Gateway Deployed on a VM

If the gateway you want to delete are deployed on a virtual machine (VM), we suggest that you take the following actions to clean up resources:

- Delete the gateway. For instructions, see Deleting Your Gateway by Using the AWS Storage Gateway Console.
- Delete all Amazon EBS snapshots you don't need. For instructions, see Deleting an Amazon EBS Snapshot in the *Amazon EC2 User Guide for Linux Instances.*

Removing Resources from a Tape Gateway Deployed on a VM

When you delete a gateway–virtual tape library (VTL), you perform additional cleanup steps before and after you delete the gateway. These additional steps help you remove resources you don't need so you don't continue to pay for them.

If the tape gateway you want to delete is deployed on a virtual machine (VM), we suggest that you take the following actions to clean up resources.

Important

Before you delete a tape gateway, you must cancel all tape retrieval operations and eject all retrieved tapes. After you have deleted the tape gateway, you must remove any resources associated with the tape gateway that you don't need to avoid paying for those resources.

When you delete a tape gateway, you can encounter one of two scenarios.

- **The tape gateway is connected to AWS** – If the tape gateway is connected to AWS and you delete the gateway, the iSCSI targets associated with the gateway (that is, the virtual tape drives and media changer) will no longer be available.

- **The tape gateway is not connected to AWS** − If the tape gateway is not connected to AWS, for example if the underlying VM is turned off or your network is down, then you cannot delete the gateway. If you attempt to do so, after your environment is back up and running you might have a tape gateway running on-premises with available iSCSI targets. However, no tape gateway data will be uploaded to, or downloaded from, AWS.

If the tape gateway you want to delete is not functioning, you must first disable it before you delete it, as described following:

- To delete tapes that have the RETRIEVED status from the library, eject the tape using your backup software. For instructions, see Archiving the Tape.

After disabling the tape gateway and deleting tapes, you can delete the tape gateway. For instructions on how to delete a gateway, see Deleting Your Gateway by Using the AWS Storage Gateway Console.

If you have tapes archived, those tapes remain and you continue to pay for storage until you delete them. For instruction on how to delete tapes from a archive. see Deleting Tapes.

Important
You are charged for a minimum of 90 days storage for virtual tapes in a archive. If you retrieve a virtual tape that has been stored in the archive for less than 90 days, you are still charged for 90 days storage.

Removing Resources from a Gateway Deployed on an Amazon EC2 Instance

If you want to delete a gateway that you deployed on an Amazon EC2 instance, we recommend that you clean up the AWS resources that were used with the gateway, specifically the Amazon EC2 instance, any Amazon EBS volumes, and also tapes if you deployed a tape gateway. Doing so helps avoid unintended usage charges.

Removing Resources from Your Cached Volumes Deployed on Amazon EC2

If you deployed a gateway with cached volumes on EC2, we suggest that you take the following actions to delete your gateway and clean up its resources:

1. In the Storage Gateway console, delete the gateway as shown in Deleting Your Gateway by Using the AWS Storage Gateway Console.

2. In the Amazon EC2 console, stop your EC2 instance if you plan on using the instance again. Otherwise, terminate the instance. If you plan on deleting volumes, make note of the block devices that are attached to the instance and the devices' identifiers before terminating the instance. You will need these to identify the volumes you want to delete.

3. In the Amazon EC2 console, remove all Amazon EBS volumes that are attached to the instance if you don't plan on using them again. For more information, see Clean Up Your Instance and Volume in the *Amazon EC2 User Guide for Linux Instances*.

Removing Resources from Your Tape Gateway Deployed on Amazon EC2

If you deployed a tape gateway, we suggest that you take the following actions to delete your gateway and clean up its resources:

1. Delete all virtual tapes that you have retrieved to your tape gateway. For more information, see Deleting Tapes.

2. Delete all virtual tapes from the tape library. For more information, see Deleting Tapes.

3. Delete the tape gateway. For more information, see Deleting Your Gateway by Using the AWS Storage Gateway Console.

4. Terminate all Amazon EC2 instances, and delete all Amazon EBS volumes. For more information, see Clean Up Your Instance and Volume in the *Amazon EC2 User Guide for Linux Instances*.

5. Delete all archived virtual tapes. For more information, see Deleting Tapes. **Important**
You are charged for a minimum of 90 days storage for virtual tapes in the archive. If you retrieve a virtual tape that has been stored in the archive for less than 90 days, you are still charged for 90 days storage.

Security

In this section, you can find information about AWS and CHAPS configuration, encrypting data and authentication and access control.

Topics

- Configuring CHAP Authentication for Your Volumes
- Encrypting Your Data Using AWS Key Management System
- Authentication and Access Control for AWS Storage Gateway

Configuring CHAP Authentication for Your Volumes

In AWS Storage Gateway, your iSCSI initiators connect to your volumes as iSCSI targets. Storage Gateway uses Challenge-Handshake Authentication Protocol (CHAP) to authenticate iSCSI and initiator connections. CHAP provides protection against playback attacks by requiring authentication to access storage volume targets. For each volume target, you can define one or more CHAP credentials. You can view and edit these credentials for the different initiators in the Configure CHAP credentials dialog box.

To configure CHAP credentials

1. In the AWS Storage Gateway Console, choose **Volumes** and select the volume for which you want to configure CHAP credentials.

2. On the **Actions** menu, choose **Configure CHAP authentication**.

3. For **Initiator name**, type the name of your initiator. The name must be at least 1 character and at most 255 characters long.

4. For **Initiator secret**, provide the secret phrase you want to used to authenticate your iSCSI initiator. The initiator secret phrase must be at least 12 characters and at most 16 characters long.

5. For **Target secret**, provide the secret phrase you want used to authenticate your target for mutual CHAP. The target secret phrase must be at least 12 characters and at most 16 characters long.

6. Choose **Save** to save your entries.

To view or update CHAP credentials, you must have the necessary IAM role permissions to that allows you to perform that operation.

Viewing and Editing CHAP Credentials

You can add, remove or update CHAP credentials for each user. To view or edit CHAP credentials, you must have the necessary IAM role permissions that allows you to perform that operation and the gateway the initiator target is attached to must be a functioning gateway.

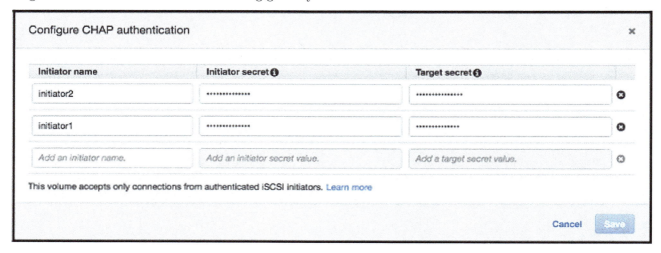

To add CHAP credentials

1. In the AWS Storage Gateway Console, choose **Volumes** and select the volume for which you want to add CHAP credentials.

2. On the **Actions** menu, choose **Configure CHAP authentication**.

3. In the Configure CHAPS page, provide the **Initiator name**, **Initiator secret**, and **Target secret** in the respective boxes and choose **Save**.

To remove CHAP credentials

1. In the AWS Storage Gateway Console, choose **Volumes** and select the volume for which you want to remove CHAP credentials.

2. On the **Actions** menu, choose **Configure CHAP authentication**.

3. Click the **X** next to the credentials you want to remove and choose **Save**.

To update CHAP credentials

1. In the AWS Storage Gateway Console, choose **Volumes** and select the volume for which you want to update CHAP.

2. On the **Actions** menu, choose **Configure CHAP authentication**.

3. In Configure CHAP credentials page, change the entries for the credentials you to update.

4. Choose **Save**.

Encrypting Your Data Using AWS Key Management System

AWS Storage Gateway uses AWS Key Management Service (AWS KMS) to support encryption. Storage Gateway is integrated with AWS KMS so you can use the Customer Master Keys (CMKs) in your account to protect the data that Storage Gateway receives, stores, or manages. Currently, you can do this by using the AWS Storage Gateway API.

- To use the Storage Gateway API to encrypt data written to a file share, see CreateNFSFileShare in the *AWS Storage Gateway API Reference.*
- To use the Storage Gateway API to encrypt data written to a cached volume, see CreateCachediSCSIVolume in the *AWS Storage Gateway API Reference.*
- To use the Storage Gateway API to encrypt data written to a virtual tape, see CreateTapes in the *AWS Storage Gateway API Reference.*

When using AWS KMS to encrypt your data keep the following in mind:

- AWS Storage Gateway currently doesn't support creating a snapshot of an encrypted cached volume.
- AWS Storage Gateway currently doesn't support creating an unencrypted volume from a recovery point of a KMS-encrypted volume.
- AWS Storage Gateway currently doesn't support creating a volume from a KMS-encrypted EBS snapshot.
- Your data is encrypted at rest. That is, the data is encrypted in Amazon S3.
- IAM users must have the required permissions to call the AWS KMS APIs. For more information, see Using IAM Policies with AWS KMS in the *AWS Key Management Service Developer Guide*
- If you delete or disable your Customer Master Key (CMK) or revoke the grant token, you wouldn't be able to access the data on the volume or tape. For more information, see Deleting Customer Master Keys in the *AWS Key Management Service Developer Guide.*

For more information about AWS KMS see What is AWS Key Management Service?.

Authentication and Access Control for AWS Storage Gateway

Access to AWS Storage Gateway requires credentials that AWS can use to authenticate your requests. Those credentials must have permissions to access AWS resources, such as a gateway, file share, volume, or tape. The following sections provide details on how you can use AWS Identity and Access Management (IAM) and AWS Storage Gateway to help secure your resources by controlling who can access them:

- Authentication
- Access Control

Authentication

You can access AWS as any of the following types of identities:

- **AWS account root user** – When you first create an AWS account, you begin with a single sign-in identity that has complete access to all AWS services and resources in the account. This identity is called the AWS account *root user* and is accessed by signing in with the email address and password that you used to create the account. We strongly recommend that you do not use the root user for your everyday tasks, even the administrative ones. Instead, adhere to the best practice of using the root user only to create your first IAM user. Then securely lock away the root user credentials and use them to perform only a few account and service management tasks.

- **IAM user** – An IAM user is an identity within your AWS account that has specific custom permissions (for example, permissions to create a gateway in AWS Storage Gateway). You can use an IAM user name and password to sign in to secure AWS webpages like the AWS Management Console, AWS Discussion Forums, or the AWS Support Center.

  In addition to a user name and password, you can also generate access keys for each user. You can use these keys when you access AWS services programmatically, either through one of the several SDKs or by using the AWS Command Line Interface (CLI). The SDK and CLI tools use the access keys to cryptographically sign your request. If you don't use AWS tools, you must sign the request yourself. AWS Storage Gateway supports *Signature Version 4*, a protocol for authenticating inbound API requests. For more information about authenticating requests, see Signature Version 4 Signing Process in the *AWS General Reference*.

- **IAM role** – An IAM role is an IAM identity that you can create in your account that has specific permissions. It is similar to an *IAM user*, but it is not associated with a specific person. An IAM role enables you to obtain temporary access keys that can be used to access AWS services and resources. IAM roles with temporary credentials are useful in the following situations:

  - **Federated user access** – Instead of creating an IAM user, you can use existing user identities from AWS Directory Service, your enterprise user directory, or a web identity provider. These are known as *federated users*. AWS assigns a role to a federated user when access is requested through an identity provider. For more information about federated users, see Federated Users and Roles in the *IAM User Guide*.

  - **AWS service access** – You can use an IAM role in your account to grant an AWS service permissions to access your account's resources. For example, you can create a role that allows Amazon Redshift to access an Amazon S3 bucket on your behalf and then load data from that bucket into an Amazon Redshift cluster. For more information, see Creating a Role to Delegate Permissions to an AWS Service in the *IAM User Guide*.

- **Applications running on Amazon EC2** – You can use an IAM role to manage temporary credentials for applications that are running on an EC2 instance and making AWS API requests. This is preferable to storing access keys within the EC2 instance. To assign an AWS role to an EC2 instance and make it available to all of its applications, you create an instance profile that is attached to the instance. An instance profile contains the role and enables programs that are running on the EC2 instance to get temporary credentials. For more information, see Using an IAM Role to Grant Permissions to Applications Running on Amazon EC2 Instances in the *IAM User Guide*.

Access Control

You can have valid credentials to authenticate your requests, but unless you have permissions you cannot create or access AWS Storage Gateway resources. For example, you must have permissions to create a gateway in AWS Storage Gateway.

The following sections describe how to manage permissions for AWS Storage Gateway. We recommend that you read the overview first.

- Overview of Managing Access Permissions to Your AWS Storage Gateway
- Identity-Based Policies (IAM Policies)

Overview of Managing Access Permissions to Your AWS Storage Gateway

Every AWS resource is owned by an AWS account, and permissions to create or access a resource are governed by permissions policies. An account administrator can attach permissions policies to IAM identities (that is, users, groups, and roles), and some services (such as AWS Lambda) also support attaching permissions policies to resources.

Note

An *account administrator* (or administrator user) is a user with administrator privileges. For more information, see IAM Best Practices in the IAM User Guide.

When granting permissions, you decide who is getting the permissions, the resources they get permissions for, and the specific actions that you want to allow on those resources.

Topics

- AWS Storage Gateway Resources and Operations
- Understanding Resource Ownership
- Managing Access to Resources
- Specifying Policy Elements: Actions, Effects, Resources, and Principals
- Specifying Conditions in a Policy

AWS Storage Gateway Resources and Operations

In AWS Storage Gateway, the primary resource is a *gateway*. Storage Gateway also supports the following additional resource types: *file share, volume*, * virtual tape*, *iSCSI target*, and *vtl device*. These are referred to as *subresources* and they don't exist unless they are associated with a gateway.

These resources and subresources have unique Amazon Resource Names (ARNs) associated with them as shown in the following table.

Resource Type	ARN Format
Gateway ARN	`arn:aws:storagegateway:region:account-id:gateway/gateway-id`
File Share ARN	`arn:aws:storagegateway:region:account-id:share/share-id`
Volume ARN	`arn:aws:storagegateway:region:account-id:gateway/gateway-id/volume/volume-id`
Tape ARN	`arn:aws:storagegateway:region:account-id:tape/tapebarcode`
Target ARN (iSCSI target)	`arn:aws:storagegateway:region:account-id:gateway/gateway-id/target/iSCSItarget`
VTL Device ARN	`arn:aws:storagegateway:region:account-id:gateway/gateway-id/device/vtldevice`

Note

AWS Storage Gateway resource IDs are in uppercase. When you use these resource IDs with the Amazon EC2 API, Amazon EC2 expects resource IDs in lowercase. You must change your resource ID to lowercase to use it with the EC2 API. For example, in Storage Gateway the ID for a volume might be `vol-1122AABB`. When you use this ID with the EC2 API, you must change it to `vol-1122aabb`. Otherwise, the EC2 API might not behave as expected. ARNs for gateways activated prior to September 2, 2015, contain the gateway name instead of the gateway ID. To obtain the ARN for your gateway, use the `DescribeGatewayInformation` API operation.

To grant permissions for specific API operations, such as creating a tape, AWS Storage Gateway provides a set of API actions for you to create and manage these resources and subresources. For a list of API actions, see Actions in the *AWS Storage Gateway API Reference*.

To grant permissions for specific API operations, such as creating a tape, AWS Storage Gateway defines a set of actions that you can specify in a permissions policy to grant permissions for specific API operations. An API operation can require permissions for more than one action. For a table showing all the AWS Storage Gateway API actions and the resources they apply to, see AWS Storage Gateway API Permissions: Actions, Resources, and Conditions Reference.

Understanding Resource Ownership

A *resource owner* is the AWS account that created the resource. That is, the resource owner is the AWS account of the *principal entity* (the root account, an IAM user, or an IAM role) that authenticates the request that creates the resource. The following examples illustrate how this works:

- If you use the root account credentials of your AWS account to activate a gateway, your AWS account is the owner of the resource (in AWS Storage Gateway, the resource is the gateway).
- If you create an IAM user in your AWS account and grant permissions to the `ActivateGateway` action to that user, the user can activate a gateway. However, your AWS account, to which the user belongs, owns the gateway resource.
- If you create an IAM role in your AWS account with permissions to activate a gateway, anyone who can assume the role can activate a gateway. Your AWS account, to which the role belongs, owns the gateway resource.

Managing Access to Resources

A permissions policy describes who has access to what. The following section explains the available options for creating permissions policies.

Note
This section discusses using IAM in the context of AWS Storage Gateway. It doesn't provide detailed information about the IAM service. For complete IAM documentation, see What is IAM in the IAM User Guide. For information about IAM policy syntax and descriptions, see AWS IAM Policy Reference in the IAM User Guide.

Policies attached to an IAM identity are referred to as *identity-based* policies (IAM polices) and policies attached to a resource are referred to as *resource-based* policies. AWS Storage Gateway supports only identity-based policies (IAM policies).

Topics

- Identity-Based Policies (IAM Policies)
- Resource-Based Policies

Identity-Based Policies (IAM Policies)

You can attach policies to IAM identities. For example, you can do the following:

- **Attach a permissions policy to a user or a group in your account** – An account administrator can use a permissions policy that is associated with a particular user to grant permissions for that user to create an AWS Storage Gateway resource, such as a gateway, volume, or tape.

- **Attach a permissions policy to a role (grant cross-account permissions)** – You can attach an identity-based permissions policy to an IAM role to grant cross-account permissions. For example, the administrator in Account A can create a role to grant cross-account permissions to another AWS account (for example, Account B) or an AWS service as follows:

  1. Account A administrator creates an IAM role and attaches a permissions policy to the role that grants permissions on resources in Account A.

  2. Account A administrator attaches a trust policy to the role identifying Account B as the principal who can assume the role.

  3. Account B administrator can then delegate permissions to assume the role to any users in Account B. Doing this allows users in Account B to create or access resources in Account A. The principal in the trust policy can also be an AWS service principal if you want to grant an AWS service permissions to assume the role.

  For more information about using IAM to delegate permissions, see Access Management in the *IAM User Guide*.

The following is an example policy that grants permissions to all `List*` actions on all resources. This action is a read-only action. Thus, the policy doesn't allow the user to change the state of the resources.

```
{
    "Version": "2012-10-17",
    "Statement": [
        {
            "Sid": "AllowAllListActionsOnAllResources",
            "Effect": "Allow",
            "Action": [
                "storagegateway:List*"
            ],
            "Resource": "*"
        }
    ]
}
```

For more information about using identity-based policies with AWS Storage Gateway, see Using Identity-Based Policies (IAM Policies) for AWS Storage Gateway. For more information about users, groups, roles, and permissions, see Identities (Users, Groups, and Roles in the *IAM User Guide*.

Resource-Based Policies

Other services, such as Amazon S3, also support resource-based permissions policies. For example, you can attach a policy to an S3 bucket to manage access permissions to that bucket. AWS Storage Gateway doesn't support resource-based policies.

Specifying Policy Elements: Actions, Effects, Resources, and Principals

For each AWS Storage Gateway resource (see AWS Storage Gateway API Permissions: Actions, Resources, and Conditions Reference), the service defines a set of API operations (see Actions). To grant permissions for these API operations, AWS Storage Gateway defines a set of actions that you can specify in a policy. For example, for the AWS Storage Gateway gateway resource, the following actions are defined: `ActivateGateway`, `DeleteGateway`, and `DescribeGatewayInformation`. Note that, performing an API operation can require permissions for more than one action.

The following are the most basic policy elements:

- **Resource** – In a policy, you use an Amazon Resource Name (ARN) to identify the resource to which the policy applies. For AWS Storage Gateway resources, you always use the wildcard character (*) in IAM policies. For more information, see AWS Storage Gateway Resources and Operations.
- **Action** – You use action keywords to identify resource operations that you want to allow or deny. For example, depending on the specified `Effect`, the `storagegateway:ActivateGateway` permission allows or denies the user permissions to perform the AWS Storage Gateway `ActivateGateway` operation.
- **Effect** – You specify the effect when the user requests the specific action—this can be either allow or deny. If you don't explicitly grant access to (allow) a resource, access is implicitly denied. You can also explicitly deny access to a resource, which you might do to make sure that a user cannot access it, even if a different policy grants access.
- **Principal** – In identity-based policies (IAM policies), the user that the policy is attached to is the implicit principal. For resource-based policies, you specify the user, account, service, or other entity that you want to receive permissions (applies to resource-based policies only). AWS Storage Gateway doesn't support resource-based policies.

To learn more about IAM policy syntax and descriptions, see AWS IAM Policy Reference in the *IAM User Guide*.

For a table showing all of the AWS Storage Gateway API actions, see AWS Storage Gateway API Permissions: Actions, Resources, and Conditions Reference.

Specifying Conditions in a Policy

When you grant permissions, you can use the IAM policy language to specify the conditions when a policy should take effect when granting permissions. For example, you might want a policy to be applied only after a specific date. For more information about specifying conditions in a policy language, see Condition in the *IAM User Guide*.

To express conditions, you use predefined condition keys. There are no condition keys specific to Storage Gateway. However, there are AWS-wide condition keys that you can use as appropriate. For a complete list of AWS-wide keys, see Available Keys in the *IAM User Guide*.

Using Identity-Based Policies (IAM Policies) for AWS Storage Gateway

This topic provides examples of identity-based policies in which an account administrator can attach permissions policies to IAM identities (that is, users, groups, and roles).

Important
We recommend that you first review the introductory topics that explain the basic concepts and options available for you to manage access to your AWS Storage Gateway resources. For more information, see Overview of Managing Access Permissions to Your AWS Storage Gateway.

The sections in this topic cover the following:

- Permissions Required to Use the Storage Gateway Console
- AWS Managed Policies for AWS Storage Gateway
- Customer Managed Policy Examples

The following shows an example of a permissions policy.

```
1  {
2      "Version": "2012-10-17",
3      "Statement": [
4          {
5              "Sid": "AllowsSpecifiedActionsOnAllGateways",
6              "Effect": "Allow",
7              "Action": [
8                  "storagegateway:ActivateGateway",
9                  "storagegateway:ListGateways"
10             ],
11             "Resource": "arn:aws:storagegateway:us-west-2:account-id:gateway/*"
12         },
13         {
14             "Sid": "AllowsSpecifiedEC2ActionsOnAllGateways",
15             "Effect": "Allow",
16             "Action": [
17                 "ec2:DescribeSnapshots",
18                 "ec2:DeleteSnapshot"
19             ],
20             "Resource": "*"
21         }
22     ]
23 }
```

The policy has two statements (note the `Action` and `Resource` elements in both the statements):

- The first statement grants permissions for two Storage Gateway actions (`storagegateway:ActivateGateway` and `storagegateway:ListGateways`) on a gateway resource using the *Amazon Resource Name (ARN)* for the gateway. The ARN specifies a wildcard character (*) because you don't know the gateway ID until after you create a gateway. **Note**
ARNs uniquely identify AWS resources. For more information, see Amazon Resource Names (ARNs) and AWS Service Namespaces in the *AWS General Reference*.

  The wildcard character (*) at the end of the gateway ARN means that this statement can match any gateway ID. In this case, the statement allows the `storagegateway:ActivateGateway` and `storagegateway:ListGateways` actions on any gateway in the specified region, `us-west-2`, and the specified ID identifies the account that is owner of the gateway resource. For information about how to use a wildcard character (*) in a policy, see Example 2: Allow Read-Only Access to a Gateway.

To limit permissions for a particular action to a specific gateway only, create a separate statement for that action in the policy and specify the gateway ID in that statement.

- The second statement grants permissions for the `ec2:DescribeSnapshots` and `ec2:DeleteSnapshot` actions. These Amazon Elastic Compute Cloud (Amazon EC2) actions require permissions because snapshots generated from AWS Storage Gateway are stored in Amazon Elastic Block Store (Amazon EBS) and managed as Amazon EC2 resources, and thus they require corresponding EC2 actions. For more information, see Actions in the *Amazon EC2 API Reference*. Because these Amazon EC2 actions don't support resource-level permissions, the policy specifies the wildcard character (*) as the `Resource` value instead of specifying a gateway ARN.

For a table showing all of the AWS Storage Gateway API actions and the resources that they apply to, see AWS Storage Gateway API Permissions: Actions, Resources, and Conditions Reference.

Permissions Required to Use the Storage Gateway Console

To use the Storage Gateway console, you need to grant read-only permissions. If you plan to describe snapshots, you also need to grant permissions for additional actions as shown in the following permissions policy:

```
1  {
2      "Version": "2012-10-17",
3      "Statement": [
4          {
5              "Sid": "AllowsSpecifiedEC2ActionOnAllGateways",
6              "Effect": "Allow",
7              "Action": [
8                  "ec2:DescribeSnapshots"
9              ],
10             "Resource": "*"
11         }
12     ]
13 }
```

This additional permission is required because the Amazon EBS snapshots generated from AWS Storage Gateway are managed as Amazon EC2 resources.

To set up the minimum permissions required to navigate the Storage Gateway console, see Example 2: Allow Read-Only Access to a Gateway.

AWS Managed Policies for AWS Storage Gateway

AWS addresses many common use cases by providing standalone IAM policies that are created and administered by AWS. Managed policies grant necessary permissions for common use cases so you can avoid having to investigate what permissions are needed. For more information about AWS managed policies, see AWS Managed Policies in the *IAM User Guide*.

The following AWS managed policies, which you can attach to users in your account, are specific to Storage Gateway:

- **AWSStorageGatewayReadOnlyAccess** – Grants read-only access to AWS Storage Gateway resources.
- **AWSStorageGatewayFullAccess** – Grants full access to AWS Storage Gateway resources.

Note
You can review these permissions policies by signing in to the IAM console and searching for specific policies there.

You can also create your own custom IAM policies to allow permissions for AWS Storage Gateway API actions. You can attach these custom policies to the IAM users or groups that require those permissions.

Customer Managed Policy Examples

In this section, you can find example user policies that grant permissions for various Storage Gateway actions. These policies work when you are using AWS SDKs and the AWS CLI. When you are using the console, you need to grant additional permissions specific to the console, which is discussed in Permissions Required to Use the Storage Gateway Console.

Note
All examples use the US West (Oregon) Region (`us-west-2`) and contain fictitious account IDs.

Topics

- Example 1: Allow Any AWS Storage Gateway Actions on All Gateways
- Example 2: Allow Read-Only Access to a Gateway
- Example 3: Allow Access to a Specific Gateway
- Example 4: Allow a User to Access a Specific Volume
- Example 5: Allow All Actions on Gateways with a Specific Prefix

Example 1: Allow Any AWS Storage Gateway Actions on All Gateways

The following policy allows a user to perform all the AWS Storage Gateway actions. The policy also allows the user to perform Amazon EC2 actions (DescribeSnapshots and DeleteSnapshot) on the Amazon EBS snapshots generated from AWS Storage Gateway.

```
1  {
2      "Version": "2012-10-17",
3      "Statement": [
4          {
5              "Sid": "AllowsAllAWSStorageGatewayActions",
6              "Action": [
7                  "storagegateway:*"
8              ],
9              "Effect": "Allow",
10             "Resource": "*"
11         },
12         {
13             "Sid": "AllowsSpecifiedEC2Actions",
14             "Action": [
15                 "ec2:DescribeSnapshots",
16                 "ec2:DeleteSnapshot"
17             ],
18             "Effect": "Allow",
19             "Resource": "*"
20         }
21     ]
22 }
```

Example 2: Allow Read-Only Access to a Gateway

The following policy allows all `List*` and `Describe*` actions on all resources. Note that these actions are read-only actions. Thus, the policy doesn't allow the user to change the state of any resources—that is, the policy doesn't allow the user to perform actions such as `DeleteGateway`, `ActivateGateway`, and `ShutdownGateway`.

The policy also allows the `DescribeSnapshots` Amazon EC2 action. For more information, see DescribeSnapshots in the *Amazon EC2 API Reference*.

```
1  {
2      "Version": "2012-10-17",
3      "Statement": [
4          {
5              "Sid": "AllowReadOnlyAccessToAllGateways",
6              "Action": [
7                  "storagegateway:List*",
8                  "storagegateway:Describe*"
9              ],
10             "Effect": "Allow",
11             "Resource": "*"
12         },
13         {
14             "Sid": "AllowsUserToDescribeSnapshotsOnAllGateways",
15             "Action": [
16                 "ec2:DescribeSnapshots"
17             ],
18             "Effect": "Allow",
19             "Resource": "*"
20         }
21     ]
22 }
```

In the preceding policy, instead of a using a wildcard character (*), you can scope resources covered by the policy to a specific gateway, as shown in the following example. The policy then allows the actions only on the specific gateway.

```
1  "Resource": [
2              "arn:aws:storagegateway:us-west-2:123456789012:gateway/gateway-id/",
3              "arn:aws:storagegateway:us-west-2:123456789012:gateway/gateway-id/*"
4          ]
```

Within a gateway, you can further restrict the scope of the resources to only the gateway volumes, as shown in the following example:

```
1  "Resource": "arn:aws:storagegateway:us-west-2:123456789012:gateway/gateway-id/volume/*"
```

Example 3: Allow Access to a Specific Gateway

The following policy allows all actions on a specific gateway. The user is restricted from accessing other gateways you might have deployed.

```
1  {
2      "Version": "2012-10-17",
3      "Statement": [
4          {
5              "Sid": "AllowReadOnlyAccessToAllGateways",
6              "Action": [
7                  "storagegateway:List*",
8                  "storagegateway:Describe*"
9              ],
```

```
10        "Effect": "Allow",
11        "Resource": "*"
12      },
13      {
14        "Sid": "AllowsUserToDescribeSnapshotsOnAllGateways",
15        "Action": [
16          "ec2:DescribeSnapshots"
17        ],
18        "Effect": "Allow",
19        "Resource": "*"
20      },
21      {
22        "Sid": "AllowsAllActionsOnSpecificGateway",
23        "Action": [
24          "storagegateway:*"
25        ],
26        "Effect": "Allow",
27        "Resource": [
28          "arn:aws:storagegateway:us-west-2:123456789012:gateway/gateway-id/",
29          "arn:aws:storagegateway:us-west-2:123456789012:gateway/gateway-id/*"
30        ]
31      }
32    ]
33 }
```

The preceding policy works if the user to which the policy is attached uses either the API or an AWS SDK to access the gateway. However, if the user is going to use the AWS Storage Gateway console, you must also grant permissions to allow the ListGateways action, as shown in the following example:

```
1  {
2    "Version": "2012-10-17",
3    "Statement": [
4      {
5        "Sid": "AllowsAllActionsOnSpecificGateway",
6        "Action": [
7          "storagegateway:*"
8        ],
9        "Effect": "Allow",
10        "Resource": [
11          "arn:aws:storagegateway:us-west-2:123456789012:gateway/gateway-id/",
12          "arn:aws:storagegateway:us-west-2:123456789012:gateway/gateway-id/*"
13        ]
14      },
15      {
16        "Sid": "AllowsUserToUseAWSConsole",
17        "Action": [
18          "storagegateway:ListGateways"
19        ],
20        "Effect": "Allow",
21        "Resource": "*"
22      }
23    ]
24 }
```

Example 4: Allow a User to Access a Specific Volume

The following policy allows a user to perform all actions to a specific volume on a gateway. Because a user doesn't get any permissions by default, the policy restricts the user to accessing only a specific volume.

```
1  {
2      "Version": "2012-10-17",
3      "Statement": [
4          {
5              "Sid": "GrantsPermissionsToSpecificVolume",
6              "Action": [
7                  "storagegateway:*"
8              ],
9              "Effect": "Allow",
10             "Resource": "arn:aws:storagegateway:us-west-2:123456789012:gateway/gateway-id/volume
                   /volume-id"
11         },
12         {
13             "Sid": "GrantsPermissionsToUseStorageGatewayConsole",
14             "Action": [
15                 "storagegateway:ListGateways"
16             ],
17             "Effect": "Allow",
18             "Resource": "*"
19         }
20     ]
21 }
```

The preceding policy works if the user to whom the policy is attached uses either the API or an AWS SDK to access the volume. However, if this user is going to use the AWS Storage Gateway console, you must also grant permissions to allow the ListGateways action, as shown in the following example:

```
1  {
2      "Version": "2012-10-17",
3      "Statement": [
4          {
5              "Sid": "GrantsPermissionsToSpecificVolume",
6              "Action": [
7                  "storagegateway:*"
8              ],
9              "Effect": "Allow",
10             "Resource": "arn:aws:storagegateway:us-west-2:123456789012:gateway/gateway-id/volume
                   /volume-id"
11         },
12         {
13             "Sid": "GrantsPermissionsToUseStorageGatewayConsole",
14             "Action": [
15                 "storagegateway:ListGateways"
16             ],
17             "Effect": "Allow",
18             "Resource": "*"
19         }
20     ]
21 }
```

Example 5: Allow All Actions on Gateways with a Specific Prefix

The following policy allows a user to perform all AWS Storage Gateway actions on gateways with names that start with DeptX. The policy also allows the DescribeSnapshots Amazon EC2 action which is required if you plan to describe snapshots.

```
1  {
2      "Version": "2012-10-17",
3      "Statement": [
4          {
5              "Sid": "AllowsActionsGatewayWithPrefixDeptX",
6              "Action": [
7                  "storagegateway:*"
8              ],
9              "Effect": "Allow",
10             "Resource": "arn:aws:storagegateway:us-west-2:123456789012:gateway/DeptX"
11         },
12         {
13             "Sid": "GrantsPermissionsToSpecifiedAction",
14             "Action": [
15                 "ec2:DescribeSnapshots"
16             ],
17             "Effect": "Allow",
18             "Resource": "*"
19         }
20     ]
21 }
```

The preceding policy works if the user to whom the policy is attached uses either the API or an AWS SDK to access the gateway. However, if this user plans to use the AWS Storage Gateway console, you must grant additional permissions as described in Example 3: Allow Access to a Specific Gateway.

AWS Storage Gateway API Permissions: Actions, Resources, and Conditions Reference

When you are setting up Access Control and writing permissions policies that you can attach to an IAM identity (identity-based policies), you can use the following table as a reference. The table lists each AWS Storage Gateway API operation, the corresponding actions for which you can grant permissions to perform the action, and the AWS resource for which you can grant the permissions. You specify the actions in the policy's `Action` field, and you specify the resource value in the policy's `Resource` field.

You can use AWS-wide condition keys in your AWS Storage Gateway policies to express conditions. For a complete list of AWS-wide keys, see Available keys in the *IAM User Guide*.

Note
To specify an action, use the `storagegateway:` prefix followed by the API operation name (for example, `storagegateway:ActivateGateway`). For each AWS Storage Gateway action, you can specify a wildcard character (*) as the resource.

If you see an expand arrow () in the upper-right corner of the table, you can open the table in a new window. To close the window, choose the close button (**X**) in the lower-right corner.

For a list of Storage Gateway resources with the ARN format, see AWS Storage Gateway Resources and Operations.

AWS Storage Gateway API and Required Permissions for Actions

Storage Gateway API Operations	Required Permissions (API Actions)	Resources
ActivateGateway	`storagegateway: ActivateGateway`	*
AddCache	`storagegateway:AddCache`	`arn:aws:storagegateway :region:account-id: gateway/gateway-id`
AddTagsToResource	`storagegateway: AddTagsToResource`	`arn:aws:storagegateway :region:account-id: gateway/gateway-id` or `arn:aws:storagegateway :region:account-id: gateway/gateway-id /volume/volume-id` or `arn:aws:storagegateway: region:account-id:tape/ tapebarcode`
AddUploadBuffer	`storagegateway: AddUploadBuffer`	`arn:aws:storagegateway :region:account-id: gateway/gateway-id`
AddWorkingStorage	`storagegateway: AddWorkingStorage`	arn:aws:storagegate-way:region:account-id:gateway/gateway-id
CancelArchival	`storagegateway: CancelArchival`	arn:aws:storagegateway:re-gion:account-id:tape/tapebar-code
CancelRetrieval	`storagegateway: CancelRetrieval`	arn:aws:storagegateway:re-gion:account-id:tape/tapebar-code

Storage Gateway API Operations	Required Permissions (API Actions)	Resources
CreateCachediSCSIVolume	`storagegateway: CreateCachediSCSIVolume`	arn:aws:storagegateway:region:account-id:gateway/gateway-id
CreateNFSFileShare	`storagegateway: CreateNFSFileShare`	arn:aws:storagegateway:region:account-id:gateway/gateway-id
CreateSnapshot	`storagegateway: CreateSnapshot`	`arn:aws:storagegateway :region:account-id: gateway/gateway-id/ volume/volume-id`
CreateSnapshotFromVolumeRecoveryPoint	`storagegateway: CreateSnapshotFromVolumeRe`	`arn:aws:storagegateway :region:account-id: gateway/gateway-id/ volume/volume-id`
CreateStorediSCSIVolume	`storagegateway: CreateStorediSCSIVolume`	`arn:aws:storagegateway :region:account-id: gateway/gateway-id`
CreateTapes	`storagegateway: CreateTapes`	`arn:aws:storagegateway :region:account-id: gateway/gateway-id`
DeleteBandwidthRateLimit	`storagegateway: DeleteBandwidthRateLimit`	`arn:aws:storagegateway :region:account-id: gateway/gateway-id`
DeleteChapCredentials	`storagegateway: DeleteChapCredentials`	arn:aws:storagegateway:region:account-id:gateway/gateway-id/target/iSCSItarget
DeleteFileShare	`storagegateway: DeleteFileShare`	`arn:aws:storagegateway: region:account-id:share/ share-id`
DeleteGateway	`storagegateway: DeleteGateway`	`arn:aws:storagegateway :region:account-id: gateway/gateway-id`
DeleteSnapshotSchedule	`storagegateway: DeleteSnapshotSchedule`	`arn:aws:storagegateway :region:account-id: gateway/gateway-id/ volume/volume-id`
DeleteTape	`storagegateway: DeleteTape`	`arn:aws:storagegateway :region:account-id: gateway/gateway-id`
DeleteTapeArchive	`storagegateway: DeleteTapeArchive`	`*`
DeleteVolume	`storagegateway: DeleteVolume`	`arn:aws:storagegateway :region:account-id: gateway/gateway-id/ volume/volume-id`
DescribeBandwidthRateLimit	`storagegateway: DescribeBandwidthRateLimit`	`arn:aws:storagegateway :region:account-id: gateway/gateway-id`
DescribeCache	`storagegateway: DescribeCache`	`arn:aws:storagegateway :region:account-id: gateway/gateway-id`

Storage Gateway API Operations	Required Permissions (API Actions)	Resources
DescribeCachediSCSIVolumes	`storagegateway:` `DescribeCachediSCSIVolumes`	`arn:aws:storagegateway` `:region:account-id:` `gateway/gateway-id/` `volume/volume-id`
DescribeChapCredentials	`storagegateway:` `DescribeChapCredentials`	arn:aws:storagegateway:region:account-id:gateway/gateway-id/target/iSCSItarget
DescribeGatewayInformation	`storagegateway:` `DescribeGatewayInformation`	`arn:aws:storagegateway` `:region:account-id:` `gateway/gateway-id`
DescribeMaintenanceStartTime	`storagegateway:` `DescribeMaintenanceStartTi`	`arn:aws:storagegateway` `:region:account-id:` `gateway/gateway-id`
DescribeNFSFileShares	`storagegateway:` `DescribeNFSFileShares`	`arn:aws:storagegateway:` `region:account-id:share/` `share-id`
DescribeSnapshotSchedule	`storagegateway:` `DescribeSnapshotSchedule`	arn:aws:storagegateway:region:account-id:gateway/gateway-id/volume/volume-id
DescribeStorediSCSIVolumes	`storagegateway:` `DescribeStorediSCSIVolumes`	`arn:aws:storagegateway` `:region:account-id:` `gateway/gateway-id/` `volume/volume-id`
DescribeTapeArchives	`storagegateway:` `DescribeTapeArchives`	*
DescribeTapeRecoveryPoints	`storagegateway:` `DescribeTapeRecoveryPoints`	`arn:aws:storagegateway` `:region:account-id:` `gateway/gateway-id`
DescribeTapes	`storagegateway:` `DescribeTapes`	`arn:aws:storagegateway` `:region:account-id:` `gateway/gateway-id`
DescribeUploadBuffer	`storagegateway:` `DescribeUploadBuffer`	`arn:aws:storagegateway` `:region:account-id:` `gateway/gateway-id`
DescribeVTLDevices	`storagegateway:` `DescribeVTLDevices`	`arn:aws:storagegateway` `:region:account-id:` `gateway/gateway-id`
DescribeWorkingStorage	`storagegateway:` `DescribeWorkingStorage`	`arn:aws:storagegateway` `:region:account-id:` `gateway/gateway-id`
DisableGateway	`storagegateway:` `DisableGateway`	`arn:aws:storagegateway` `:region:account-id:` `gateway/gateway-id`
ListFileShares	`storagegateway:` `ListFileShares`	`arn:aws:storagegateway` `:region:account-id:` `gateway/gateway-id`
ListGateways	`storagegateway:` `ListGateways`	*

Storage Gateway API Operations	Required Permissions (API Actions)	Resources
ListLocalDisks	`storagegateway: ListLocalDisks`	`arn:aws:storagegateway :region:account-id: gateway/gateway-id`
ListTagsForResource	`storagegateway: ListTagsForResource`	arn:aws:storagegate-way:region:account-id:gateway/gateway-id or arn:aws:storage-gateway:region:account-id:gateway/gateway-id/volume/volume-id or arn:aws:storagegateway:region:account-id:tape/tapebar-code
ListTapes	`storagegateway:ListTapes`	arn:aws:storagegate-way:region:account-id:gateway/gateway-id
ListVolumeInitiators	`storagegateway: ListVolumeInitiators`	arn:aws:storagegate-way:region:account-id:gateway/gateway-id/volume/volume-id
ListVolumeRecoveryPoints	`storagegateway: ListVolumeRecoveryPoints`	`arn:aws:storagegateway :region:account-id: gateway/gateway-id`
ListVolumes	`storagegateway: ListVolumes`	`arn:aws:storagegateway :region:account-id: gateway/gateway-id`
RefreshCache	`storagegateway: RefreshCache`	`arn:aws:storagegateway: region:account-id:share/ share-id`
RemoveTagsFromResource	`storagegateway: RemoveTagsFromResource`	arn:aws:storagegate-way:region:account-id:gateway/gateway-id or arn:aws:storage-gateway:region:account-id:gateway/gateway-id/volume/volume-id or arn:aws:storagegateway:region:account-id:tape/tapebar-code
ResetCache	`storagegateway: ResetCache`	`arn:aws:storagegateway :region:account-id: gateway/gateway-id`
RetrieveTapeArchive	`storagegateway: RetrieveTapeArchive`	`arn:aws:storagegateway :region:account-id: gateway/gateway-id`
RetrieveTapeRecoveryPoint	`storagegateway: RetrieveTapeRecoveryPoint`	`arn:aws:storagegateway :region:account-id: gateway/gateway-id`
ShutdownGateway	`storagegateway: ShutdownGateway`	`arn:aws:storagegateway :region:account-id: gateway/gateway-id`

Storage Gateway API Operations	Required Permissions (API Actions)	Resources

StartGateway	`storagegateway:`
	`StartGateway`
		`arn:aws:storagegateway`
		`:region:account-id:`
		`gateway/gateway-id`

UpdateBandwidthRateLimit	`storagegateway:` `UpdateBandwidthRateLimit`	arn:aws:storagegateway:region:account-id:gateway/gateway-id
UpdateChapCredentials	`storagegateway:` `UpdateChapCredentials`	arn:aws:storagegateway:region:account-id:gateway/gateway-id/target/iSCSItarget
UpdateGatewayInformation	`storagegateway:` `UpdateGatewayInformation`	arn:aws:storagegateway:region:account-id:gateway/gateway-id

UpdateGatewaySoftwareNow	`storagegateway:`
	`UpdateGatewaySoftwareNow`
		`arn:aws:storagegateway`
		`:region:account-id:`
		`gateway/gateway-id`

UpdateMaintenanceStartTime	`storagegateway:`
	`UpdateMaintenanceStartTime`
		`arn:aws:storagegateway`
		`:region:account-id:`
		`gateway/gateway-id`

UpdateNFSFileShare	`storagegateway:`
	`UpdateNFSFileShare`
		`arn:aws:storagegateway:`
		`region:account-id:share/`
		`share-id`

UpdateSnapshotSchedule	`storagegateway:`
	`UpdateSnapshotSchedule`
		`arn:aws:storagegateway`
		`:region:account-id:`
		`gateway/gateway-id/`
		`volume/volume-id`

UpdateVTLDeviceType	`storagegateway:` `UpdateVTLDeviceType`	arn:aws:storagegateway:region:account-id:gateway/gateway-id/device/vtldevice

Related Topics

- Access Control
- Customer Managed Policy Examples

Troubleshooting Your Gateway

Following, you can find information about troubleshooting issues related to gateways, file shares, volumes, virtual tapes, and snapshots. The on-premises gateway troubleshooting information covers gateways deployed on both the VMware ESXi and Microsoft Hyper-V clients. The troubleshooting information for file shares apply to the file gateway type. The troubleshooting information for volumes applies to the volume gateway type. The troubleshooting information for tapes applies to the tape gateway type.

Topics

- Troubleshooting On-Premises Gateway Issues
- Troubleshooting Your Microsoft Hyper-V Setup
- Troubleshooting Amazon EC2 Gateway Issues
- Troubleshooting File Share Issues
- Troubleshooting Volume Issues
- Troubleshooting Virtual Tape Issues
- Best Practices for Recovering Your Data

Troubleshooting On-Premises Gateway Issues

The following table lists typical issues that you might encounter working with your on-premises gateways.

Topics

- Enabling AWS Support To Help Troubleshoot Your Gateway Hosted On-Premises

Issue	Action to Take
You cannot find the IP address of your gateway.	Use the hypervisor client to connect to your host to find the gateway IP address. [See the AWS documentation website for more details] If you are still having trouble finding the gateway IP address: [See the AWS documentation website for more details]
You're having network or firewall problems.	[See the AWS documentation website for more details]
Your gateway's activation fails when you click the Proceed to Activation button in the AWS Storage Gateway Management Console.	[See the AWS documentation website for more details]
You need to remove a disk allocated as upload buffer space. For example, you might want to reduce the amount of upload buffer space for a gateway, or you might need to replace a disk used as an upload buffer that has failed.	For instructions about removing a disk allocated as upload buffer space, see Removing Upload Buffer Capacity
You need to improve bandwidth between your gateway and AWS.	You can improve the bandwidth from your gateway to AWS by setting up your Internet connection to AWS on a network adapter (NIC) separate from that connecting your applications and the gateway VM. Taking this approach is useful if you have a high-bandwidth connection to AWS and you want to avoid bandwidth contention, especially during a snapshot restore. For high-throughput workload needs, you can use AWS Direct Connect to establish a dedicated network connection between your on-premises gateway and AWS. To measure the bandwidth of the connection from your gateway to AWS, use the `CloudBytesDownloaded` and `CloudBytesUploaded` metrics of the gateway. For more on this subject, see Measuring Performance Between Your Gateway and AWS. Improving your Internet connectivity helps to ensure that your upload buffer does not fill up.
Throughput to or from your gateway drops to zero.	[See the AWS documentation website for more details] You can view the throughput to and from your gateway from the Amazon CloudWatch console. For more information about measuring throughput to and from your gateway to AWS, see Measuring Performance Between Your Gateway and AWS.

Issue	Action to Take
You are having trouble importing (deploying) AWS Storage Gateway on Microsoft Hyper-V.	See Troubleshooting Your Microsoft Hyper-V Setup, which discusses some of the common issues of deploying a gateway on Microsoft Hyper-V.
You receive a message that says: "The data that has been written to the volume in your gateway isn't securely stored at AWS".	You receive this message if your gateway VM was created from a clone or snapshot of another gateway VM. If this isn't the case, contact AWS Support.

Enabling AWS Support To Help Troubleshoot Your Gateway Hosted On-Premises

AWS Storage Gateway provides a local console you can use to perform several maintenance tasks, including enabling AWS Support to access your gateway to assist you with troubleshooting gateway issues. By default, AWS Support access to your gateway is disabled. You enable this access through the host's local console. To give AWS Support access to your gateway, you first log in to the local console for the host, navigate to the storage gateway's console, and then connect to the support server.

To enable AWS Support access to your gateway

1. Log in to your host's local console.

    - VMware ESXi—for more information, see Accessing the Gateway Local Console with VMware ESXi.
    - Microsoft Hyper-V—for more information, see Access the Gateway Local Console with Microsoft Hyper-V.

    The local console looks like the following.

2. At the prompt, type **5** to open the AWS Storage Gateway console.

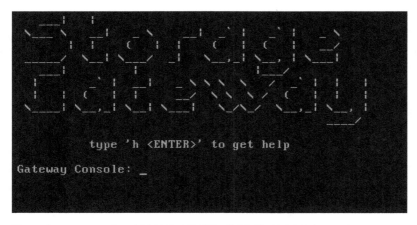

3. Type **h** to open the **AVAILABLE COMMANDS** window.

4. In the **AVAILABLE COMMANDS** window, type **open-support-channel** to connect to customer support for AWS Storage Gateway. You must allow TCP port 22 to initiate a support channel to AWS. When you connect to customer support, Storage Gateway assigns you a support number. Make a note of your support number.

```
AVAILABLE COMMANDS
type 'man <command name>' to find out more information about commands

ip                      Show / manipulate routing, devices, and tunnels
save-routing-table      Save newly added routing table entry
ifconfig                View or configure network interfaces
iptables                Administration tool for IPv4 packet filtering and NAT
save-iptables           Persist IP tables
testconn                Test network connectivity
man                     Display command manual pages
open-support-channel    Connect to Storage Gateway Support
h                       Display available command list
exit                    Return to Storage Gateway Configuration menu

Gateway Console: open-support-channel
```

Note

The channel number is not a Transmission Control Protocol/User Datagram Protocol (TCP/UDP) port number. Instead, the gateway makes a Secure Shell (SSH) (TCP 22) connection to Storage Gateway servers and provides the support channel for the connection.

5. Once the support channel is established, provide your support service number to AWS Support so AWS Support can provide troubleshooting assistance.

6. When the support session is completed, type **q** to end it.

7. Type **exit** to log out of the AWS Storage Gateway console.

8. Follow the prompts to exit the local console.

Troubleshooting Your Microsoft Hyper-V Setup

The following table lists typical issues that you might encounter when deploying AWS Storage Gateway on the Microsoft Hyper-V platform.

Issue	Action to Take
You try to import a gateway and receive the error message: "Import failed. Unable to find virtual machine import file under location 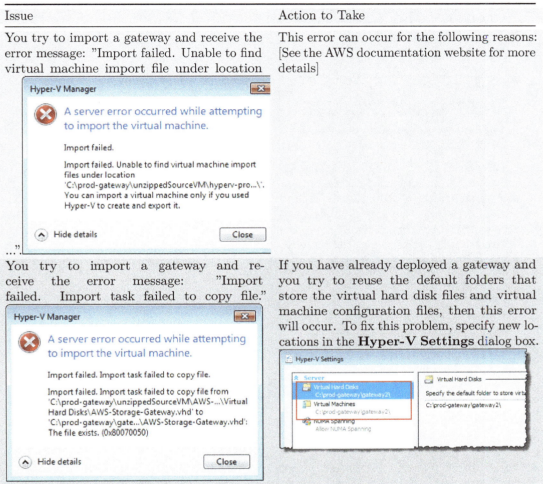 ..."	This error can occur for the following reasons: [See the AWS documentation website for more details]
You try to import a gateway and receive the error message: "Import failed. Import task failed to copy file." 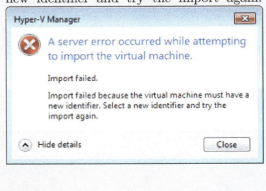	If you have already deployed a gateway and you try to reuse the default folders that store the virtual hard disk files and virtual machine configuration files, then this error will occur. To fix this problem, specify new locations in the **Hyper-V Settings** dialog box.
You try to import a gateway and receive an error message: "Import failed. Import failed because the virtual machine must have a new identifier. Select a new identifier and try the import again."	When you import the gateway make sure you select the **Copy the virtual machine** option and check the **Duplicate all files** option in the **Import Virtual Machine** dialog box to create a new unique ID for the VM. The following example shows the options in the **Import Virtual Machine** dialog box that you should use. 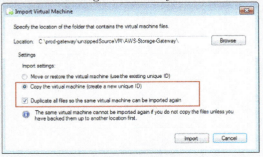

271

Issue	Action to Take
You try to start a gateway VM and receive an error message "The child partition processor setting is incompatible with parent partition." 	This error is likely caused by a CPU discrepancy between the required CPUs for the gateway and the available CPUs on the host. Ensure that the VM CPU count is supported by the underlying hypervisor. For more information about the requirements for AWS Storage Gateway, see Requirements.
You try to start a gateway VM and receive an error message "Failed to create partition: Insufficient resources exist to complete the requested service." 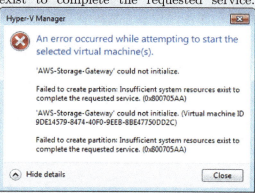	This error is likely caused by a RAM discrepancy between the required RAM for the gateway and the available RAM on the host. For more information about the requirements for AWS Storage Gateway, see Requirements.
Your snapshots and gateway software updates are occurring at slightly different times than expected.	The gateway VM's clock might be offset from the actual time, known as clock drift. Check and correct the VM's time using local gateway console's time synchronization option. For more information, see Synchronizing Your Gateway VM Time.
You need to put the unzipped Microsoft Hyper-V AWS Storage gateway files on the host file system.	Access the host as you do a typical Microsoft Windows server. For example, if the hypervisor host is name **hyperv-server**, then you can use the following UNC path \\hyperv-server\c$, which assumes that the name **hyperv-server** can be resolved or is defined in your local hosts file.

Issue	Action to Take
You are prompted for credentials when connecting to hypervisor. 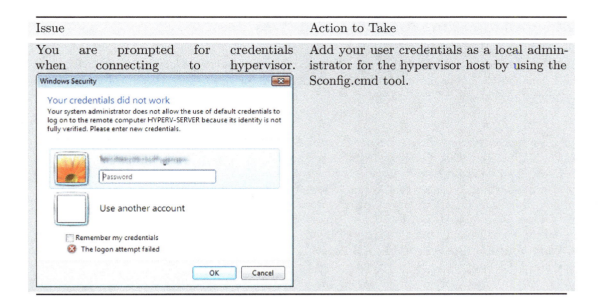	Add your user credentials as a local administrator for the hypervisor host by using the Sconfig.cmd tool.

Troubleshooting Amazon EC2 Gateway Issues

In the following sections, you can find typical issues that you might encounter working with your gateway deployed on Amazon EC2. For more information about the difference between an on-premises gateway and a gateway deployed in Amazon EC2, see Deploying a Volume or Tape Gateway on an Amazon EC2 Host.

Topics

- Your Gateway Activation Hasn't Occurred After a Few Moments
- You Can't Find Your EC2 Gateway Instance in the Instance List
- You Created an Amazon EBS Volume But Can't Attach it to Your EC2 Gateway Instance
- You Can't Attach an Initiator to a Volume Target of Your EC2 Gateway
- You Get a Message That You Have No Disks Available When You Try to Add Storage Volumes
- You Want to Remove a Disk Allocated as Upload Buffer Space to Reduce Upload Buffer Space
- Throughput to or from Your EC2 Gateway Drops to Zero
- You Want Your File Gateway to Use a C5 or M5 EC2 Instance Type Instead of C4 or M4
- You Want AWS Support to Help Troubleshoot Your EC2 Gateway

Your Gateway Activation Hasn't Occurred After a Few Moments

Check the following in the Amazon EC2 console:

- Port 80 is enabled in the security group you associated with the instance. For more information about adding a security group rule, see Adding a Security Group Rule in the *Amazon EC2 User Guide for Linux Instances.*
- The gateway instance is marked as running. In the Amazon EC2 console, the **State** value for the instance should be RUNNING.
- Make sure that your Amazon EC2 instance type meets the minimum requirements, as described in Storage Requirements.

After correcting the problem, try activating the gateway again by going to the AWS Storage Gateway console, choosing **Deploy a new Gateway on Amazon EC2**, and re-entering the IP address of the instance.

You Can't Find Your EC2 Gateway Instance in the Instance List

If you didn't give your instance a resource tag and you have many instances running, it can be hard to tell which instance you launched. In this case, you can take the following actions to find the gateway instance:

- Check the name of the Amazon Machine Image (AMI) on the **Description** tab of the instance. An instance based on the AWS Storage Gateway AMI should start with the text **aws-storage-gateway-ami**.
- If you have several instances based on the AWS Storage Gateway AMI, check the instance launch time to find the correct instance.

You Created an Amazon EBS Volume But Can't Attach it to Your EC2 Gateway Instance

Check that the Amazon EBS volume in question is in the same Availability Zone as the gateway instance. If there is a discrepancy in Availability Zones, create a new Amazon EBS volume in the same Availability Zone as your instance.

You Can't Attach an Initiator to a Volume Target of Your EC2 Gateway

Check that the security group that you launched the instance with includes a rule that allows the port that you are using for iSCSI access. The port is usually set as 3260. For more information on connecting to volumes, see Connecting to Your Volumes to a Windows Client.

You Get a Message That You Have No Disks Available When You Try to Add Storage Volumes

For a newly activated gateway, no volume storage is defined. Before you can define volume storage, you must allocate local disks to the gateway to use as an upload buffer and cache storage. For a gateway deployed to Amazon EC2, the local disks are Amazon EBS volumes attached to the instance. This error message likely occurs because no Amazon EBS volumes are defined for the instance.

Check block devices defined for the instance that is running the gateway. If there are only two block devices (the default devices that come with the AMI), then you should add storage. For more information on doing so, see Deploying a Volume or Tape Gateway on an Amazon EC2 Host. After attaching two or more Amazon EBS volumes, try creating volume storage on the gateway.

You Want to Remove a Disk Allocated as Upload Buffer Space to Reduce Upload Buffer Space

Follow the steps in Adding and Removing Upload Buffer.

Throughput to or from Your EC2 Gateway Drops to Zero

Verify that the gateway instance is running. If the instance is starting due to a reboot, for example, wait for the instance to restart.

Also, verify that the gateway IP has not changed. If the instance was stopped and then restarted, the IP address of the instance might have changed. In this case, you need to activate a new gateway.

You can view the throughput to and from your gateway from the Amazon CloudWatch console. For more information about measuring throughput to and from your gateway to AWS, see Measuring Performance Between Your Gateway and AWS.

You Want Your File Gateway to Use a C5 or M5 EC2 Instance Type Instead of C4 or M4

Do the following:

1. Create a new file gateway using the c5 or m5 Amazon EC2 AMI.
2. Create a new file share on the new gateway and configure it to point to your Amazon S3 bucket.
3. Mount your new file share to your client.
4. Make sure that your file gateway that is using a c4 or m4 EC2 AMI has finished uploading all data to S3 (that is, the `CachePercentDirty` value is 0).
5. Shut down the file gateway that is using a c4 or m4 AMI and delete the gateway if you no longer need it.

For information about instance type requirements, see Hardware and Storage Requirements.

Warning
You can't use the elastic IP address of the Amazon EC2 instance used as the target address.

You Want AWS Support to Help Troubleshoot Your EC2 Gateway

AWS Storage Gateway provides a local console you can use to perform several maintenance tasks, including enabling AWS Support to access your gateway to assist you with troubleshooting gateway issues. By default, AWS Support access to your gateway is disabled. You enable this access through the Amazon EC2 local console. You log in to the Amazon EC2 local console through a Secure Shell (SSH). To successfully log in through SSH, your instance's security group must have a rule that opens TCP port 22.

Note

If you add a new rule to an existing security group, the new rule applies to all instances that use that security group. For more information about security groups and how to add a security group rule, see Amazon EC2 Security Groups in the *Amazon EC2 User Guide*.

To let AWS Support connect to your gateway, you first log in to the local console for the Amazon EC2 instance, navigate to the storage gateway's console, and then provide the access.

To enable AWS support access to a gateway deployed on an Amazon EC2 instance

1. Log in to the local console for your Amazon EC2 instance. For instructions, go to Connect to Your Instancein the *Amazon EC2 User Guide*.

   You can use the following command to log in to the EC2 instance's local console.

   1 `ssh -i PRIVATE-KEY sguser@INSTANCE-PUBLIC-DNS-NAME`

Note

The *PRIVATE-KEY* is the `.pem` file containing the private certificate of the EC2 key pair that you used to launch the Amazon EC2 instance. For more information, see Retrieving the Public Key for Your Key Pair in the *Amazon EC2 User Guide*.

The *INSTANCE-PUBLIC-DNS-NAME* is the public Domain Name System (DNS) name of your Amazon EC2 instance that your gateway is running on. You obtain this public DNS name by selecting the Amazon EC2 instance in the EC2 console and clicking the **Description** tab.

1 `The local console looks like the following\.`

```
AWS Storage Gateway Configuration

###############################################################
##   Currently connected network adapters:
##
##   eth0: 10.222.0.40
###############################################################

1: SOCKS Proxy Configuration
2: Test Network Connectivity
3: Gateway Console
4: View System Resource Check (0 Errors)

0: Stop AWS Storage Gateway

Press "x" to exit session

Enter command: _
```

1. At the prompt, type **3** to open the AWS Storage Gateway console.

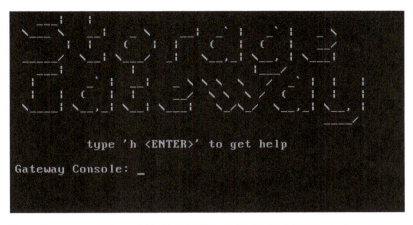

```
                type 'h <ENTER>' to get help

Gateway Console: _
```

2. Type **h** to open the **AVAILABLE COMMANDS** window.

3. In the **AVAILABLE COMMANDS** window, type **open-support-channel** to connect to customer support for AWS Storage Gateway. You must allow TCP port 22 to initiate a support channel to AWS. When you connect to customer support, Storage Gateway assigns you a support number. Make a note of your support number.

```
AVAILABLE COMMANDS
type 'man <command name>' to find out more information about commands

ip                        Show / manipulate routing, devices, and tunnels
save-routing-table        Save newly added routing table entry
ifconfig                  View or configure network interfaces
iptables                  Administration tool for IPv4 packet filtering and NAT
save-iptables             Persist IP tables
testconn                  Test network connectivity
man                       Display command manual pages
open-support-channel      Connect to Storage Gateway Support
h                         Display available command list
exit                      Return to Storage Gateway Configuration menu

Gateway Console: open-support-channel
```

Note

The channel number is not a Transmission Control Protocol/User Datagram Protocol (TCP/UDP) port number. Instead, the gateway makes a Secure Shell (SSH) (TCP 22) connection to Storage Gateway servers and provides the support channel for the connection.

4. Once the support channel is established, provide your support service number to AWS Support so AWS Support can provide troubleshooting assistance.

5. When the support session is completed, type **q** to end it.

6. Type **exit** to exit the AWS Storage Gateway console.

7. Follow the console menus to log out of the AWS Storage Gateway instance.

Troubleshooting File Share Issues

You can find information following about actions to take if you experience unexpected issues with your file share.

Topics

- Your File Share Is Stuck in CREATING Status
- You Can't Create a File Share
- Multiple File Shares Can't Write to the Mapped Amazon S3 Bucket
- You Can't Upload Files into Your S3 Bucket
- Object Versioning May Impact What You See in Your File System

Your File Share Is Stuck in CREATING Status

When your file share is being created, the status is CREATING. The status transitions to AVAILABLE status after the file share is created. If your file share gets stuck in the CREATING status, do the following:

1. Open the Amazon S3 console at https://console.aws.amazon.com/s3/.

2. Make sure the Amazon S3 bucket that you mapped your file share to exists. If the bucket doesn't exist, create it. After you create the bucket, the file share status transitions to AVAILABLE. For information about how to create an Amazon S3 bucket, see Create a Bucket in the *Amazon Simple Storage Service Console User Guide*.

3. Make sure your bucket name complies with the rules for bucket naming in Amazon S3. For more information, see Rules for Bucket Naming in the *Amazon Simple Storage Service Developer Guide*.

4. Make sure the IAM role you used to access the Amazon S3 bucket has the correct permissions and verify that the Amazon S3 bucket is listed as a resource in the IAM policy. For more information, see Granting Access to an Amazon S3 Bucket.

You Can't Create a File Share

1. If you can't create a file share because your file share is stuck in CREATING status, verify that the Amazon S3 bucket you mapped your file share to exists. For information on how to do so, see Your File Share Is Stuck in CREATING Status, preceding.

2. If the Amazon S3 bucket exists, then verify that AWS Security Token Service is enabled in the region where you are creating the file share. If a security token is not enabled, you should enable it. For information about how to enable a token using AWS Security Token Service, see Activating and Deactivating AWS STS in an AWS Region in the *IAM User Guide*.

Multiple File Shares Can't Write to the Mapped Amazon S3 Bucket

We don't recommend configuring your Amazon S3 bucket to allow multiple file shares to write to one S3 bucket. This approach can cause unpredictable results.

Instead, we recommend that you allow only one file share to write to each S3 bucket. You create a bucket policy to allow only the role associated with your file share to write to the bucket. For more information, see File Share Best Practices.

You Can't Upload Files into Your S3 Bucket

If you can't upload files into your Amazon S3 bucket, do the following:

1. Make sure you have granted the required access for the file gateway to upload files into your S3 bucket. For more information, see Granting Access to an Amazon S3 Bucket.

2. Make sure the role that created the bucket has permission to write to the S3 bucket. For more information, see File Share Best Practices.

Object Versioning May Impact What You See in Your File System

If your Amazon S3 bucket has objects written to it by another client, your view of the S3 bucket might not be up-to-date as a result of S3 bucket object versioning.You should always refresh your cache before examining files of interest.

*Object versioning *is an optional S3 bucket feature that helps protect data by storing multiple copies of the same-named object. Each copy has a separate ID value, for example `file1.jpg`: ID="xxx" and `file1.jpg`: ID="yyy". The number of identically named objects and their lifetimes is controlled by S3 lifecycle policies. For more details on these S3 concepts, see Using Versioning and Object Lifecycle Management in the *Amazon S3 Developer Guide. *

When you delete a versioned object, that object is flagged with a delete marker but retained. Only an S3 bucket owner can permanently delete an object with versioning turned on.

In your file gateway, files shown are the most recent versions of objects in an S3 bucket at the time the object was fetched or the cache was refreshed. File gateway ignore any older versions or any objects marked for deletion. When reading a file, you read data from the latest version. When you write a file in your file share, your file gateway creates a new version of a named object with your changes, and that version becomes the latest version.

Your file gateway continues to read from the earlier version, and updates that you make are based on the earlier version should a new version be added to the S3 bucket outside of your application. To read the latest version of an object, use the RefreshCache API action or refresh from the console as described in Refreshing Objects in Your Amazon S3 Bucket. We don't recommend that objects or files be written to your file gateway S3 bucket from outside of the file share.

Use of versioned S3 buckets can greatly increase the amount of storage in S3 because each modification to a file creates a new version. By default, S3 continues to store all of these versions unless you specifically create a policy to override this behavior and limit the number of versions that are kept. If you notice unusually large storage usage with object versioning enabled, check that you have your storage policies set appropriately. An increase in the number of `HTTP 503-slow down` responses for browser requests can also be the result of problems with object versioning.

If you enable object versioning after installing a file gateway, all unique objects are retained (`ID=NULL`) and you can see them all in the file system. New versions of objects are assigned a unique ID (older versions are retained). Based on the object's timestamp only the newest versioned object is viewable in the NFS file system.

After you enable object versioning, your S3 bucket can't be returned to a nonversioned state. You can, however, suspend versioning. When you suspend versioning, a new object is assigned an ID. If the same named object exists with an `ID=NULL` value, the older version is overwritten. However, any version that contains a non-`NULL` ID is retained. Timestamps identify the new object as the current one, and that is the one that appears in the NFS file system.

Troubleshooting Volume Issues

You can find information about the most typical issues you might encounter when working with volumes, and actions that we suggest that you take to fix them.

Topics

- The Console Says That Your Volume Is Not Configured
- The Console Says That Your Volume Is Irrecoverable
- Your Cached Gateway is Unreachable And You Want to Recover Your Data
- The Console Says That Your Volume Has PASS THROUGH Status
- You Want to Verify Volume Integrity and Fix Possible Errors
- Your Volume's iSCSI Target Doesn't Appear in Windows Disk Management Console
- You Want to Change Your Volume's iSCSI Target Name
- Your Scheduled Volume Snapshot Did Not Occur
- You Need to Remove or Replace a Disk That Has Failed
- Throughput from Your Application to a Volume Has Dropped to Zero
- A Cache Disk in Your Gateway Encounters a Failure
- A Volume Snapshot Has PENDING Status Longer Than Expected

The Console Says That Your Volume Is Not Configured

If the AWS Storage Gateway console indicates that your volume has a status of UPLOAD BUFFER NOT CONFIGURED, add upload buffer capacity to your gateway. You cannot use a gateway to store your application data if the upload buffer for the gateway is not configured. For more information, see To configure upload buffer or cache storage .

The Console Says That Your Volume Is Irrecoverable

For stored volumes, if the AWS Storage Gateway console indicates that your volume has a status of IRRECOVERABLE, you can no longer use this volume. You can try to delete the volume in the AWS Storage Gateway console. If there is data on the volume, then you can recover the data when you create a new volume based on the local disk of the VM that was initially used to create the volume. When you create the new volume, select **Preserve existing data**. Make sure to delete pending snapshots of the volume before deleting the volume. For more information, see Deleting a Snapshot. If deleting the volume in the AWS Storage Gateway console does not work, then the disk allocated for the volume might have been improperly removed from the VM and cannot be removed from the appliance.

For cached volumes, if the AWS Storage Gateway console indicates that your volume has a status of IRRECOVERABLE, you can no longer use this volume. If there is data on the volume, you can create a snapshot of the volume and then recover your data from the snapshot or you can clone the volume from the last recovery point. You can delete the volume after you have recovered your data. For more information, see Your Cached Gateway is Unreachable And You Want to Recover Your Data.

For stored volumes, you can create a new volume from the disk that was used to create the irrecoverable volume. For more information, see Creating a Volume. For information about volume status, see Understanding Volume Status.

Your Cached Gateway is Unreachable And You Want to Recover Your Data

When your gateway becomes unreachable (such as when you shut it down), you have the option of either creating a snapshot from a volume recovery point and using that snapshot, or cloning a new volume from the last recovery point for an existing volume. Cloning from a volume recovery point is faster and more cost effective than creating a snapshot. For more information about cloning a volume, see Cloning a Volume.

AWS Storage Gateway provides recovery points for each volume in a cached volume gateway architecture. A *volume recovery point* is a point in time at which all data of the volume is consistent and from which you can create a snapshot or clone a volume.

The Console Says That Your Volume Has PASS THROUGH Status

In some cases, the AWS Storage Gateway console might indicate that your volume has a status of PASSTHROUGH. A volume can have PASSTHROUGH status for several reasons. Some reasons require action, and some do not.

An example of when you should take action if your volume has the PASS THROUGH status is when your gateway has run out of upload buffer space. To verify if your upload buffer was exceeded in the past, you can view the UploadBufferPercentUsed metric in the Amazon CloudWatch console; for more information, see Monitoring the Upload Buffer. If your gateway has the PASS THROUGH status because it has run out of upload buffer space, you should allocate more upload buffer space to your gateway. Adding more buffer space will cause your volume to transition from PASS THROUGH to BOOTSTRAPPING to AVAILABLE automatically. While the volume has the BOOTSTRAPPING status, the gateway reads data off the volume's disk, uploads this data to Amazon S3, and catches up as needed. When the gateway has caught up and saved the volume data to Amazon S3, the volume status becomes AVAILABLE and snapshots can be started again. Note that when your volume has the PASS THROUGH or BOOTSTRAPPING status, you can continue to read and write data from the volume disk. For more information about adding more upload buffer space, see Adding and Removing Upload Buffer.

To take action before the upload buffer is exceeded, you can set a threshold alarm on a gateway's upload buffer. For more information, see To set an upper threshold alarm for a gateway's upload buffer.

In contrast, an example of not needing to take action when a volume has the PASS THROUGH status is when the volume is waiting to be bootstrapped because another volume is currently being bootstrapped. The gateway bootstraps volumes one at a time.

Infrequently, the PASS THROUGH status can indicate that a disk allocated for an upload buffer has failed. In this is the case, you should remove the disk. For more information, see Removing Upload Buffer Capacity. For information about volume status, see Understanding Volume Status.

You Want to Verify Volume Integrity and Fix Possible Errors

If you want to verify volume integrity and fix possible errors, and your gateway uses Microsoft Windows initiators to connect to its volumes, you can use the Windows CHKDSK utility to verify the integrity of your volumes and fix any errors on the volumes. Windows can automatically run the CHKDSK tool when volume corruption is detected, or you can run it yourself.

Your Volume's iSCSI Target Doesn't Appear in Windows Disk Management Console

If your volume's iSCSI target does not show up in the Disk Management Console in Windows, check that you have configured the upload buffer for the gateway. For more information, see To configure upload buffer or cache storage .

You Want to Change Your Volume's iSCSI Target Name

If you want to change the iSCSI target name of your volume, you must delete the volume and add it again with a new target name. If you do so, you can preserve the data on the volume.

Your Scheduled Volume Snapshot Did Not Occur

If your scheduled snapshot of a volume did not occur, check whether your volume has the PASSTHROUGH status, or if the gateway's upload buffer was filled just prior to the scheduled snapshot time. You can check the `UploadBufferPercentUsed` metric for the gateway in the Amazon CloudWatch console and create an alarm for this metric. For more information, see Monitoring the Upload Buffer and To set an upper threshold alarm for a gateway's upload buffer.

You Need to Remove or Replace a Disk That Has Failed

If you need to replace a volume disk that has failed or replace a volume because it isn't needed, you should remove the volume first using the AWS Storage Gateway console. For more information, see To remove a volume. You then use the hypervisor client to remove the backing storage:

- For VMware ESXi, remove the backing storage as described in Deleting a Volume.
- For Microsoft Hyper-V, remove the backing storage.

Throughput from Your Application to a Volume Has Dropped to Zero

If throughput from your application to a volume has dropped to zero, try the following:

- If you are using the VMware vSphere client, check that your volume's **Host IP** address matches one of the addresses that appears in the vSphere client on the **Summary** tab. You can find the **Host IP** address for a storage volume in the AWS Storage Gateway console in the **Details** tab for the volume. A discrepancy in the IP address can occur, for example, when you assign a new static IP address to your gateway. If there is a discrepancy, restart your gateway from the AWS Storage Gateway console as shown in Shutting Down Your Gateway VM. After the restart, the **Host IP** address in the **ISCSI Target Info** tab for a storage volume should match an IP address shown in the vSphere client on the **Summary** tab for the gateway.
- If there is no IP address in the **Host IP** box for the volume and the gateway is online. For example, this could occur if you create a volume associated with an IP address of a network adapter of a gateway that has two or more network adapters. When you remove or disable the network adapter that the volume is associated with, the IP address might not appear in the **Host IP** box. To address this issue, delete the volume and then re-create it preserving its existing data.
- Check that the iSCSI initiator your application uses is correctly mapped to the iSCSI target for the storage volume. For more information about connecting to storage volumes, see Connecting to Your Volumes to a Windows Client.

You can view the throughput for volumes and create alarms from the Amazon CloudWatch console. For more information about measuring throughput from your application to a volume, see Measuring Performance Between Your Application and Gateway.

A Cache Disk in Your Gateway Encounters a Failure

If one or more cache disks in your gateway encounters a failure, the gateway prevents read and write operations to your virtual tapes and volumes. To resume normal functionality, reconfigure your gateway as described following:

- If the cache disk is inaccessible or unusable, delete the disk from your gateway configuration.
- If the cache disk is still accessible and useable, reconnect it to your gateway.

Note
If you delete a cache disk, tapes or volumes that have clean data (that is, for which data in the cache disk and Amazon S3 are synchronized) will continue to be available when the gateway resumes normal functionality. For example, if your gateway has three cache disks and you delete two, tapes or volumes that are clean will have

AVAILABLE status. Other tapes and volumes will have IRRECOVERABLE status.

If you use ephemeral disks as cache disks for your gateway or mount your cache disks on an ephemeral drive, your cache disks will be lost when you shut down the gateway. Shutting down the gateway when your cache disk and Amazon S3 are not synchronized can result in data loss. As a result, we don't recommend using ephemeral drives or disks.

A Volume Snapshot Has PENDING Status Longer Than Expected

If a volume snapshot remains in PENDING state longer than expected, the gateway VM might have crashed unexpectedly or the status of a volume might have changed to PASS THROUGH or IRRECOVERABLE. If any of these are the case, the snapshot remains in PENDING status and the snapshot does not successfully complete. In these cases, we recommend that you delete the snapshot. For more information, see Deleting a Snapshot.

When the volume returns to AVAILABLE status, create a new snapshot of the volume. For information about volume status, see Understanding Volume Status.

Troubleshooting Virtual Tape Issues

You can find information following about actions to take if you experience unexpected issues with your virtual tapes.

Topics

- Recovering a Virtual Tape From An Unrecoverable Gateway
- Troubleshooting Irrecoverable Tapes

Recovering a Virtual Tape From An Unrecoverable Gateway

Although it is rare, your tape gateway might encounter an unrecoverable failure. Such a failure can occur in your hypervisor host, the gateway itself, or the cache disks. If a failure occurs, you can recover your tapes by following the troubleshooting instructions in this section.

Topics

- You Need to Recover a Virtual Tape from a Malfunctioning Tape Gateway
- You Need to Recover a Virtual Tape from a Malfunctioning Cache Disk

You Need to Recover a Virtual Tape from a Malfunctioning Tape Gateway

If your tape gateway or the hypervisor host encounters an unrecoverable failure, you can recover any data that has already been uploaded to AWS to another tape gateway.

Note that the data written to a tape might not be completely uploaded until that tape has been successfully archived into VTS. The data on tapes recovered to another gateway in this manner may be incomplete or empty. We recommend performing an inventory on all recovered tapes to ensure they contain the expected content.

To recover a tape to another tape gateway

1. Identify an existing functioning tape gateway to serve as your recovery target gateway. If you don't have a tape gateway to recover your tapes to, create a new tape gateway. For information about how to create a gateway, see Choosing a Gateway Type.

2. Open the AWS Storage Gateway console at https://console.aws.amazon.com/storagegateway/home.

3. In the navigation pane, choose **Gateways**, and then choose the tape gateway you want to recover tapes from.

4. Choose the **Details** tab. A tape recovery message is displayed in the tab.

5. Choose **Create recovery tapes** to disable the gateway.

6. In the dialog box that appears, choose **Disable gateway**.

   This process permanently halts normal function of your tape gateway and exposes any available recovery points. For instructions, see Disabling Your Tape Gateway.

7. From the tapes that the disabled gateway displays, choose the virtual tape and the recovery point you want to recover. A virtual tape can have multiple recovery points.

8. To begin recovering any tapes you need to the target tape gateway, choose **Create recovery tape**.

9. In the **Create recovery tape** dialog box, verify the barcode of the virtual tape you want to recover.

10. For **Gateway**, choose the tape gateway you want to recover the virtual tape to.

11. Choose **Create recovery tape**.

12. Delete the failed tape gateway so you don't get charged. For instructions, see Deleting Your Gateway by Using the AWS Storage Gateway Console and Removing Associated Resources.

Storage Gateway moves the tape from the failed tape gateway to the tape gateway you specified. The tape gateway marks the tape status as RECOVERED.

You Need to Recover a Virtual Tape from a Malfunctioning Cache Disk

If your cache disk encounters an error, the gateway prevents read and write operations on virtual tapes in the gateway. For example, an error can occur when a disk is corrupted or removed from the gateway. The AWS Storage Gateway console displays a message about the error.

In the error message, Storage Gateway prompts you to take one of two actions that can recover your tapes:

- **Shut Down and Re-Add Disks **– Take this approach if the disk has intact data and has been removed. For example, if the error occurred because a disk was removed from your host by accident but the disk and the data is intact, you can re-add the disk. To do this, see the procedure later in this topic.
- **Reset Cache Disk** – Take this approach if the cache disk is corrupted or not accessible. If the disk error causes the cache disk to be inaccessible, unusable, or corrupted, you can reset the disk. If you reset the cache disk, tapes that have clean data (that is, tapes for which data in the cache disk and Amazon S3 are synchronized) will continue to be available for you to use. However, tapes that have data that is not synchronized with Amazon S3 are automatically recovered. The status of these tapes is set to RECOVERED, but the tapes will be read-only. For information about how to remove a disk from your host, see Adding and Removing Upload Buffer. **Important**
  If the cache disk you are resetting contains data that has not been uploaded to Amazon S3 yet, that data can be lost. After you reset cache disks, no configured cache disks will be left in the gateway, so you must configure at least one new cache disk for your gateway to function properly.

To reset the cache disk, see the procedure later in this topic.

To shut down and re-add a disk

1. Shut down the gateway. For information about how to shut down a gateway, see Shutting Down Your Gateway VM.

2. Add the disk back to your host, and make sure the disk node number of the disk has not changed. For information about how to add a disk, see Adding and Removing Upload Buffer.

3. Restart the gateway. For information about how to restart a gateway, see Shutting Down Your Gateway VM.

After the gateway restarts, you can verify the status of the cache disks. The status of a disk can be one of the following:

- **present** – The disk is available to use.
- **missing** – The disk is no longer connected to the gateway.
- **mismatch** – The disk node is occupied by a disk that has incorrect metadata, or the disk content is corrupted.

To reset and reconfigure a cache disk

1. In the **A disk error has occurred** error message illustrated preceding, choose **Reset Cache Disk**.

2. On the **Configure Your Activated Gateway** page, configure the disk for cache storage. For information about how to do so, see Configuring Local Disks.

3. After you have configured cache storage, shut down and restart the gateway as described in the previous procedure.

The gateway should recover after the restart. You can then verify the status of the cache disk.

To verify the status of a cache disk

1. Open the AWS Storage Gateway console at https://console.aws.amazon.com/storagegateway/home.

2. In the navigation pane, choose **Gateways**, and then choose your gateway.

3. On the **Actions** menu, choose **Configure Local Storage** to display the **Configure Local Storage** dialog box. This dialog box shows all local disks in the gateway.

The cache disk node status is displayed next to the disk.

Note
If you don't complete the recovery process, the gateway displays a banner that prompts you to configure local storage.

Troubleshooting Irrecoverable Tapes

If your virtual tape fails unexpectedly, AWS Storage Gateway sets the status of the failed virtual tape to IRRECOVERABLE. The action you take depends on the circumstances. You can find information following on some issues you might find, and how to troubleshoot them.

You Need to Recover Data From an IRRECOVERABLE Tape

If you have a virtual tape with the status IRRECOVERABLE, and you need to work with it, try one of the following:

- Activate a new tape gateway if you don't have one activated. For more information, see Choosing a Gateway Type.
- Disable the tape gateway that contains the irrecoverable tape, and recover the tape from a recovery point to the new tape gateway. For more information, see You Need to Recover a Virtual Tape from a Malfunctioning Tape Gateway. **Note**
  You have to reconfigure your iSCSI initiator and backup application to use the new tape gateway. For more information, see Connecting Your VTL Devices.

You Don't Need an IRRECOVERABLE Tape That Isn't Archived

If you have a virtual tape with the status IRRECOVERABLE, you don't need it, and the tape has never been archived, you should delete the tape. For more information, see Deleting Tapes.

A Cache Disk in Your Gateway Encounters a Failure

If one or more cache disks in your gateway encounters a failure, the gateway prevents read and write operations to your virtual tapes and volumes. To resume normal functionality, reconfigure your gateway as described following:

- If the cache disk is inaccessible or unusable, delete the disk from your gateway configuration.
- If the cache disk is still accessible and useable, reconnect it to your gateway.

Note
If you delete a cache disk, tapes or volumes that have clean data (that is, for which data in the cache disk and Amazon S3 are synchronized) will continue to be available when the gateway resumes normal functionality. For example, if your gateway has three cache disks and you delete two, tapes or volumes that are clean will have AVAILABLE status. Other tapes and volumes will have IRRECOVERABLE status.
If you use ephemeral disks as cache disks for your gateway or mount your cache disks on an ephemeral drive, your cache disks will be lost when you shut down the gateway. Shutting down the gateway when your cache disk and Amazon S3 are not synchronized can result in data loss. As a result, we don't recommend using ephemeral drives or disks.

Best Practices for Recovering Your Data

Although it is rare, your gateway might encounter an unrecoverable failure. Such a failure can occur in your virtual machine (VM), the gateway itself, the local storage, or elsewhere. If a failure occurs, we recommend that you follow the instructions in the appropriate section following to recover your data.

Important
AWS Storage Gateway doesn't support recovering a gateway VM from a snapshot that is created by your hypervisor or from your Amazon EC2 ami. If your gateway VM malfunctions, activate a new gateway and recover your data to that gateway using the instructions following.

Topics

- Recovering from an Unexpected Virtual Machine Shutdown
- Recovering Your Data from a Malfunctioning Gateway or VM
- Retrieving Your Data from an Irrecoverable Volume
- Recovering Your Data from an Irrecoverable Tape
- Recovering Your Data from a Malfunctioning Cache Disk
- Recovering Your Data from a Corrupted File System
- Recovering Your Data From An Inaccessible Data Center

Recovering from an Unexpected Virtual Machine Shutdown

If your VM shuts down unexpectedly, for example during a power outage, your gateway becomes unreachable. When power and network connectivity are restored, your gateway becomes reachable and starts to function normally. Following are some steps you can take at that point to help recover your data:

- If an outage causes network connectivity issues, you can troubleshoot the issue. For information about how to test network connectivity, see Testing Your Gateway Connection to the Internet.
- For cached volumes and tapes setups, when your gateway becomes reachable, your volumes or tapes go into BOOTSTRAPPING status. This functionality ensures that your locally stored data continues to be synchronized with AWS. For more information on this status, see Understanding Volume Status.
- If your gateway malfunctions and issues occur with your volumes or tapes as a result of an unexpected shutdown, you can recover your data. For information about how to recover your data, see the sections following that apply to your scenario.

Recovering Your Data from a Malfunctioning Gateway or VM

If your gateway or virtual machine malfunctions, you can recover data that has been uploaded to AWS and stored on a volume in Amazon S3. For cached volumes gateways, you recover data from a recovery snapshot. For stored volumes gateways, you can recover data from your most recent Amazon EBS snapshot of the volume. For tape gateways, you recover one or more tapes from a recovery point to a new tape gateway.

If your cached volumes gateway becomes unreachable, you can use the following steps to recover your data from a recovery snapshot:

1. In the AWS Management Console, choose the malfunctioning gateway, choose the volume you want to recover, and then create a recovery snapshot from it.

2. Deploy and activate a new volume gateway. Or, if you have an existing functioning volume gateway, you can use that gateway to recover your volume data.

3. Find the snapshot you created and restore it to a new volume on the functioning gateway.

4. Mount the new volume as an iSCSI device on your on-premises application server.

For detailed information on how to recover cached volumes data from a recovery snapshot, see Your Cached Gateway is Unreachable And You Want to Recover Your Data.

If your tape gateway or the hypervisor host encounters an unrecoverable failure, you can use the following steps to recover the tapes from the malfunctioning tape gateway to another tape gateway:

1. Identify a tape gateway you want to use as the recovery target or create you can create a new one.

2. Disable the malfunctioning gateway.

3. Create recovery tapes for each tape you want to recover and specify the target tape gateway.

4. Delete the malfunctioning tape gateway.

For detailed information on how to recover the tapes from a malfunctioning tape gateway to another tape gateway, see You Need to Recover a Virtual Tape from a Malfunctioning Tape Gateway.

Retrieving Your Data from an Irrecoverable Volume

If the status of your volume is IRRECOVERABLE, you can no longer use this volume.

For stored volumes, you can retrieve your data from the irrecoverable volume to a new volume by using the following steps:

1. Create a new volume from the disk that was used to create the irrecoverable volume.

2. Preserve existing data when you are creating the new volume.

3. Delete all pending snapshot jobs for the irrecoverable volume.

4. Delete the irrecoverable volume from the gateway.

For cached volumes, we recommend using the last recovery point to clone a new volume.

For detailed information about how to retrieve your data from an irrecoverable volume to a new volume, see The Console Says That Your Volume Is Irrecoverable.

Recovering Your Data from an Irrecoverable Tape

If your tape encounters a failure and the status of the tape is IRRECOVERABLE, we recommend you use one of the following options to recover your data or resolve the failure depending on your situation:

- If you need the data on the irrecoverable tape, you can recover the tape to a new gateway.

- If you don't need the data on the tape, and the tape has never been archived, you can simply delete the tape from your tape gateway.

  For detailed information about how to recover your data or resolve the failure if your tape is IRRECOVERABLE, see Troubleshooting Irrecoverable Tapes.

Recovering Your Data from a Malfunctioning Cache Disk

If your cache disk encounters a failure, we recommend you use the following steps to recover your data depending on your situation:

- If the malfunction occurred because a cache disk was removed from your host, shut down the gateway, re-add the disk, and restart the gateway.
- If the cache disk is corrupted or not accessible, shut down the gateway, reset the cache disk, reconfigure the disk for cache storage, and restart the gateway.

For detailed information, see You Need to Recover a Virtual Tape from a Malfunctioning Cache Disk.

Recovering Your Data from a Corrupted File System

If your file system gets corrupted, you can use the **fsck** command to check your file system for errors and repair it. If you can repair the file system, you can then recover your data from the volumes on the file system, as described following:

1. Shut down your virtual machine and use the AWS Storage Gateway Management Console to create a recovery snapshot. This snapshot represents the most current data stored in AWS. **Note** You use this snapshot as a fallback if your file system can't be repaired or the snapshot creation process can't be completed successfully.

   For information about how to create a recovery snapshot, see Your Cached Gateway is Unreachable And You Want to Recover Your Data.

2. Use the **fsck** command to check your file system for errors and attempt a repair.

3. Restart your gateway VM.

4. When your hypervisor host starts to boot up, press and hold down shift key to enter the grub boot menu.

5. From the menu, press **e** to edit.

6. Choose the kernel line (the second line), and then press **e** to edit.

7. Append the following option to the kernel command line: **init=/bin/bash**. Use a space to separate the previous option from the option you just appended.

8. Press **Return** to save the changes.

9. Press **b** to boot your computer with the modified kernel option. Your computer will boot to a `bash#` prompt.

10. Type **/sbin/fsck** to run this command manually from the prompt, to check and repair your file system.

11. When the file system check and repair is complete, reboot the instance. The grub settings will revert to the original values, and the gateway will boot up normally.

12. Wait for snapshots that are in-progress from the original gateway to complete, and then validate the snapshot data.

You can continue to use the original volume as-is, or you can create a new gateway with a new volume based on either the recovery snapshot or the completed snapshot. Alternatively, you can create a new volume from any of your completed snapshots from this volume.

Recovering Your Data From An Inaccessible Data Center

If your gateway or data center becomes inaccessible for some reason, you can recover your data to a another gateway in a different data center or recover to a gateway hosted on an Amazon EC2 instance. If you don't have access to another data center, we recommend creating the gateway on an Amazon EC2 instance. The steps you follow depends on the gateway type you are covering the data from.

To recover data from a volume gateway in an inaccessible data center

1. Create and activate a new volume gateway on an Amazon EC2 host. For more information, see Deploying a Volume or Tape Gateway on an Amazon EC2 Host. **Note** Gateway stored volumes can't be hosted on Amazon EC2 instance.

2. Create a new volume and choose the EC2 gateway as the target gateway. For more information, see Creating a Volume.

   Create the new volume based on an Amazon EBS snapshot or clone from last recovery point of the volume you want to recover.

If your volume is based on a snapshot, provide the snapshot id.

If you are cloning a volume from a recovery point, choose the source volume.

To recover data from a tape gateway in an inaccessible data center

1. Create and activate a new tape gateway on an Amazon EC2 host. For more information, see Deploying a Volume or Tape Gateway on an Amazon EC2 Host.

2. Recover the tapes from the source gateway in the data center to the new gateway you created on Amazon EC2 For more information, see Recovering a Virtual Tape From An Unrecoverable Gateway.

   Your tapes should be covered to the new Amazon EC2 gateway.

To recover data from a file gateway in an inaccessible data center

For file gateway, you map a new file share to the Amazon S3 that contains the data you want to recover.

1. Create and activate a new file gateway on an Amazon EC2 host. For more information, see Deploying File Gateway on an Amazon EC2 Host.

2. Create a new file share on the EC2 gateway you created. For more information, see Creating a File Share.

3. Mount your file share on your client and map the it to the Amazon S3 bucket that contains the data you want to recover. For more information, see Using Your File Share.

Additional AWS Storage Gateway Resources

In this section, you can find information about AWS and third-party software, tools, and resources that can help you set up or manage your gateway, and also about AWS Storage Gateway limits.

Topics

- Host Setup
- Volume Gateway
- Tape Gateway
- Getting an Activation Key for Your Gateway
- Connecting iSCSI Initiators
- Using AWS Direct Connect with AWS Storage Gateway
- Port Requirements
- Connecting to Your Gateway
- Understanding AWS Storage Gateway Resources and Resource IDs
- Tagging Storage Gateway Resources
- Working with Open-Source Components for AWS Storage Gateway
- AWS Storage Gateway Limits

Host Setup

Topics

- Configuring VMware for Storage Gateway
- Deploying a Volume or Tape Gateway on an Amazon EC2 Host
- Deploying File Gateway on an Amazon EC2 Host

Configuring VMware for Storage Gateway

When configuring VMware for AWS Storage Gateway, make sure to synchronize your VM time with your host time, configure VM to use paravirtualized disk controllers when provisioning storage and provide protection from failures in the infrastructure layer supporting a gateway VM.

Topics

- Synchronizing VM Time with Host Time
- Configuring the AWS Storage Gateway VM to Use Paravirtualized Disk Controllers
- Using AWS Storage Gateway with VMware High Availability

Synchronizing VM Time with Host Time

To successfully activate your gateway, you must ensure that your VM time is synchronized to the host time, and that the host time is correctly set. In this section, you first synchronize the time on the VM to the host time. Then you check the host time and, if needed, set the host time and configure the host to synchronize its time automatically to a Network Time Protocol (NTP) server.

Important
Synchronizing the VM time with the host time is required for successful gateway activation.

To synchronize VM time with host time

1. Configure your VM time.

    1. In the vSphere client, open the context (right-click) menu for your gateway VM, and choose **Edit Settings**.

        The **Virtual Machine Properties** dialog box opens.

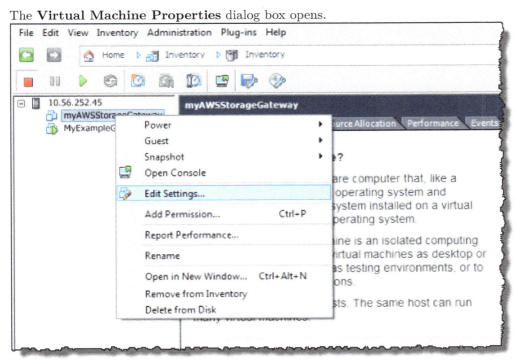

    2. Choose the **Options** tab, and choose **VMware Tools** in the options list.

    3. Check the **Synchronize guest time with host** option, and then choose **OK**.

The VM synchronizes its time with the host.

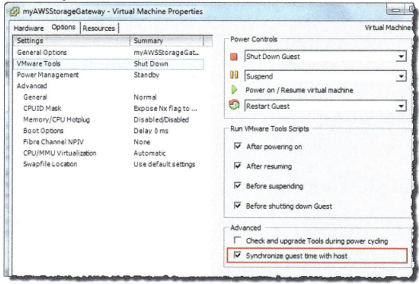

2. Configure the host time.

It is important to make sure that your host clock is set to the correct time. If you have not configured your host clock, perform the following steps to set and synchronize it with an NTP server.

1. In the VMware vSphere client, select the vSphere host node in the left pane, and then choose the **Configuration** tab.

2. Select **Time Configuration** in the **Software** panel, and then choose the **Properties** link.

The **Time Configuration** dialog box appears.

3. In the **Date and Time** panel, set the date and time.

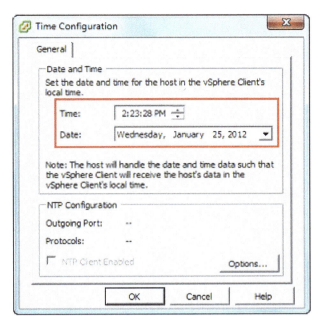

4. Configure the host to synchronize its time automatically to an NTP server.

   1. Choose **Options** in the **Time Configuration** dialog box, and then in the **NTP Daemon (ntpd) Options** dialog box, choose **NTP Settings** in the left pane.

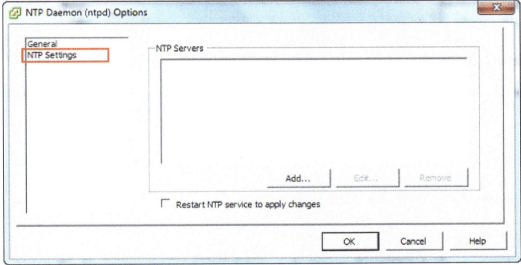

   2. Choose **Add** to add a new NTP server.

   3. In the **Add NTP Server** dialog box, type the IP address or the fully qualified domain name of an NTP server, and then choose **OK**.

      You can use `pool.ntp.org` as shown in the following example.

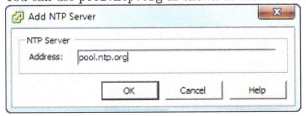

4. In the **NTP Daemon (ntpd) Options** dialog box, choose **General** in the left pane.

5. In the **Service Commands** pane, choose **Start** to start the service.

Note that if you change this NTP server reference or add another later, you will need to restart the service to use the new server.

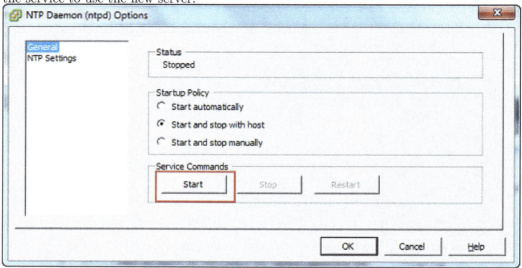

5. Choose **OK** to close the **NTP Daemon (ntpd) Options** dialog box.

6. Choose **OK** to close the **Time Configuration** dialog box.

Configuring the AWS Storage Gateway VM to Use Paravirtualized Disk Controllers

In this task, you set the iSCSI controller so that the VM uses paravirtualization. *Paravirtualization* is a mode where the gateway VM works with the host operating system so the console can identify the virtual disks that you add to your VM.

Note

You must complete this step to avoid issues in identifying these disks when you configure them in the gateway console.

To configure your VM to use paravirtualized controllers

1. In the VMware vSphere client, open the context (right-click) menu for your gateway VM, and then choose **Edit Settings**.

2. In the **Virtual Machine Properties** dialog box, choose the **Hardware** tab, select the **SCSI controller 0**, and then choose **Change Type**.

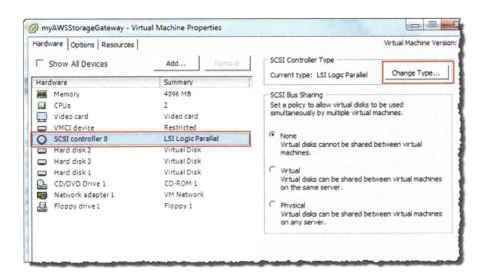

3. In the **Change SCSI Controller Type** dialog box, select the **VMware Paravirtual** SCSI controller type, and then choose **OK**.

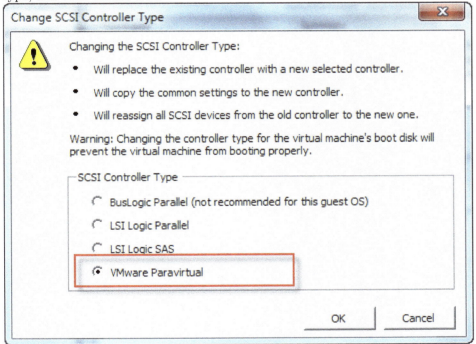

Using AWS Storage Gateway with VMware High Availability

VMware High Availability (HA) is a component of vSphere that can provide protection from failures in the infrastructure layer supporting a gateway VM. VMware HA does this by using multiple hosts configured as a cluster so that if a host running a gateway VM fails, the gateway VM can be restarted automatically on another host within the cluster. For more information about VMware HA, see VMware HA: Concepts and Best Practices on the VMware website.

To use AWS Storage Gateway with VMware HA, we recommend doing the following things:

- Deploy the VMware ESX `.ova` downloadable package that contains the AWS Storage Gateway VM on only one host in a cluster.

- When deploying the `.ova` package, select a data store that is not local to one host. Instead, use a data store that is accessible to all hosts in the cluster. If you select a data store that is local to a host and the host fails, then the data source might not be accessible to other hosts in the cluster and failover to another host might not succeed.

- To prevent your initiator from disconnecting from storage volume targets during failover, follow the recommended iSCSI settings for your operating system. In a failover event, it can take from a few seconds to several minutes for a gateway VM to start in a new host in the failover cluster. The recommended iSCSI timeouts for both Windows and Linux clients are greater than the typical time it takes for failover to occur. For more information on customizing Windows clients' timeout settings, see Customizing Your Windows iSCSI Settings. For more information on customizing Linux clients' timeout settings, see Customizing Your Linux iSCSI Settings.

- With clustering, if you deploy the `.ova` package to the cluster, select a host when you are prompted to do so. Alternately, you can deploy directly to a host in a cluster.

Deploying a Volume or Tape Gateway on an Amazon EC2 Host

You can deploy and activate a volume or tape gateway on an Amazon EC2 instance. Gateways hosted on Amazon EC2 instances can be used for disaster recovery and data mirroring. The EC2 Amazon Machine Image (AMI) is available in the AWS Marketplace For volume gateway and tape gateways, we recommend using the **1-Click Launch**.

Provisioning an Amazon EC2 Host by Using 1-Click Launch

To deploy a gateway on an Amazon EC2 instance

1. On the **Select host platform** page, choose **Amazon EC2**.

2. Choose **Launch with AWS Marketplace**. You are redirected to AWS Marketplace where you launch the EC2 AMI.

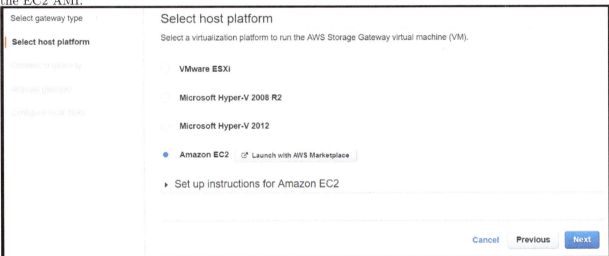

3. On AWS Marketplace, choose **Continue**.

4. Choose **1-Click Launch**. Doing this launches the AMI with default settings.

5. If this is your first time using an AWS Storage Gateway AMI, choose **Accept Terms** to accept the terms of service.

6. Review the default settings. You can accept and use these default settings or modify them to meet your needs.

   The 1-Click Launch feature comes with an autogenerated security group that is named AWS Storage Gateway-1-0-AutogenByAWSMP. For information about security group settings, see Configuring Security Groups for Your Amazon EC2 Gateway Instance.

7. After reviewing all your settings, choose **Launch with 1-Click**.

8. Choose **Return to Product Page** and locate your instance on the Amazon EC2 console. **Important** EC2 instances launched with the 1-Click Launch functionality come with one root Amazon EBS volume. You need to add additional EBS volumes to your instance as a separate step after the instance is launched. For information about how to add EBS volumes, see Attaching an Amazon EBS Volume to an Instance.

9. In the Amazon EC2 console, choose your Amazon EC2 instance, choose the **Description** tab at the bottom, and then note the IP address. You will use this IP address to connect to the gateway.

Deploying File Gateway on an Amazon EC2 Host

You can deploy and activate a file gateway on an Amazon EC2 instance. The file gateway Amazon Machine Image (AMI) is available as a community AMI.

To deploy a gateway on an Amazon EC2 instance

1. On the **Choose host platform** page, choose **Amazon EC2**.

2. Choose **Launch instance** to launch a storage gateway EC2 AMI. You are redirected to the EC2 community AMI page where you can choose an instance type.

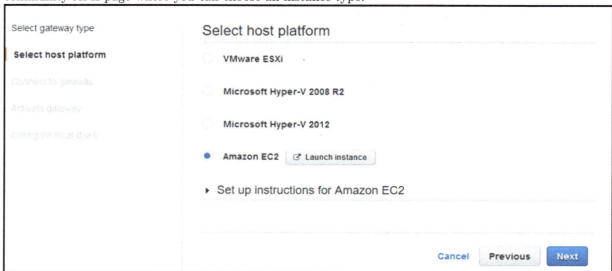

3. On the **Choose an Instance Type** page, choose the hardware configuration of your instance. AWS Storage Gateway is supported on instance types that meet certain minimum requirements. We recommend starting with the m4xlarge instance type, which meets the minimum requirements for your gateway to function properly. For more information, see Hardware Requirements.

   You can resize your instance after you launch, if necessary. For more information, see Resizing Your Instance in the *Amazon EC2 User Guide for Linux Instances*.

4. Choose **Next: Configure Instance Details**.

5. On the **Configure Instance Details** page, choose a value for **Auto-assign Public IP**. If your instance should be accessible from the public Internet, verify that **Auto-assign Public IP** is set to **Enable**. If your instance should not be accessible from the Internet, choose **Auto-assign Public IP** for **Disable**.

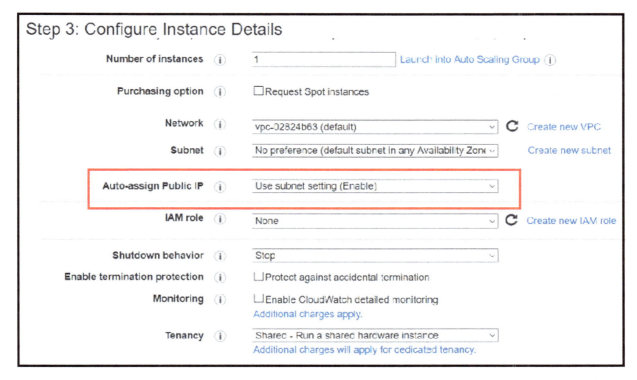

Step 3: Configure Instance Details

Number of instances (i)	1	Launch into Auto Scaling Group (i)
Purchasing option (i)	☐Request Spot instances	
Network (i)	vpc-02824b63 (default) ⌄ C	Create new VPC
Subnet (i)	No preference (default subnet in any Availability Zone ⌄	Create new subnet
Auto-assign Public IP (i)	Use subnet setting (Enable) ⌄	
IAM role (i)	None ⌄ C	Create new IAM role
Shutdown behavior (i)	Stop ⌄	
Enable termination protection (i)	☐Protect against accidental termination	
Monitoring (i)	☐Enable CloudWatch detailed monitoring Additional charges apply.	
Tenancy (i)	Shared - Run a shared hardware instance ⌄ Additional charges will apply for dedicated tenancy.	

6. On the **Configure Instance Details** page, choose the AWS Identity and Access Management (IAM) role that you want to use for your gateway.

7. Choose **Next: Add Storage**.

8. On the **Add Storage** page, choose **Add New Volume** to add storage to your file gateway instance. You need at least one Amazon EBS volume to configure for cache storage.

   The following table recommends sizes for local disk storage for your deployed gateway.
   [See the AWS documentation website for more details] **Note**
   You can configure one or more local drives for your cache and upload buffer, up to the maximum capacity. When adding cache or upload buffer to an existing gateway, it's important to create new disks in your host (hypervisor or Amazon EC2 instance). Don't change the size of existing disks if the disks have been previously allocated as either a cache or upload buffer.

9. On the **Step 5: Add Tags** page, you can add an optional tag to your instance. Then choose **Next: Configure Security Group**.

10. On the **Configure Security Group** page, add firewall rules to specific traffic to reach our instance. You can create a new security group or choose an existing security group. **Important**
    Besides the Storage Gateway activation and Secure Shell (SSH) access ports, NFS clients require access to additional ports. For detailed information, see Network and Firewall Requirements.

11. Choose **Review and Launch** to review your configuration.

12. On the **Review Instance Launch** page, choose **Launch**.

13. In the **Select an existing key pair or create a new key pair** dialog box, choose **Choose an existing key pair**, and then select the key pair that you created when getting set up. When you are ready, choose the acknowledgment box, and then choose **Launch Instances**.

14. A confirmation page lets you know that your instance is launching. Choose **View Instances** to close the confirmation page and return to the console. On the **Instances** screen, you can view the status of your instance. It takes a short time for an instance to launch. When you launch an instance, its initial state is **pending**. After the instance starts, its state changes to **running**, and it receives a public DNS name

15. Select your instance, take note of the public IP address in the **Description** tag and return to the Connect to gateway page on the Storage Gateway console to continue your gateway setup.

The following table lists the available Storage Gateway AMIs by region.

Region	AMI Name	AMI ID	EC2 Console Link
ap-northeast-1	aws-storage-gateway-file-2018-03-01	ami-946d2cf2	Launch instance
ap-northeast-2	aws-storage-gateway-file-2018-03-01	ami-5974d937	Launch instance
ap-south-1	aws-storage-gateway-file-2018-03-01	ami-4e9fc021	Launch instance
ap-southeast-1	aws-storage-gateway-file-2018-03-01	ami-ae94dfd2	Launch instance
ap-southeast-2	aws-storage-gateway-file-2018-03-01	ami-7118de13	Launch instance
ca-central-1	aws-storage-gateway-file-2018-03-01	ami-17961173	Launch instance
eu-central-1	aws-storage-gateway-file-2018-03-01	ami-010f636e	Launch instance
eu-west-1	aws-storage-gateway-file-2018-03-01	ami-e19dd998	Launch instance
eu-west-2	aws-storage-gateway-file-2018-03-01	ami-07779360	Launch instance
eu-west-3	aws-storage-gateway-file-2018-03-01	ami-3e79cf43	Launch instance
sa-east-1	aws-storage-gateway-file-2018-03-01	ami-a34a01cf	Launch instance
us-east-1	aws-storage-gateway-file-2018-03-01	ami-edd92c90	Launch instance
us-east-2	aws-storage-gateway-file-2018-03-01	ami-1ce9de79	Launch instance
us-west-1	aws-storage-gateway-file-2018-03-01	ami-5a969d3a	Launch instance
us-west-2	aws-storage-gateway-file-2018-03-01	ami-5c3fb724	Launch instance

Volume Gateway

Topics

- Adding and Removing Disks for Your Gateway
- Adding and Removing Amazon EBS Volumes for Your Gateway Hosted on Amazon EC2

Adding and Removing Disks for Your Gateway

You can add or remove underlying disks from your gateway as described following. For example, you might add disks to your gateway to use as an upload buffer or cache storage if you need additional upload buffer space or cache storage. You can also remove the underlying disks from your gateway. For example, you might want to remove a failed disk from your gateway.

Important
When adding cache or upload buffer to an existing gateway, it is important to create new disks in your host (hypervisor or Amazon EC2 instance). Don't change the size of existing disks if the disks have been previously allocated as either a cache or upload buffer.

Topics

- Remove a Disk from a Gateway Hosted on VMware ESXi
- Remove a Disk from Gateway Hosted on Microsoft Hyper-V

Remove a Disk from a Gateway Hosted on VMware ESXi

You can use the following procedure to remove a disk from your gateway hosted on VMware hypervisor.

To remove a disk allocated for the upload buffer (VMware ESXi)

1. In the vSphere client, open the context (right-click) menu, choose the name of your gateway VM, and then choose **Edit Settings**.

2. On the **Hardware** tab of the **Virtual Machine Properties** dialog box, select the disk allocated as upload buffer space, and then choose **Remove**.

   Verify that the **Virtual Device Node** value in the **Virtual Machine Properties** dialog box has the same value that you noted previously. Doing this helps ensure that you remove the correct disk.

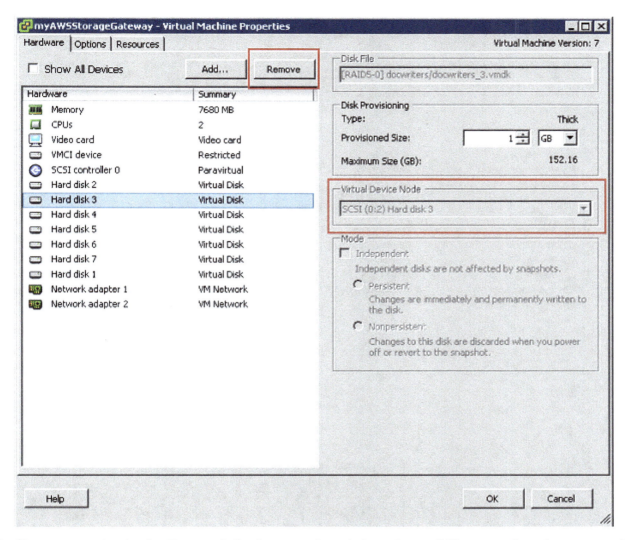

3. Choose an option in the **Removal Options** panel, and then choose **OK** to complete the process of removing the disk.

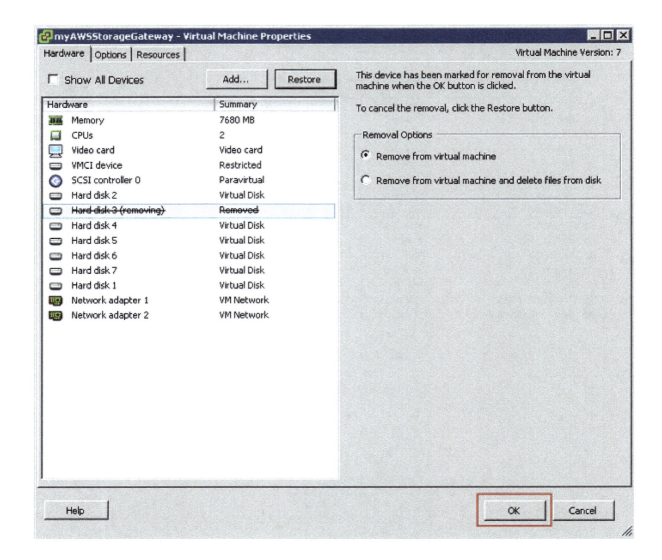

Remove a Disk from Gateway Hosted on Microsoft Hyper-V

Using the following procedure, you can remove a disk from your gateway hosted on a Microsoft Hyper-V hypervisor.

To remove an underlying disk allocated for the upload buffer (Microsoft Hyper-V)

1. In the Microsoft Hyper-V Manager, open the context (right-click) menu, choose the name of your gateway VM, and then choose **Settings**.

2. In the **Hardware** list of the **Settings** dialog box, select the disk to remove, and then choose **Remove**.

   The disks you add to a gateway appear under the **SCSI Controller** entry in the **Hardware** list. Verify that the **Controller** and **Location** value are the same value that you noted previously. Doing this helps ensure that you remove the correct disk.

   The first SCSI controller displayed in the Microsoft Hyper-V Manager is controller 0.

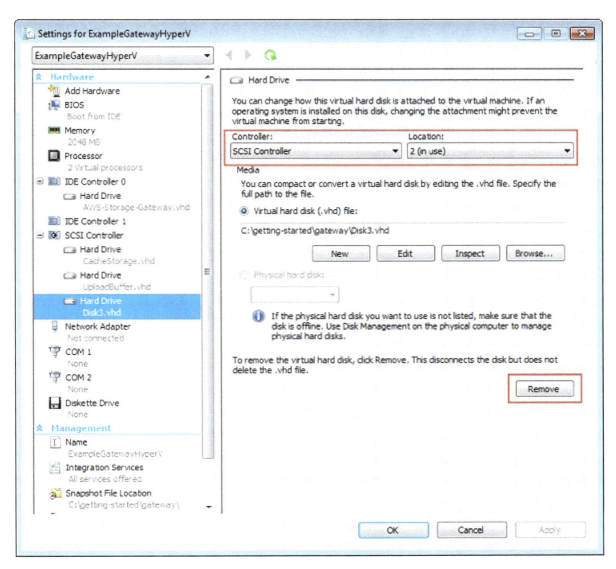

3. Choose **OK** to apply the change.

Adding and Removing Amazon EBS Volumes for Your Gateway Hosted on Amazon EC2

When you initially configured your gateway to run as an Amazon EC2 instance, you allocated Amazon EBS volumes for use as an upload buffer and cache storage. Over time, as your applications needs change, you can allocate additional Amazon EBS volumes for this use. You can also reduce the storage you allocated by removing previously allocated Amazon EBS volumes. For more information about Amazon EBS, see Amazon Elastic Block Store (Amazon EBS) in the *Amazon EC2 User Guide for Linux Instances.*

Before you add more storage to the gateway, you should review how to size your upload buffer and cache storage based on your application needs for a gateway. To do so, see Sizing the Upload Buffer and Adding and Removing Upload Buffer.

There are limits to the maximum storage you can allocate as an upload buffer and cache storage. You can attach as many Amazon EBS volumes to your instance as you want, but you can only configure these volumes as upload buffer and cache storage space up to these storage limits. For more information, see AWS Storage Gateway Limits.

To create an Amazon EBS volume, attach it, and configure it for your gateway

1. Create an Amazon EBS volume. For instructions, see Creating or Restoring an Amazon EBS Volume in the *Amazon EC2 User Guide for Linux Instances.*

2. Attach the Amazon EBS volume to your Amazon EC2 instance. For instructions, see Attaching an Amazon EBS Volume to an Instance in the *Amazon EC2 User Guide for Linux Instances.*

3. Configure the Amazon EBS volume you added as either an upload buffer or cache storage. For instructions, see Managing Local Disks for Your AWS Storage Gateway.

There are times you might find you don't need the amount of storage you allocated for the upload buffer.

To remove an Amazon EBS volume Warning
These steps apply only for Amazon EBS volumes allocated as upload buffer space. If you remove an Amazon EBS volume that is allocated as cache storage from a gateway, virtual tapes on the gateway will have the IRRECOVERABLE status, and you risk data loss. For more information on the IRRECOVERABLE status, see Understanding Tape Status Information in a VTL.

1. Shut down the gateway by following the approach described in the Shutting Down Your Gateway VM section.

2. Detach the Amazon EBS volume from your Amazon EC2 instance. For instructions, see Detaching an Amazon EBS Volume from an Instance in the *Amazon EC2 User Guide for Linux Instances.*

3. Delete the Amazon EBS volume. For instructions, see Deleting an Amazon EBS Volume in the *Amazon EC2 User Guide for Linux Instances.*

4. Start the gateway by following the approach described in the Shutting Down Your Gateway VM section.

Tape Gateway

Topics

- Working with VTL Devices
- Working With Tapes

Working with VTL Devices

Your tape gateway setup provides the following SCSI devices, which you select when activating your gateway.

Topics

- Selecting a Medium Changer After Gateway Activation
- Updating the Device Driver for Your Medium Changer

For medium changers, AWS Storage Gateway works with the following:

- AWS-Gateway-VTL—This device is provided with the gateway.

- STK-L700—This device emulation is provided with the gateway.

  When activating your tape gateway, you select your backup application from the list and storage gateway uses the appropriate medium changer. If your backup application is not listed, you choose **Other** and then choose the medium changer that works with backup application.

  The type of medium changer you choose depends on the backup application you plan to use. The following table lists third-party backup applications that have been tested and found to be compatible with tape gateways. This table includes the medium changer type recommended for each backup application. [See the AWS documentation website for more details] **Important** We highly recommend that you choose the medium changer that's listed for your backup application. Other medium changers might not function properly. You can choose a different medium changer after the gateway is activated. For more information, see Selecting a Medium Changer After Gateway Activation.

For tape drives, AWS Storage Gateway works with the following:

- IBM-ULT3580-TD5—This device emulation is provided with the gateway.

Selecting a Medium Changer After Gateway Activation

After your gateway is activated, you can choose to select a different medium changer type.

Important
If your tape gateway uses the Symantec Backup Exec 2014 or NetBackup 7.x backup software, you must select the AWS-Gateway-VTL device type. For more information on how to change the medium changer after gateway activation for these applications, see Best Practices for using Symantec Backup products (NetBackup, Backup Exec) with the Amazon Web Services (AWS) Storage Tape Gateway in *Symantec Support*.

To select a different medium changer type after gateway activation

1. Stop any related jobs that are running in your backup software.

2. On the Windows server, open the iSCSI initiator properties window.

3. Choose the **Targets** tab to display the discovered targets.

4. On the Discovered targets pane, choose the medium changer you want to change, choose **Disconnect**, and then choose **OK**.

5. On the AWS Storage Gateway console, choose **Gateways** from the navigation pane, and then choose the gateway whose medium changer you want to change.

6. Choose the **VTL Devices** tab, select the medium changer you want to change, and then choose the **Change Media Changer** button,

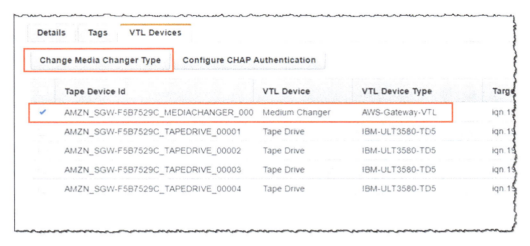

7. In the Change Media Changer Type dialog box that appears, select the media changer you want from the drop-down list box and then choose **Save**.

Updating the Device Driver for Your Medium Changer

Depending on the backup software you use on your Windows server, you might need to update the driver for your medium changer.

1. Open Device Manager on your Windows server, and expand the **Medium Changer devices** tree.

2. Open the context (right-click) menu for **Unknown Medium Changer**, and choose **Update Driver Software** to open the **Update Driver Software-unknown Medium Changer** window.

3.

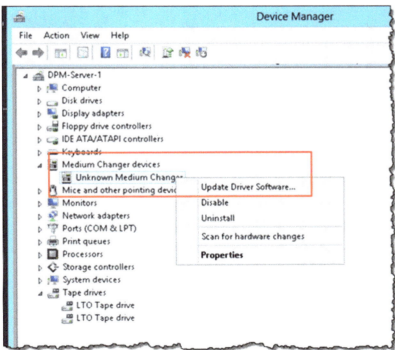

In the **How do you want to search for driver software?** section, choose **Browse my computer for driver software**.

1. Choose **Let me pick from a list of device drivers on my computer**. **Note**
   We recommend using the Sony TSL-A500C Autoloader driver with the Veeam Backup & Replication V7, Veeam Backup & Replication V8, and Microsoft System Center 2012 R2 Data Protection Manager backup software. This Sony driver has been tested with these types of backup software.

2. In the **Select the device driver you want to install for this hardware** section, clear the **Show compatible hardware** check box, choose **Sony** in the **Manufacturer** list, choose **Sony - TSL-A500C Autoloader** in the **Model** list, and then choose **Next**.

3. In the warning box that appears, choose **Yes**. If the driver is successfully installed, close the **Update drive software** window.

Working With Tapes

AWS Storage Gateway provides one virtual tape library (VTL) for each tape gateway you activate. Initially, the library contains no tapes, but you can create tapes whenever you need to. Your application can read and write to any tapes available on your tape gateway. A tape's status must be AVAILABLE for you to write to the tape. These tapes are backed by Amazon Simple Storage Service (Amazon S3)—that is, when you write to these tapes, the tape gateway stores data in Amazon S3. For more information, see Understanding Tape Status Information in a VTL.

Topics

- Archiving Tapes
- Canceling Tape Archival

The tape library shows tapes in your tape gateway. The library shows the tape barcode, status, and size, amount of the tape used, and the gateway the tape is associated with.

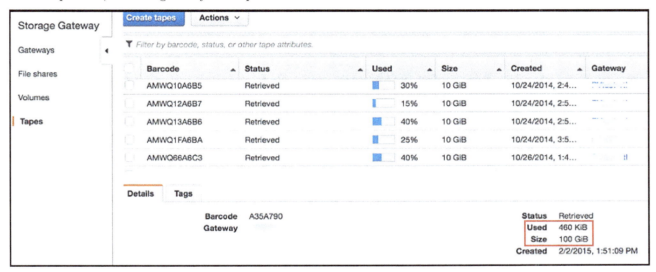

When you have a large number of tapes in the library, the console supports searching for tapes by barcode, by status, or by both. When you search by barcode, you can filter by status and gateway.

To search by barcode, status, and gateway

1. Open the AWS Storage Gateway console at https://console.aws.amazon.com/storagegateway/home.

2. In the navigation pane, choose **Tapes**, and then type a value in the search box. The value can be the barcode, status, or gateway. By default, AWS Storage Gateway searches for all virtual tapes. However, you can also filter your search by status.

   If you filter for status, tapes that match your criteria appear in the library in the AWS Storage Gateway console.

   If you filter for gateway, tapes that are associated with that gateway appear in the library in the AWS Storage Gateway console. **Note**
   By default, AWS Storage Gateway displays all tapes regardless of status.

Archiving Tapes

You can archive the virtual tapes that are in your tape gateway. When you archive a tape, AWS Storage Gateway moves the tape to the archive.

313

To archive a tape, you use your backup software. Tape archival process consists of three stages, seen as the tape statuses **IN TRANSIT TO VTS**, **ARCHIVING**, and **ARCHIVED**:

- To archive a tape, use the command provided by your backup application. When the archival process begins the tape status changes to **IN TRANSIT TO VTS** and the tape is no longer accessible to your backup application. In this stage, your tape gateway is uploading data to AWS. If needed, you can cancel the archival in progress. For more information about canceling archival, see Canceling Tape Archival.
  Note
  The steps for archiving a tape depend on your backup application. For detailed instructions, see the documentation for your backup application.
- After the data upload to AWS completes, the tape status changes to **ARCHIVING** and AWS Storage Gateway begins moving the tape to the archive. You cannot cancel the archival process at this point.
- After the tape is moved to the archive, its status changes to **ARCHIVED** and you can retrieve the tape to any of your gateways. For more information about tape retrieval, see Retrieving Archived Tapes.

The steps involved in archiving a tape depend on your backup software. For instructions on how to archive a tape by using Symantec NetBackup software, see Archiving the Tape.

Canceling Tape Archival

After you start archiving a tape, you might decide you need your tape back. For example, you might want to cancel the archival process, get the tape back because the archival process is taking too long, or read data from the tape. A tape that is being archived goes through three statuses, as shown following:

- IN TRANSIT TO VTS: Your tape gateway is uploading data to AWS.
- ARCHIVING: Data upload is complete and the tape gateway is moving the tape to the archive.
- ARCHIVED: The tape is moved and the archive and is available for retrieval.

You can cancel archival only when the tape's status is IN TRANSIT TO VTS. Depending on factors such as upload bandwidth and the amount of data being uploaded, this status might or might not be visible in the AWS Storage Gateway console. To cancel a tape archival, use the CancelRetrieval action in the API reference.

Getting an Activation Key for Your Gateway

To get an activation key for your gateway, you make a web request to the gateway VM and it returns a redirect that contains the activation key. This activation key is passed as one of the parameters to the `ActivateGateway` API action to specify the configuration of your gateway. The request you make to the gateway VM contains the AWS Region in which activation occurs.

The URL returned by the redirect in the response contains a query string parameter called `activationkey`. This query string parameter is your activation key. The format of the query string looks like the following: `http://gateway_ip_address/?activationRegion=activation_region`.

Topics

- AWS CLI
- Linux (bash/zsh)
- Microsoft Windows PowerShell

AWS CLI

If you haven't already done so, you must install and configure the AWS CLI. To do this, follow these instructions in the *AWS Command Line Interface User Guide:*

- Installing the AWS Command Line Interface
- Configuring the AWS CLI

The following example shows you how to use the AWS CLI to fetch the HTTP response, parse HTTP headers and get the activation key.

```
1 wget 'ec2_instance_ip_address/?activationRegion=eu-west-2' 2>&1 | \
2 grep -i location | \
3 grep -i key | \
4 cut -d'=' -f2 |\
5 cut -d'&' -f1
```

Linux (bash/zsh)

The following example shows you how to use Linux (bash/zsh) to fetch the HTTP response, parse HTTP headers, and get the activation key.

```
1 function get-activation-key() {
2   local ip_address=$1
3   local activation_region=$2
4   if [[ -z "$ip_address" || -z "$activation_region" ]]; then
5     echo "Usage: get-activation-key ip_address activation_region"
6     return 1
7   fi
8   if redirect_url=$(curl -f -s -S -w '%{redirect_url}' "http://$ip_address/?activationRegion=
        $activation_region"); then
9     activation_key_param=$(echo "$redirect_url" | grep -oE 'activationKey=[A-Z0-9-]+')
10    echo "$activation_key_param" | cut -f2 -d=
11  else
12    return 1
13  fi
14 }
```

Microsoft Windows PowerShell

The following example shows you how to use Microsoft Windows PowerShell to fetch the HTTP response, parse HTTP headers, and get the activation key.

```
1  function Get-ActivationKey {
2    [CmdletBinding()]
3    Param(
4      [parameter(Mandatory=$true)][string]$IpAddress,
5      [parameter(Mandatory=$true)][string]$ActivationRegion
6    )
7    PROCESS {
8      $request = Invoke-WebRequest -UseBasicParsing -Uri "http://$IpAddress/?activationRegion=
           $ActivationRegion" -MaximumRedirection 0 -ErrorAction SilentlyContinue
9      if ($request) {
10       $activationKeyParam = $request.Headers.Location | Select-String -Pattern "activationKey=([
             A-Z0-9-]+)"
11       $activationKeyParam.Matches.Value.Split("=")[1]
12     }
13   }
14 }
```

Connecting iSCSI Initiators

When managing your gateway, you work with file shares, volumes or virtual tape library (VTL) devices that are exposed as Internet Small Computer System Interface (iSCSI) targets. For file gateways the iSCSI targets are file share, For volume gateways, the iSCSI targets are volumes. For tape gateways, the targets are VTL devices. As part of this work, you do such tasks as connecting to those targets, customizing iSCSI settings, connecting from a Red Hat Linux client, and configuring Challenge-Handshake Authentication Protocol (CHAP).

Topics

- Connecting to Your Volumes to a Windows Client
- Connecting Your VTL Devices to a Windows client
- Connecting Your Volumes or VTL Devices to a Linux Client
- Customizing iSCSI Settings
- Configuring CHAP Authentication for Your iSCSI Targets

The iSCSI standard is an Internet Protocol (IP)–based storage networking standard for initiating and managing connections between IP-based storage devices and clients. The following list defines some of the terms that are used to describe the iSCSI connection and the components involved.

**iSCSI initiator **
The client component of an iSCSI network. The initiator sends requests to the iSCSI target. Initiators can be implemented in software or hardware. AWS Storage Gateway only supports software initiators.

iSCSI target
The server component of the iSCSI network that receives and responds to requests from initiators. Each of your volumes is exposed as an iSCSI target. Connect only one iSCSI initiator to each iSCSI target.

Microsoft iSCSI initiator
The software program on Microsoft Windows computers that enables you to connect a client computer (that is, the computer running the application whose data you want to write to the gateway) to an external iSCSI-based array (that is, the gateway). The connection is made using the host computer's Ethernet network adapter card. The Microsoft iSCSI initiator is already installed on Windows Server 2008 R2, Windows 7, Windows Server 2008, and Windows Vista. On these operating systems, you don't need to install the initiator.

Red Hat iSCSI initiator
The iscsi-initiator-utils Resource Package Manager (RPM) package provides you with an iSCSI initiator implemented in software for Red Hat Linux. The package includes a server daemon for the iSCSI protocol.

Each type of gateway can connect to iSCSI devices, and you can customize those connections, as described following.

Connecting to Your Volumes to a Windows Client

A volume gateway exposes volumes you have created for the gateway as iSCSI targets. For more information, see Connecting Your Volumes to Your Client.

Note
To connect to your volume target, your gateway must have an upload buffer configured. If an upload buffer is not configured for your gateway, then the status of your volumes is displayed as UPLOAD BUFFER NOT CONFIGURED. To configure an upload buffer for a gateway in a stored volumes setup, see To configure upload buffer or cache storage . To configure an upload buffer for a gateway in a cached volumes setup, see To configure upload buffer or cache storage .

The following diagram highlights the iSCSI target in the larger picture of the AWS Storage Gateway architecture. For more information, see How AWS Storage Gateway Works (Architecture).

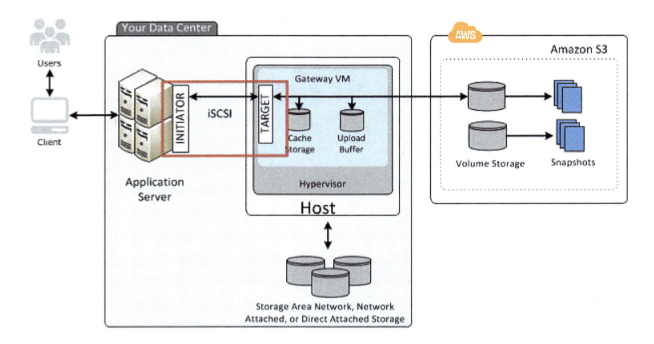

You can connect to your volume from either a Windows or Red Hat Linux client. You can optionally configure CHAP for either client type.

Your gateway exposes your volume as an iSCSI target with a name you specify, prepended by `iqn.1997-05.com.amazon:`. For example, if you specify a target name of `myvolume`, then the iSCSI target you use to connect to the volume is `iqn.1997-05.com.amazon:myvolume`. For more information about how to configure your applications to mount volumes over iSCSI, see Connecting to Your Volumes to a Windows Client.

To	See
Connect to your volume from Windows.	Connecting Your Volumes to Your Client in the Getting Started section
Connect to your volume from Red Hat Linux.	Connecting to a Microsoft Windows Client
Configure CHAP authentication for Windows and Red Hat Linux.	Configuring CHAP Authentication for Your iSCSI Targets

To connect your Windows client to a storage volume

1. On the **Start** menu of your Windows client computer, type **iscsicpl.exe** in the **Search Programs and files** box, locate the iSCSI initiator program, and then run it. **Note**
   You must have administrator rights on the client computer to run the iSCSI initiator.

2. If prompted, choose **Yes** to start the Microsoft iSCSI initiator service.

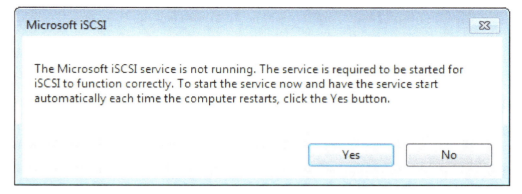

Microsoft iSCSI

The Microsoft iSCSI service is not running. The service is required to be started for iSCSI to function correctly. To start the service now and have the service start automatically each time the computer restarts, click the Yes button.

Yes   No

3. In the **iSCSI Initiator Properties** dialog box, choose the **Discovery** tab, and then choose the **Discovery Portal** button.

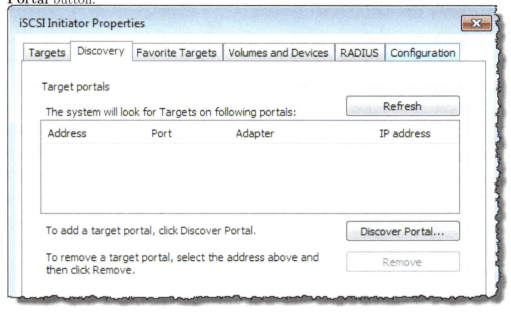

iSCSI Initiator Properties

Targets | Discovery | Favorite Targets | Volumes and Devices | RADIUS | Configuration

Target portals

The system will look for Targets on following portals: Refresh

Address   Port   Adapter   IP address

To add a target portal, click Discover Portal.   Discover Portal...

To remove a target portal, select the address above and then click Remove.   Remove

4. In the **Discover Target Portal** dialog box, type the IP address of your iSCSI target for **IP address or DNS name**, and then choose **OK**. To get the IP address of your gateway, check the **Gateway** tab on the AWS Storage Gateway console. If you deployed your gateway on an Amazon EC2 instance, you can find the public IP or DNS address in the **Description** tab on the Amazon EC2 console.

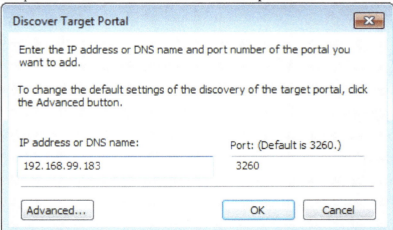

Discover Target Portal

Enter the IP address or DNS name and port number of the portal you want to add.

To change the default settings of the discovery of the target portal, click the Advanced button.

IP address or DNS name: Port: (Default is 3260.)
192.168.99.183   3260

Advanced...   OK   Cancel

The IP address now appears in the **Target portals** list on the **Discovery** tab.

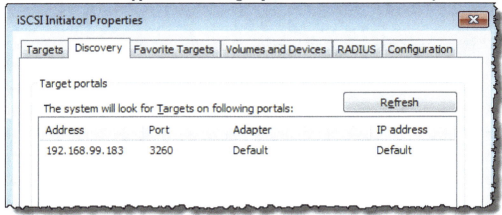

5. Connect the new target portal to the storage volume target on the gateway:

   1. Choose the **Targets** tab.

      The new target portal is shown with an inactive status. Note that the target name shown should be the same as the name you specified for your storage volume in step 1.

   2. Select the target, and then choose **Connect**.

      If the target name is not populated already, type the name of the target as shown in step 1 in the **Connect to Target** dialog box, select the check box next to **Add this connection to the list of Favorite Targets**, and then choose **OK**.

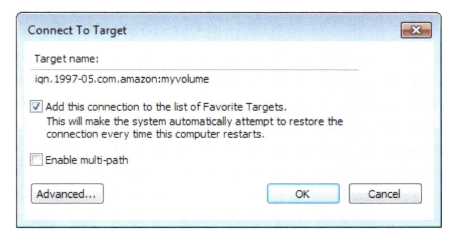

3. In the **Targets** tab, ensure that the target **Status** has the value **Connected** indicating the target is connected, and then choose **OK**.

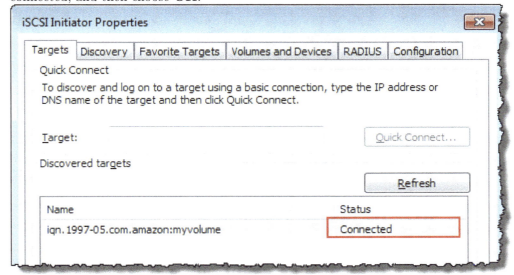

You can now initialize and format this storage volume for Windows so you can begin saving data on it. You do this by using the Windows Disk Management tool.

Note
Although it is not required for this exercise, we highly recommend that you customize your iSCSI settings for a real-world application as discussed in Customizing Your Windows iSCSI Settings.

Connecting Your VTL Devices to a Windows client

A tape gateway exposes several tape drives and a media changer, referred to collectively as VTL devices, as iSCSI targets. For more information, see Requirements.

Note
You connect only one application to each iSCSI target.

The following diagram highlights the iSCSI target in the larger picture of the AWS Storage Gateway architecture. For more information on AWS Storage Gateway architecture, see Tape Gateways.

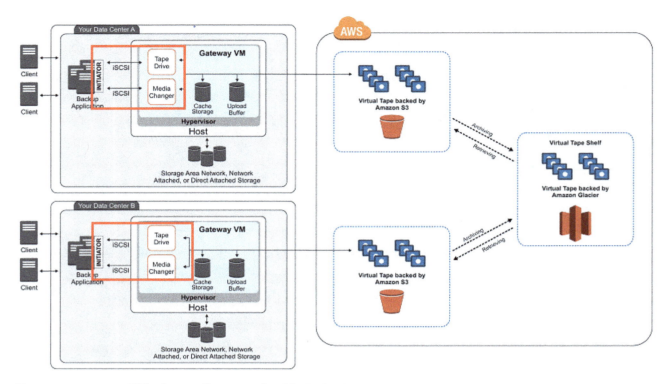

To connect your Windows client to the VTL devices

1. On the **Start** menu of your Windows client computer, type **iscsicpl.exe** in the **Search Programs and files** box, locate the iSCSI initiator program, and then run it. **Note**
   You must have administrator rights on the client computer to run the iSCSI initiator.

2. If prompted, choose **Yes** to start the Microsoft iSCSI initiator service.

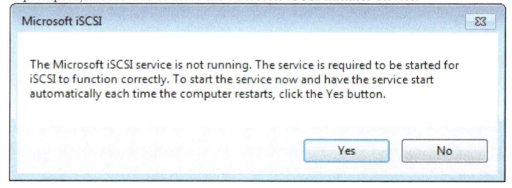

3. In the **iSCSI Initiator Properties** dialog box, choose the **Discovery** tab, and then choose **Discover Portal**.

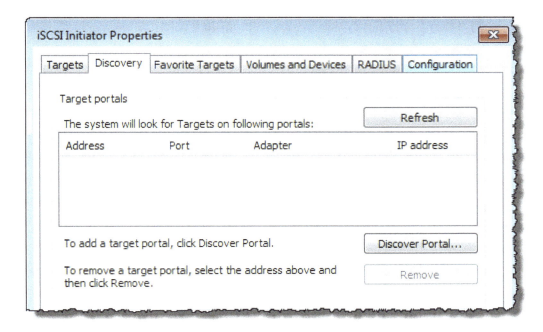

4. In the **Discover Target Portal** dialog box, type the IP address of your tape gateway for **IP address or DNS name**, and then choose **OK**. To get the IP address of your gateway, check the **Gateway** tab on the AWS Storage Gateway console. If you deployed your gateway on an Amazon EC2 instance, you can find the public IP or DNS address in the **Description** tab on the Amazon EC2 console.

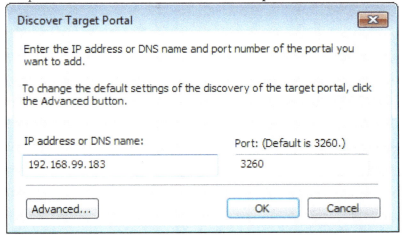

5. Choose the **Targets** tab, and then choose **Refresh**. All 10 tape drives and the medium changer appear in the **Discovered targets** box. The status for the targets is **Inactive**.

The following screenshot shows the discovered targets.

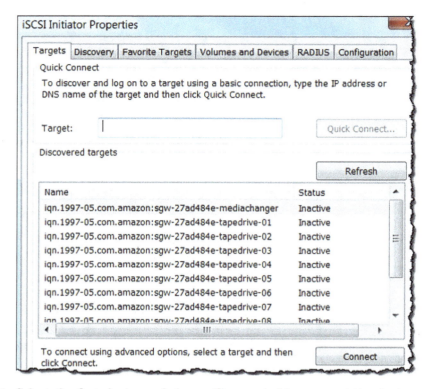

6. Select the first device and choose **Connect**. You connect the devices one at a time.

7. In the **Connect to Target** dialog box, choose **OK**.

8. Repeat steps 6 and 7 for each of the devices to connect all of them, and then choose **OK** in the **iSCSI Initiator Properties** dialog box.

On a Windows client, the driver provider for the tape drive must be Microsoft. Use the following procedure to verify the driver provider, and update the driver and provider if necessary.

To verify the driver provider and if necessary update the provider and driver on a Windows client

1. On your Windows client, start Device Manager.

2. Expand **Tape drives**, choose the context (right-click) menu for a tape drive, and choose **Properties**.

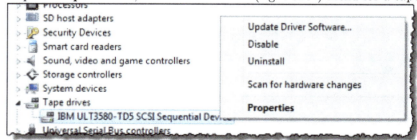

3. In the **Driver** tab of the **Device Properties** dialog box, verify **Driver Provider** is Microsoft.

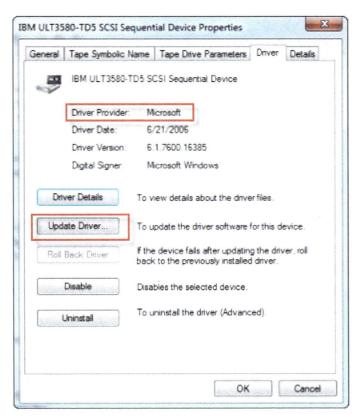

4. If **Driver Provider** is not Microsoft, set the value as follows:

   1. Choose **Update Driver**.

   2. In the **Update Driver Software** dialog box, choose **Browse my computer for driver software**.

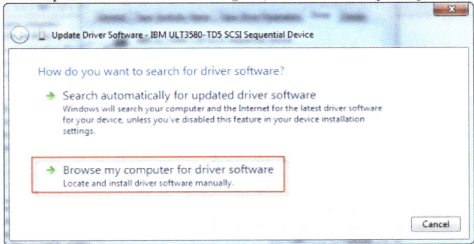

   3. In the **Update Driver Software** dialog box, choose **Let me pick from a list of device drivers on my computer**.

4. Select **LTO Tape drive** and choose **Next**.

5. Choose **Close** to close the **Update Driver Software** window, and verify that the **Driver Provider** value is now set to Microsoft.

5. Repeat steps 4.1 through 4.5 to update all the tape drives.

Connecting Your Volumes or VTL Devices to a Linux Client

Topics

When using Red Hat Enterprise Linux (RHEL), you use the iscsi-initiator-utils RPM package to connect to your gateway iSCSI targets (volumes or VTL devices).

To connect a Linux client to the iSCSI targets

1. Install the iscsi-initiator-utils RPM package, if it isn't already installed on your client.

You can use the following command to install the package.

```
1 sudo yum install iscsi-initiator-utils
```

2. Ensure that the iSCSI daemon is running.

    1. Verify that the iSCSI daemon is running using one of the following commands.

        For RHEL 5 or 6, use the following command.

        ```
        1 sudo /etc/init.d/iscsi status
        ```

        For RHEL 7, use the following command.

        ```
        1 sudo service iscsid status
        ```

    2. If the status command doesn't return a status of *running*, then start the daemon using one of the following commands.

        For RHEL 5 or 6, use the following command.

        ```
        1 sudo /etc/init.d/iscsi start
        ```

        For RHEL 7, use the following command. For RHEL 7, you usually don't need to explicitly start the iscsid service.

        ```
        1 sudo service iscsid start
        ```

3. To discover the volume or VTL device targets defined for a gateway, use the following discovery command.

```
1 sudo /sbin/iscsiadm --mode discovery --type sendtargets --portal [GATEWAY_IP]:3260
```

Substitute your gateway's IP address for the *[GATEWAY_IP]* variable in the preceding command. You can find the gateway IP in the **iSCSI Target Info** properties of a volume on the AWS Storage Gateway console.

The output of the discovery command will look like the following example output.

For volume gateways: `[GATEWAY_IP]:3260, 1 iqn.1997-05.com.amazon:myvolume`

For tape gateways: `iqn.1997-05.com.amazon:[GATEWAY_IP]-tapedrive-01`

Your iSCSI qualified name (IQN) will be different than what is shown preceding, because IQN values are unique to an organization. The name of the target is the name that you specified when you created the volume. You can also find this target name in the **iSCSI Target Info** properties pane when you select a volume on the AWS Storage Gateway console.

4. To connect to a target, use the following command.

    Note that you need to specify the correct *[GATEWAY_IP]* and IQN in the connect command. **Warning** For gateways that are deployed on an Amazon EC2 instance, accessing the gateway over a public Internet connection is not supported. The elastic IP address of the Amazon EC2 instance cannot be used as the target address.

```
1 sudo /sbin/iscsiadm --mode node --targetname iqn.1997-05.com.amazon:[ISCSI_TARGET_NAME] --
   portal [GATEWAY_IP]:3260,1 --login
```

5. To verify that the volume is attached to the client machine (the initiator), use the following command.

```
1 ls -l /dev/disk/by-path
```

The output of the command will look like the following example output.

```
lrwxrwxrwx. 1 root root 9 Apr 16 19:31 ip-[GATEWAY_IP]:3260-iscsi-iqn.1997-05.com.
amazon:myvolume-lun-0 -> ../../sda
```

We highly recommend that after you set up your initiator you customize your iSCSI settings as discussed in Customizing Your Linux iSCSI Settings.

Customizing iSCSI Settings

After setting up your initiator, we highly recommend that you customize your iSCSI settings to prevent the initiator from disconnecting from targets.

By increasing the iSCSI timeout values as shown in the following steps, you make your application better at dealing with write operations that take a long time and other transient issues such as network interruptions.

Note
Before making changes to the registry, you should make a backup copy of the registry. For information on making a backup copy and other best practices to follow when working with the registry, see Registry best practices in the *Microsoft TechNet Library.*

Topics

- Customizing Your Windows iSCSI Settings
- Customizing Your Linux iSCSI Settings

Customizing Your Windows iSCSI Settings

When using a Windows client, you use the Microsoft iSCSI initiator to connect to your gateway volume. For instructions on how to connect to your volumes, see Connecting Your Volumes to Your Client.

For a tape gateway setup, connecting to your VTL devices by using a Microsoft iSCSI initiator is a two-step process:

1. Connect your tape gateway devices to your Windows client.

2. If you are using a backup application, configure the application to use the devices.

The Getting Started example setup provides instructions for both these steps. It uses the Symantec NetBackup backup application. For more information, see Connecting Your VTL Devices and Configuring NetBackup Storage Devices.

To customize your Windows iSCSI settings

1. Increase the maximum time for which requests are queued.

   1. Start Registry Editor (`Regedit.exe`).

   2. Navigate to the globally unique identifier (GUID) key for the device class that contains iSCSI controller settings, shown following. **Warning**
      Make sure you are working in the **CurrentControlSet** subkey and not another control set such as **ControlSet001** or **ControlSet002**.

   i `HKEY_Local_Machine\SYSTEM\CurrentControlSet\Control\Class\{4D36E97B-E325-11CE-BFC1`
      `-08002BE10318}`

   3. Find the subkey for the Microsoft iSCSI initiator, shown following as *[<Instance Number].*

      The key is represented by a four-digit number, such as 0000.

   i `HKEY_Local_Machine\SYSTEM\CurrentControlSet\Control\Class\{4D36E97B-E325-11CE-BFC1`
      `-08002BE10318}\[<Instance Number]`

Depending on what is installed on your computer, the Microsoft iSCSI initiator might not be the subkey 0000. You can ensure that you have selected the correct subkey by verifying that the string `DriverDesc` has the value `Microsoft iSCSI Initiator`, as shown in the following example.

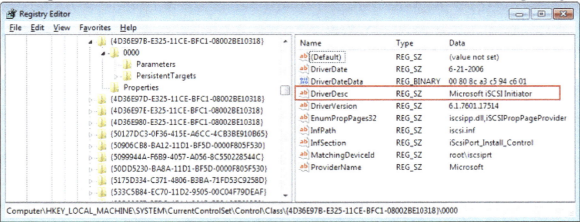

4. To show the iSCSI settings, choose the **Parameters** subkey.

5. Open the context (right-click) menu for the **MaxRequestHoldTime** DWORD (32-bit) value, choose **Modify**, and then change the value to 600.

This value represents a hold time of 600 seconds. The example following shows the **MaxRequestHoldTime** DWORD value with a value of 600.

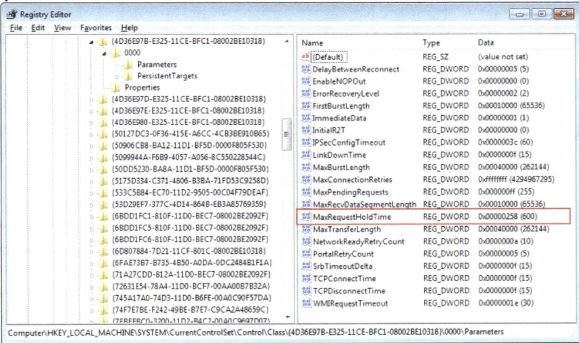

2. Increase the disk timeout value, as shown following:

1. Start Registry Editor (`Regedit.exe`), if you haven't already.

2. Navigate to the **Disk** subkey in the **Services** subkey of the **CurrentControlSet**, shown following.

```
1 HKEY_Local_Machine\SYSTEM\CurrentControlSet\Services\Disk
```

3. Open the context (right-click) menu for the **TimeOutValue** DWORD (32-bit) value, choose **Modify**, and then change the value to 600.

This value represents a timeout of 600 seconds. The example following shows the **TimeOutValue** DWORD value with a value of 600.

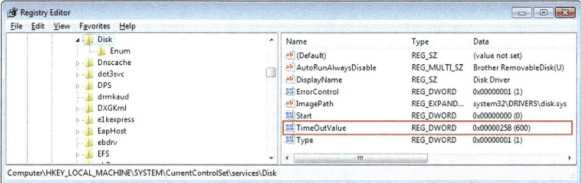

3. To ensure that the new configuration values take effect, restart your system.

Before restarting, you must make sure that the results of all write operations to volumes are flushed. To do this, take any mapped storage volume disks offline before restarting.

Customizing Your Linux iSCSI Settings

After setting up your initiator, we highly recommend that you customize your iSCSI settings to prevent the initiator from disconnecting from targets. By increasing the iSCSI timeout values as shown following, you make your application better at dealing with write operations that take a long time and other transient issues such as network interruptions.

Note
Commands might be slightly different for other types of Linux. The following examples are based on Red Hat Linux.

To customize your Linux iSCSI settings

1. Increase the maximum time for which requests are queued.

   1. Open the `/etc/iscsi/iscsid.conf` file and find the following lines.

   ```
   1 node.session.timeo.replacement_timeout = [replacement_timeout_value]
   2 node.conn[0].timeo.noop_out_interval = [noop_out_interval_value]
   3 node.conn[0].timeo.noop_out_timeout = [noop_out_timeout_value]
   ```

   2. Set the *[replacement_timeout_value]* value to 600.

   Set the *[noop_out_interval_value]* value to 60.

   Set the *[noop_out_timeout_value]* value to 600.

   All three values are in seconds. **Note**
   The `iscsid.conf` settings must be made before discovering the gateway. If you have already discovered your gateway or logged in to the target, or both, you can delete the entry from the discovery database using the following command. Then you can rediscover or log in again to pick up the new configuration.

   ```
   1 iscsiadm -m discoverydb -t sendtargets -p [GATEWAY_IP]:3260 -o delete
   ```

2. Increase the disk timeout value in the rules file.

   1. If you are using the RHEL 5 initiator, open the `/etc/udev/rules.d/50-udev.rules` file and find the following line.

```
1 ACTION=="add", SUBSYSTEM=="scsi" , SYSFS{type}=="0|7|14", \
2 RUN+="/bin/sh -c 'echo [timeout] > /sys$$DEVPATH/timeout'"
```

This rules file does not exist in RHEL 6 or 7 initiators, so you must create it using the following rule.

```
1 ACTION=="add", SUBSYSTEMS=="scsi" , ATTRS{model}=="Storage Gateway",
2 RUN+="/bin/sh -c 'echo [timeout] > /sys$$DEVPATH/timeout'"
```

To modify the timeout value in RHEL 6, use the following command and then add the lines of code shown preceding.

```
1 sudo vim /etc/udev/rules.d/50-udev.rules
```

To modify the timeout value in RHEL 7, use the following command and then add the lines of code shown preceding.

```
1 sudo su -c "echo 600 > /sys/block/[device name]/device/timeout"
```

2. Set the *[timeout]* value to 600.

   This value represents a timeout of 600 seconds.

3. Restart your system to ensure that the new configuration values take effect.

   Before restarting, you must make sure that the results of all write operations to your volumes are flushed. To do this, unmount storage volumes before restarting.

4. You can test the configuration by using the following command.

```
1 udevadm test [PATH_TO_ISCSI_DEVICE]
```

This command shows the udev rules that are applied to the iSCSI device.

Configuring CHAP Authentication for Your iSCSI Targets

AWS Storage Gateway supports authentication between your gateway and iSCSI initiators by using Challenge-Handshake Authentication Protocol (CHAP). CHAP provides protection against playback attacks by periodically verifying the identity of an iSCSI initiator as authenticated to access a volume and VTL device target.

To set up CHAP, you must configure it both on the AWS Storage Gateway console and in the iSCSI initiator software that you use to connect to the target. Storage Gateway uses mutual CHAP, which is when the initiator authenticates the target and the target authenticates the initiator.

To set up mutual CHAP for your targets

1. Configure CHAP on the AWS Storage Gateway console, as discussed in To configure CHAP for a volume target on the AWS Storage Gateway console.

2. In your client initiator software, complete the CHAP configuration:
   - To configure mutual CHAP on a Windows client, see To configure mutual CHAP on a Windows client.
   - To configure mutual CHAP on a Red Hat Linux client, see To configure mutual CHAP on a Red Hat Linux client.

To configure CHAP for a volume target on the AWS Storage Gateway console

In this procedure, you specify two secret keys that are used to read and write to a volume. These same keys are used in the procedure to configure the client initiator.

1. On the AWS Storage Gateway console, choose **Volumes** in the navigation pane.

2. On the **Actions** menu, choose **Configure CHAP Authentication**.

3. Provide the requested information in the **Configure CHAP Authentication** dialog box, shown in the screenshot following:

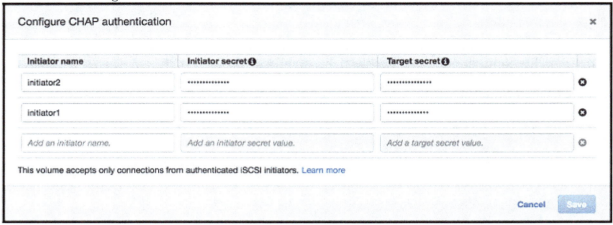

1. For **Initiator Name**, type the name of your iSCSI initiator.

   You can find the initiator name by using your iSCSI initiator software. For example, for Windows clients, the name is the value on the **Configuration** tab of the iSCSI initiator. For more information, see To configure mutual CHAP on a Windows client. **Note**
   To change an initiator name, you must first disable CHAP, change the initiator name in your iSCSI initiator software, and then enable CHAP with the new name.

2. For **Secret used to Authenticate Initiator**, type the secret requested.

   This secret must be a minimum of 12 characters and a maximum of 16 characters long. This value is the secret key that the initiator (that is, the Windows client) must know to participate in CHAP with the target.

3. For **Secret used to Authenticate Target (Mutual CHAP)**, type the secret requested.

   This secret must be a minimum of 12 characters and a maximum of 16 characters long. This value is the secret key that the target must know to participate in CHAP with the initiator. **Note**
   The secret used to authenticate the target must be different than the secret to authenticate the initiator.

4. Choose **Save**.

4. Choose the **Details** tab and confirm that **iSCSI CHAP authentication** is set to **true**.

To configure CHAP for a VTL device target on the AWS Storage Gateway console

In this procedure, you specify two secret keys that are used to read and write to a virtual tape. These same keys are used in the procedure to configure the client initiator.

1. In the navigation pane, choose **Gateways**.

2. Choose your gateway, and then choose the **VTL Devices** tab to display all your VTL devices.

3. Choose the device you want to configure CHAP for.

4. Provide the requested information in the **Configure CHAP Authentication** dialog box, shown in the screenshot following:

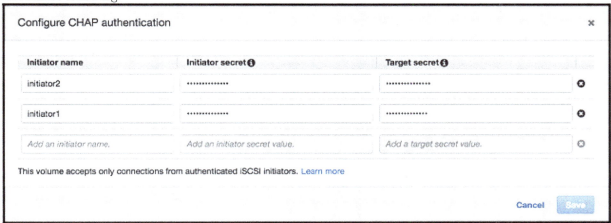

1. For **Initiator Name**, type the name of your iSCSI initiator.

   You can find the initiator name by using your iSCSI initiator software. For example, for Windows clients, the name is the value on the **Configuration** tab of the iSCSI initiator. For more information, see To configure mutual CHAP on a Windows client. **Note**
   To change an initiator name, you must first disable CHAP, change the initiator name in your iSCSI initiator software, and then enable CHAP with the new name.

2. For **Secret used to Authenticate Initiator**, type the secret requested.

   This secret must be a minimum of 12 characters and a maximum of 16 characters long. This value is the secret key that the initiator (that is, the Windows client) must know to participate in CHAP with the target.

3. For **Secret used to Authenticate Target (Mutual CHAP)**, type the secret requested.

   This secret must be a minimum of 12 characters and a maximum of 16 characters long. This value is the secret key that the target must know to participate in CHAP with the initiator. **Note**
   The secret used to authenticate the target must be different than the secret to authenticate the initiator.

4. Choose **Save**.

5. On the **VTL Devices** tab, confirm that the iSCSI CHAP authentication field is set to **true**.

To configure mutual CHAP on a Windows client

In this procedure, you configure CHAP in the Microsoft iSCSI initiator using the same keys that you used to configure CHAP for the volume on the console.

1. If the iSCSI initiator is not already started, on the **Start** menu of your Windows client computer, choose **Run**, type **iscsicpl.exe**, and then choose **OK** to run the program.

2. Configure mutual CHAP configuration for the initiator (that is, the Windows client):

   1. Choose the **Configuration** tab.

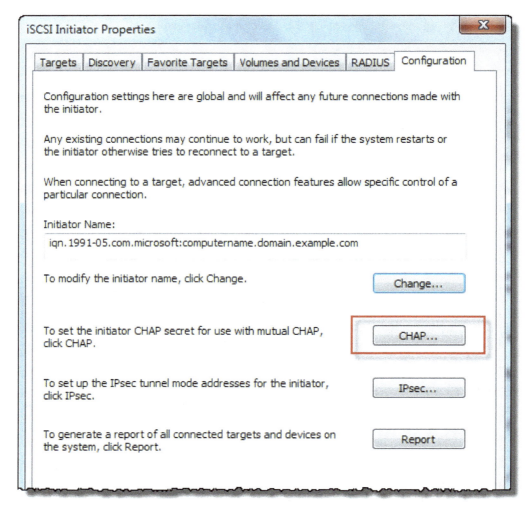

The **Initiator Name** value is unique to your initiator and company. The name shown preceding is the value that you used in the **Configure CHAP Authentication** dialog box of the AWS Storage Gateway console.

The name shown in the example image is for demonstration purposes only.

2. Choose **CHAP**.

3. In the **iSCSI Initiator Mutual Chap Secret** dialog box, type the mutual CHAP secret value.

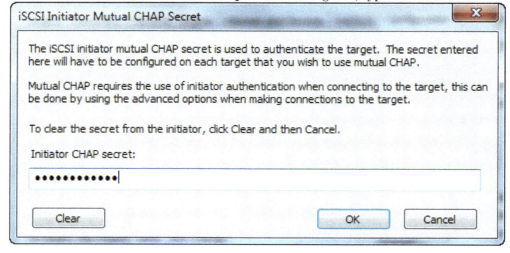

In this dialog box, you enter the secret that the initiator (the Windows client) uses to authenticate the target (the storage volume). This secret allows the target to read and write to the initiator. This secret is the same as the secret typed into the **Secret used to Authenticate Target (Mutual CHAP)** box in the **Configure CHAP Authentication** dialog box. For more information, see Configuring CHAP Authentication for Your iSCSI Targets.

4. If the key that you typed is less than 12 characters or more than 16 characters long, an **Initiator CHAP secret** error dialog box appears.

Choose **OK**, and then type the key again.

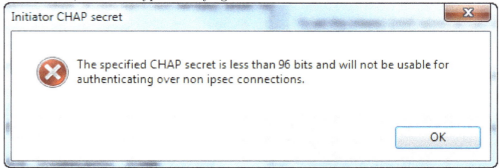

3. Configure the target with the initiator's secret to complete the mutual CHAP configuration.

1. Choose the **Targets** tab.

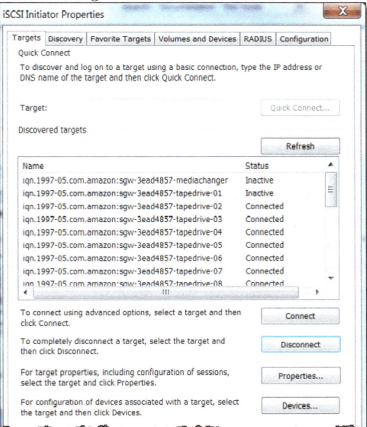

2. If the target that you want to configure for CHAP is currently connected, disconnect the target by selecting it and choosing **Disconnect**.

335

3. Select the target that you want to configure for CHAP, and then choose **Connect**.

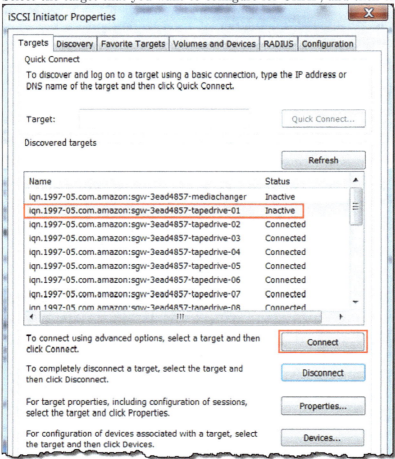

4. In the **Connect to Target** dialog box, choose **Advanced**.

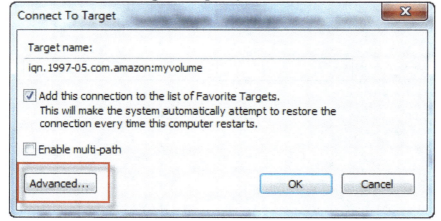

5. In the **Advanced Settings** dialog box, configure CHAP.

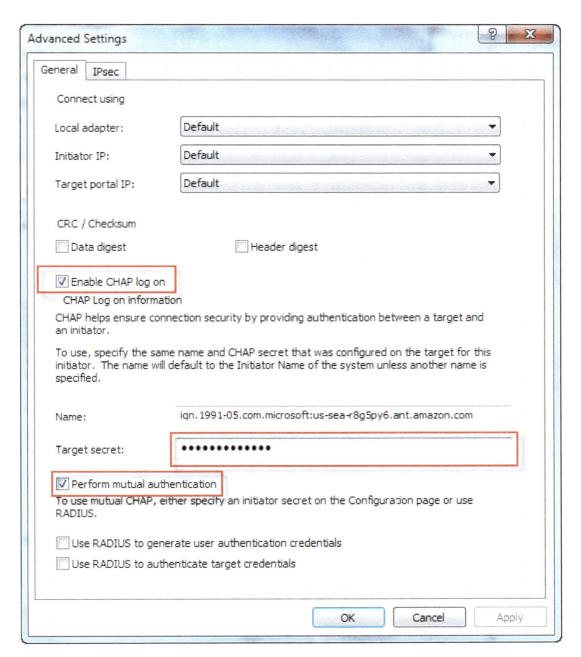

1. Select **Enable CHAP log on**.

2. Type the secret that is required to authenticate the initiator. This secret is the same as the secret typed into the **Secret used to Authenticate Initiator** box in the **Configure CHAP Authentication** dialog box. For more information, see Configuring CHAP Authentication for Your iSCSI Targets.

3. Select **Perform mutual authentication**.

4. To apply the changes, choose **OK**.

6. In the **Connect to Target** dialog box, choose **OK**.

4. If you provided the correct secret key, the target shows a status of **Connected**.

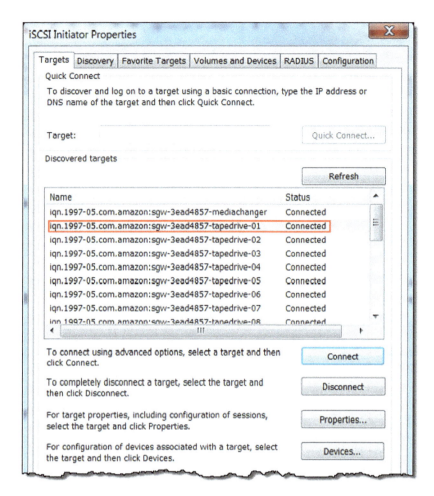

To configure mutual CHAP on a Red Hat Linux client

In this procedure, you configure CHAP in the Linux iSCSI initiator using the same keys that you used to configure CHAP for the volume on the AWS Storage Gateway console.

1. Ensure that the iSCSI daemon is running and that you have already connected to a target. If you have not completed these two tasks, see Connecting to a Microsoft Windows Client.

2. Disconnect and remove any existing configuration for the target for which you are about to configure CHAP.

    1. To find the target name and ensure it is a defined configuration, list the saved configurations using the following command.

    ```
    1 sudo /sbin/iscsiadm --mode node
    ```

    2. Disconnect from the target.

    The following command disconnects from the target named **myvolume** that is defined in the Amazon iSCSI qualified name (IQN). Change the target name and IQN as required for your situation.

    ```
    1 sudo /sbin/iscsiadm --mode node --logout GATEWAY_IP:3260,1 iqn.1997-05.com.amazon:
        myvolume
    ```

    3. Remove the configuration for the target.

    The following command removes the configuration for the **myvolume** target.

```
1 sudo /sbin/iscsiadm --mode node --op delete --targetname iqn.1997-05.com.amazon:
    myvolume
```

3. Edit the iSCSI configuration file to enable CHAP.

    1. Get the name of the initiator (that is, the client you are using).

    The following command gets the initiator name from the `/etc/iscsi/initiatorname.iscsi` file.

```
1 sudo cat /etc/iscsi/initiatorname.iscsi
```

    The output from this command looks like this:

    `InitiatorName=iqn.1994-05.com.redhat:8e89b27b5b8`

    2. Open the `/etc/iscsi/iscsid.conf` file.

    3. Uncomment the following lines in the file and specify the correct values for *username*, *password*, *username_in*, and *password_in*.

```
1 node.session.auth.authmethod = CHAP
2 node.session.auth.username = username
3 node.session.auth.password = password
4 node.session.auth.username_in = username_in
5 node.session.auth.password_in = password_in
```

    For guidance on what values to specify, see the following table.
    [See the AWS documentation website for more details]

    4. Save the changes in the configuration file, and then close the file.

4. Discover and log in to the target. To do so, follow the steps in Connecting to a Microsoft Windows Client.

Using AWS Direct Connect with AWS Storage Gateway

AWS Direct Connect links your internal network to the AWS Cloud. By using AWS Direct Connect with AWS Storage Gateway, you can create a connection for high-throughput workload needs, providing a dedicated network connection between your on-premises gateway and AWS.

Storage Gateway uses public endpoints. With an AWS Direct Connect connection in place, you can create a public virtual interface to allow traffic to be routed to the Storage Gateway endpoints. The public virtual interface bypasses internet service providers in your network path. The Storage Gateway service public endpoint can be in the same AWS Region as the AWS Direct Connect location, or it can be in a different AWS Region.

The following illustration shows an example of how AWS Direct Connect works with Storage Gateway.

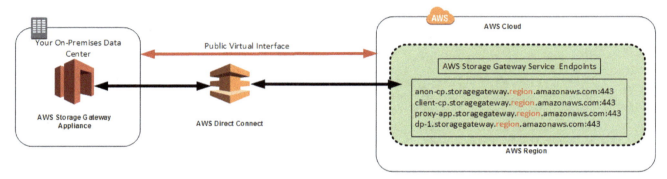

The following procedure assumes that you have created a functioning gateway.

To use AWS Direct Connect with Storage Gateway

1. Create and establish an AWS Direct Connect connection between your on-premises data center and your Storage Gateway endpoint. For more information about how to create a connection, see Getting Started with AWS Direct Connect in the *AWS Direct Connect User Guide.*

2. Connect your on-premises Storage Gateway appliance to the AWS Direct Connect router.

3. Create a public virtual interface, and configure your on-premises router accordingly. For more information, see Creating a Virtual Interface in the *AWS Direct Connect User Guide.*

For details about AWS Direct Connect, see What is AWS Direct Connect? in the *AWS Direct Connect User Guide.*

Port Requirements

AWS Storage Gateway requires the following ports for its operation. Some ports are common to all gateway types and are required by all gateway types. Other ports are required by specific gateway types. In this section, you can find an illustration of the required ports and a list of the ports required by each gateway type.

File Gateways

The following illustration shows the ports to open for file gateways' operation.

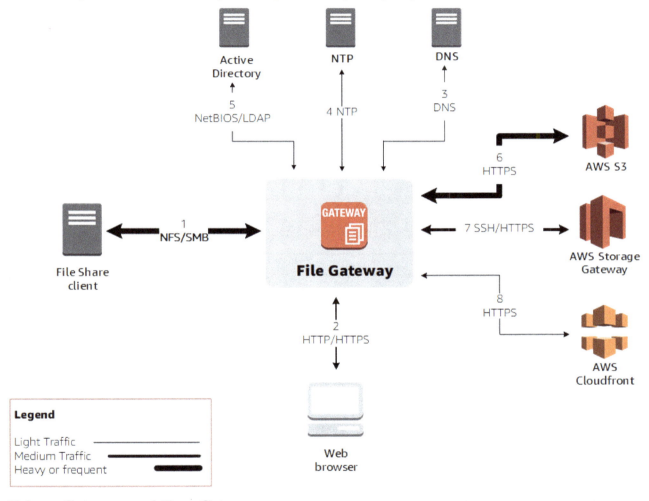

Volume Gateways and Tape Gateways

The following illustration shows the ports to open for volume gateways' and tape gateways' operation.

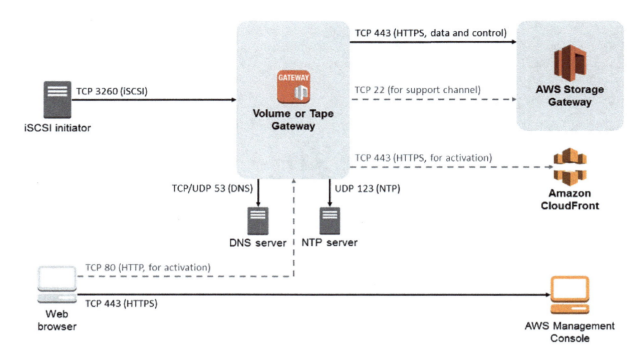

The following ports are common to all gateway types and are required by all gateway types.

From	To	Protocol	Port	How Used
Storage Gateway VM	AWS	Transmission Control Protocol (TCP)	443 (HTTPS)	For communication from an AWS Storage Gateway VM to an AWS service endpoint. For information about service endpoints, see Allowing AWS Storage Gateway Access Through Firewalls and Routers.

From	To	Protocol	Port	How Used
Your web browser	Storage Gateway VM	TCP	80 (HTTP)	By local systems to obtain the Storage Gateway activation key. Port 80 is used only during activation of a Storage Gateway appliance. A Storage Gateway VM doesn't require port 80 to be publicly accessible. The required level of access to port 80 depends on your network configuration. If you activate your gateway from the AWS Storage Gateway Management Console, the host from which you connect to the console must have access to your gateway's port 80.
Storage Gateway VM	Domain Name Service (DNS) server	User Datagram Protocol (UDP)/UDP	53 (DNS)	For communication between a Storage Gateway VM and the DNS server.
Storage Gateway VM	AWS	TCP	22 (Support channel)	Allows AWS Support to access your gateway to help you with troubleshooting gateway issues. You don't need this port open for the normal operation of your gateway, but it is required for troubleshooting.

From	To	Protocol	Port	How Used
Storage Gateway VM	Network Protocol (NTP) server	Time (NTP) UDP	123 (NTP)	Used by local systems to synchronize VM time to the host time. A Storage Gateway VM is configured to use the following NTP servers: [See the AWS documentation website for more details]

The following table lists the required ports that must be opened for a file gateway using either the Network File System (NFS) or Server Message Block (SMB) protocol. These port rules are part of your security group definition.

Rule	Network Element	File Share Type	Protocol	Port	Inbound	Out-bound	Re-quired?	Notes
1	File share client	NFS	TCP/UDP Data	111				File sharing data transfer (for NFS only)
			TCP/UDP NFS	2049				File sharing data transfer (for NFS only)
			TCP/UDP NFSv3	20048				File sharing data transfer (for NFS only)
		SMB	TCP/UDP SMBv2	139				File sharing data transfer session service (for SMB only); replaces ports 137–139 for Microsoft Windows NT and later

Rule	Network Element	File Share Type	Protocol	Port	Inbound	Out-bound	Re-quired?	Notes
			TCP/UDP SMBv3	445				File sharing data transfer session service (for SMB only); replaces ports 137–139 for Microsoft Windows NT and later
2	Web browser	NFS and SMB	TCP HTTP	80				AWS Management Console (activation only)
			TCP HTTPS	443				AWS Management Console (all other operations)
3	DNS	NFS and SMB	TCP/UDP DNS	53				IP name resolution
4	NTP	NFS and SMB	UDP NTP	123				Time synchronization service
5	Microsoft Active Directory	SMB	UDP Net-BIOS	137				Name service (not used for NFS)
			UDP Net-BIOS	138				Datagram service
			TCP LDAP	389				Directory System Agent (DSA); client connection

Rule	Network Element	File Share Type	Protocol	Port	Inbound	Outbound	Required?	Notes
			TCP LDAPS	636				LDAPS—Lightweight Directory Access Protocol (LDAP) over Secure Socket Layer (SSL)
6	Amazon S3	NFS and SMB	HTTPS data	443				Storage data transfer
7	Storage Gateway	NFS and SMB	TCP SSH	22				Support channel
			TCP HTTPS	443				Management control
8	Amazon CloudFront	NFS and SMB	TCP HTTPS	443				For activation

In addition to the common ports, volume and tape gateways require the following port.

From	To	Protocol	Port	How Used
iSCSI initiators	Storage Gateway VM	TCP	3260 (iSCSI)	By local systems to connect to iSCSI targets exposed by a gateway.

Connecting to Your Gateway

After you choose a host and deploy your gateway VM, you connect and activate your gateway. To do this, you need the IP address of your gateway VM. You get the IP address from your gateway's local console. You log in to the local console and get the IP address from the top of the console page.

For gateways deployed on-premises, you can also get the IP address from your hypervisor. For Amazon EC2 gateways, you can also get the IP address of your Amazon EC2 instance from the Amazon EC2 Management Console. To find how to get your gateway's IP address, see one of the following:

- VMware host: Accessing the Gateway Local Console with VMware ESXi
- HyperV host: Access the Gateway Local Console with Microsoft Hyper-V
- EC2 host: Getting an IP Address from an Amazon EC2 Host

When you locate the IP address, take note of it. Then return to the AWS Storage Gateway console and type the IP address into the console.

Getting an IP Address from an Amazon EC2 Host

To get the IP address of the Amazon EC2 instance your gateway is deployed on, log in to the EC2 instance's local console. Then get the IP address from the top of the console page. For instructions, see Logging In to Your Amazon EC2 Gateway Local Console.

You can also get the IP address from the Amazon EC2 Management Console. We recommend using the public IP address for activation. To get the public IP address, use procedure 1. If you choose to use the elastic IP address instead, see procedure 2.

Procedure 1: To connect to your gateway using the public IP address

1. Open the Amazon EC2 console at https://console.aws.amazon.com/ec2/.

2. In the navigation pane, choose **Instances**, and then select the EC2 instance that your gateway is deployed on.

3. Choose the **Description** tab at the bottom, and then note the public IP. You use this IP address to connect to the gateway. Return to the AWS Storage Gateway console and type in the IP address.

If you want to use the elastic IP address for activation, use the procedure following.

Procedure 2: To connect to your gateway using the elastic IP address

1. Open the Amazon EC2 console at https://console.aws.amazon.com/ec2/.

2. In the navigation pane, choose **Instances**, and then select the EC2 instance that your gateway is deployed on.

3. Choose the **Description** tab at the bottom, and then note the **Elastic IP** value. You use this elastic IP address to connect to the gateway. Return to the AWS Storage Gateway console and type in the elastic IP address.

4. After your gateway is activated, choose the gateway that you just activated, and then choose the **VTL devices** tab in the bottom panel.

5. Get the names of all your VTL devices.

6. For each target, run the following command to configure the target.

   ```
   iscsiadm -m node -o new -T [$TARGET_NAME] -p [$Elastic_IP]:3260
   ```

7. For each target, run the following command to log in.

   ```
   iscsiadm -m node -p [$ELASTIC_IP]:3260 --login
   ```

Your gateway is now connected using the elastic IP address of the EC2 instance.

Understanding AWS Storage Gateway Resources and Resource IDs

In AWS Storage Gateway, the primary resource is a *gateway* but other resource types include: *volume*, * virtual tape*, *iSCSI target*, and *vtl device*. These are referred to as *subresources* and they don't exist unless they are associated with a gateway.

These resources and subresources have unique Amazon Resource Names (ARNs) associated with them as shown in the following table.

Resource Type	ARN Format
Gateway ARN	`arn:aws:storagegateway:region:account-id:gateway/gateway-id`
File Share ARN	`arn:aws:storagegateway:region:account-id:share/share-id`
Volume ARN	`arn:aws:storagegateway:region:account-id:gateway/gateway-id/volume/volume-id`
Tape ARN	`arn:aws:storagegateway:region:account-id:tape/tapebarcode`
Target ARN (iSCSI target)	`arn:aws:storagegateway:region:account-id:gateway/gateway-id/target/iSCSItarget`
VTL Device ARN	`arn:aws:storagegateway:region:account-id:gateway/gateway-id/device/vtldevice`

AWS Storage Gateway also supports the use of EC2 instances and EBS volumes and snapshots. These resources are Amazon EC2 resources that are used in AWS Storage Gateway.

Working with Resource IDs

When you create a resource, Storage Gateway assigns the resource a unique resource ID. This resource ID is part of the resource ARN. A resource ID takes the form of a resource identifier, followed by a hyphen, and a unique combination of eight letters and numbers. For example, a gateway ID is of the form `sgw-12A3456B` where `sgw` is the resource identifier for gateways. A volume ID takes the form `vol-3344CCDD` where `vol` is the resource identifier for volumes.

For virtual tapes, you can prepend a up to a four character prefix to the barcode ID to help you organize your tapes.

AWS Storage Gateway resource IDs are in uppercase. However, when you use these resource IDs with the Amazon EC2 API, Amazon EC2 expects resource IDs in lowercase. You must change your resource ID to lowercase to use it with the EC2 API. For example, in Storage Gateway the ID for a volume might be `vol-1122AABB`. When you use this ID with the EC2 API, you must change it to `vol-1122aabb`. Otherwise, the EC2 API might not behave as expected.

Important

IDs for Storage Gateway volumes and Amazon EBS snapshots created from gateway volumes are changing to a longer format. Starting in December 2016, all new volumes and snapshots will be created with a 17-character string. Starting in April 2016, you will be able to use these longer IDs so you can test your systems with the new format. For more information, see Longer EC2 and EBS Resource IDs.

For example, a volume ARN with the longer volume ID format will look like this:

`arn:aws:storagegateway:us-west-2:111122223333:gateway/sgw-12A3456B/volume/vol-1122AABBCCDDEEFFG.`

A snapshot ID with the longer ID format will look like this: `snap-78e226633445566ee`.

For more information, see Announcement: Heads-up – Longer AWS Storage Gateway volume and snapshot IDs coming in 2016.

Tagging Storage Gateway Resources

In AWS Storage Gateway, you can use tags to manage your resources. Tags let you add metadata to your resources and categorize your resources to make them easier to manage. Each tag consists of a key-value pair, which you define. You can add tags to gateways, volumes, and virtual tapes. You can search and filter these resources based on the tags you add.

As an example, you can use tags to identify Storage Gateway resources used by each department in your organization. You might tag gateways and volumes used by your accounting department like this: (key= `department` and `value=accounting`). You can then filter with this tag to identify all gateways and volumes used by your accounting department and use the information to determine cost. For more information, see Using Cost Allocation Tags and Working with Tag Editor.

If you archive a virtual tape that is tagged, the tape maintains its tags in the archive. Similarly, if you retrieve a tape from the archive to another gateway, the tags are maintained in the new gateway.

Tags don't have any semantic meaning but rather are interpreted as strings of characters.

The following restrictions apply to tags:

- Tag keys and values are case-sensitive.
- The maximum number of tags for each resource is 10.
- Tag keys cannot begin with `aws:`. This prefix is reserved for AWS use.
- Valid characters for the key property are UTF-8 letters and numbers, space, and special characters + - = . _ : / and @.

Working with Tags

You can work with tags by using the Storage Gateway console, the Storage Gateway API, or the Storage Gateway Command Line Interface (CLI). The following procedures show you how to add, edit, and delete a tag on the console.

To add a tag

1. Open the AWS Storage Gateway console at https://console.aws.amazon.com/storagegateway/home.

2. In the navigation pane, choose the resource you want to tag.

   For example, to tag a gateway, choose **Gateways**, and then choose the gateway you want to tag from the list of gateways.

3. Choose **Tags**, and then choose **Add/edit tags**.

4. In the **Add/edit tags** dialog box, choose **Create tag**.

5. Type a key for **Key** and a value for **Value**. For example, you can type **Department** for the key and **Accounting** for the value. **Note**
   You can leave the **Value** box blank.

6. Choose **Create Tag** to add more tags. You can add multiple tags to a resource.

7. When you're done adding tags, choose **Save**.

To edit a tag

1. Open the AWS Storage Gateway console at https://console.aws.amazon.com/storagegateway/home.

2. Choose the resource whose tag you want to edit.

3. Choose **Tags** to open the **Add/edit tags** dialog box.

4. Choose the pencil icon next to the tag you want edit, and then edit the tag.

5. When you're done editing the tag, choose **Save**.

To delete a tag

1. Open the AWS Storage Gateway console at https://console.aws.amazon.com/storagegateway/home.

2. Choose the resource whose tag you want to delete.

3. Choose **Tags**, and then choose **Add/edit tags** to open the **Add/edit tags** dialog box.

4. Choose the **X** icon next to the tag you want to delete, and then choose **Save**.

Working with Open-Source Components for AWS Storage Gateway

The source code for certain open-source software components that are included with the AWS Storage Gateway software is available for download at the following locations:

- https://s3.amazonaws.com/aws-storage-gateway-terms/sources.tar for gateways deployed on VMware ESXi.
- https://s3.amazonaws.com/aws-storage-gateway-terms/sources_hyperv.tar for gateways deployed on Microsoft Hyper-V

This product includes software developed by the OpenSSL Project for use in the OpenSSL Toolkit (http://www.openssl.org/).

The packages that make up the AWS Storage Gateway VM are tracked and monitored for security vulnerabilities. When updates are issued, they are applied to each gateway and the updated packages will increment their version number, although the major version number of the Linux distribution might not increment.

AWS Storage Gateway Limits

In this topic, you can find information about file share, volume, tape, configuration, and performance limits for Storage Gateway.

Topics

- Limits For File Shares
- Limits for Volumes
- Limits for Tapes
- Configuration and Performance Limits
- Recommended Local Disk Sizes For Your Gateway

Limits For File Shares

The following table lists limits for file shares.

Description	File Gateway
Maximum number of file shares per Amazon S3 bucket. There is a one-to-one mapping between a file share and an S3 bucket	1
Maximum number of file shares per gateway	10
The maximum size of an individual file, which is the maximum size of an individual object in Amazon S3 If you write a file larger than 5 TB, you get a "file too large" error message and only the first 5 TB of the file is uploaded.	5 TB

Limits for Volumes

The following table lists limits for volumes.

Description	Cached Volumes	Stored Volumes
Maximum size of a volume If you create a snapshot from a cached volume that is more than 16 TiB in size, you cannot restore it to an Amazon Elastic Block Store (Amazon EBS) volume; however, it can be restored to a Storage Gateway volume.	32 TiB	16 TiB
Maximum number of volumes for a gateway	32	32
Total size of all volumes for a gateway	1,024 TiB	512 TiB

Limits for Tapes

The following table lists limits for tapes.

Description	Tape Gateway
Minimum size of a virtual tape	100 GiB
Maximum size of a virtual tape	2.5 TiB
Maximum number of virtual tapes for a virtual tape library (VTL)	1,500
Total size of all tapes in a virtual tape library (VTL)	1 PiB
Maximum number of virtual tapes in archive	No limit
Total size of all tapes in a archive	No limit

Configuration and Performance Limits

The following table lists limits for configuration and performance.

Description	File Gateway	Cached Volumes	Stored Volumes	Tape Gateway
Maximum upload rate The maximum upload rate was achieved by using 100 percent sequential write operations and 256 KB I/Os. Depending on your I/O mix and network conditions, the actual rate might be lower.	–	120 MB/s	120 MB/s	120 MB/s
Maximum download rate	–	20 MB/s	20 MB/s	20 MB/s

Recommended Local Disk Sizes For Your Gateway

The following table recommends sizes for local disk storage for your deployed gateway.

Gateway Type	Cache (Minimum)	Cache (Maximum)	Upload Buffer (Minimum)	Upload Buffer (Maximum)	Other Required Local Disks
File gateway	150 GiB	16 TiB	—	—	—
Cached volume gateway	150 GiB	16 TiB	150 GiB	2 TiB	—
Stored volume gateway	—	—	150 GiB	2 TiB	1 or more for stored volume or volumes
Tape gateway	150 GiB	16 TiB	150 GiB	2 TiB	—

Note
You can configure one or more local drives for your cache and upload buffer, up to the maximum capacity.

When adding cache or upload buffer to an existing gateway, it's important to create new disks in your host (hypervisor or Amazon EC2 instance). Don't change the size of existing disks if the disks have been previously allocated as either a cache or upload buffer.

API Reference for AWS Storage Gateway

In addition to using the console, you can use the AWS Storage Gateway API to programmatically configure and manage your gateways. This section describes the AWS Storage Gateway operations, request signing for authentication and the error handling. For information about the regions and endpoints available for AWS Storage Gateway, see Regions and Endpoints.

Note
You can also use the AWS SDKs when developing applications with AWS Storage Gateway. The AWS SDKs for Java, .NET, and PHP wrap the underlying AWS Storage Gateway API, simplifying your programming tasks. For information about downloading the SDK libraries, see Sample Code Libraries.

Topics

- AWS Storage Gateway Required Request Headers
- Signing Requests
- Error Responses
- Actions

AWS Storage Gateway Required Request Headers

This section describes the required headers that you must send with every POST request to AWS Storage Gateway. You include HTTP headers to identify key information about the request including the operation you want to invoke, the date of the request, and information that indicates the authorization of you as the sender of the request. Headers are case insensitive and the order of the headers is not important.

The following example shows headers that are used in the ActivateGateway operation.

```
1 POST / HTTP/1.1
2 Host: storagegateway.us-east-2.amazonaws.com
3 Content-Type: application/x-amz-json-1.1
4 Authorization: AWS4-HMAC-SHA256 Credential=AKIAIOSFODNN7EXAMPLE/20120425/us-east-2/
      storagegateway/aws4_request, SignedHeaders=content-type;host;x-amz-date;x-amz-target,
      Signature=9cd5a3584d1d67d57e61f120f35102d6b3649066abdd4bf4bbcf05bd9f2f8fe2
5 x-amz-date: 20120912T120000Z
6 x-amz-target: StorageGateway_20120630.ActivateGateway
```

The following are the headers that must include with your POST requests to AWS Storage Gateway. Headers shown below that begin with "x-amz" are AWS-specific headers. All other headers listed are common header used in HTTP transactions.

Header	Description
Authorization	The authorization header contains several of pieces of information about the request that enable AWS Storage Gateway to determine if the request is a valid action for the requester. The format of this header is as follows (line breaks added for readability): Authorization: AWS4-HMAC_SHA456 Credentials=YourAccessKey/yyyymmd-d/region/storagegateway/aws4_request, SignedHeaders=content-type;host;x-amz-date;x-amz-target, Signature=Calculat-edSignature In the preceding syntax, you specify *YourAccessKey*, the year, month, and day (*yyyymmdd*), the *region*, and the *CalculatedSignature*. The format of the authorization header is dictated by the requirements of the AWS V4 Signing process. The details of signing are discussed in the topic Signing Requests.
Content-Type	Use `application/x-amz-json-1.1` as the content type for all requests to AWS Storage Gateway. Content-Type: application/x-amz-json-1.1
Host	Use the host header to specify the AWS Storage Gateway endpoint where you send your request. For example, `storagegateway.us-east-2.amazonaws.com` is the endpoint for the US East (Ohio) region. For more information about the endpoints available for AWS Storage Gateway, see Regions and Endpoints. Host: storagegateway.region.amazonaws.com
x-amz-date	You must provide the time stamp in either the HTTP `Date` header or the AWS `x-amz-date` header. (Some HTTP client libraries don't let you set the `Date` header.) When an `x-amz-date` header is present, the AWS Storage Gateway ignores any `Date` header during the request authentication. The `x-amz-date` format must be ISO8601 Basic in the YYYYMMDD'T'HHMMSS'Z' format. If both the `Date` and `x-amz-date` header are used, the format of the Date header does not have to be ISO8601. x-amz-date: YYYYM-MDD'T'HHMMSS'Z'

Header	Description
x-amz-target	This header specifies the version of the API and the operation that you are requesting. The target header values are formed by concatenating the API version with the API name and are in the following format. x-amz-target: StorageGateway_APIversion.operationName The *operationName* value (e.g. "ActivateGateway") can be found from the API list, API Reference for AWS Storage Gateway.

Signing Requests

AWS Storage Gateway requires that you authenticate every request you send by signing the request. To sign a request, you calculate a digital signature using a cryptographic hash function. A cryptographic hash is a function that returns a unique hash value based on the input. The input to the hash function includes the text of your request and your secret access key. The hash function returns a hash value that you include in the request as your signature. The signature is part of the **Authorization** header of your request.

After receiving your request, AWS Storage Gateway recalculates the signature using the same hash function and input that you used to sign the request. If the resulting signature matches the signature in the request, AWS Storage Gateway processes the request. Otherwise, the request is rejected.

AWS Storage Gateway supports authentication using AWS Signature Version 4. The process for calculating a signature can be broken into three tasks:

- Task 1: Create a Canonical Request

  Rearrange your HTTP request into a canonical format. Using a canonical form is necessary because AWS Storage Gateway uses the same canonical form when it recalculates a signature to compare with the one you sent.

- Task 2: Create a String to Sign

  Create a string that you will use as one of the input values to your cryptographic hash function. The string, called the *string to sign*, is a concatenation of the name of the hash algorithm, the request date, a *credential scope* string, and the canonicalized request from the previous task. The *credential scope* string itself is a concatenation of date, region, and service information.

- Task 3: Create a Signature

  Create a signature for your request by using a cryptographic hash function that accepts two input strings: your *string to sign* and a *derived key*. The *derived key* is calculated by starting with your secret access key and using the *credential scope* string to create a series of Hash-based Message Authentication Codes (HMACs).

Example Signature Calculation

The following example walks you through the details of creating a signature for ListGateways. The example could be used as a reference to check your signature calculation method. Other reference calculations are included in the Signature Version 4 Test Suite of the Amazon Web Services Glossary.

The example assumes the following:

- The time stamp of the request is "Mon, 10 Sep 2012 00:00:00" GMT.
- The endpoint is the US East (Ohio) region.

The general request syntax (including the JSON body) is:

```
1 POST / HTTP/1.1
2 Host: storagegateway.us-east-2.amazonaws.com
3 x-amz-Date: 20120910T000000Z
4 Authorization: SignatureToBeCalculated
5 Content-type: application/x-amz-json-1.1
6 x-amz-target: StorageGateway_20120630.ListGateways
7 {}
```

The canonical form of the request calculated for [Task 1: Create a Canonical Request](#SignatureCalculation-Task1) is:

```
1  POST
2  /
3
4  content-type:application/x-amz-json-1.1
5  host:storagegateway.us-east-2.amazonaws.com
6  x-amz-date:20120910T000000Z
7  x-amz-target:StorageGateway_20120630.ListGateways
8
9  content-type;host;x-amz-date;x-amz-target
10 44136fa355b3678a1146ad16f7e8649e94fb4fc21fe77e8310c060f61caaff8a
```

The last line of the canonical request is the hash of the request body. Also, note the empty third line in the canonical request. This is because there are no query parameters for this API (or any AWS Storage Gateway APIs).

The *string to sign* for [Task 2: Create a String to Sign](#SignatureCalculationTask2) is:

```
1 AWS4-HMAC-SHA256
2 20120910T000000Z
3 20120910/us-east-2/storagegateway/aws4_request
4 92c0effa6f9224ac752ca179a04cecbede3038b0959666a8160ab452c9e51b3e
```

The first line of the *string to sign* is the algorithm, the second line is the time stamp, the third line is the *credential scope*, and the last line is a hash of the canonical request from Task 1.

For [Task 3: Create a Signature](#SignatureCalculationTask3), the *derived key* can be represented as:

```
1 derived key = HMAC(HMAC(HMAC(HMAC("AWS4" + YourSecretAccessKey,"20120910"),"us-east-2"),"
    storagegateway"),"aws4_request")
```

If the secret access key, wJalrXUtnFEMI/K7MDENG/bPxRfiCYEXAMPLEKEY, is used, then the calculated signature is:

```
1 6d4c40b8f2257534dbdca9f326f147a0a7a419b63aff349d9d9c737c9a0f4c81
```

The final step is to construct the `Authorization` header. For the demonstration access key AKIAIOSFODNN7EXAMPLE, the header (with line breaks added for readability) is:

```
1 Authorization: AWS4-HMAC-SHA256 Credential=AKIAIOSFODNN7EXAMPLE/20120910/us-east-2/
    storagegateway/aws4_request,
2 SignedHeaders=content-type;host;x-amz-date;x-amz-target,
3 Signature=6d4c40b8f2257534dbdca9f326f147a0a7a419b63aff349d9d9c737c9a0f4c81
```

Error Responses

Topics

- Exceptions
- Operation Error Codes
- Error Responses

This section provides reference information about AWS Storage Gateway errors. These errors are represented by an error exception and an operation error code. For example, the error exception `InvalidSignatureException` is returned by any API response if there is a problem with the request signature. However, the operation error code `ActivationKeyInvalid` is returned only for the ActivateGateway API.

Depending on the type of error, AWS Storage Gateway may return only just an exception, or it may return both an exception and an operation error code. Examples of error responses are shown in the Error Responses.

Exceptions

The following table lists AWS Storage Gateway API exceptions. When an AWS Storage Gateway operation returns an error response, the response body contains one of these exceptions. The `InternalServerError` and `InvalidGatewayRequestException` return one of the operation error codes Operation Error Codes message codes that give the specific operation error code.

Exception	Message	HTTP Status Code
IncompleteSignatureException	The specified signature is incomplete.	400 Bad Request
InternalFailure	The request processing has failed due to some unknown error, exception or failure.	500 Internal Server Error
InternalServerError	One of the operation error code messages Operation Error Codes.	500 Internal Server Error
InvalidAction	The requested action or operation is invalid.	400 Bad Request
InvalidClientTokenId	The X.509 certificate or AWS Access Key ID provided does not exist in our records.	403 Forbidden
InvalidGatewayRequestException	One of the operation error code messages in Operation Error Codes.	400 Bad Request
InvalidSignatureException	The request signature we calculated does not match the signature you provided. Check your AWS Access Key and signing method.	400 Bad Request
MissingAction	The request is missing an action or operation parameter.	400 Bad Request
MissingAuthenticationToken	The request must contain either a valid (registered) AWS Access Key ID or X.509 certificate.	403 Forbidden

Exception	Message	HTTP Status Code
RequestExpired	The request is past the expiration date or the request date (either with 15 minute padding), or the request date occurs more than 15 minutes in the future.	400 Bad Request
SerializationException	An error occurred during serialization. Check that your JSON payload is well-formed.	400 Bad Request
ServiceUnavailable	The request has failed due to a temporary failure of the server.	503 Service Unavailable
SubscriptionRequiredException	The AWS Access Key Id needs a subscription for the service.	400 Bad Request
ThrottlingException	Rate exceeded.	400 Bad Request
UnknownOperationException	An unknown operation was specified. Valid operations are listed in Operations in AWS Storage Gateway.	400 Bad Request
UnrecognizedClientException	The security token included in the request is invalid.	400 Bad Request
ValidationException	The value of an input parameter is bad or out of range.	400 Bad Request

Operation Error Codes

The following table shows the mapping between AWS Storage Gateway operation error codes and APIs that can return the codes. All operation error codes are returned with one of two general exceptions—`InternalServerError` and `InvalidGatewayRequestException`—described in Exceptions.

Operation Error Code	Message	Operations That Return this Error Code
ActivationKeyExpired	The specified activation key has expired.	ActivateGateway
ActivationKeyInvalid	The specified activation key is invalid.	ActivateGateway
ActivationKeyNotFound	The specified activation key was not found.	ActivateGateway
BandwidthThrottleScheduleNotFound	The specified bandwidth throttle was not found.	DeleteBandwidthRateLimit
CannotExportSnapshot	The specified snapshot cannot be exported.	CreateCachediSCSIVolume CreateStorediSCSIVolume
InitiatorNotFound	The specified initiator was not found.	DeleteChapCredentials
DiskAlreadyAllocated	The specified disk is already allocated.	AddCache AddUploadBuffer AddWorkingStorage CreateStorediSCSIVolume
DiskDoesNotExist	The specified disk does not exist.	AddCache AddUploadBuffer AddWorkingStorage CreateStorediSCSIVolume
DiskSizeNotGigAligned	The specified disk is not gigabyte-aligned.	CreateStorediSCSIVolume

Operation Error Code	Message	Operations That Return this Error Code
DiskSizeGreaterThanVolumeMaxSize	The specified disk size is greater than the maximum volume size.	CreateStorediSCSIVolume
DiskSizeLessThanVolumeSize	The specified disk size is less than the volume size.	CreateStorediSCSIVolume
DuplicateCertificateInfo	The specified certificate information is a duplicate.	ActivateGateway
GatewayInternalError	A gateway internal error occurred.	AddCache AddUploadBuffer AddWorkingStorage CreateCachediSCSIVolume CreateSnapshot CreateStorediSCSIVolume CreateSnapshotFromVolumeRecoveryPoint DeleteBandwidthRateLimit DeleteChapCredentials DeleteVolume DescribeBandwidthRateLimit DescribeCache DescribeCachediSCSIVolumes DescribeChapCredentials DescribeGatewayInformation DescribeMaintenanceStartTime DescribeSnapshotSchedule DescribeStorediSCSIVolumes DescribeWorkingStorage ListLocalDisks ListVolumes ListVolumeRecoveryPoints ShutdownGateway StartGateway UpdateBandwidthRateLimit UpdateChapCredentials UpdateMaintenanceStartTime UpdateGatewaySoftwareNow UpdateSnapshotSchedule

Operation Error Code	Message	Operations That Return this Error Code
GatewayNotConnected	The specified gateway is not connected.	AddCache AddUploadBuffer AddWorkingStorage CreateCachediSCSIVolume CreateSnapshot CreateStorediSCSIVolume CreateSnapshotFromVolumeRecoveryPoint DeleteBandwidthRateLimit DeleteChapCredentials DeleteVolume DescribeBandwidthRateLimit DescribeCache DescribeCachediSCSIVolumes DescribeChapCredentials DescribeGatewayInformation DescribeMaintenanceStartTime DescribeSnapshotSchedule DescribeStorediSCSIVolumes DescribeWorkingStorage ListLocalDisks ListVolumes ListVolumeRecoveryPoints ShutdownGateway StartGateway UpdateBandwidthRateLimit UpdateChapCredentials UpdateMaintenanceStartTime UpdateGatewaySoftwareNow UpdateSnapshotSchedule

Operation Error Code	Message	Operations That Return this Error Code
GatewayNotFound	The specified gateway was not found.	AddCache AddUploadBuffer AddWorkingStorage CreateCachediSCSIVolume CreateSnapshot CreateSnapshotFromVolumeRecoveryPoint CreateStorediSCSIVolume DeleteBandwidthRateLimit DeleteChapCredentials DeleteGateway DeleteVolume DescribeBandwidthRateLimit DescribeCache DescribeCachediSCSIVolumes DescribeChapCredentials DescribeGatewayInformation DescribeMaintenanceStartTime DescribeSnapshotSchedule DescribeStorediSCSIVolumes DescribeWorkingStorage ListLocalDisks ListVolumes ListVolumeRecoveryPoints ShutdownGateway StartGateway UpdateBandwidthRateLimit UpdateChapCredentials UpdateMaintenanceStartTime UpdateGatewaySoftwareNow UpdateSnapshotSchedule

Operation Error Code	Message	Operations That Return this Error Code
GatewayProxyNetworkConnectionBusy	The specified gateway proxy network connection is busy.	AddCache AddUploadBuffer AddWorkingStorage CreateCachediSCSIVolume CreateSnapshot CreateSnapshotFromVolumeRecoveryPoint CreateStorediSCSIVolume DeleteBandwidthRateLimit DeleteChapCredentials DeleteVolume DescribeBandwidthRateLimit DescribeCache DescribeCachediSCSIVolumes DescribeChapCredentials DescribeGatewayInformation DescribeMaintenanceStartTime DescribeSnapshotSchedule DescribeStorediSCSIVolumes DescribeWorkingStorage ListLocalDisks ListVolumes ListVolumeRecoveryPoints ShutdownGateway StartGateway UpdateBandwidthRateLimit UpdateChapCredentials UpdateMaintenanceStartTime UpdateGatewaySoftwareNow UpdateSnapshotSchedule

Operation Error Code	Message	Operations That Return this Error Code
InternalError	An internal error occurred.	ActivateGateway AddCache AddUploadBuffer AddWorkingStorage CreateCachediSCSIVolume CreateSnapshot CreateSnapshotFromVolumeRecoveryPoint CreateStorediSCSIVolume DeleteBandwidthRateLimit DeleteChapCredentials DeleteGateway DeleteVolume DescribeBandwidthRateLimit DescribeCache DescribeCachediSCSIVolumes DescribeChapCredentials DescribeGatewayInformation DescribeMaintenanceStartTime DescribeSnapshotSchedule DescribeStorediSCSIVolumes DescribeWorkingStorage ListLocalDisks ListGateways ListVolumes ListVolumeRecoveryPoints ShutdownGateway StartGateway UpdateBandwidthRateLimit UpdateChapCredentials UpdateMaintenanceStartTime UpdateGatewayInformation UpdateGatewaySoftwareNow UpdateSnapshotSchedule

Operation Error Code	Message	Operations That Return this Error Code
InvalidParameters	The specified request contains invalid parameters.	ActivateGateway AddCache AddUploadBuffer AddWorkingStorage CreateCachediSCSIVolume CreateSnapshot CreateSnapshotFromVolumeRecoveryPoint CreateStorediSCSIVolume DeleteBandwidthRateLimit DeleteChapCredentials DeleteGateway DeleteVolume DescribeBandwidthRateLimit DescribeCache DescribeCachediSCSIVolumes DescribeChapCredentials DescribeGatewayInformation DescribeMaintenanceStartTime DescribeSnapshotSchedule DescribeStorediSCSIVolumes DescribeWorkingStorage ListLocalDisks ListGateways ListVolumes ListVolumeRecoveryPoints ShutdownGateway StartGateway UpdateBandwidthRateLimit UpdateChapCredentials UpdateMaintenanceStartTime UpdateGatewayInformation UpdateGatewaySoftwareNow UpdateSnapshotSchedule
LocalStorageLimitExceeded	The local storage limit was exceeded.	AddCache AddUploadBuffer AddWorkingStorage
LunInvalid	The specified LUN is invalid.	CreateStorediSCSIVolume
MaximumVolumeCountExceeded	The maximum volume count was exceeded.	CreateCachediSCSIVolume CreateStorediSCSIVolume DescribeCachediSCSIVolumes DescribeStorediSCSIVolumes
NetworkConfigurationChanged	The gateway network configuration has changed.	CreateCachediSCSIVolume CreateStorediSCSIVolume

Operation Error Code	Message	Operations That Return this Error Code
NotSupported	The specified operation is not supported.	ActivateGateway AddCache AddUploadBuffer AddWorkingStorage CreateCachediSCSIVolume CreateSnapshot CreateSnapshotFromVolumeRecoveryPoint CreateStorediSCSIVolume DeleteBandwidthRateLimit DeleteChapCredentials DeleteGateway DeleteVolume DescribeBandwidthRateLimit DescribeCache DescribeCachediSCSIVolumes DescribeChapCredentials DescribeGatewayInformation DescribeMaintenanceStartTime DescribeSnapshotSchedule DescribeStorediSCSIVolumes DescribeWorkingStorage ListLocalDisks ListGateways ListVolumes ListVolumeRecoveryPoints ShutdownGateway StartGateway UpdateBandwidthRateLimit UpdateChapCredentials UpdateMaintenanceStartTime UpdateGatewayInformation UpdateGatewaySoftwareNow UpdateSnapshotSchedule
OutdatedGateway	The specified gateway is out of date.	ActivateGateway
SnapshotInProgressException	The specified snapshot is in progress.	DeleteVolume
SnapshotIdInvalid	The specified snapshot is invalid.	CreateCachediSCSIVolume CreateStorediSCSIVolume
StagingAreaFull	The staging area is full.	CreateCachediSCSIVolume CreateStorediSCSIVolume
TargetAlreadyExists	The specified target already exists.	CreateCachediSCSIVolume CreateStorediSCSIVolume
TargetInvalid	The specified target is invalid.	CreateCachediSCSIVolume CreateStorediSCSIVolume DeleteChapCredentials DescribeChapCredentials UpdateChapCredentials
TargetNotFound	The specified target was not found.	CreateCachediSCSIVolume CreateStorediSCSIVolume DeleteChapCredentials DescribeChapCredentials DeleteVolume UpdateChapCredentials

Operation Error Code	Message	Operations That Return this Error Code
UnsupportedOperationFor-GatewayType	The specified operation is not valid for the type of the gateway.	AddCache AddWorkingStorage CreateCachediSCSIVolume CreateSnapshotFromVolumeRecoveryPoint CreateStorediSCSIVolume DeleteSnapshotSchedule DescribeCache DescribeCachediSCSIVolumes DescribeStorediSCSIVolumes DescribeUploadBuffer DescribeWorkingStorage ListVolumeRecoveryPoints
VolumeAlreadyExists	The specified volume already exists.	CreateCachediSCSIVolume CreateStorediSCSIVolume
VolumeIdInvalid	The specified volume is invalid.	DeleteVolume
VolumeInUse	The specified volume is already in use.	DeleteVolume
VolumeNotFound	The specified volume was not found.	CreateSnapshot CreateSnapshotFromVolumeRecoveryPoint DeleteVolume DescribeCachediSCSIVolumes DescribeSnapshotSchedule DescribeStorediSCSIVolumes UpdateSnapshotSchedule
VolumeNotReady	The specified volume is not ready.	CreateSnapshot CreateSnapshotFromVolumeRecoveryPoint

Error Responses

When there is an error, the response header information contains:

- Content-Type: application/x-amz-json-1.1
- An appropriate **4xx** or **5xx** HTTP status code

The body of an error response contains information about the error that occurred. The following sample error response shows the output syntax of response elements common to all error responses.

```
1 {
2     "__type": "String",
3     "message": "String",
4     "error":
5         { "errorCode": "String",
6           "errorDetails": "String"
7         }
8 }
```

The following table explains the JSON error response fields shown in the preceding syntax.

___type
One of the exceptions from Exceptions.
Type: String

error

Contains API-specific error details. In general errors (i.e., not specific to any API), this error information is not shown.

Type: Collection

errorCode

One of the operation error codes .

Type: String

errorDetails

This field is not used in the current version of the API.

Type: String

message

One of the operation error code messages.

Type: String

Error Response Examples

The following JSON body is returned if you use the DescribeStorediSCSIVolumes API and specify a gateway ARN request input that does not exist.

```
1 {
2   "__type": "InvalidGatewayRequestException",
3   "message": "The specified volume was not found.",
4   "error": {
5     "errorCode": "VolumeNotFound"
6   }
7 }
```

The following JSON body is returned if AWS Storage Gateway calculates a signature that does not match the signature sent with a request.

```
1 {
2   "__type": "InvalidSignatureException",
3   "message": "The request signature we calculated does not match the signature you provided."
4 }
```

Operations in AWS Storage Gateway

For a list of AWS Storage Gateway operations, see Actions in the *AWS Storage Gateway API Reference*.

Document History for AWS Storage Gateway

The following table describes important changes to the documentation since the last release of the *AWS Storage Gateway User Guide*.

- **API version**: 2013-06-30
- **Latest documentation update**: June 20, 2018

Change	Description	Date Changed
Support for Server Message Block (SMB) protocol	File gateway added support for the Server Message Block (SMB) protocol to file shares. For more information, see Creating an SMB File Share.	In this release
Support for file share, cached volumes, and virtual tape encryption	You can now use AWS Key Management Service (AWS KMS) to encrypt data written to a file share, cached volume or a virtual tape. Currently, you can do this by using the AWS Storage Gateway API Reference. For more information, see Encrypting Your Data Using AWS Key Management System.	June 12, 2018
Support for NovaStor DataCenter/Network	Tape gateways now support NovaStor DataCenter/Network. You can now use NovaStor DataCenter/Network version 6.4 or 7.1 to back up your data to Amazon S3 and archive directly to Amazon Glacier. For more information, see Testing Your Setup by Using NovaStor DataCenter/Network.	May 24, 2018
Support for S3 One Zone_IA storage class	For file gateways, you can now choose S3 One Zone_IA as the default storage class for your file shares. Using this storage class, you can store your object data in a single Availability Zone in Amazon S3. For more information, see Creating a File Share.	April 4, 2018
New region	Tape Gateway is now available in the Asia Pacific (Singapore) region. For detailed information, see Regions.	April 3, 2018

Change	Description	Date Changed
Support for refresh cache notification, requester pays, and canned ACLs for Amazon S3 buckets.	With file gateways, you can now be notified when the gateway finishes refreshing the cache for your Amazon S3 bucket. For more information, see RefreshCache.html in the *AWS Storage Gateway API Reference*. File gateways now enable the requester or reader instead of the bucket owner to pay for access charges. File gateways now enable you to give full control to the owner of the S3 bucket that maps to the NFS file share. For more information, see Creating a File Share.	March 1, 2018
Support for Dell EMC NetWorker V9.x	Tape gateways now support Dell EMC NetWorker V9.x. You can now use Dell EMC NetWorker V9.x to back up your data to Amazon S3 and archive directly to Amazon Glacier. For more information, see Testing Your Setup by Using Dell EMC NetWorker.	February 27, 2018
New region	AWS Storage Gateway is now available in the EU (Paris) region. For detailed information, see Regions.	December 18, 2017
Support for file upload notification and guessing of the MIME type	File gateways now enable you to get notification when all files written to your NFS file share have been uploaded to Amazon S3. For more information, see NotifyWhenUploaded in the *AWS Storage Gateway API Reference*. File gateways now enable guessing of the MIME type for uploaded objects based on file extensions. For more information, see Creating a File Share.	November 21, 2017
Support for VMware ESXi Hypervisor version 6.5	AWS Storage Gateway now supports VMware ESXi Hypervisor version 6.5. This is in addition to version 4.1, 5.0, 5.1, 5.5, and 6.0. For more information, see Supported Hypervisors and Host Requirements.	September 13, 2017

Change	Description	Date Changed
Compatibility with Commvault 11	Tape gateways are now compatible with Commvault 11. You can now use Commvault to back up your data to Amazon S3 and archive directly to Amazon Glacier. For more information, see Testing Your Setup by Using Commvault .	September 12, 2017
File gateway support for Microsoft Hyper-V hypervisor	You can now deploy a file gateway on a Microsoft Hyper-V hypervisor. For information, see Supported Hypervisors and Host Requirements.	June 22, 2017
Support for three to five hour tape retrieval from archive	For a tape gateway, you can now retrieve your tapes from archive in three to five hours. You can also determine the amount of data written to your tape from your backup application or your virtual tape library (VTL). For more information, see Viewing Tape Usage.	May 23, 2017
New region	AWS Storage Gateway is now available in the Asia Pacific (Mumbai) Region. For detailed information, see Regions.	May 02, 2017
Updates to file share settings Support for cache refresh for file shares	File gateways now add mount options to the file share settings. You can now set squash and read-only options for your file share. For more information, see Creating a File Share. File gateways now can find objects in the Amazon S3 bucket that were added or removed since the gateway last listed the bucket's contents and cached the results. For more information, see RefreshCache in the API Reference.	March 28, 2017
Support for cloning a volume	For cached volume gateways, AWS Storage Gateway now supports the ability to clone a volume from an existing volume. For more information, see Cloning a Volume.	March 16, 2017

Change	Description	Date Changed
Support for file gateways on Amazon EC2	AWS Storage Gateway now provides the ability to deploy a file gateway in Amazon EC2. You can launch a file gateway in Amazon EC2 using the Storage Gateway Amazon Machine Image (AMI) now available as a community AMI. For information about how to create a file gateway and deploy it on an EC2 instance, see Creating a Gateway. For information about how to launch a file gateway AMI, see Deploying File Gateway on an Amazon EC2 Host. In addition, file gateway now supports for HTTP proxy configuration. For more information, see Routing Your On-Premises Gateway Through a Proxy.	February 08, 2017
Compatibility with Arcserve 17	Tape gateway is now compatible with Arcserve 17. You can now use Arcserve to back up your data to Amazon S3 and archive directly to Amazon Glacier. For more information, see Testing Your Setup by Using Arcserve Backup r17.0.	January 17, 2017
New region	AWS Storage Gateway is now available in the EU (London) region. For detailed information, see Regions.	December 13, 2016
New region	AWS Storage Gateway is now available in the Canada (Central) region. For detailed information, see Regions.	December 08, 2016
Support for File gateway	In addition to volume gateways and tape gateway, AWS Storage Gateway now provides File Gateway. File Gateway combines a service and virtual software appliance, enabling you to store and retrieve objects in Amazon S3 using industry-standard file protocols such as Network File System (NFS). The gateway provides access to objects in Amazon S3 as files on a NFS mount point.	November 29, 2016

Change	Description	Date Changed
Backup Exec 16	Tape gateway is now compatible with Backup Exec 16. You can now use Backup Exec 16 to back up your data to Amazon S3 and archive directly to Amazon Glacier. For more information, see Testing Your Setup by Using Backup Exec.	November 7, 2016
Compatibility with Micro Focus (HPE) Data Protector 9.x	Tape gateway is now compatible with Micro Focus (HPE) Data Protector 9.x. You can now use HPE Data Protector to back up your data to Amazon S3 and archive directly to Amazon Glacier. For more information, see Testing Your Setup by Using Micro Focus (HPE) Data Protector.	November 2, 2016
New region	AWS Storage Gateway is now available in the US East (Ohio) region. For detailed information, see Regions.	October 17, 2016
AWS Storage Gateway console redesign	The AWS Storage Gateway Management Console has been redesigned to make it easier to configure, manage, and monitor your gateways, volumes, and virtual tapes. The user interface now provides views that can be filtered and provides direct links to integrated AWS services such as CloudWatch and Amazon EBS. For more information, see Sign Up for AWS Storage Gateway.	August 30, 2016
Compatibility with Veeam Backup & Replication V9 Update 2 or later	Tape gateway is now compatible with Veeam Backup & Replication V9 Update 2 or later (that is, version 9.0.0.1715 or later). You can now use Veeam Backup Replication V9 Update 2 or later to back up your data to Amazon S3 and archive directly to Amazon Glacier. For more information, see Testing Your Setup by Using Veeam Backup & Replication.	August 15, 2016

Change	Description	Date Changed
Longer volume and snapshot IDs	AWS Storage Gateway is introducing longer IDs for volumes and snapshots. You can enable the longer ID format for your volumes, snapshots, and other supported AWS resources. For more information, see Understanding AWS Storage Gateway Resources and Resource IDs.	April 25, 2016
New region Support for storage up to 512 TiB in size for stored volumes Other gateway updates and enhancements to the AWS Storage Gateway local console	Tape gateway is now available in the Asia Pacific (Seoul) region. For more information, see Regions. For stored volumes, you can now create up to 32 storage volumes up to 16 TiB in size each, for a maximum of 512 TiB of storage. For more information, see Stored Volumes Architecture and AWS Storage Gateway Limits. Total size of all tapes in a virtual tape library is increased to 1 PiB. For more information, see AWS Storage Gateway Limits. You can now set the password for your VM local console on the AWS Storage Gateway Console. For information, see Setting the Local Console Password from the Storage Gateway Console..	March 21, 2016
Compatibility with for Dell EMC NetWorker 8.x	Tape gateway is now compatible with Dell EMC NetWorker 8.x. You can now use Dell EMC NetWorker to back up your data to Amazon S3 and archive directly to Amazon Glacier. For more information, see Testing Your Setup by Using Dell EMC NetWorker.	February 29, 2016

Change	Description	Date Changed
Support for VMware ESXi Hypervisor version 6.0 and Red Hat Enterprise Linux 7 iSCSI initiator Content restructure	AWS Storage Gateway now supports the VMware ESXi Hypervisor version 6.0 and the Red Hat Enterprise Linux 7 iSCSI initiator. For more information, see Supported Hypervisors and Host Requirements and Supported iSCSI Initiators. This release includes this improvement: The documentation now includes a Managing Your Activated Gateway section that combines management tasks that are common to all gateway solutions. Following, you can find instructions on how you can manage your gateway after you have deployed and activated it. For more information, see Managing Your Gateway.	October 20, 2015
Support for storage up to 1,024 TiB in size for cached volumes Support for the VMXNET3 (10 GbE) network adapter type in VMware ESXi hypervisor Performance enhancements Miscellaneous enhancements and updates to the AWS Storage Gateway local console	For cached volumes, you can now create up to 32 storage volumes at up to 32 TiB each for a maximum of 1,024 TiB of storage. For more information, see Cached Volumes Architecture and AWS Storage Gateway Limits. If your gateway is hosted on a VMware ESXi hypervisor, you can reconfigure the gateway to use the VMXNET3 adapter type. For more information, see Configuring Network Adapters for Your Gateway. The maximum upload rate for AWS Storage Gateway has increased to 120 MB a second, and the maximum download rate has increased to 20 MB a second. For more information, see Configuration and Performance Limits. The AWS Storage Gateway local console has been updated and enhanced with additional features to help you perform maintenance tasks. For more information, see Configuring Your Gateway Network.	September 16, 2015

Change	Description	Date Changed
Support for tagging	AWS Storage Gateway now supports resource tagging. You can now add tags to gateways, volumes, and virtual tapes to make them easier to manage. For more information, see Tagging Storage Gateway Resources.	September 2, 2015
Compatibility with Quest (formerly Dell) NetVault Backup 10.0	Tape gateway is now compatible with Quest NetVault Backup 10.0. You can now use Quest NetVault Backup 10.0 to back up your data to Amazon S3 and archive directly to Amazon Glacier. For more information, see Testing Your Setup by Using Quest NetVault Backup.	June 22, 2015
Support for 16 TiB storage volumes for stored volumes gateway setups Support for system resource checks on the AWS Storage Gateway local console Support for the Red Hat Enterprise Linux 6 iSCSI initiator	AWS Storage Gateway now supports 16 TiB storage volumes for stored volumes gateway setups. You can now create 12 16 TiB storage volumes for a maximum of 192 TiB of storage. For more information, see Stored Volumes Architecture. You can now determine whether your system resources (virtual CPU cores, root volume size, and RAM) are sufficient for your gateway to function properly. For more information, see Viewing Your Gateway System Resource Status or Viewing Your Gateway System Resource Status. AWS Storage Gateway now supports the Red Hat Enterprise Linux 6 iSCSI initiator. For more information, see Requirements. This release includes the following AWS Storage Gateway improvements and updates: [See the AWS documentation website for more details]	June 3, 2015

Change	Description	Date Changed
Support for Microsoft Hyper-V hypervisor versions 2012 and 2012 R2	AWS Storage Gateway now supports Microsoft Hyper-V hypervisor versions 2012 and 2012 R2. This is in addition to support for Microsoft Hyper-V hypervisor version 2008 R2. For more information, see Supported Hypervisors and Host Requirements.	April 30, 2015
Compatibility with Symantec Backup Exec 15	Tape gateway is now compatible with Symantec Backup Exec 15. You can now use Symantec Backup Exec 15 to back up your data to Amazon S3 and archive directly to Amazon Glacier. For more information, see Testing Your Setup by Using Backup Exec.	April 6, 2015
CHAP authentication support for storage volumes	AWS Storage Gateway now supports configuring CHAP authentication for storage volumes. For more information, see Creating a Volume.	April 2, 2015
Support for VMware ESXi Hypervisor version 5.1 and 5.5	AWS Storage Gateway now supports VMware ESXi Hypervisor versions 5.1 and 5.5. This is in addition to support for VMware ESXi Hypervisor versions 4.1 and 5.0. For more information, see Supported Hypervisors and Host Requirements.	March 30, 2015
Support for Windows CHKDSK utility	AWS Storage Gateway now supports the Windows CHKDSK utility. You can use this utility to verify the integrity of your volumes and fix errors on the volumes. For more information, see Troubleshooting Volume Issues.	March 04, 2015

Change	Description	Date Changed
Integration with AWS Cloud-Trail to capture API calls	AWS Storage Gateway is now integrated with AWS Cloud-Trail. AWS CloudTrail captures API calls made by or on behalf of AWS Storage Gateway in your AWS account and delivers the log files to an Amazon S3 bucket that you specify. For more information, see Logging AWS Storage Gateway API Calls by Using AWS CloudTrail. This release includes the following AWS Storage Gateway improvement and update:[See the AWS documentation website for more details]	December 16, 2014
Compatibility with additional backup software and medium changer	Tape gateway is now compatible with the following backup software: [See the AWS documentation website for more details]You can now use these four backup software products with the Storage Gateway virtual tape library (VTL) to back up to Amazon S3 and archive directly to Amazon Glacier. For more information, see Testing Your Gateway Setup. AWS Storage Gateway now provides an additional medium changer that works with the new backup software. This release includes miscellaneous AWS Storage Gateway improvements and updates.	November 3, 2014
EU (Frankfurt) region	AWS Storage Gateway is now available in the EU (Frankfurt) region. For detailed information, see Regions.	October 23, 2014

Change	Description	Date Changed
Content restructure	Created a Getting Started section that is common to all gateway solutions. Following, you can find instructions for you to download, deploy, and activate a gateway. After you deploy and activate a gateway, you can proceed to further instructions specific to stored volumes, cached volumes, and tape gateway setups. For more information, see Creating a Tape Gateway.	May 19, 2014
Compatibility with Symantec Backup Exec 2012	Tape gateway is now compatible with Symantec Backup Exec 2012. You can now use Symantec Backup Exec 2012 to back up your data to Amazon S3 and archive directly to Amazon Glacier. For more information, see Testing Your Setup by Using Backup Exec.	April 28, 2014
Support for Windows Server Failover Clustering Support for VMware ESX initiator Support for performing configuration tasks on AWS Storage Gateway local console	[See the AWS documentation website for more details]	January 31, 2014
Support for virtual tape library (VTL) and introduction of API version 2013-06-30	AWS Storage Gateway connects an on-premises software appliance with cloud-based storage to integrate your on-premises IT environment with the AWS storage infrastructure. In addition to volume gateways (cached volumes and stored volumes), AWS Storage Gateway now supports gateway–virtual tape library (VTL). You can configure tape gateway with up to 10 virtual tape drives per gateway. Each virtual tape drive responds to the SCSI command set, so your existing on-premises backup applications will work without modification. For more information, see the following topics in the *AWS Storage Gateway User Guide*. [See the AWS documentation website for more details]	November 5, 2013

Change	Description	Date Changed
Support for Microsoft Hyper-V	AWS Storage Gateway now provides the ability to deploy an on-premises gateway on the Microsoft Hyper-V virtualization platform. Gateways deployed on Microsoft Hyper-V have all the same functionality and features as the existing on-premises storage gateway. To get started deploying a gateway with Microsoft Hyper-V, see Supported Hypervisors and Host Requirements.	April 10, 2013
Support for deploying a gateway on Amazon EC2	AWS Storage Gateway now provides the ability to deploy a gateway in Amazon Elastic Compute Cloud (Amazon EC2). You can launch a gateway instance in Amazon EC2 using the AWS Storage Gateway AMI available in AWS Marketplace. To get started deploying a gateway using the AWS Storage Gateway AMI, see Deploying a Volume or Tape Gateway on an Amazon EC2 Host.	January 15, 2013

Change	Description	Date Changed
Support for cached volumes and introduction of API Version 2012-06-30	In this release, AWS Storage Gateway introduces support for cached volumes. Cached volumes minimize the need to scale your on-premises storage infrastructure, while still providing your applications with low-latency access to their active data. You can create storage volumes up to 32 TiB in size and mount them as iSCSI devices from your on-premises application servers. Data written to your cached volumes is stored in Amazon Simple Storage Service (Amazon S3), with only a cache of recently written and recently read data stored locally on your on-premises storage hardware. Cached volumes allow you to utilize Amazon S3 for data where higher retrieval latencies are acceptable, such as for older, infrequently accessed data, while maintaining storage on-premises for data where low-latency access is required. In this release, AWS Storage Gateway also introduces a new API version that, in addition to supporting the current operations, provides new operations to support cached volumes. For more information on the two AWS Storage Gateway solutions, see How AWS Storage Gateway Works (Architecture). You can also try a test setup. For instructions, see Creating a Tape Gateway.	October 29, 2012
API and IAM support	In this release, AWS Storage Gateway introduces API support as well as support for AWS Identity and Access Management(IAM). [See the AWS documentation website for more details]	May 9, 2012
Static IP support	You can now specify a static IP for your local gateway. For more information, see Configuring Your Gateway Network.	March 5, 2012

Change	Description	Date Changed
New guide	This is the first release of *AWS Storage Gateway User Guide*.	January 24, 2012